German infantry and a camouflaged panzer. The tank is of Czechoslovakian manufacture.

RETREAT
TO THE REICH

RETREAT
TO THE REICH

The German Defeat
in France, 1944

Samuel W. Mitcham, Jr.

 PRAEGER

Westport, Connecticut
London

Library of Congress Cataloging-in-Publication Data

Mitcham, Samuel W.
    Retreat to the Reich : the German defeat in France, 1944 / Samuel W. Mitcham, Jr.
        p.   cm.
    Includes bibliographical references and index.
    ISBN 0–275–96857–X (alk. paper)
    1. World War, 1939–1945—Campaigns—France.   2. Germany—Armed
    Forces—History—20th century.   I. Title.
    D761.M58   2000
    940.54'214—dc21   99–086096

British Library Cataloguing in Publication Data is available.

Library of Congress Catalog Card Number: 99–086096
ISBN: 0–275–96857–X

First published in 2000

Praeger Publishers, 88 Post Road West, Westport, CT 06881
An imprint of Greenwood Publishing Group, Inc.
www.praeger.com

Printed in the United States of America

∞

The paper used in this book complies with the
Permanent Paper Standard issued by the National
Information Standards Organization (Z39.48–1984).

10 9 8 7 6 5 4 3 2 1

CONTENTS

Contents

Photo essay follows page 129.

TABLES AND FIGURES

Tables and Figures

RETREAT
TO THE REICH

CHAPTER I

SETTING THE STAGE FOR DISASTER

On July 17, 1944, a pair of German soldiers dragged an unconscious officer into the Catholic hospital near Vimoutiers, France. His left cheekbone was destroyed, he had many shell splinters and fragments in his head, his skull was fractured, his left eye was injured, and his temple was penetrated. At first the medical staff gave him no chance to live.

What had happened to him was not unusual. Throughout Normandy this violent summer, Allied fighter-bombers were plastering any German vehicle that moved during daylight hours, killing or wounding tens of thousands of German soldiers, immolating tanks and armored vehicles, reducing German facilities to rubble, cutting their supply lines, and making it impossible for the Germans to launch anything resembling a major counterattack. Now not even Dr. Joseph Goebbels's propaganda machine talked about throwing the Allies back into the sea; it spoke only of how the German soldiers on the Western Front were bravely holding their positions—which, for once, was nothing but the truth. This task had just become infinitely more difficult, however, because of the identity of the unconscious officer. He was arguably Germany's most gifted tactician, a fearless leader, and the man who had imposed stalemate on the Western Allies in Normandy, despite the fact that he was heavily outnumbered in every material category. He was a man among men, the holder of Germany's highest decorations, including the Knight's Cross with Oak Leaves, Sword and Diamonds, the commander in chief of Army Group B, and a field marshal—the highest rank in the German Army. More important, he was the man most respected by the German soldier and most feared and respected by the men on the other side of the line. He was Generalfeldmarschall Erwin Rommel—the Desert Fox.

It had all begun many years before, when Germany lost World War I and made the transition from the Second Reich (empire) to a democratic

1

form of government called the Weimar Republic. Led to believe that the peace treaty ending the war would be predicated on U.S. President Woodrow Wilson's Fourteen Points, the German people had instead been handed the very harsh Treaty of Versailles, which they called the "treaty of shame," because Germany had to admit that it alone was responsible for World War I, when clearly this was not true. The treaty was also tantamount to economic rape. In rapid succession, over a period of only 5 years, Germany had lost a world war; witnessed the collapse of its royal house (which had ruled Prussia for 19 generations and 507 years); was forced to give up all its colonies and one-eighth of its national land area, as well as its entire air force, virtually all of its navy, and most of its army; had to pay huge reparations; underwent a civil war (which the Germans called "the war after the war"); and underwent a period of unbelievable hyperinflation, during which the value of the mark fell from 8 marks to 1 American dollar to 4,210,500 million marks to 1 dollar. The price of an egg increased from 25 pfennings (one-fourth of a mark) in 1918 to 80 billion marks in 1923. A newspaper now cost 300 billion marks, and a beer cost 150 billion marks. Had the American dollar inflated at the same rate, a postage stamp would have cost 11,900 million dollars.[1]

The brilliant economic policies of Dr. Hjalmar Horace Greeley Schacht, the Reich currency commissioner and president of the Reichsbank, changed all that and temporarily restored the German economy. By November 1923, the mark was stabilized at 4.2 per American dollar. It was too late for the Weimar Republic, however. German faith in democracy had been completely shattered. Now, like a tree without roots, it was subject to falling under the force of the first moderate wind that struck it.

The next wind, however, was far from moderate: It was the Great Depression of 1929, which shook Germany to its core. Factories closed, wages fell, and tent colonies of middle-class people—now homeless—surrounded every city. In Berlin alone, a city of 4 million people, there were 750,000 unemployed. By 1932, German unemployment exceeded 5.5 million, out of a work force of 29 million, and nobody knows how many other Germans, who had exhausted both their unemployment benefits and their hopes, simply no longer bothered to register.

Onto this stage walked Adolf Hitler, undisputed leader (Fuehrer) of the National Socialist German Workers' Party (Nationalsozialistische Deutsche Arbeitpartei), called the NSDAP or Nazi Party for short. An undeniably brilliant orator and a master politician, he promised to return Germany to greatness. More important, he offered her people hope for the future. Hungry and desperate, they turned to him in droves. In 1933, he became the legally elected chancellor of Germany.

At first, it seemed to the Germans that Hitler was keeping his word—

and, for a time, he did. This was certainly not because integrity was a hallmark of his character—it was not—but because he was blindly ambitious and he really did have certain core beliefs, perverted though some of them were. The general German public, along with its military leaders, was unable to tell the difference. In addition, admittedly Hitler did some positive things for Germany in the 1930s. He stimulated the economy with his public works programs, built the autobahns, eliminated unemployment, restored a measure of political stability to Germany for the first time since 1918, drastically reduced crime, eliminated street violence (largely by suppressing his own Storm Troopers) and reintroduced compulsory military service to the nation. It must be recalled that the typical German male of that time felt that he had been cheated of his birthright if he did not have the opportunity to serve in the military. *Heerlos, Wehrlos, Ehrlos*—no army, no defense, no honor—was an often-repeated slogan during the Versailles years, and Hitler's restoration of universal military suffrage was celebrated by the masses and seen even by most anti-Nazis as a definite positive.

Hitler's foreign policy prior to 1939 was also a brilliant success. After establishing the Luftwaffe and keeping his promise to make Germany strong again, he launched the *Blumenkrieg*—his "Flower Wars." In three dizzying years, he reannexed the Saar to the Reich, remilitarized the Rhineland, annexed Austria, reclaimed the Sudetenland, and reduced the hated Czechoslovakian Republic to military and diplomatic impotence. In achieving all of this, however, the German people paid a price. They lost their political freedom. As Hitler pursued his agenda, he outlawed all other political parties, established the Nazi dictatorship, abolished the Weimar Republic, and established the Third Reich. By February 1938, he had even brought the army under his control. The Germans in general, however, were happy with the exchange, and when they spoke of freedom at all, they spoke of losing the freedom to starve.

Only gradually did this opinion begin to change. The first shudders were felt on Crystal Night, also known as the Night of the Broken Glass, November 9–10, 1938, when rampaging Brownshirts and other Nazis smashed the windows of Jewish homes, shops, businesses, and synagogues. Not confining themselves to windows, the Nazis wrecked and plundered 267 synagogues, 815 shops and businesses, and a large number of private homes. At least 36 Jews were killed, 20,000 Jews were arrested, and about 6 million marks worth of damage was done. The Nazi government blamed the victims, confiscated the insurance money, and imposed a billion-marks fine on the Jewish community.[2]

This lawless outrage decisively turned world public opinion against Germany, but most Germans passively accepted even this. The economy, after all, was fine. Then, on March 15, 1939, the Fuehrer occupied the rump Czechoslovakian state. Unlike the case with Hitler's previous foreign adventures, there was no way this newly annexed region could be considered German. Perhaps Hitler had been serious in 1924 when he wrote *Mein Kampf* and spoke of lebensraum (living space), which Germany would have to take in the East, or so the more thoughtful and intelligent Germans wondered. If so, they realized, lebensraum could only be taken by means of another major European war—perhaps even a second world war. The remaining Germans who thought this way, however, dared not verbalize it publicly, for fear of the Gestapo. It was too late now to object to the Nazis; Hitler was firmly at the controls, and there was no one left who could fire the engineer. He would be able to take the train wherever he wished, and they would have to stay on for the ride.

In 1939, Hitler finally miscalculated and drove the train over the edge and into the abyss. Thinking that the British and French would back down when faced with a physical confrontation, he invaded Poland on September 1. London and Paris declared war on September 3. They refused to make peace even after the Wehrmacht (German armed forces) overran Poland in less than four weeks.

Thanks primarily to his exhalted General Staff, which Hitler feared and hated but with whom he had to work, the German Army had grown from 100,000 men in 1933 to 2.5 million in 1939. Hitler used this superb instrument to conquer Poland in 1939; the Netherlands, Belgium, Luxembourg, and France in 1940; and Yugoslavia, Greece, Crete, and most of Libya in 1941. Then Hitler made a second fatal mistake. Without subduing or making peace with the United Kingdom, he invaded the Soviet Union on June 22, 1941. By the end of the year, his invasion had been checked at Leningrad and turned back before the gates of Moscow, and he was at war with the United States. By December 1941, those who were in a position to know knew Germany could not win the war. The Third Reich and its partners were outnumbered almost 2 to 1 in population, and Italy, militarily speaking, counted for little (Table 1.1). Worse still, all three of the Reich's principal opponents outproduced her industrially. Table 1.2, for example, shows German and Japanese aircraft production for 1942 and 1943 versus those for the United States, the Soviet Union, and Great Britain. Ratios were similar in every material category. Nevertheless, Hitler—an inveterate gambler—pressed recklessly on, and the Wehrmacht suffered defeat after defeat. The German 6th Army was encircled and destroyed at Stalingrad, costing the Reich 230,000 men. The Battle of Britain was lost, England recovered, the U.S. two- and four-engine bombers arrived in Great Britain in significant numbers, and German cities were devastated by Anglo-American bombs. The Allies won the Battle of the Atlantic, and despite an occasional success, the armies of the Reich were pushed steadily back in the East, losing tens of thousands of men, hundreds of tanks and assault guns, and tons of ma-

Table 1.1
Population, Major Allied and Axis Countries, 1939 Estimates

Allies	
Soviet Union	167,300,000
United States	130,000,000
United Kingdom	47,700,000
Total	345,000,000
Axis	
Germany	68,400,000
Japan	70,600,000
Italy	43,800,000
Total	182,800,000

terial in the process. Meanwhile, in North Africa, German supply lines collapsed and Army Group Afrika was forced to surrender in May 1943, costing Germany another 130,000 men. The loss of Sicily, the defection of Italy, and the Allied invasion of Italy followed. By early 1944, the Wehrmacht was on the defensive everywhere, and Hitler's empire faced its greatest challenge: the invasion of Western Europe.

In 1944, everyone knew that the Allies would attempt to return to France via amphibious landings. This invasion represented both the greatest threat to and the greatest opportunity for Nazi Germany. If the Reich could repulse the invasion, the Allies would not be able to mount another for perhaps a year. A score of divisions—including several elite panzer and SS (Schutzstaffel) panzer formations—would be released for the Eastern Front. Allied military and political leadership would be thrown into chaos, the Churchill government might fall, and it was conceivable that the Allied coalition might fall apart altogether. Even if the Wehrmacht was not able to reestablish German military superiority in Europe, it might at least be able to reestablish a balance of power and force the Allies to accept a negotiated peace. Even if this failed, German scientists would have another year to develop or perfect their "miracle weapons," including new and more dangerous U-boats, flying bombs, guided rockets, jet airplanes, and perhaps even atomic bombs. On the other hand, if the invasion succeeded, there would be little hope left for the Third Reich.

Since March 1942, OB West (the German abbreviation for *Oberbefehlshaber West*, the commander in chief, West, or his headquarters) was Field Marshal Gerd von Rundstedt, a 69-year-old Prussian aristocrat who had served the Fatherland since 1892.[3] (See Appendix I for a table of comparative ranks.) An officer of the Old School, Rundstedt planned to fight

Table 1.2
Military Aircraft Production (All Types)

Country	1942	1943
United States	47,836	85,898
Soviet Union	25,436	34,900
United Kingdom	23,672	26,263
Germany	15,409	24,807
Japan	8,861	16,693
Allied Total	96,944	147,061
Axis Total	24,270	41,500

a conventional, 1940-type battle. He intended to let the Allies land, build up, and move inland; then he would attack and decisively defeat them with his highly regarded panzer divisions somewhere in the interior of France, far beyond the range of Allied naval gunfire. For this purpose he created Panzer Group West under the command of his friend and fellow aristocrat, General of Panzer Troops Leo Geyr von Schweppenburg, and gave him control of all 10 of OB West's panzer and panzer grenadier divisions.[4] What von Rundstedt, von Geyr, and their colleagues had failed to grasp was that the days of the blitzkrieg were over. Allied aerial domination had made this type of strategy obsolete. It was simply impossible for Germany to fight a 1940- or 1941-type battle in 1944—at least on the Western Front. To make matters worse, Rundstedt was content to isolate himself in St. Germain, his luxurious headquarters in Paris, with his cigarettes, brandy, cognac, and cheap detective novels (which he loved), and he did not stay abreast of recent developments in his profession. Even his friend von Geyr admitted to his interrogators in 1947: "Of all the German generals, Field Marshal von Rundstedt knew the least of panzer tactics. He was an infantryman of the last generation. He and his staff were armchair strategists who didn't like dirt, noise and tanks in general—as far as I know, Field Marshal von Rundstedt was never in a tank. Do not misunderstand me, however," Geyr quickly added, "I have the greatest respect for von Rundstedt, but he was too old for this war."[5]

Rundstedt's staff adopted the same attitude as their commander. When Vice Admiral Friedrich Ruge visited Rundstedt's headquarters, he found "a fatalistic acceptance of the deteriorating situation and a lack of alertness in looking for possible improvements."[6] OB West was further handicapped by its amiable but mediocre chief of staff, Lieutenant General Guenther Blumentritt, who, as General von Geyr recalled, was "unsuited [for his post] in ability or character."[7] Blumentritt, in fact,

suspected that the entire invasion was a colossal bluff that might v
not take place at all.[8] With these generals in charge, little was done
improve the "Atlantic Wall," as the propaganda ministry dubbed t
German coastal defenses of Western Europe.

By December 1943, Adolf Hitler and his chief military adviser, Colon
General Alfred Jodl, the chief of operations of Oberkommando des Wehr
macht (the High Command of the Armed Forces, or OKW), among oth·
ers, had begun to suspect that something was wrong in the West.[9] To
investigate matters, Hitler summoned Field Marshal Rommel to Rastenburg, his headquarters in East Prussia. At the time, Rommel was in
charge of Army Group B z.b.V. ("for special purposes"), but neither he
nor his skeleton staff had a specific assignment.[10] The Fuehrer felt they
could do useful work by assessing the state of the German defenses in
Denmark, the Netherlands, Belgium, and France. This appointment left
Rundstedt wondering if the younger and much more energetic Rommel
had been earmarked to succeed him.

Rommel conducted a whirlwind inspection of the defensive sectors
from Denmark to the Pyrenees Mountains on the Spanish frontier from
December 11 to 23, 1943, and was not at all impressed by what he saw.
The Atlantic Wall had been touted by the German media as an invincible
barrier against which the invading Allies would dash all of their hopes,
but a soldier of Rommel's caliber saw through this curtain of deception
almost immediately. He was soon denouncing it as a farce—an "enormous bluff" and a "figment of Hitler's *Wolkenkuckucksheim*" (cloud
cuckoo land).[11] Later, he bitterly denounced it as "the Propaganda Wall."
Meanwhile, on December 15, he stopped in Paris to discuss the situation
with Gerd von Rundstedt.

It is hard to imagine two officers more diverse than Rommel and von
Rundstedt. From all appearances, Rommel was the quintessential pro-
totype of a Nazi general—young, tough, blunt, energetic, uncompromis-
ingly competent, and a man of action. Rundstedt was elderly, aloof,
cynical, tired, and somewhat jaded—the product of a bygone era. Their
backgrounds were equally divergent. Rundstedt was a Prussian aristocrat, whereas Rommel was the son and grandson of schoolteachers.
Rundstedt was prone to compromise, even on matters of principle, and
he enjoyed luxurious living and the finer things of life, whereas Rommel
had simple, puritanical tastes and absolutely refused to compromise on
matters of principle. Finally, Rundstedt had made his way to the top of
his profession as a General Staff officer, whereas Rommel earned his
spurs on the front lines, where he had won the *Pour le Merite*, all four
grades of the Knight's Cross, and the Wounded Badge—five times. A
clash between the pair seemed inevitable. To everyone's surprise, however, the two marshals quickly developed an understanding and even a

Figure 1.1
Northwest Europe

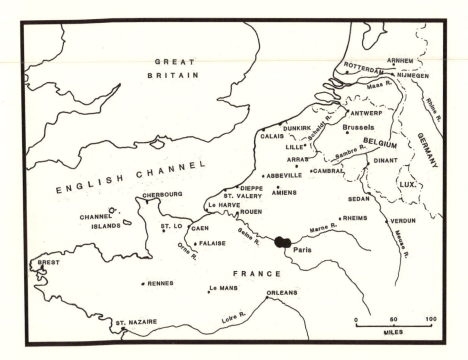

faint liking for one another. This was because Rundstedt compromised again. Even though he and Rommel had serious disagreements over how the West should be defended (see below), he offered Rommel command of his two largest armies and the sectors most seriously threatened by an Allied invasion. Even though Rundstedt was giving up a great deal, Rommel would now be subordinated to Rundstedt; therefore, there would be no danger of the Desert Fox replacing him as OB West. (Rundstedt had no way of knowing that his fears were completely unfounded.) The two marshals jointly proposed to Fuehrer Headquarters that Army Group B be subordinate to OB West and that it be given responsibility for northern France, Belgium, and the Netherlands. A surprised Hitler was not particularly pleased by this development because he had planned to use Rommel on the Eastern Front, but in the end, he acquiesced. Erwin Rommel was given the 7th and 15th Armies and Wehrmacht Command Netherlands. The Desert Fox received his most difficult command. Figure 1.1 shows his principal area of operations.

Hitler added some surprising clauses to the terms of Rommel's appointment: He was given a measure of authority over Rundstedt's other

Table 1.3
The Order of Battle of OB West, May 1, 1944

OB West: Field Marshal Gerd von Rundstedt

Army Group B: Field Marshal Erwin Rommel
Armed Forces Netherlands: General of Fliers Friedrich Christiansen
15th Army: Colonel General Hans von Salmuth
7th Army: Colonel General Friedrich Dollmann

Armeegruppe G[1]: Colonel General Johannes Blaskowitz
19th Army: General of Infantry Georg von Sodenstern[2]
1st Army: Colonel General Johannes Blaskowitz[3]

Panzer Group West: General of Panzer Troops Baron Leo Geyr von Schweppenburg

1st Parachute Army[4]: Luftwaffe Colonel General Kurt Student

Notes:
[1]An Armeegruppe was not a regular Heeresgruppe (army group) but, rather, was an ad hoc headquarters, normally intermediate between an army and an army group in the chain of command. This one was activated on April 28, 1944, and was eventually upgraded to full army group (Heeresgruppe) status.
[2]Succeeded by General of Infantry Friedrich Wiese on June 29, 1944.
[3]Succeeded as commander of the 1st Army on May 3, 1944, by General of Panzer Troops Joachim Lemelsen. On June 4, Lemelsen was replaced by General of Infantry Kurt von der Chevallerie.
[4]At this time, 1st Parachute Army was employed as a training command only. It had no organic combat divisions.

two armies in matters of coastal defense. He was ordered to inspect their sectors and show himself publicly, to deceive the enemy as to what his area of responsibility was and to advance the myth that there were more troops south of the Loire than there were. Early that spring, Hitler even proposed that if the enemy attacked in southern France, Rommel would immediately assume command there, leaving Rundstedt to command in the North. The OB West, however, objected to this confusing arrangement, and it was dropped.

Perhaps to counter Rommel's growing influence in the West, Field Marshal von Rundstedt created a new command: Armeegruppe G, under Colonel General Johannes Blaskowitz. It controlled the 1st and 19th Armies, which were responsible for the defense of southwestern and southern France, respectively. Table 1.3 shows the German Order of Battle on May 1, 1944.

Rommel had a formidable task, and he did everything humanly possible to prepare his men for it. The lethargy he found at Rundstedt's headquarters had pervaded the entire Western Front; now Rommel shook them out of it. With that intangible gift he had for instilling a fighting spirit and an aggressive attitude in his men, the Desert Fox hurled himself into his work. The rank and file were eager to serve under a military genius of Rommel's caliber, and morale soared, even as their workload increased. In six months, Rommel laid three times as many mines as OB West had laid in the previous four years. He built fortifications, constructed strong points and bunkers at and near the coast, laid hundreds of thousands of offshore obstacles (many with mines or heavy shells attached, in order to blow up landing craft), constructed many *Scheinbatterien* (dummy batteries) to deceive enemy fighter-bombers, flooded selected areas to drown enemy paratroopers, and erected scores of antiglider poles, which the troops called "Rommel asparagus." He could do little, however, to improve the fragmented German command structure (he had no control over and little influence with the navy or the Luftwaffe—including the III Flak Corps); he could do nothing about the manpower drain to the Eastern Front; nor could he deploy the panzer divisions that were in France in the manner that he knew was best. "Our friends in the East cannot imagine what they're in for here," Rommel said. He added:

It's not a matter of fanatical hordes to be driven forward in masses against our line, with no regard for casualties and little recourse to tactical craft; here we are facing an enemy who applies all his native intelligence to the use of his many technical resources, who spares no expenditure of material and whose every operation goes its course as though it had been the subject of repeated rehearsal.[12]

Of the German commanders in the West, only Rommel had faced the British since 1940 or the Americans since 1918. Only he had experienced Anglo-American air power firsthand, when it devastated his Panzer Army Afrika at Alam Halfa Ridge and El Alamein and later when it smashed Army Group Afrika in Tunisia. Only he understood that the magnitude of Anglo-American air superiority would not influence the success of the invasion—it would decide it in favor of the Allies—unless the German Army could mount a major armored thrust within 48 hours of the initial landings and hurl the invading force back into the sea. To accomplish this task, it would be necessary to position all 10 of OB West's mobile divisions very near the coast. This strategy, however, was in diametric opposition to Rundstedt's, which called for concentrating the panzer divisions in the interior of France—well out of the range of the big guns of the Royal and U.S. navies. Typically, Rundstedt remained aloof of the debate and did not involve himself personally; his point of view was represented by Baron Leo Geyr von Schweppenburg.

Hitler should have chosen between Rommel's coastal defense theory and Geyr's armored counterattack theory; instead, he compromised between them. He gave Army Group B three panzer divisions: the 2nd, 21st, and 116th; three others (the 9th, 11th, and 2nd SS) were assigned to the soon-to-be activated Army Group G, which was responsible for the defense of southern France. This left Geyr's Panzer Group West with only 4 mobile divisions—the 1st SS Panzer, the 12th SS Panzer, the 17th SS Panzer Grenadier, and Panzer Lehr—instead of its original 10. Even these could not be employed without OKW's permission. Rundstedt now had no armor under his personal command. The compromise satisfied no one. Rommel still did not have the strength to execute his plans for an immediate counterattack, whereas von Geyr and Rundstedt no longer had the armor necessary to fight their kind of battle in the interior of France. In short, by compromising, Hitler made both defensive theories impossible. Figure 1.2 shows the dispositions of OB West just before D-Day.

While the army generals reorganized, improved the coastal defenses, and debated strategies, the Allied air forces swept the Luftwaffe from the skies of France.

In February 1944, the 8th U.S. Air Force under Lieutenant General James H. Doolittle began a program of bombing deliberately aimed at provoking aerial battles with the Luftwaffe. Although the German fighters, led by Lieutenant General Adolf Galland, put up quite a struggle, they were unable to overcome the swarms of U.S. Army Air Force (USAAF) and Royal Air Force (RAF) Spitfires, Hurricanes, Mustangs, Lightnings, and Mosquitoes that protected the bomber streams. Even when they were able to break through the fighter screens, the bombers themselves fairly bristled with guns. Although the Allies suffered heavier losses, they could afford them; the Luftwaffe—whose training establishment had already virtually collapsed—was already facing a shortage of experienced fighter pilots. Due to the demands of the various fronts, demand for fighter pilots exceeded supply as early as 1939. To meet this demand quickly, the pilot training program of the Luftwaffe had been steadily reduced from 260 hours of flight time per student in 1940 to as little as 50 in 1944, and even then it could not keep up with losses. The new, green German pilots were no match for the superbly trained British and American aviators. Many of the German pilots could not even land properly. In May 1944, for example, the Luftwaffe lost 712 aircraft to hostile action and 656 in flying accidents.[13] The burden of the battle fell more and more on the veteran aviators, whose numbers were steadily reduced. As a result, by June, the Luftwaffe had been decisively defeated, and Allied bombers were flying over Berlin in broad daylight, unchallenged except by anti-aircraft guns.

In the West, the situation was even worse. Here Luftwaffe Field Mar-

Figure 1.2
Dispositions, OB West, June 5, 1944

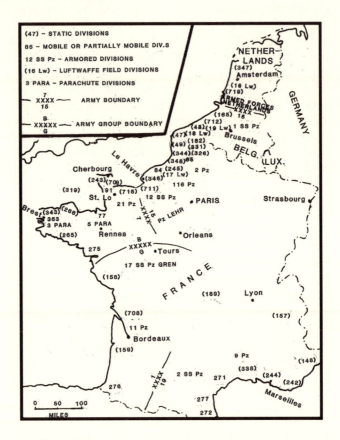

shal Hugo Sperrle, the commander in chief of the 3rd Air Fleet and senior air force commander in the West since 1940, had "gone to seed" in the luxurious city of Paris.[14] A large, ugly bear of a man, he is most famous for inventing the terror raid while commanding the Condor Legion in Spain. Now, however, he headquartered in a palace, developed a taste for gourmet food and fine wines, and ate, drank, and gambled to excess. He did nothing to maintain the quality of his command, which both deteriorated alarmingly and bloated remarkably. By 1944, for example, nearly 340,000 of the Wehrmacht personnel in the West were in the Luftwaffe,[15] but according to Rommel's chief of staff, Sperrle had only 90 bombers and 70 fighter aircraft in his entire air fleet as of June 1, 1944.[16] Even if flak troops (100,000 men) and ground paratrooper units (30,000 men) are deducted, the size of the Luftwaffe's ground and service establishments versus the number of airplanes they could put into the air is still enormous.[17]

Hitler, Hermann Goering, and their staffs played right into the Allies' hands by dissipating their remaining air power on strategically senseless terror raids against civilian targets in England. Despite Rommel's pleas that the bombers concentrate against Allied embarkation ports (especially Portsmouth and Southampton), the attacks attempted to answer terror with terror and focused on the heavily defended city of London. When this so-called "Baby Blitz" began on January 21, 1944, Attack Command England had 462 operational aircraft. By the end of May, only 107 remained. Conditions deteriorated to the point that the Luftwaffe had to abandon its airfields near the coast and retreat to the interior of France.[18]

U.S. General Dwight D. Eisenhower, the Supreme Allied commander, finally gained control over the Allied strategic air forces in April 1944 and used them with devastating effect against two main targets: the French rail system and the French highway system. Against Rommel's wishes, but with the full backing of Hermann Goering, General of Flak Artillery Wolfgang Pickert, the commander of the III Flak Corps, had scattered his command all over the map.[19] It thus had a presence everywhere but no real strength anywhere. Both III Flak and 3rd Air Fleet were totally unable to protect the rail network, as hundreds of Allied bombers, fighters, and fighter-bombers shot up hundreds of locomotives and blew up bridges faster than the Germans could repair them. (Rommel wanted the flak corps concentrated in Normandy, which he suspected might be the target of the invasion.) By the middle of May, every bridge on the Seine below Paris and every bridge on the Loire below Orleans had been knocked out; by the end of April, 600 army supply trains were backlogged in France alone. Repairs simply could not keep up with the destruction. Before the aerial onslaught began, the German transportation staff was running more than 100 supply trains per day in France. By the end of May, only 20 trains per day were operating in the country, and traffic over the Seine, Oise, and Meuse rivers was at a complete standstill. By June 6, the French National Railway was operating at only 10% of its normal capacity.[20]

Although not hit as hard as the railroads, the French road system was by no means neglected by the Allied airmen. Normandy and the approach routes to it were subjects of particular attention from the Allied bombers and fighter-bombers, and the region had, for all practical purposes, become a strategic island. German reinforcements to the invasion sector would have to get there via overland march using a badly damaged road system, adding days to their travel time when hours counted. When Hitler finally released the 1st SS Panzer Division from OKW reserve and ordered it to Normandy, for example, it took the division seven days to cover the 186 miles (300 kilometers) from Louvain, Belgium, to Paris. This trip normally took only one day by train—and the 1st SS was still 90 miles from the combat zone.[21] From here, it had to proceed by road and was exposed to repeated attacks by fighter-bomber squadrons reserved specifically for that purpose.

When evaluating the German Wehrmacht in the Battle of Normandy and the French campaign of 1944, perhaps the factor that should be considered more serious than any other in the outcome of the battle is the deterioration in quality of the German Army and Luftwaffe vis-à-vis their opponents. Five years of war had definitely taken their toll, and the quality of the German Army facing Eisenhower's invasion in 1944 was far below that which had so triumphantly overrun France in six glorious weeks in 1940. True, their panzers were better in 1944 than they had been in 1939, but the secret of the blitzkrieg had never been in its equipment. In 1940, for example, most of the German panzers were inferior to those employed by their French and British counterparts, which they crushed so thoroughly and destroyed so utterly. (Not a single French armored unit escaped; virtually every British tank was destroyed or had to be abandoned at Dunkirk.) The secret to the blitzkrieg lay in the ranks; it was found in the hearts and minds of the men who executed it. Now most of these men were crippled or dead or were rotting away in a prisoner-of-war camp. The days of the quick, decisive campaign were over; now it was a war of attrition. And Germany was near the end of its manpower reserves. By the spring of 1944, the Fatherland had suffered more than 2.5 million casualties. In the West, it faced a serious shortage of first-rate combat troops. Of the 4.27 million men in the German Army in December 1943, more than 1.5 million were over 34 years of age. Many below 34 were very young (17–19), were victims of third-degree frostbite, were ethnic Germans (Volksdeutsche), or were "Eastern Troops" (Osttruppen)—non-Germans recruited from occupied countries. The average age in the whole army was 31.5 years, or more than 6 years older than the average for the American army in 1943. In the LXXXIV Corps, which defended Normandy, 8 of 42 rifle battalions were made up of Osttruppen,[22] who were mainly recruited out of prisoner-of-war camps. Many of them chose to serve in the Nazi army as an alternative to starving to death. Their loyalty to the Third Reich was dubious at best.

By 1944, the Eastern Front was taxing Hitler's empire to the breaking point. In 1943, German losses in Russia reached 2.086 million, of which 677,000 were permanent (killed, missing, permanently incapacitated, or captured), and this figure excludes losses in any other sector, including North Africa, where two armies had been lost. Of the 151 German divisions fighting on the Russian Front, 10 panzer and 50 infantry divisions

Table 1.4
Dispositions of German Divisions by Theater, June 1, 1944

Theater	Army	Luftwaffe Field	SS	Total
East	149	—	8	157
Finland	6	—	1	7
Norway-Denmark	15	—	—	15
Western	47	3	4	54
Italy	23	3	1	27
Balkans	8	—	7	15
Total	248	6	21	275

Source: Albert Seaton, *The Russo-German War, 1941–45* (New York: 1971), p. 458.

were classified as "fought out." The abbreviation "KG" now appeared with alarming frequency on the German Order of Battle charts. It stood for *Kampfgruppe* ("battle group")—a division that had been reduced by casualties to the value of a regimental-sized battle group. And still the Russians kept on coming. To meet this threat, Hitler called on units stationed in the West. By October 1943, he had transferred 36 infantry and 17 mobile (panzer and panzer grenadier) divisions from OB West to other fronts. A few of these were sent to Italy, but almost all of them ended up in the East. Despite these reinforcements, the situation in Russia remained critical. In the spring of 1944, the Red Army still fielded more than 5 million troops in 300 divisions, despite horrendous casualties. Germany had only 2 million men in 157 divisions.[23] Table 1.4 shows the dispositions of Germany's divisions by theater as of June 1, 1944, and clearly shows the manpower drain caused by the Eastern Front.

Many of the divisions in Rundstedt's command were units previously mauled in the East. Many of them (though by no means all) had six understrength infantry battalions, instead of the nine full-strength infantry battalions that was standard for a German infantry division in 1939. In fact, the standard German infantry division at full establishment in 1939 had 17,200 men. This establishment had been reduced to 13,656 by 1943, and a full-strength 1944-type division had only 12,769 men, but very few of the 1944-type divisions were at 100% strength.

The material requirements of the Eastern Front also put a catastrophic strain on the German war effort. First priority of equipment was to the East until January 1944, because tank losses there were tremendous. Between October and December 1943, 979 Panzer Mark IIIs and IVs were lost, along with 444 assault guns (see Appendix III for a description of the various Allied and German tanks.) In the last six months of 1943,

Germany lost 2,235 field guns and 1,692 antitank guns on the Russian Front alone. By February 1944, however, the threat in the West became real enough for Hitler to order an increase in tank delivery to OB West. Although the bulk of new Panzer Mark VI (PzKw VI or "Tiger") tanks still went east, PzKw V "Panther" (PzKw V) output was mostly sent to France. By the end of April, OB West had 1,608 German-made tanks and assault guns, of which 674 were PzKw IVs and 514 were Panthers.[24] This still fell far short of the great concentrations that occurred in the Soviet Union. During the Battle of Kursk in July 1943, for example, Hitler's legions lost almost 2,000 tanks. On June 1, 1944, at approximately its peak strength, OB West could muster only 1,552 tanks.[25]

The Wehrmacht was not only short of tanks in 1944—it was short of practically everything else as well. Rundstedt's regiments were forced to improvise as a result and were equipped with the most astonishing collection of obsolete, foreign, and captured equipment one could imagine. One division's artillery regiment had so many different kinds of obsolete and foreign guns that it called itself "the travelling artillery museum of Europe." The 7th Army alone had 92 different kinds of artillery pieces, which used 252 types of ammunition, of which 47 were no longer manufactured.[26] Rundstedt's trucks were of German, French, Italian, Russian, or Czech manufacture, whereas many of his "mobile" regiments were equipped with bicycles. The 243rd Infantry Division was a real hybrid: It included one motorized regiment, one bicycle regiment, and one "marching" infantry regiment. Like virtually all of the German infantry divisions, its artillery and supply trains were horse-drawn. In most infantry divisions, only the ambulance company was fully motorized.

The Allies landed on the Cotentin peninsula on the coast of Normandy on D-Day, June 6, 1944 (Figure 1.3). Under the overall command of General Eisenhower's Supreme Headquarters, Allied Expeditionary Force (SHAEF), their ground forces on D-Day were commanded by the British 21st Army Group (General Sir Bernard L. Montgomery), which controlled the British 2nd Army (Lieutenant General Sir Miles Dempsey), and the U.S. 1st Army (Lieutenant General Omar Bradley). They achieved surprise at three levels. They landed at Normandy, when most German generals expected them to land at Pas de Calais, in the zone of the 15th Army; they came at low tide, not at high tide, as expected by Rommel (leaving many of the offshore obstacles high and dry but exposing their assault elements to German machine guns for a longer period as they ran across open beach); and they came in near–gale force conditions, instead of in calm weather, as everyone predicted.

At the higher levels, German reaction was slow and poor. Of the senior German leaders who played a prominent part in the battle that day, only

Figure 1.3
D-Day: The Allied Assault

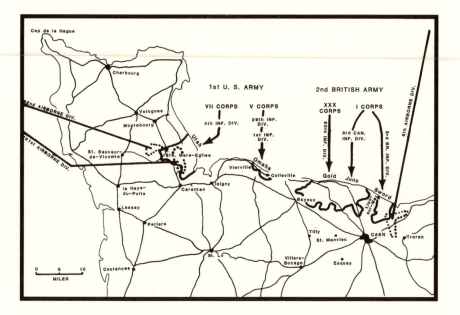

General of Artillery Erich Marcks stands out as the one man who grasped the situation quickly, issued the correct orders, and consistently did the right thing.[27] Rommel had made perhaps the worst mistake of his military career the day before when, after consulting the meteorological reports, he concluded that the weather would be too poor for an invasion and left for Germany. He planned to spend a day at home near Ulm (June 6 was his wife's birthday) and then go on to Berchtesgaden, to try to persuade Hitler to give him more divisions. Rommel's chief of staff, Lieutenant General Hans Speidel, now de facto army group commander, concluded that the predawn parachute drops were a diversion and went back to bed. (Some of them were; some, obviously, were not.) He did not telephone Rommel at home until around 10:15 A.M.—eight hours after the invasion began. At 7 A.M., Jodl had concluded that the invasion was a diversionary attack and rejected Rundstedt's request to move the 12th SS Panzer Division behind the invasion beaches. He also turned down OB West's request to alert the Panzer Lehr Division. Rundstedt refused to appeal directly to Hitler (which, as a field marshal, he had the right to do) because he would not deal with the man he habitually referred to as "that Bohemian corporal." He spent the day at his headquarters, fuming. Jodl did not allow anyone to wake Hitler until 10 A.M. Even then it would be five hours before the Fuehrer released the

12th SS and Panzer Lehr Divisions. When they finally were released, Colonel General Friedrich Dollmann, the commander of the German 7th Army, ordered Panzer Lehr to head for the beaches—in broad daylight.[28] As a result, this elite division lost 80 AFVs (armored fighting vehicles—tanks, armored cars, armored personnel carriers, etc.) to Allied fighter-bombers on its approach march and was crippled before it even reached the invasion beaches.

Meanwhile, 3,467 Allied heavy bombers and 1,645 medium bombers, protected and assisted by 5,409 fighters and fighter-bombers, dropped 11,912 tons of bombs. Within a few hours, they dropped more bombs on Normandy than they had on Hamburg the year before—and Hamburg was the most heavily bombed city in 1943.[29] Then, at 5:30 A.M., the Allied fleets attacked the surviving German batteries with a devastating bombardment from six battleships, 23 cruisers, and 104 destroyers. Shortly thereafter, the actual landings began. Eisenhower came with 7,000 ships and more than 190,000 men. By the end of the day, the U.S. 82nd and 101st Airborne Divisions, the British 6th Airborne Division, the U.S. 1st, 4th, and 29th Infantry Divisions, the British 3rd and 50th Infantry Divisions, and the Canadian 3rd Infantry Division had landed on five separate beaches. An impressive assortment of armored, armored artillery, combat engineer, and Ranger battalions had landed as well.

Because Hitler had rejected Rommel's pleas to position the panzer divisions near the coast, only 1 was available, and it was the worst: the 21st Panzer Division. Although its human material was excellent, one of its two tank battalions was equipped with 80 obsolete Czech tanks that were too light for modern warfare and had not been manufactured since 1941. Its other tank battalion had 40 PzKw IVs, but they were also obsolete and were fitted with short-barreled guns. (Both battalions were controlled by the 100th Panzer Regiment, which had four additional panzers in its staff company.) The division's two panzer grenadier regiments (the 125th and 192nd) were also equipped with inferior and obsolete equipment.

The 21st Panzer also had the poorest divisional commander in France. Major General Edgar Feuchtinger had commanded the 227th Artillery Regiment—a horse-drawn unit!—on the northern (Leningrad) sector of the Eastern Front for 14 months. Apparently wounded in action in August 1942, he was without an assignment until May 15, 1943, when he assumed command of the 21st. He was totally unqualified for this position and owed it solely to his Nazi Party contacts—he had been deeply involved in organizing the Nuremberg Rallies for the NSDAP prior to the war. When reports arrived that the invasion might have begun, he could not be found. He was in Paris with his Ia (operations officer—see Appendix II for German staff abbreviations), taking a spot of unauthorized leave in a sleazy Parisian night club. Based upon his subsequent performance, it would have been better for the German Army had his staff left him in the bar.[30] He did not feel he could move his unit without the permission of OKW, and he adamantly refused to do so, despite pleas, curses, orders and threats from Lieutenant General Wilhelm Richter, whose 716th Infantry Division was being slaughtered on the beaches.[31] When Feuchtinger finally did decide to attack, around 6:30 A.M., he decided to move against the British 6th Airborne Division—*away* from the invasion beaches. It was 2:30 P.M. before General Marcks could get the division under his control and get its 100th Panzer and 192nd Panzer Grenadier Regiments in position to attack the British. The 100th Panzer lost 50 of its 124 tanks to fighter-bombers on the approach march. Then it lost 16 more tanks to British guns before it could even get within range of the enemy positions. Its regimental commander, Hermann von Oppeln-Bronikowski, wisely called off the attack after 15 minutes.[32] The depressed colonel watched despondently as the German troops fell back toward Caen, alone or in small groups. One of them was Wilhelm Richter, the commander of the 716th Infantry Division, who "was almost demented with grief," von Oppeln recalled. "My troops are lost," Richter said as tears flowed from his eyes. "My whole division is finished!"[33] This was nothing but the truth. His Osttruppen had surrendered immediately after the Allies landed—as soon as they had a chance, in fact— but his German soldiers had resisted gallantly and in some cases to the last man. Montgomery had planned to capture Caen (a city of 42,000) on D-Day and be 30 miles inland by nightfall. Due to the efforts of the 716th and its sister unit, Lieutenant General Dietrich Kraiss's 352nd Infantry Division, he did not even cover the 10 miles to Caen. In fact, Colonel Ernst Goth's 916th Grenadier Regiment of the 352nd almost defeated the American landings on Omaha Beach and inflicted more than 3,000 casualties on the U.S. 1st Infantry Division during the initial assault wave—1 casualty for every six feet of beach. The U.S. Rangers, who attacked Pointe du Hoc on the right flank of Omaha Beach, suffered more than 50% casualties, whereas the U.S. 111th Field Artillery Battalion lost all but one of its howitzers and the U.S. 58th Armored Field Artillery Battalion lost all of its amphibious tanks and most of its men. The U.S. 29th Infantry Division also suffered serious losses on Omaha Beach.

Despite locally heavy losses, however, the invasion was an unqualified Allied success. They were firmly lodged on four of their five invasion beaches by nightfall and had beaten back the only panzer division in a position to threaten their landings. By day's end, the Anglo-Americans had lost more than 10,000 men but had put 156,000 men ashore and had pushed their way inland an average depth of 4 to 6 miles along a 24-mile front. They had scattered the German 716th Infantry Division (which had lost more than 6,000 men) and had severely damaged the 352nd Infantry and 21st Panzer. The assault landings were now over.

Now the second phase of the Normandy campaign—the battle of the hedgerows—was about to begin.

The hedgerows of Normandy were nothing like the harmless, decorative bush the average American today associates with the term *hedge*. If you go there today, you will see that few of them remain. In 1944 they were everywhere. They were mounds of earth and stone several feet thick and four to eight feet tall, overgrown with bushes, thornbush, tangled vegetation, and small trees, with a drainage ditch on either side. Used to separate fields, they offered the Germans one excellent defensive position after another. A single machine gun hidden in the hedge could mow down many advancing soldiers, and snipers could be (and were) posted everywhere. Defenders, properly dug in at the base of a hedgerow, were impervious to any kind of artillery or mortar fire except a direct hit. The Norman fields were so small that for the Germans to abandon one hedgerow and to retreat to another involved the loss of very little land indeed. (There were an average of 500 small fields per square mile in Normandy, and the hedgerow country was 60 miles long and 25 miles wide.)[34] The Norman roads also aided the defense. They were usually old trails, worn down over centuries. Overlooked by the hedges, they were death traps for tanks. The alternative for a Sherman—climbing over a hedge—was worse. As it climbed, its main battle gun and machine guns pointed toward the sky, and it exposed its very thin underbelly (its weakest point) to the Germans, many of whom were equipped with *Panzerfausten*: shoulder-fired antitank weapons that allowed them to get very close to Allied armor. It short, Normandy offered Hitler's legions some of the best defensive terrain in Europe. It was therefore imperative for the Allies to quickly break out of hedgerow country (called *bocage* by the French), or the Germans might be able to stalemate them.

That is exactly what happened. Hurriedly, Rommel brought up Panzer Group West to deliver his counterattack with the Panzer Lehr Division on the left, 12th SS Panzer in the center, and what was left of 21st Panzer on the right. With equal haste, the British disembarked their 7th Armoured Division and a number of independent British and Canadian armored brigades. When Panzer Group West finally launched its counterattack on June 9, it was at least two days too late. The fighting itself was inconclusive, but with the Allies growing stronger every hour, it was clear that the invasion had succeeded. By June 12, the Allies had 15 divisions ashore and 5 more landed from June 13 to 19 (including the U.S. 2nd Armored and the British 11th Armoured), along with several separate armored brigades and dozens of battalions of artillery, engineers, and tanks. Rommel initially left Panzer Group West, along with the bulk of his armor, to cover his right flank in front of Caen against the British, while Dollmann's 7th Army (especially LXXXIV Corps) dealt with the Americans in front of St.-Lô. Due to the swampy nature of the terrain in which they were forced to operate, the Americans were severely cramped for space, but they initially did not have to deal with Tigers and Panthers either, as the British did.

For the Allies, the main problem was the hedgerows. No sooner did they take one than they were confronted with another. For the Germans, the main problem was Allied fighter-bombers, which the German soldiers called "Jabos." They made resupply difficult and daytime movement nearly impossible and blasted headquarters, armored concentrations, and anything else that moved—and some things that did not. Panzer Group West's CP (Command Post), for example, was blown away because it exercised sloppy camouflage and radio discipline. Geyr was wounded, his chief of staff, Major General Ritter und Elder Sigismund-Helmut von Dawans, was killed, along with the Ia and the entire operation's staff (about 19 men), who were buried in one mass grave.[35] Other units that were veterans of the Eastern Front also learned that the Western Front was a more exacting war than that in Russia. Lack of radio discipline was probably responsible for the naval shelling of the Headquarters of 12th SS Panzer Division, during which its commander, SS Lieutenant General Fritz Witt, was killed. SS General Sepp Dietrich, the commander of the I SS Panzer Corps, lost 16 of his 20 radios in two days. The Allies also had 640 big naval guns, which materially aided the Jabos in blasting Army Group B. Even so, because of the nature of hedgerow fighting, Allies losses exceeded German losses through the middle of July, if only slightly. On the other hand, the Anglo-Americans could afford these losses; OB West could not.

Despite these losses, Hitler, OKW, and even Rundstedt were convinced that the Normandy landings were a diversion. U.S. Lieutenant General George S. Patton's 1st Army Group had been set up as a diversionary force, and it did a marvelous job with fake troop movements, radio traffic dummy installations, and other forms of "disinformation." All of its divisions were fictitious; nevertheless, on June 12, OB West reported to OKW that the enemy still had 20 to 30 uncommitted field divisions and four airborne divisions. Rundstedt said that he excepted a second invasion to come either in the Somme (Pas de Calais) area or in Belgium.

Inside OKW, only Jodl expressed any disagreement with Rundstedt's appreciation of the situation. Although he did not consider further landings out of the question, he wanted to reinforce 7th Army in Normandy, using forces from Italy if necessary.[36]

The first strategic objective of the Allied invasion was plain to anyone who could read a map: It was the port of Cherbourg on the northern tip of the Cotentin peninsula. It was defended by Lieutenant General Karl-Wilhelm von Schlieben, the commander of the 709th Infantry Division.[37] Now dubbed Group von Schlieben, his forces included what was left of the 709th Infantry, the 91st Air Landing Division (which had suffered serious losses to U.S. paratroopers and fighter-bombers on D-Day), the 243rd Infantry Division, the 77th Infantry Division, elements of the 265th Infantry Division (already a Kampfgruppe), the 456th and 457th Motorized Artillery Battalions, the 100th Mortar Regiment, most of the 25th Flak Regiment, and a few miscellaneous units. Mostly understrength even before the battle began and without transport, it faced five American divisions, all but one of which were at or near full strength and 100% mobile. (The exception was the 82nd Airborne Division.) They also had complete command of the air and sea. The battle began on June 12, and on June 15, the U.S. VII Corps under Lieutenant General J. Lawton ("Lightning Joe") Collins broke through and, two days later, reached the west coast of the Cotentin. About half of the 77th Infantry Division broke out against orders and escaped to the south. The 91st Air Landing and a fragment of the 243rd Infantry survived because the breakout occurred north of their positions. Schlieben retreated into Cherbourg, but Collins pursued rapidly and there was fighting in the suburbs by June 22. Hitler ordered Schlieben to fight to the last man. He surrendered on the afternoon of June 26, and the last pockets of resistance (Cap de la Hague, on the northwest corner of the peninsula) capitulated on July 1—more than two weeks behind Eisenhower's schedule. Hitler nevertheless denounced Schlieben as "[a] disgrace to his uniform and the lowest form of a German general!"[38]

During the Cherbourg campaign, Collins's VII Corps lost 22,000 men, including 2,811 killed, 13,564 wounded, and 5,665 missing. German losses were estimated at 47,070 killed, wounded, or captured, including 826 officers and six generals[39] They had liberated their first major French city, Rommel now had 47,000 fewer men with which to fight, and by July 1, more than 900,000 Allied soldiers had landed in France. Rommel had roughly a third that number. And still Hitler and OKW continued to believe that the Normandy landings were a diversion—the real landings would yet come at Pas de Calais, in the zone of 15th Army. For this reason, every request Rommel or Rundstedt made to transfer divisions from 15th Army to Normandy was rejected. Nineteen German divisions lay idle, awaiting an invasion that had already come.

On the other hand, the capture of Cherbourg was not the victory the Allies had hoped for. They had hoped to capture a major port; instead, they found a field of ruins. "The demolition of the port of Cherbourg is a masterful job, beyond a doubt the most complete, intensive, and best-planned demolition in history," the senior American engineer in the sector reported. The U.S. Army's official history recorded: "[T]he whole port was as nearly a wreck as demolitions could make it." The Wehrmacht had scuttled 55 ships, barges, and other craft. Cranes were wrecked and overturned; bridges, piers, wharves, and quays were dynamited, railroads were uprooted, and mines were everywhere, both on land and underwater. Some were delayed-action mines, which worked on timers. Some detonated up to 85 days after they were set. It was three weeks before the Americans could get the slightest use out of it, and the harbor remained essentially unusable until September. Hitler was so pleased when he heard how badly wrecked the port was that he awarded Rear Admiral Walther Hennecke, the Naval Commander, Normandy, the Knight's Cross even though he was in captivity.[40]

Meanwhile, the first effective V-1 rocket launch was fired on June 16. Traveling at 400 miles per hour, it crossed the English Channel and landed in the London area. Utter confusion resulted. Although they caused relatively few casualties (about 6,000 killed and 17,000 wounded in the Greater London area), they nevertheless had a significant impact on the campaign. The area of northern France and Belgium now became a focus of Allied strategy solely because the V-1 launching sites were here. Also, the V-1 attacks improved German morale. If their cities were being devastated and their families were being killed or endangered, so too were the British. The German *Feldgrau* (field gray) were not aware of how exaggerated propaganda ministry reports tended to be. Some of them believed all of southern England was in flames, and the death total there exceeded 10 million instead of several hundred. (*Feldgrau*, incidentally, is the term the German enlisted men used to describe themselves— companions in misfortune with the British "Tommy" and the American "GI.")

The Allies continued to attack throughout June and into July. The British tried again and again to capture Caen and push onto the Falaise Plain, beyond *bocage* country, while the Americans drove on the important road junction of St.-Lô (Figure 1.4). Formerly a charming little city, it had been a favorite place for German soldiers on leave; now 95% of its buildings had been destroyed by the American bombers, and still its defenders held out. This city, however, was not as important as Caen, because the hedgerows continue for miles south of St.-Lô. The Germans launched another major counterattack on June 29. Directed by Headquarters (HQ), Panzer Group West (which had been rebuilt), it failed miserably, although the newly committed II SS Panzer Corps (9th and 10th SS Panzer Divisions) did manage to recapture the critical Hill 112 west of Caen the following day. Meanwhile, Colonel General Dollmann collapsed and died of a heart attack at his forward command post on June 29. Much to the disgust of von Rundstedt and Rommel, Hitler pro-

Figure 1.4
The Normandy Front, July 1, 1944

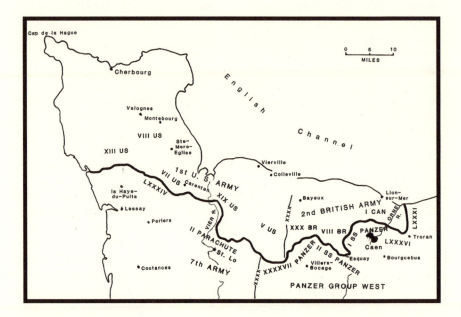

moted SS General Paul Hausser, the commander of the II SS Panzer Corps, to the vacant post, rejecting Rommel's nominee, 1st Army Commander General of Infantry Kurt von der Chevallerie.[41]

Even now, Hitler refused to believe the major Allied invasion had come. He and OKW were being deceived by U.S. Lieutenant General George S. Patton's 1st Army Group, which lurked in southeastern England with 45 divisions, poised to strike across the English Channel against the 15th Army at Pas de Calais. All of these divisions were bogus, but Hitler and his High Command did not know that. In addition to being deceived by the Allies, they were being deceived by their own intelligence service as well.

The Abwehr was never very good. By early 1944, its estimates amounted to little more than educated guesswork. At that time, it estimated that there were 90 Allied divisions and 22 independent brigades in the United Kingdom, which was more than twice the real figure (37 divisions). By June 1, Eisenhower had 2,876,000 men in 45 full-strength divisions, all of which were fully mobile.

Colonel Baron Alexis von Roenne, the chief of the German Army intelligence in the West, was only too eager to accept Patton's ghost army group as a genuine force. For months he had been deliberately exaggerating the strength of the Western Allies. We will never know why for sure.

Baron von Roenne was a strong anti-Nazi and was deeply involved in the plot to assassinate Hitler and was executed shortly thereafter. Was he engaged in high treason and attempting to assist in the military defeat of Nazi Germany when he deliberately introduced false data into the planning process? Or was he just trying to force an element of reality into the strategic planning at Fuehrer Headquarters? Either way, it proved much easier for Roenne to add divisions to the Allied Order of Battle estimate than for anyone to ever take them off again. As late as June 26, Army Group B's intelligence section (Lieutenant Colonel Staubwasser) estimated that there were 67 enemy divisions in England, of which 57 were fit for combat. In reality, Eisenhower had 15 divisions in England: all awaiting transport to Normandy.

On January 21, 1944, Admiral Wilhelm Canaris was in Italy, telling Field Marshal Albert Kesselring that there was absolutely no chance of a second Allied landing in Italy. The next day, the entire U.S. VI Corps landed at Anzio. This latest in a series of gross military intelligence failures was it for Canaris, insofar as Hitler was concerned. He suspended Canaris from office and ordered Himmler to absorb the Abwehr into the SS intelligence service. The change did little good, as many of the same people remained in charge, and by the fifth year of the war, most of Germany's best agents had already been arrested. As a result, the performance of Germany military intelligence continued to be abysmal. On July 3, OKW estimated that the Allies had landed 225,000 to 250,000 men with 43,000 vehicles in Normandy. The actual total was 929,000 men, 177,000 vehicles, and 586,000 tons of equipment. Rommel was outnumbered roughly 3 to 1, but the Fuehrer would not believe it.[42] On June 20, he even ordered Rommel to launch a counterattack and throw the Allies back into the sea!

As a result of orders of this nature, Rommel and Hitler had their final clash on the Obersalzberg on June 30. Hitler repeated his orders to von Rundstedt and Rommel and insisted that every inch of ground be held. All thought of mobile warfare was to be forgotten. The Desert Fox, backed by Rundstedt, made no secret of the fact that the war was lost. When Rommel insisted upon addressing the overall strategic situation, not just a narrow discussion of the invasion front, the Fuehrer ordered him to leave the room. Rommel turned on his heel and walked out. He never saw Hitler again.

"Why must our battles be directed by idiots far from the scene who have no conception of what's going on in Normandy?" Rommel snapped bitterly to General Speidel and Admiral Ruge.[43] When he returned to his desk, he found an estimate of the situation, written by Geyr and Hausser, the new commander of the 7th Army. It called for a retreat to the Orne River–Bully–Avenay–Villers-Bocage–Caumont line, which would have a double advantage. It would shorten the German line and thus require fewer units to defend it, and it would place most of the army group out of the range of Allied naval guns. On the other hand, it would allow the Allies to advance beyond the hedgerows and put them on terrain favorable for armored operations. Obviously this proposal was in diametric opposition to the orders Hitler had just given. Rommel signed it anyway and forwarded it to OB West. Rundstedt quickly endorsed it as well, asked for permission to evacuate Caen, and forwarded it to Berchtesgaden. The Desert Fox went one step further and, on July 1, unilaterally placed every Luftwaffe and naval unit in Army Group B's territory under the command of the army. Hitler was furious when he learned of this development.[44]

Meanwhile, Rundstedt telephoned Berlin on July 1 and spoke to Field Marshal Wilhelm Keitel, the commander in chief of OKW, to report the failure of a local attack.[45] While they were on the telephone, they began discussing the general strategic situation, which Keitel knew was hopeless. "What shall we do? What shall we do?" Keitel moaned.

Rundstedt already had enough of Hitler, his lackeys, and their interference in the Normandy campaign. Later he told his captors:

I knew all along the German position in France was hopeless [after the June 9 attack failed], and that eventually the war would be lost. But if I had been given a free hand to conduct operations, I think I could have made the Allies pay a fearful price for their victory. I had planned to fight a slow retiring action, exacting a heavy toll for each bit of ground I gave up. I had hoped this might have brought about a political decision which would have saved Germany from complete and utter defeat. But I did not have my way.[46]

By now, Rundstedt could see that Hitler and the Nazis would not even seek a negotiated peace, that Keitel, Jodl, and others were going to continue to interfere in the business of OB West and Army Group B, and that he quite possibly would be held responsible for the loss of the West. Suddenly the old man lost his temper. "Make peace, you fools!" he shouted into the receiver. "What else can you do?" Then he slammed down the telephone.

The Geyr-Hausser memo arrived in Berchtesgaden that same day. Jodl recommended that it be rejected on the grounds that what it really called for was the evacuation of France, even though the enemy had committed hardly a third of his available forces(!). Hitler also rejected the proposal and countered with another hold-every-position order. Allied breakthroughs were to be halted by local counterattacks.

The next day, Colonel Heinrich Borgmann, one of Hitler's military adjutants, arrived at Rundstedt's Headquarters in Paris. He presented him with the Oak Leaves to his Knight's Cross (a decoration normally only presented by the Fuehrer in person) and handed him an envelope.

Inside was a polite, handwritten note from Hitler, ordering Rundstedt into retirement due to his health and age. For the second time in three years, Hitler had relieved him of his command.

Rundstedt's reaction was one of relief. "I thank God that I won't be in command during the coming catastrophe!" he told Rommel.[47]

Also relieved of his command that day was General of Panzer Troops Baron Leo Geyr von Schweppenburg. Hitler did not act as politely toward him, and there were no handwritten notes or decorations. Geyr's chief of staff was sacked as well.[48] In addition, Rommel's order of the previous day (placing the Luftwaffe and naval units in France under army command) was rescinded by order of the Fuehrer.

Geyr was replaced by General of Panzer Troops Hans Eberbach, who had spent the last three years commanding 5th Panzer Brigade, 4th Panzer Division, and XXXXVIII Panzer Corps on the Eastern Front.[49] Geyr, at least, had been replaced by a man who knew his business, and he adapted quickly to conditions on the Western Front. Rommel nevertheless protested Geyr's removal to OKW but was brushed off by Keitel. Major General Alfred Gause, Rommel's former chief of staff in Africa and in the early days of Army Group B, was named Eberbach's chief of staff.

Rommel was next in line for the job at OB West, but he, of course, was passed over. Instead, Hitler gave the supreme command in the West to Field Marshal Guenther von Kluge. "I will be next [to be fired]," Rommel said when he heard the news.

Prior to arriving at St. Germain, Kluge had spent several days at Berchtesgaden, where Hitler, Jodl, and Field Marshal Wilhelm Keitel, the commander in chief of the High Command of the Armed Forces (OKW), convinced him that Rommel was an undisciplined defeatist. The crisis on the Western Front, they told him, was solely due to poor generalship. When he first visited Rommel's Headquarters at la Roche Guyon on July 5, Kluge was excited and optimistic in the extreme. He had come to "straighten out" the Desert Fox. He began the conference by listing Rommel's sins: He was too pessimistic and too easily influenced by the "allegedly overpowering effect of the enemy's weapons"; he was too obstinate; he did not carry out the Fuehrer's orders as wholeheartedly as he should. He told Rommel that even he must learn to obey orders without question from now on.

Rommel exploded. He had never been the type to take unwarranted criticism lying down. This insult was doubly offensive because it had been delivered in the presence of Dr. Speidel and Colonel Hans-Georg Tempelhoff, the army group's operations officer. He rejected Hitler's criticisms as unjustified and demanded that Kluge visit the front before drawing any conclusions. He then proceeded to censure Hitler, the High

Command, and Kluge himself in no uncertain terms. The argument grew so violent that Kluge ordered everyone to leave the room except Rommel and himself. The argument then increased in fury, ending with Kluge yelling that, up to now, Rommel had not really commanded anything more than a division, and Rommel screaming back that Kluge understood nothing about the situation because he had yet to meet the British in battle. (Neither insult was true.) Even after Kluge did visit the front and came around to Rommel's viewpoint, the relationship between the two never really healed.[50]

Of his new commander, General Blumentritt, the chief of staff of OB West, wrote: "Field Marshal von Kluge was a robust, aggressive type of soldier. At the start he was very cheerful and confident—like all newly appointed commanders. . . . Within a few days he became very sober and quiet. Hitler did not like the changing tone of his reports."[51]

It took Kluge only one visit to the front to change his mind completely. After that, he let Rommel conduct his own battle and did not interfere in the affairs of Army Group B from that point on.

NOTES

1. Richard Hawser, *Putsch!* (New York: 1971), pp. 288–89.

2. Robert Goralski, *World War II Almanac, 1931–1945* (New York: 1981), p. 75.

3. Gerd von Rundstedt was born at Aschersleben in the Harz Mountain region on December 12, 1875. His father was a hussar (cavalry) officer. He was educated at cadet schools and graduated from Gross Lichterfelde, the German equivalent of West Point. He entered the army in 1892 at the age of 16 as a senior officer cadet and was commissioned second lieutenant in the 83rd Royal Prussian Infantry Regiment the following year. He became a member of the General Staff in 1909. He spent most of World War I on the Eastern Front, became a corps chief of staff, and returned home a major. He rose rapidly after the war and assumed command of the 2nd Cavalry Division in 1928. He was briefly commander of the 3rd Infantry Division (1932) before assuming command of Army Group 1 (1933–38). He retired in 1938 but was recalled to active duty in 1939 and led Army Group South in the Polish campaign. He later commanded Army Group B (later South) in France (1940) and southern Russia (1941). Hitler sacked him for the first time in December 1941, but after Sepp Dietrich told the Fuehrer that he had done Rundstedt an injustice, Hitler recalled Rundstedt to duty as OB West in March 1942. For the best biography of Rundstedt, see Charles Messenger, *The Last Prussian: A Biography of Field Marshal Gerd von Rundstedt, 1875–1953* (London: 1991). Also see Guenther Blumentritt's earlier *Von Rundstedt: The Soldier and the Man* (London: 1952).

4. Geyr was born in Potsdam on February 2, 1886, the son of an old military family. He entered the service as a *Fahnenjunker* (officer-cadet) in 1904 and was commissioned in the family regiment, the 26th Light Dragoons (2nd Wuerttemberg Dragoons) in 1905. He was appointed to the War Academy in 1911 and spent most of World War I in General Staff positions, although he did briefly

command a battalion in 1917. A sophisticated and urbane person, bright, articulate, and well educated, and with great social skills, Geyr represented Germany as military attaché in London, Brussels, and The Hague in the 1930s and was an excellent military diplomat. Seeing that the future belonged to the panzer branch, he befriended Heinz Guderian and transferred to the tank arm in 1937. He commanded the 3rd Panzer Division (1937–40), XXIV Panzer Corps (1940–42), XXXX Panzer Corps (1942), and LVIII Reserve Panzer Corps (late 1942–43), before being assigned to OB West in July 1943 as commander of the then-forming Panzer Group West.

5. Baron Leo Geyr von Schweppenburg, "Panzer Tactics in Normandy," U.S. Army ETHINT 3, an interrogation conducted at Irschenhausen, Germany, December 11, 1947. On file, U.S. National Archives.

6. Friedrich Ruge, "The Invasion of Normandy," in H. A. Jacobsen and J. Rohwer, eds., *Decisive Battles of World War II: The German View* (New York: 1965), p. 321 (hereafter cited as "Ruge, 'Invasion' "). Friedrich Ruge was born in Leipzig on December 24, 1894, and entered the navy in 1914. Commissioned two years later, he spent most of World War I in torpedo boats. He joined the minesweepers in 1928 and became chief of the branch in 1937. Later he was commander of Minesweepers, West (1939–41) and led a battle group during the invasion of Norway. He was commander of Naval Security Forces, West, in 1941, and in 1943, he headed a special naval staff in Tunisia. In May 1943, he became commander of German Naval Forces, Italy, and in November 1943, he was assigned to Army Group B as naval adviser, largely because of his friendship with Rommel's then–chief of staff, Lieutenant General Alfred Gause.

In August 1944, Ruge would be reassigned to German naval headquarters and was chief of the Office of Naval Construction in November 1944 until the end of the war. Here he helped facilitate the building of the new Type XXI U-boat. He joined the West German Navy in 1956 and was inspector of the navy (1956–61). He retired in 1961 and wrote prolifically about the German Navy in World War I and II and about the Battle of Normandy and Field Marshal Rommel. He died in Tuebingen on July 3, 1985. Hans H. Hildebrand and Ernst Henriot, *Deutschland Admirale, 1849–1945* (Osnabrueck: 1990), Volume 3, pp. 164–65 (hereafter cited as "Hildebrand and Henriot").

7. Leo Geyr von Scheppenburg, "Panzer Group West (Mid-1943–15 July 1944)," Foreign Military Studies *MS # 258*, Office of the Chief of Military History, Washington, D.C. (hereafter referred to as "Geyr *MS # 258*." Another draft of the same manuscript will be referred to as "Geyr *MS # 466*").

Guenther Blumentritt was born in Munich in 1892. He had previously served as Rundstedt's operations officer in the Polish and French campaigns, was Field Marshal Hans von Kluge's chief of staff when he commanded the 4th Army (late 1940–early 1942), and was chief of operations at OKH (Oberkommando des Heeres, the High Command of the Army). He was dismissed from this post when Hitler suddenly fired his boss, Colonel General Franz Halder, as chief of the General Staff of the Army and replaced him with Kurt Zeitzler. Blumentritt became chief of staff of OB West on September 24, 1942, and was promoted to general of infantry on April 1, 1944. Wolf Keilig, *Die General des Heeres* (Friedberg: 1983), p. 38 (hereafter cited as "Keilig").

8. Geyr *MS # 466*.

9. Albert Seaton, *The Fall of Fortress Europe, 1943–1945* (New York: 1981), p. 11 (hereafter cited as "Seaton, *Fortress*").

10. Army Group B had been in Italy, where it had briefly shared military hegemony with Field Marshal Albert Kesselring's Army Group C, with B in control of the north and C in the south. This situation had proven to be unworkable, and Hitler had been forced to choose between the two. Because Kesselring felt that defending Italy south of Rome was feasible, and because Rommel wanted to retreat to the Alps, Hitler placed Kesselring in overall command. Rommel and his staff left Italy in late November 1943.

11. Cornelius Ryan, *The Longest Day* (New York, 1959; reprint ed., New York, 1959), p. 23 (hereafter cited as "Ryan, *Longest*").

12. Erwin Rommel, *The Rommel Papers*, B. H. Liddell Hart ed. (New York: 1953) (hereafter cited as "Rommel").

13. Gordon A. Harrison, *Cross-Channel Attack*, United States Army in World War II, European Theater of Operations, Office of the Chief of Military History (Washington, D.C.: 1951), p. 266 (hereafter cited as "Harrison").

14. Hugo Sperrle was born in 1885 and joined the army as an infantryman in 1903. During World War I, he joined the flying service and was commander of all aviation units attached to 7th Army at the end of the war. He remained in the army until 1935, when he transferred to the Luftwaffe as a major general. He was the first commander of the Condor Legion in Spain, where he pioneered the use of the terror bombing attack. He assumed command of the 3rd Air Fleet in 1938 and led it with considerable success against France in 1940. Promoted to field marshal on July 19, 1940, he was less successful in the Battle of Britain. He remained in France until he was relieved of his command. He was later tried as a war criminal at Nuremberg but was acquitted. Embittered after the war, he died in relative poverty in Munich in 1953.

15. Seaton, *Fortress*, p. 107.

16. Hans Speidel, *Invasion, 1944* (Chicago: 1950; reprint ed., New York: 1950), p. 107 (hereafter cited as "Speidel").

17. Seaton, *Fortress*, p. 107.

18. Speidel, pp. 46–47.

19. Wolfgang Pickert (born 1897) commanded the 9th Flak Division on the Eastern Front until it was destroyed at Stalingrad. He flew out of the pocket just before the end, allegedly because he was wounded. He was promoted to general of flak artillery on March 1, 1945, and ended the war as the general of the flak arm at OKL, the High Command of the Luftwaffe. He was still alive in the 1980s (Rudolf Absolon, comp., *Rangliste der Generale der deutschen Luftwaffe nach dem Stand vom 20 April 1945* [Friedberg: 1984], p. 30). Throughout his career on the Western Front, he refused to employ his anti-aircraft units as the army generals requested.

The III Flak Corps was formed from Headquarters, 11th Motorized Flak Division. It included the 431st, 653rd, 37th, and 79th Flak Regiments. Georg Tessin, *Verbaende und Truppen der deutschen Wehrmacht und Waffen-SS im Zweiten Weltkrieg, 1939–1945* (Osnabrueck: 1973), Volume 2, p. 161 (hereafter cited as "Tessin").

20. Harrison, pp. 225–27; Ruge, "Invasion," pp. 323–29; Charles MacDonald

and Martin Blumenson, "Recovery of France," in Vincent J. Esposito, ed., *A Concise History of World War II* (New York: 1964), p. 80; and Speidel, pp. 46–47.

21. Alfred C. Mierzejewski, "Railroads," in David G. Chandler and James L. Collins, Jr., eds. *The D-Day Encyclopedia* (New York: 1993), p. 448 (hereafter cited as "Chandler and Collins").

22. Harrison, pp. 146, 238; Rommel, p. 481.

23. Harrison, p. 144; Rommel, p. 481; also see John Toland, *Adolf Hitler* (New York: 1976; reprint ed., New York: 1977), p. 1072 (hereafter cited as "Toland").

24. Harrison, p. 241.

25. Bryan Perrett, *Knights of the Black Cross* (New York: 1986), p. 196.

26. Friedrich Ruge, *Rommel in Normandy*, Ursula R. Moessner, trans. (San Rafael, Calif.: 1979), p. 60 (hereafter cited as "Ruge, *Rommel*").

27. Erich Marcks was born in Berlin in 1891, the son of a university professor and a prominent Bismarck scholar. Young Marcks entered the army as a *Fahnenjunker* (officer-cadet) in the artillery in 1910. He was severely wounded in the face during World War I and bore the scars the rest of his life. His nose was particularly disfigured. Upon recovery, Marcks became a staff officer and joined the General Staff in 1917. After the war, he served in the Freikorps and later worked in the Defence Ministry for General Kurt von Schleicher. Later, when Schleicher was chancellor (1932–33), Marcks was his press secretary. He was also press secretary for Schleicher's predecessor and puppet, Franz von Papen. (Schleicher was murdered by the Gestapo in 1934.) Marcks, meanwhile, rejoined the army as a major in 1933, successively serving as commander of a battalion (1933–35), chief of staff of VIII Corps (1935–39), chief of staff of 18th Army (1939–40), and commander of the 101st Jaeger Division (1940–41). He fought in Poland, France, and Russia and played a prominent part in planning the invasion of the Soviet Union. On the fifth day of the invasion, he was seriously wounded and lost his left leg. Marcks returned to duty as commander of the 337th Infantry Division in March 1942 and later commanded LXVI and LXXXVII Corps, all in the West (1942–44). He was promoted to general of artillery on October 1, 1942, and assumed command of LXXXIV Corps on August 1, 1943. He was fatally wounded near St.-Lô. Sources differ as to the exact day. See Otto Jacobsen, *Erich Marcks, Soldat und Gelehrter* (Goettingen: 1971).

28. A Bavarian artillery officer and a man who was very good at military politics, Friedrich Dollmann was born in 1882. A colonel by 1930, he commanded 6th Artillery Regiment (1931–32) and was Artillery Commander VII and deputy commander of the 7th Infantry Division in Munich (1932–33). After serving as inspector of artillery (1933–34), he assumed command of Wehrkreis IX (1934–39), the main component of which became IX Corps upon mobilization in August 1939. Dollmann had commanded the 7th Army since October 1939 but had only seen action once in World War II—and on a secondary sector at that. He had commanded an army of occupation in France since 1940 and had never faced the Anglo-Americans in battle. His performance as commander of the 7th Army left much to be desired in 1944. Although he was an early supporter of National Socialism within the military, he became deeply troubled by their actions and had ceased to support them by 1944.

29. Paul Carell, *Invasion: They're Coming!* (Boston: 1965; reprint ed., New York: 1966), p. 55 (hereafter cited as "Carell").

30. Hans von Luck, *Panzer Commander* (New York: 1989), p. 159.

31. Carell, p. 97.

32. Hermann von Oppeln-Bronikowski was born in Berlin on January 2, 1899. He was educated at various cadet schools and entered the army as a senior cadet in 1917. He was commissioned in the 10th Ulan Regiment later that year. He remained in the cavalry branch until 1940. He commanded II/10th Cavalry Regiment (a reconnaissance unit) in Poland. Later he served on the staff of the General of Mobile Troops and led an ad hoc panzer brigade on the Eastern Front in 1941. Here he survived the destruction of his tank by enemy fire on at least three occasions. An incredibly brave officer, he commanded the 35th, 204th, and 11th Panzer Regiments (1941–autumn, 1943) but was not given his own division, almost certainly due to the fact he had a drinking problem. He was known to come in drunk at 8 A.M. Oppeln assumed command of the 100th Panzer Regiment in late 1943. In October 1944, he was given command of the 20th Panzer Division on the Eastern Front and was promoted to major general in 1945. A holder of the Knight's Cross with Oak Leaves, Swords and Diamonds, he survived the war and settled in Hanover (Keilig, p. 247).

33. Ryan, *Longest*, p. 297.

34. Martin Blumenson and the Editors of Time-Life Books, *Liberation* (Alexandria, Va.: 1978), p. 20 (hereafter cited as "Blumenson, *Liberation*").

35. Sigismund-Helmut von Dawans was born in 1899 and received his commission in 1918. Discharged in 1919, he reentered the service in 1924 and was on the staff of I Corps when World War II broke out. He served as Ia, 19th Panzer Division (1940–41); chief of staff, XIII Corps (1941–42); chief of staff, III Panzer Corps (1942–43); and chief of staff, 4th Army (1943). He became chief of staff of Panzer Group West in December 1943. After the RAF attack, Dawans and 16 others were buried together in a mass grave, located in one of the bomb craters.

36. Seaton, *Fortress*, p. 116.

37. Karl-Wilhelm von Schlieben was born in Eisenach in 1894. He joined the Imperial Army as a *Fahnenjunker* (officer-cadet) when World War I broke out and was commissioned shortly thereafter in the elite 3rd Foot Grenadier Regiment. He remained in the Reichsheer during the Weimar period. He was adjutant of Wehrkreis XIII when World War II started. Later he commanded the 108th Rifle Regiment (1940–42), 4th Rifle Brigade (1942), and 18th Panzer Division (1943). He was without a command for four months after the 18th was disbanded and, in December 1943, was given command of the 709th Infantry Division—a definite demotion. He was nevertheless promoted to lieutenant general on May 1, 1944.

Schlieben was held in British prisons until October 1947. He died in Giessen on June 18, 1964. Keilig, p. 302. Florian Berberich, "Karl-Wilhelm von Schlieben," in Chandler and Collins, pp. 482–83.

38. William B. Breuer, *Hitler's Fortress Cherbourg* (New York: 1984), p. 114 (hereafter cited as "Breuer, *Cherbourg*").

39. Harrison, pp. 441, 447.

40. Ibid, p. 441. Rear Admiral Walther Hennecke was born on May 23, 1898, in Bethelm/Hanover. He entered the Imperial Navy as a war volunteer in 1915 and was commissioned ensign in 1917. He spent most of his career on line ships and commanded the obsolete battleship *Schleswig-Holstein* from May to October

1941. He spent most of World War II, however, as commander of the Ship Artillery School. He assumed command in Normandy on May 6, 1943, and was promoted to rear admiral on March 1, 1944. Released from captivity on April 18, 1947, he died on New Year's Day in 1984. Hildebrand and Henriot, Volume 2, pp. 59–60.

41. Paul Hausser was, in the view of many, the single greatest influence on the military development of the Waffen-SS. He was born in Brandenburg on October 7, 1880, the son of a Prussian officer. Educated in various cadet and military prep schools, he graduated from Gross Lichterfelde (Imperial Germany's West Point) in 1899 and was assigned to the 155th Infantry Regiment. He became a member of the General Staff in 1912 . He spent most of World War I in General Staff positions, although he did command a company for a time. After the armistice, he served in the Freikorps (fighting against the Poles) and joined the Reichsheer. He retired as a major general (with an honorary promotion to lieutenant general) in 1932.

When Himmler offered him the job of training his SS-Verfuegungstruppe (SS-VT or Special Purposes Troops, the embryo of the Waffen-SS), Hausser joined the SS in 1934. He soon became responsible for the military training of all SS troops except the "Death's Head" concentration camp guards units. He assumed command of the SS-VT Division when it was formed in late 1939 and led it with distinction in the Netherlands, Belgium, and France in 1940. This unit later became the 2nd SS Panzer Division "Das Reich." Hausser led "Das Reich" on the Eastern Front until October 1941, when he was wounded in action and lost his right eye. After he returned to field duty in 1942, he was given command of the SS Panzer Corps (later II SS Panzer), which he led until 1944. An outstanding training commander and an excellent divisional commander, he led his corps with mixed results. He was a relatively poor army commander. Wounded at Falaise, he did not return to active duty until January 1945, when he was given command of Army Group G. By now thoroughly disillusioned with Hitler and the Nazi leadership, he was sacked at the end of March for refusing to obey one of Hitler's senseless "hold at all costs" orders.

Despite his prominence in the Waffen-SS, SS Colonel General Hausser was not subjected to a long imprisonment. A staunch defender of the Waffen-SS until the end, Paul Hausser died on December 28, 1972, at the age of 92.

42. Speidel, pp. 103–4.

43. Ruge, "Invasion," pp. 342–43; Carell, pp. 201–2.

44. Seaton, *Fortress*, p. 118.

45. Wilhelm Keitel was born on the family estate of Helmscherode in 1882. Although he would have preferred to have spent his life as a farmer, his family's farm was not large enough to support his and his father's family, so he joined the army as an artillery *Fahnenjunker* in 1901. As a battery commander, he was severely wounded by a shell splinter on the Western Front during World War I. Upon recovery, he was posted to the General Staff as a captain in 1915. Although later known as "Lakeitel" (*lakei* means "lackey" in German), he definitely had organizational talents. Except for a brief tour as commander of the 6th Artillery Regiment, he served in the Defense Ministry from 1925 to 1933, rising to the head of the Organizations Office. After briefly commanding the 22nd Infantry Division in Bremen, Keitel returned to Berlin in October 1935 as head of the

General Office of the War Ministry. When the war minister, Field Marshal von Blomberg, fell from power in February 1938, the position of war minister was abolished and Keitel became commander in chief of the High Command of the Armed Forces (OKW), although he was largely a figurehead and the real power lay with Hitler. Keitel was hanged at Nuremberg as a war criminal on October 16, 1946.

46. Matthew Cooper, *The German Army, 1933–1945* (Briarcliff Manor, N.Y.: 1978), p. 504.

47. Breuer, *Cherbourg*, p. 256.

48. Geyr's forced retirement lasted only a few weeks. On July 21, 1944, the day after the unsuccessful attempt on Hitler's life, his friend Heinz Guderian became the new chief of the General Staff of the Army. The following month, Guderian managed to get Geyr installed as his successor as inspector general of panzer troops. Captured by the Americans at the end of the war, Geyr was a prolific writer about military affairs. Until the end of his life, Geyr maintained that he was right and Rommel was wrong concerning the use of German strategic reserves in Normandy. It is difficult to follow his logic, however. He died at Irschenhausen on January 27, 1974.

49. Heinrich Eberbach was born in Stuttgart in 1895 and joined the Imperial Army in 1914. Commissioned second lieutenant in the infantry in 1915, he was captured on the Western Front and held prisoner for more than a year. After the war, he was not selected for retention in the Reichsheer, so, like many military officers, he joined the police. Eberbach saw the potential of motorized warfare early on and was active in developing paramilitary motorized police units. He returned to the army as a major in armored branch in 1935 and commanded the 35th Panzer Regiment (1938–41), distinguishing himself in Poland and France. He then successively led the 5th Panzer Brigade, 4th Panzer Division, and XXXXVIII Panzer Corps on the Eastern Front (1941–44), before assuming command of Panzer Group West, which was upgraded to 5th Panzer Army on August 6, 1944. He was still alive in West Germany in the 1970s. Friedrich von Stauffenberg, "Panzer Commanders of the Western Front," unpublished manuscript in the possession of the author (hereafter cited as "Stauffenberg MS").

50. Speidel, pp. 105–6; David Irving, *The Trail of the Fox* (New York: 1977), p. 403 (hereafter cited as "Irving, *Trail*").

51. B. H. Liddell Hart, *The Other Side of the Hill* (London: 1951), p. 413 (hereafter cited as "Hart, *Hill*").

CHAPTER II

HANS VON KLUGE AND THE CONSPIRACY OF JULY 20

Guenther Hans von Kluge was born in Posen, Prussia, on October 30, 1882. After attending various cadet schools, he was admitted to Gross Lichterfelde, Germany's equivalent of West Point, from which he graduated shortly after the turn of the century. On March 22, 1901, he joined the 46th Field Artillery Battalion at Wolfenbuettel as a second lieutenant. By the late 1900s, he was a first lieutenant and a battalion adjutant. Then he was selected for General Staff training and was sent to the War Academy in Berlin. Only about 15% of applicants at that time passed the preliminary tests for admission to the War Academy; fully two-thirds of these never graduated. Kluge did graduate, however, and his future in the army was assured. In 1913 he was on the Greater General Staff in Berlin. When World War I broke out in 1914, he went to France as a captain on the staff of the XXI Corps. Later he led a battalion on the Western Front (November 1915–April 1916) before resuming his General Staff appointments with the 89th Infantry Division (1916–18) and the Alpine Corps (1918). Captain von Kluge fought in the battles around Artois and in Flanders and was seriously wounded near Verdun in 1918.[1]

By the end of the war, Kluge was recognized as an energetic and efficient staff officer. He was selected for retention in the Reichsheer and was assigned to the staff of the 3rd Infantry Division in 1921. He served in staff positions in the Defense Ministry (1923–26), as commander of the V Battalion, 3rd Artillery Regiment at Sagan (1926–28), and as chief of staff of the 1st Cavalry Division at Frankfurt-an-der-Oder (1928–30). In 1930 he succeeded Baron Werner von Fritsch as commander of the 2nd Artillery Regiment, and in 1931 he was named *Artilleriefuehrer* III and deputy commander of the 3rd Infantry Division. Successively promoted to major (1923), lieutenant colonel (1927), and colonel (1930), he was promoted to major general and named Inspector of Signal Troops in

February 1933. Fourteen months later he was promoted to lieutenant general and, in October 1934, became commander of the 6th Infantry Division at Muenster. He continued his rapid advancement in September 1935, when he was named commander of Wehrkreis VI (VI Military District) at Muenster, controlling the 6th Infantry Division and the 9th Frontier Command. This was at the beginning of Hitler's rapid military expansion, and the 16th and 26th Infantry Divisions at Rheine and Cologne, respectively, were created under Kluge's general direction. He was promoted to general of artillery on August 1, 1936.[2]

Kluge was a firm supporter of his friend Werner von Fritsch, the commander in chief of the army from 1934 to 1938.[3] In January 1938, Fritsch was forced into retirement on phoney charges of homosexuality, trumped up by Heinrich Himmler, head of the SS, and his deputy, Reinhard Heydrich, chief of the SD (Sicherheitsdienst, or Security Service). Kluge let it be known that he was outraged and that something should be done about Himmler and the Nazis. It was one of the few times in his professional career he stood up for something as a matter of principle, and it cost him. General of Artillery Walther von Brauchitsch, the new commander in chief of the army, "sold out" to the Nazis.[4] They paid off his estranged wife, who agreed to accept a quiet divorce (and a large amount of cash from the NSDAP). Brauchitsch then married his beautiful, 100% Nazi mistress and dismissed a number of officers thought to be unfavorably disposed toward Hitler and/or the party. One of those forced into retirement was Hans von Kluge.

Kluge was a traditional Prussian officer who showed considerable military talent. He was also marked, as Robert Wistrich wrote, by a "vacillating character and weakminded opportunism."[5] He had a sharp brain and recognized the monstrosity of the Nazi regime, but he also realized that there was considerable scope for personal and professional advancement if he cooperated with it. He also knew what the right thing to do was. Throughout World War II, Kluge realized he should join the anti-Hitler conspiracy but vacillated between duty to the Fatherland and personal gain. He never really did choose between the two, but his forced retirement clearly convinced him that he would have to at least pretend to play along with the Nazis.

Hitler almost pushed the world into war in September 1938. Even with the ink still wet on the Munich Accords, he continued his military expansion. Unfortunately, the Third Reich lacked good officers at every level. Those it had were excellent, but there were not enough of them. The Treaty of Versailles, it will be recalled, had limited Germany to 4,000 army officers, and Hitler had only renounced it three and a half years before. (Ludwig Beck, the chief of the General Staff until August 1938, had estimated that 7% of the men in the army should be officers in case of war but that it could get by with 3% during a peacetime expansion.

In 1938, the army could not even maintain that level, despite the fact that it had recalled reserve, territorial, retired, and police officers to active duty.) With a shortage of experienced commanders, especially after the purges following the dismissal of Fritsch and the defense minister, Field Marshal Werner von Blomberg,[6] Hitler was persuaded to recall Kluge and give him command of Army Group 6, which was formed in October. Headquartered in Hanover in northern Germany, it included Wehrkreise IX, X, and XI, with six infantry divisions.[7]

For the invasion of Poland, Brauchitsch changed the name of Army Group 6 to 4th Army and earmarked it to direct the secondary attack: the drive across the "Polish Corridor" that separated East Prussia from the rest of the Reich. Hermann Goering had a great personal hatred for Hans von Kluge, however, and persuaded the Fuehrer to veto his appointment. Brauchitsch appealed to Hitler to reconsider. (Perhaps Brauchitsch felt guilty about the way he treated Kluge the year before, or perhaps he just did not like having his appointments interfered with by the likes of Goering.) Unlike his deputy, Adolf Hitler had nothing personal against Kluge and did not distrust him any more than any other General Staff officer. He did, however, doubt Kluge's ability. Even so, he allowed himself to be overruled by the commander in chief of the army. Hans von Kluge, however, was clearly on probation; he would have to prove himself in Poland.[8]

Kluge passed the test with flying colors. He knifed through the Polish Corridor in three days, smashing a Polish Army in the progress, and linked up with 3rd Army, coming out of East Prussia. He then turned and drove aggressively on Warsaw from the northwest. Shortly thereafter his airplane crashed, and he spent the rest of the campaign in a hospital or on rehabilitation leave. Hitler had seen enough, however; he never doubted Kluge's abilities again.

Promoted to colonel general after Poland, Kluge quickly recovered and led 4th Army in the French campaign, and again he distinguished himself in a secondary role. He played a part in the delay at Dunkirk, advising Gerd von Rundstedt, his army group commander, to halt the panzer divisions on May 23.[9] The magnitude of this mistake was not known for some time, however, and it did not affect Kluge's advancement. He was promoted to field marshal on July 19, 1940, at the age of 57.

Unlike most German generals, Kluge was in favor of the invasion of the Soviet Union, which began on June 22, 1941. Kluge's 4th Army initially contained 21 infantry and two security divisions and was the largest to cross the border. On June 26, however, Hitler decreed that Kluge hand his infantry over to the 2nd Army and take charge of the 2nd and 3rd Panzer Groups (later Armies), which were led by Heinz Guderian and Hermann Hoth, respectively. Hitler took this step over the pointed objections of Field Marshal Fedor von Bock, the army group commander, who did not think Kluge could handle the task.[10] Guderian mercilessly criticized Kluge's handling of armored formations, but his remarks must be taken with a grain of salt, for he was hypercritical of people he did not like, and he did not get along with Kluge at all. The two were even considering fighting a duel at one point, before cooler heads intervened. Hoth, on the other hand, was a dispassionate, objective observer, and he also was highly critical of Kluge, charging him with advancing on too wide a front and failing to seal off the Smolensk Pocket quickly enough, allowing a number of Red Army formations to escape.[11] By early August, Kluge was commanding infantry forces again.

In September, Kluge objected to making the final drive on Moscow, saying that it was too late in the season. When Hitler ordered the advance anyway, Kluge directed the main assault, but in such a slow and half-hearted manner that he came under criticism, particularly from Colonel General Erich Hoepner, whose 4th Panzer Army bore the brunt of the fighting while Kluge remained pretty much inactive.[12] The Soviets counterattacked on December 6, and on December 18, Field Marshal von Bock was relieved of the command of Army Group Center at his own request. He was replaced by Hans von Kluge.[13]

During the retreat from Moscow, Kluge extracted revenge on the generals with whom he had clashed. Within a week he signaled Fuehrer Headquarters that either he or Guderian must go. He, Kluge, was faithfully obeying Hitler's orders to stand fast and to hold at all costs, whereas Guderian was retreating when he considered the situation hopeless, whether higher headquarters approved the decision or not. On December 25, 1941, Guderian was relieved of his command. Germany lost one of its best tank commanders.

In Russia, Kluge obeyed Hitler's orders blindly. "If scapegoats were needed, von Kluge could find them," Colonel Seaton wrote later. "If heads must fall, von Kluge took good care to see that his would not be among them."[14] Among those whose heads did roll were General Ludwig Kuebler, commander of the 4th Army; Erich Hoepner, commander of the 4th Panzer Army; and, of course, Kluge's hated rival, General Guderian, commander of the 2nd Panzer Army and "father" of the blitzkrieg.[15] Several corps and divisional commanders were replaced as well. Army Group Center survived, however, and in part because Kluge was usually able to obtain Hitler's permission to retreat, even if the Fuehrer gave it only with the greatest reluctance and only when it was absolutely necessary.

Meanwhile, Hans von Kluge discovered that his own headquarters was a hotbed of anti-Nazi resistance.

The term "the German Resistance" is somewhat misleading, because it seems to imply that there was only one and that it had a sense of

unity. In fact, there were numerous resistance groups; some did not know of the existence of the others (or had only the vaguest idea of their existence and activities); and they were united only in the sense that they had one common desire: to get rid of Adolf Hitler. Some of them did not even want to eliminate the Nazi Party. Some even balked at the idea of assassinating Hitler; they feared the creation of a great Nazi martyr and wanted him arrested and tried and/or declared insane. Some feared that the killing of Hitler might create another "stabbed in the back" legend à la 1918. Others, such as Count Helmuth James von Moltke, were so repulsed by the thought of taking a human life—even Hitler's—that they rejected any violent solution whatsoever.

The opposition to Hitler first jelled into a true anti-Hitler conspiracy in 1938, during the Sudetenland crisis. It began to fall apart in the wake of British Prime Minister Sir Neville Chamberlain's sacrifice of Czechoslovakia at Munich and Hitler's subsequent occupation of the entire country. Nor was there significant opposition to Hitler's conquest of Poland in military circles; the Prussians in particular hated Poland and felt that the Poles got what they deserved in 1939. There was some military opposition to the Einsatzgruppen (SS mass murder squads) in German-occupied Poland in late 1939 (most notably from Colonel General von Blaskowitz and Major General Friedrich Mieth), but it was not particularly widespread and was more anti-SS than anti-Hitler.[16] In any case, it was soon rendered silent. Within the military, the outbreak of the war itself was opposed only by General of Infantry Georg Thomas, the chief of the Economic Office at OKW, who was against it for economic and military reasons: He did not think the German economy was strong enough to enable the Reich to win a war of attrition. He did not oppose the war on moral grounds.

There was opposition to the Fuehrer's military adventures in Scandinavia, France, and the Low Countries, most notably from Colonel Generals Walter von Reichenau, Erwin von Witzleben, and Ritter Wilhelm von Leeb[17] and from Colonel Hans Oster of the Abwehr, but only Witzleben and the debonair Oster, a confirmed monarchist and former subordinate to General Kurt von Bredow—one of the victims of the "Blood Purge" of 1934—actually wanted to do Hitler in. In fact, the Resistance had been routed and thrown into disarray in 1938, and it was five years later before it could really be called a major, organized threat again. Between October 1938 and February 1943, the closest Hitler came to being assassinated was on November 8, 1939, when former watchmaker Johann Georg Elser, acting alone, nearly succeeded in blowing him up in the Buergerbrauekeller, a Munich beer hall. There were other plots, but none came very close to succeeding. Field Marshal Erwin von Witzleben, the commander in chief of Army Group C and OB West, was also perfectly willing to put Hitler to death, if the Fuehrer would come to Paris. But

Hitler only came to the French city once in his life, and that was shortly after it fell, before Witzleben took charge. He landed unannounced at the Le Bourget Airport at 5 A.M. on June 23, took a whirlwind tour, visited the Champs-Elysees, the Opera, the Louvre, the Eiffel Tower, and the Invalides (where he saw Napoleon's tomb), and left again before most of the city woke up. Witzleben was forced to retire in March 1942, and the new OB West, Field Marshal Gerd von Rundstedt, spent most of his time in his luxurious headquarters, where he became too fond of French cognac. He was certainly not conspiracy material.

The anti-Hitler conspiracy became leaderless on November 5, 1938. On that day, Hitler made a cryptic remark to Colonel General Walther von Brauchitsch, commander in chief of the army from 1938 to 1941, concerning the "spirit of Zossen"—referring to the spirit of defeatism that he imagined existed on the Headquarters of the commander in chief of the army, then located in Zossen, about 30 miles from Berlin. General of Artillery Franz Halder, the chief of the General Staff from 1938 to 1942, took the remark to mean that Hitler knew they were plotting to overthrow him. He was immediately filled with terror. He quickly burned the plans for the coup and never again actively conspired against his master.[18] With Witzleben away from Berlin, there was no officer in a position of responsibility and/or with a powerful personality to take charge and organize an anti-Hitler putsch. One reason for this, of course, was that Hitler was still winning his victories. Another was that Brauchitsch, Halder, and most of the other generals were thoroughly intimidated by the Fuehrer. After 1939, there were few protests concerning the activities of the Einsatzgruppen; few objections concerning the Commissar Order, which specified that Soviet political officers were to be shot, even after they had been captured or had surrendered; and almost no protests about the fact that tens of thousands of Soviet prisoners were being systematically starved to death.

One man who did protest was Lieutenant Colonel Henning von Treschow. Born in Magdeburg in 1901, he came from an old Prussian officer family. He joined the army as a *Fahnenjunker* (officer-cadet) in 1917 and was commissioned into the famous 1st Foot Guards Regiment five months before the end of the war. He was a platoon leader on the Western Front when the armistice came. Discharged in 1920, he could not return to duty until 1926, due to the fact that the Treaty of Versailles limited the Officer Corps to 4,000 men. During that time, he worked for a bank and traveled around the world. Significantly, when he did return to duty, he was sponsored by Field Marshal Paul von Hindenburg and assigned to the 9th Infantry Regiment in Potsdam (called "I.R. von 9" by its detractors). He began clandestine General Staff training in 1932 and became a General Staff officer in 1936. Treschow served as operations officer of the 221st Infantry Division in the Polish campaign, after

which he joined the staff of his uncle, Colonel General (later Field Marshal) Fedor von Bock as Ia (chief of operations) of an Army Group B. He served in the conquests of the Netherlands, Belgium, and France.

Like most of the Officer Corps, Treschow initially welcomed the rise of Hitler and the NSDAP, despite his concern over their antireligious policies. By 1936, however, he was demanding that the army take measures against the SS and Gestapo, and in 1938 he advocated retaining Colonel General Baron Werner von Fritsch as commander in chief of the army, by offensive action if necessary. Exceptionally capable, Treschow was considered far and above the average General Staff officer by his superiors and was rated as one of the outstanding officers in the Wehrmacht. He was also an extremely straitlaced man with no tolerance for the unfair and the unjust, so naturally he grew to abhor Hitler and the Nazi regime. In 1938, he believed that a general European war must be prevented, since Germany could not win it; therefore, Hitler must be assassinated. As early as 1939, he told Fabian von Schlabrendorff that "both duty and honor demand from us that we should do our best to bring about the downfall of Hitler and National Socialism in order to save Germany and Europe from barbarism."[19] In 1941, Treschow pressed von Bock into protesting against the Commissar Order, but it was without effect. Considering this order barbaric and uncivilized, Treschow became an extremely active anti-Hitler conspirator. As a result of his efforts, Headquarters, Army Group Center, became the focal point of the anti-Hitler conspiracy. His recruits included Lieutenant Colonel Georg Schulze-Buettger, a former aide to Colonel General Ludwig Beck (the chief of the General Staff until 1938) and the operations officer of Army Group Center from 1941 until early 1943, when he became Ia of Army Group South and was promoted to colonel. (Schulze-Buettger became chief of staff of the 4th Panzer Army in the summer of 1944 and was later executed for his part in the conspiracy on October 13, 1944). He was replaced as Ia of Army Group Center by Lieutenant Colonel Hans-Alexander von Voss, the former army group training officer. He was another former member of "I.R. von 9," the son-in-law of General Joachim von Stuelpnagel, and a former staff officer to Field Marshal von Witzleben. He committed suicide on November 8, 1944. Voss was succeeded as training officer of Army Group Center by Major Hans-Ulrich von Oertzen, who later joined the staff of Wehrkreis III in Berlin. He committed suicide on July 21, 1944, the day after the Stauffenberg assassination attempt failed.

Another conspirator was Lieutenant Colonel Berndt von Kleist, a former member of Treschow's own 1st Prussian Foot Guards Regiment. He had lost a leg in World War I but was now back on active duty as the Chief Supply Officer of Army Group Center. He served as liaison officer between Treschow and Dr. Carl Goerdeler, the civilian head of the conspiracy, and the conspirators in Berlin.[20] Other conspirators included Colonel Baron Rudolf-Christoph von Gersdorff, the chief intelligence officer of Army Group Center; Lieutenant of Reserves Fabian von Schlabrendorff, aide to the Ia and a principal liaison officer between the army group and Berlin; Major (later Lieutenant Colonel) Horst Pretzell, operations officer in early 1942 and intelligence officer from March 1942 to February 1943; both of von Bock's aides, Major (later Lieutenant Colonel) Count Carl-Hans von Hardenberg and Lieutenant Count Heinrich von Lehndorff; and several other field and company grade officers. As a result of Treschow's efforts, the Headquarters of Army Group Center represented the strongest center of opposition to Hitler in existence from 1941 until Colonel Count von Stauffenberg became the de facto head of the conspiracy in the fall of 1943.

Treschow and the conspirators made little progress during the Russian campaign of 1941. These were the days of the blitzkrieg: the rapid advances, the double envelopments, and the magnificent victories with huge numbers of prisoners. The Fuehrer seemed to be a military genius, and the senior generals in the Soviet Union had neither the time nor inclination to engage in anti-Hitler plotting. The farsighted General Thomas toured the Eastern Front in September 1941 and tried to muster support against the regime, but without success. After the arrival of winter and the defeat before Moscow, however, the generals became more receptive to the idea of ridding themselves and Germany of Adolf Hitler and his regime. In Berlin, meanwhile, a group that included Beck, former Ambassador von Hassell, Oster, and General of Infantry Friedrich Olbricht, the chief of the General Army Office and deputy commander of the Replacement Army, combined to nominate Beck as de facto head of the conspiracy.[21] Dr. Goerdeler and his civilian confederates accepted this arrangement at the end of March 1942, although all parties agreed that a military regime would be a temporary, emergency expedient only and would yield power to a civilian-dominated government as quickly as possible. From July 1942, these groups were in permanent contact with Headquarters, Army Group Center.

That summer, Treschow instructed Lieutenant Colonel Baron von Gersdorff, the Ib of the army group, to obtain the equipment suitable for use in an assassination attempt. Unlike some of the other conspirators, Treschow was not particularly worried that "innocent people" might be killed in an assassination of Adolf Hitler. Their objective, he believed, was to save the entire German nation; if a few innocent persons died in order to save millions of other innocent people from death or terrible suffering, that was regrettable but necessary. Using this reasoning, he ruled out an assassination attempt using the most risky methods, such as an attack with a pistol or by a single marksman, because of the high possibility of failure. He instructed Gersdorff to produce a bomb. Specifically, he wanted one that occupied the smallest possible space but produced the greatest possible effect and that had an adjustable timing mechanism. Above all else, however, it must be silent. This requirement eliminated German fuses, which burned with a slight hiss. From conspirators in the Abwehr, Gersdorff obtained several samples of high-grade British explosives, some of which had been captured from British commandos at Saint Nazaire and Dieppe and some of which had been dropped to the French resistance.

In June 1942, Lieutenant Baron Philipp von Boeselager, another Treschow conspirator, joined the staff as Kluge's aide. In January 1943, he used his influence to persuade Kluge to agree to form the "Boeselager Cavalry Unit" under the command of his brother Georg, a highly decorated captain and noted pentathlon athlete.[22] The project was approved by Colonel Helmuth Stieff, the chief of the Organization Section at OKH, who saw to it that Boeselager was provided with first-rate equipment. The unit soon grew into Cavalry Regiment Center, a two-battalion formation that served as a fire brigade that was permanently at the disposal of HQ, Army Group Center. Unknown to Kluge, however, it was also permanently at the disposal of the conspiracy. Its total strength was about 2,200 men, 650 of whom were Russian Cossacks.

On March 7, 1943, Admiral Wilhelm Canaris, the head of the Abwehr (the military intelligence branch of OKW), boarded an airplane at the Berlin-Gatow airfield and took off for the headquarters of Army Group Center's HQ, then located at Smolensk.[23] He was accompanied by Major General Hans Oster,[24] Colonel Erwin Lahousen (the chief of the sabotage branch), Lahousen's special assistant Dr. Hans Dohnanyi, and several other staff officers. As they left Berlin, the officers could clearly see the effects of the last RAF raid, six days before, which had left 35,000 homeless and 700 dead. Theoretically, the purpose of the Abwehr officials was to hold a general intelligence conference with officers of Kluge's staff. Once there, however, they gave Baron von Gersdorff another box of British explosives. Meanwhile, Canaris assured von Treschow that everything was ready for a coup in Berlin. Coordination measures were discussed, and Treschow declared that the "flash"—the event initiating the anti-Hitler putsch—would take place at the next available opportunity. The "flash" was to be the assassination of Adolf Hitler.

The opportunity came six days later, when three Focke-Wulf Condors, escorted by several Me-109 fighters, landed at Smolensk, and Adolf Hitler stepped out, accompanied by General Jodl, his SS bodyguards, stenographers, aides, photographers, staff officers, and other cronies. As usual, when it came to acting against Hitler, however, Field Marshal von Kluge's nerve failed him at the decisive moment, and he forbade Treschow to make an attempt upon the Fuehrer's life. This precluded Treschow from using Boeselager's unit to gun Hitler down, but the resourceful General Staff officer had a backup plan. It had occurred to his aide, Fabian von Schlabrendorff, that easily formed British plastic explosives could be molded into a bomb that had the shape and weight of two bottles of Cointreau, a French liquor. While Hitler was eating a vegetarian lunch with Kluge and his staff, Schlabrendorff arranged for Colonel Heinz Brandt, one of Hitler's aides, to carry back the two bottles of "Cointreau" to Colonel Helmuth Stieff, head of the Army Organization Section at Rastenburg.[25] Hitler, who was now five weeks away from his fifty-fourth birthday, looked much older. His face was pale, he hunched forward in his chair, and his hands trembled when they were at rest. He hardly looked like the vigorous, awe-inspiring Fuehrer the propaganda ministry portrayed him as being. Even so, he continued to predict great victories in Russia in the coming year.

As soon as lunch was over, Hitler announced that he had to immediately return to Rastenburg. As everyone prepared to depart for the airfield, Treschow accompanied Schlabrendorff to his quarters, where they had hidden the bomb. Then they took a staff car to the airfield. Hitler was just getting ready to board the Condor when they arrived. Schlabrendorff glanced at Treschow, who answered with his eyes. The lieutenant surreptitiously depressed the fuse and handed the bomb to Colonel Brandt. It was set to explode in 30 minutes. Treschow hurried back to headquarters and put through a coded telephone call to Berlin, informing General Olbricht that the "flash" would take place in 30 minutes. They predicted that the Condor would blow apart and crash somewhere north of Minsk, 200 miles to the southwest.

The tension in Smolensk was terrible as they waited for word that the dictator's airplane had exploded. More than two hours passed; then Treschow received a telephone call from East Prussia. The Fuehrer had arrived safely; there had been no incidents. Obviously something had gone wrong. Now Treschow and Schlabrendorff had another problem: They had to recover the unexploded bomb before Brandt gave the package to Stieff, or the plot would be discovered and the conspiracy revealed. In that case, they would all end up dead or in concentration camps. Treschow had no choice but to suppress his agitation and telephone Colonel Brandt. Trying to make a joke out of the entire incident, he told Brandt that he had mistakenly sent the wrong package to Colonel Stieff. He would send someone on tomorrow's courier airplane to pick it up and to deliver the correct package.

Lieutenant von Schlabrendorff departed for Rastenburg early the next morning. He nearly had a heart attack when he entered Brandt's office because the colonel was casually tossing the "bottles" in the air from one hand to another. If he dropped it, Schlabrendorff thought, the bomb might yet explode. With his heart in his throat, he quickly retrieved the package, apologized for the mix-up, and departed as quickly as he could, despite the fact that the colonel wanted to chat. He headed for the nearby railroad station at Korschen and boarded the special OKW train leaving for Berlin. Only when he was alone and able to lock the door to his compartment did he carefully remove the wrapping paper and examine the bomb. He found that the acid capsule had shattered, that the acid had eaten through the wire, and that the firing pin had been activated; the detonator, however, had failed to function, making the bomb a dud. The Fuehrer had been lucky once more.

By now, the insiders in the army had nicknamed Kluge "Der kluge Hans"—Clever Hans, a play on words with his name, similar to "Tricky Dicky"—because he liked to play both sides of any issue and was quite good at it. No better example of this character trait can be cited than his attitude toward the Kursk offensive of 1943. In early May, he arrived for a conference at Fuehrer Headquarters, prepared to speak in favor of delaying the offensive—until he learned that Hitler had already decided to delay it. When he saw the dictator, Kluge spoke *against* a postponement. The field marshal knew he would thereby be absolved of any blame if the operation failed, which it did.

In a similar manner, he was on both sides of the anti-Hitler conspiracy. He gave it noncommittal encouragement, expressing sympathy for it but never commitment. Kluge's anti-Hitlerism, on the other hand, did not stop him from accepting a check for 250,000 reichsmarks from the Fuehrer in 1942, as a combination bonus and birthday present. This was a huge amount of money for the day.

On the fighting front, however, Kluge continued to prove himself a competent tactician. In 1942, he conducted a brilliant feint, deceiving Stalin into believing that the Germans intended to launch their summer offensive against Moscow, instead of to the south. Stalin and his generals were quite surprised (and had their huge reserves in the wrong place) when the Wehrmacht attacked on the Don and drove toward Stalingrad and the Caucasus.

Later that year, Kluge faced several minor Soviet offensives and defeated them all. Most notably, he destroyed Cavalry Corps Below (20,000 men) at Kirov, after it had broken through, and the Soviet 39th Army and XI Cavalry Corps (40,000 men) at Belyy, also after they had penetrated the German front.

On March 21, 1943, only a week after the Smolensk assassination attempt failed, the conspirators tried again. This time Colonel Baron Rudolf-Christoph von Gersdorff, the chief intelligence officer of Army Group Center, volunteered for a suicide mission.[26] Since his wife had died the previous year, he told Treschow, life had lost its joy and he was now prepared to blow himself to pieces for the Fatherland. He had learned that Hitler had agreed to visit the Zeughaus, a Berlin armory, to inspect captured Russian arms and equipment before attending the annual Heroes Memorial Day ceremonies in the capital. Since much of the equipment had been captured by Army Group Center, it was only natural that an officer from the army group be on hand, in case the Fuehrer had any technical questions, which was likely. Treschow told Gersdorff to fly to Berlin and try to learn the details of the Fuehrer's schedule; he also instructed Schlabrendorff to hand over his bomb (now outfitted with a new fuse) to Gersdorff. Gersdorff had a difficult time even getting into the Zeughaus, because he was not on the list of those permitted inside at the same time as the Fuehrer. Fortunately, Colonel General Walter Model, the commander of the 9th Army, intervened on Gersdorff's behalf, and he was in the armory when Hitler arrived at 1 P.M. Baron von Gersdorff had wanted to use the standard 4.5-second German "potato masher" grenade fuse, but it would not fit inside Schlabrendorff's bomb, so he had no choice but to use a British fuse. The most rapid such fuse in their possession had a 10-minute delay. As Hitler raced through his speech, Gersdorff made his final plans: When the Fuehrer finished his address, he would activate the bomb. After 10 minutes had elapsed, he would grab Hitler and hold him until the bomb exploded. He never had the chance, however. Hitler spoke for less than 15 minutes (a record for brevity), acknowledged the applause, and headed in the direction of Gersdorff and the captured equipment, as the colonel crushed the acid capsule and activated the bomb. The Fuehrer was closely followed by Goering, Himmler, Keitel, and Doenitz; and for a moment, the colonel thought that he might get them all. But it was not to be. Hitler all but ignored the captured equipment and almost raced for the exit. Within 2 minutes he was out of the door and gone. Defeated and horrified, Colonel von Gersdorff hurriedly looked for a place to neutralize the bomb. Fortunately he found it in a stall in a nearby men's room. He was on his way back to Russia the next day.

Throughout the summer of 1943, the conspiracy floundered due to the fact that it lacked a leader. Henning von Treschow was too junior in rank (he was not promoted to major general until late January 1944) and was too far from Berlin to be truly effective, and General Beck was a sick man, slowly recovering from a cancer operation. Never dynamic in the sense that Guderian, Rommel, or Reichenau were dynamic, the scholarly and intellectual Beck became more of an adviser to the conspirators, rather than a leader; in fact, the conspiracy had no real leader. What they needed was an energetic senior general who presently occupied a position of power and could command troops. In September 1943, they thought they had found one in Field Marshal von Kluge. It was obvious that he did not object to having conspirators on his staff. Perhaps he could be persuaded to join them. During a visit to Rastenburg, Colonel

Stieff (who had recently joined the conspiracy) approached the field marshal and had a frank conversation with him. This was followed by a meeting between Kluge, Beck, Treschow, Olbricht, and Goerdeler in Berlin. At last, the vacillating army group commander committed himself to the conspiracy and to the idea of removing Adolf Hitler by force. Significantly, however, he did not appoint von Treschow as his chief of staff because the strong-willed anti-Nazi had too much influence on him.

Kluge's leadership was short-lived. He returned to the Eastern Front and five weeks later, on October 28, suffered a near-fatal automobile accident on an icy Russian road. He was in traction for months. His replacement at Army Group Center was Field Marshal Ernst Busch, an avid Nazi. Treschow, meanwhile, was named acting commander of the 442nd Infantry Regiment on October 15. He was to lead this unit for a month, prior to taking up his new post as chief of staff of the 2nd Army on November 20, 1943. All of his efforts to place himself at Fuehrer HQ— so that he could personally direct an assassination attempt—failed.

It must be pointed out that Hitler knew how to disrupt assassination attempts. "I understand very well why 90% of the assassination attempts throughout history have been successful," he declared. "The only effective precaution is to lead an irregular life—to take a walk or a drive at a different time each day and always travel unexpectedly. Whenever I go anywhere by road, I do so as far as possible unexpectedly, and without warning the police."[27] The next man to make the Fuehrer his target, however, came closer than any of them to finishing the job. He was Claus Phillip Maria Schenck, Count von Stauffenberg.

He was born at Jettingen, Bavaria, on November 15, 1907, the third son of Alfred von Stauffenberg, the senior marshal at the court of the king of Wuerttemberg. His first two children, twin brothers christened Berthold and Alexander, had been born two years before. Claus's mother, Caroline (nee Countess von Uexkuell) lacked all of Count Alfred's considerable practical abilities but instilled in her sons a love of music, literature, and poetry. Claus's ancestors on his mother's side included Gneisenau and Yorck, major Prussian military heroes of the Napoleonic Wars.

Like Erwin Rommel, Claus von Stauffenberg was a gifted and highly intelligent Swabian. Also like Rommel, he had a high moral code and a strong and unbending personality, and he did not "suffer fools gladly." Unlike Rommel, however, Claus was a born aristocrat (the Stauffenberg castle near Hechingen can be traced back to 1262) and was the product of generations of cultured breeding, reinforced by a fine education at the strongly humanistic Eberhard Ludwig School in Stuttgart, the city where he spent much of his youth. A tall, handsome young man of considerable charm, he was somewhat arrogant and overbearing, but nevertheless he had an active social life and was an accomplished cellist, until he realized that he would never play above a certain level. Then he dropped the instrument altogether. Intellectually, he was a follower of the Symbolic poet Stefan George, an advocate of a philosophy of action and of a rebirth of Germany and a man who exerted a strange and magnetic influence upon his disciples.

Young Stauffenberg also had a powerful and dynamic personality and was a natural leader. In 1944, a Gestapo report stated that he had "a remarkable gift of oratory and a fascinating ability to captivate others."[28] He seemed destined for a distinguished career as an architect; then, for reasons that were never explained, he dropped his original life's plan and, in 1926, at the age of 19, joined the Reichsheer as an enlisted man. Naturally, he chose the 17th Cavalry—the family regiment—then stationed at Bamberg. Promoted to *Fahnenjunker* (officer-cadet) in 1927, he attended the Infantry School at Dresden for a year, followed by a year-long course at the Cavalry School at Hanover. He returned to his regiment for further training in 1929 and received his commission on January 1, 1930. He was promoted to first lieutenant on May 1, 1933.

Later that year, Stauffenberg took the Wehrkreise General Staff examination, which was mandatory for all officers with 10 years of service. As in Kluge's day, only the top 15% of those who took the exam were allowed to undergo General Staff training, and only a third of these ultimately qualified to wear the red stripes of the General Staff officer. Stauffenberg passed, attended the War Academy from 1936 to 1938, was admitted to the General Staff, and was posted to Erich Hoepner's 1st Light Division at Wueppertal as Ib (chief supply officer). He took part in the occupation of the Sudetenland (1938), the Polish campaign (1939), and the conquest of France (1940). In the meantime, the 1st Light had been reorganized as the 6th Panzer Division. In the summer of 1940, Stauffenberg was transferred to the Organizations Section of the High Command of the Army (OKH), where he remained until early 1943. Here he was deeply involved in forming anti-Communist units from the peoples of the Soviet Union, and he worked closely with former Soviet General Andrey Andreyevitch Vlasov, the former commander of the 2nd Shock Army who had been captured in July 1942. In German captivity, the six-foot five-inch giant of a man had been convinced to work for the overthrow of Stalin and communism. Due to Hitler's insistence upon treating the Russians as *Untermenschen* (subhuman), however, the anti-Stalin Russian Liberation Movement never really had a chance to grow— much to the fury of von Stauffenberg. Even so, there were some 800,000 Russian soldiers and auxiliaries in German service by 1943.[29]

In Berlin, Stauffenberg (who was now a major) was disgusted by the inefficiency of the leadership of the Wehrmacht, especially Hermann Goering and the Luftwaffe. He was also repelled by the murders of the Jews. A devout Catholic, Stauffenberg agreed with his brothers that the Jews possessed an essentially foreign, non-German character and should lead a controlled, separate existence. They could not, however, abide Nazi racial extremism and physical cruelty; supporting mass murder, of course, was unthinkable. They were also very much upset by the antireligious nature of the regime. "Men are not guaranteed a civilized existence by a state without religious background," Claus correctly proclaimed.[30] He also stated that national policy must be conducted on the basis of "morality firmly rooted in religion. A people which does not know how to pray is not fit to live." He added: "Christianity should again become the overriding spiritual force of the future."[31] With these strongly held principles and in spite of his oath as an officer, Claus von Stauffenberg eventually drew the inevitable conclusion: Hitler and the Nazis would have to be overthrown.

Because of his great organizational abilities and unusual talent, Claus von Stauffenberg was promoted to lieutenant colonel on January 1, 1943. He was unexpectedly transferred to the North African Front in February 1943 as the Ia of the 10th Panzer Division. Although surprised by his posting, Stauffenberg was nevertheless pleased, because it got him away from the circus in Berlin. His predecessor, Colonel Wilhelm Buerklin, had been badly wounded in the same explosion that had killed his brilliant divisional commander, Lieutenant General Wolfgang Fischer. Stauffenberg's tour of duty was destined to be brief, however. Near Gafsa on April 7, his Volkswagen staff vehicle was attacked by an American fighter-bomber, and he was critically wounded. At the forward military hospital near Carthage, his right hand had to be amputated above the wrist, what remained of his left eye had to be removed, and the third and fourth fingers of his left hand had to be cut off as well. Three days later he was taken to a hospital in Tunis, and on April 21, he was flown back to Munich, where he underwent knee joint and middle ear operations and a succession of head and eye operations. His wounds became infected, and he was delirious for weeks. For a long time it was uncertain if he would live; it was also questionable if he would regain his sight. Despite his pain, Stauffenberg refused all pain-killing drugs and sleeping medication—a harsh example of his belief in the superiority of mind over matter. A man in ordinary physical condition would not have survived this ordeal. When he escaped both death and blindness, von Stauffenberg concluded that God had spared his life so that he might fulfill a mission of critical importance to mankind: He had been chosen to rid the world of Adolf Hitler.

From that time until the moment of his death, Claus von Stauffenberg was *the* leader of the anti-Hitler conspiracy.

Late that summer, Stauffenberg reported himself ready for duty. The APA (Army Personnel Office) offered him the post of chief of staff to the head of the General Army Office (Allgemeine Heeresamt, or AHA), a part of the Replacement Army. Stauffenberg accepted immediately, because this appointment would place him near the center of power and perhaps give him the opportunity to carry out his mission. His superior was General of Infantry Friedrich Olbricht, who was also a member of the anti-Hitler conspiracy.[32] Stauffenberg took up his new duties in August. In early September, General Beck met von Stauffenberg and was instantly impressed that he was the man for the job of overthrowing Hitler. The former chief of the General Staff, in effect, appointed the dynamic, one-eyed colonel as the man in charge of the plot

Stauffenberg's plans for a putsch centered around Operation "Valkyrie," a contingency plan originated by Olbricht and Admiral Canaris in the winter of 1941–42. Presented to Hitler by Olbricht in early 1942, it was predicated on the possibility that the more than 4 million foreign workers and prisoners of war that would be working within the Reich by the end of 1942 might stage a revolt. He did not have much difficulty convincing Hitler that they constituted a potential threat (because they did) and that they might have to be suppressed by military force someday. This task naturally fell within the jurisdiction of the Replacement Army and its subordinate headquarters, the Wehrkreise (military districts). Part of this task would involve protecting government and party offices and headquarters, officials, and radio stations. Olbricht, of course, did not mention that "Valkyrie" would also be a natural and effective plan that could be used by the leaders of the Home Army to overthrow the Nazi regime. In any case, Hitler approved the idea, and Olbricht drafted the plan. Because the Replacement Army would have to use the units available inside the Third Reich during the period of "internal unrest," and because these units were constantly changing, "Valkyrie" had to be updated constantly. Under Olbricht and Stauffenberg, it was transformed into a military plan to overthrow the Nazi regime. The "flash" (or beginning spark) for Valkyrie would be the assassination of Adolf Hitler. The problem, however, was getting someone close enough to the Fuehrer to assassinate him. Of the conspirators, only Stieff was occasionally allowed to attend one of the dictator's conferences, and he was not willing to make the attempt himself. Treschow and Stauffenberg tried several candidates, but they all failed in turn. Then an unexpected event occurred: Stauffenberg himself was placed in a position that gave him frequent access to the Fuehrer.

While Stauffenberg was planning for the coup, he also did an excellent job as chief of staff of AHA. He had a remarkable talent for organization, and within a short period of time, he had been instrumental in organizing 15 new divisions. Even Himmler (who was now conspiring to add the Replacement Army to his empire) recognized his abilities. When he and Guderian (who had been recalled to duty in 1943 as chief of the

Panzer Inspectorate) discussed a suitable successor to Lieutenant General Adolf Heusinger, the chief of operations at OKH, Guderian recommended Stauffenberg as "the best horse in the General Staff stable." Himmler agreed at once.[33] (By 1944, OKH was directing the war on the Eastern Front, while OKW handled all other theaters.) In view of the count's growing and widespread reputation, Colonel General Fritz Fromm, the commander in chief of the Replacement Army since it was formed in September 1939, pirated Stauffenberg away from Olbricht and, on June 1, 1944, named him chief of staff of the Replacement Army.[34] He was promoted to full colonel on July 1. Colonel Ritter Albrecht Mertz von Quirnheim, a veteran General Staff officer, succeeded Stauffenberg at AHA.

Claus von Stauffenberg accompanied General Fromm to Fuehrer Headquarters at Berchtesgaden and met Adolf Hitler for the first time on June 7, 1944—the day after D-Day. Hitler had been so impressed by one of Stauffenberg's memoranda that he summoned Fromm to his first Fuehrer Conference in two and a half years. The count, on the other hand, was unimpressed by the Fuehrer, whom he found both redundant and repulsive. Also present at the meeting were Himmler, Speer, and Goering. Stauffenberg found the entire entourage "rotten and degenerate." Only Speer impressed him as being normal; the rest were "patent psychopaths."[35] Others had been so overwhelmed by Hitler's charisma and physical presence (especially his eyes) that they felt themselves unable to make an attempt on his life. Stauffenberg now knew that he would have no such qualms. By the end of June, he had decided to make the assassination attempt himself. It was regrettable that he was forced to make this decision because it cast him in a dual role: He would have to play the assassin, and then he would have to return to Berlin and direct the coup. It was a major weakness in the plan for Operation "Valkyrie." Unfortunately, there was no way around it, because Stauffenberg was the only conspirator likely to get close enough to Hitler to do him in.

In the meantime, more and more outstanding Germans joined the conspiracy. Chief among them was Erwin Rommel, perhaps the most respected military leader in the German Army. Rommel had already been primed for the conspiracy by Dr. Stroelin, the mayor of Stuttgart, who was also a member of the plot, but the Desert Fox had become more and more interested in overthrowing the Nazi regime as the time for the Allied invasion grew nearer. Sometime around May 15, Rommel met with Eduard Wagner, the deputy chief of the General Staff and chief army supply officer, and was, for the first time, informed of the existence of an active resistance, the planned revolt, and the previous attempts on Hitler's life. The politically naive Rommel was opposed to the idea of assassination because he feared the creation of a great Nazi martyr and because he wanted Hitler to be arrested and forced to stand trial for his crimes. Stauffenberg once said: "We have no real field marshals any more. They all shake in their shoes and stand to attention when the Fuehrer gives an order. They are not assertive enough with their views regarding the seriousness of the situation."[36] This remark did not apply to Rommel, whom Stauffenberg called "a great leader."[37]

As early as June 25, Rommel informed Colonel Eberhard Finckh, the deputy chief of staff of OB West, that he could be counted upon in the event of a coup, even though he still opposed assassinating Hitler. Even so, Rommel discussed the matter with other senior officers and provided a tremendous amount of momentum for the conspiracy in the West. He met with Luftwaffe Lieutenant Colonel Caesar von Hofacker, the son of Rommel's commander on the Italian Front in World War I and the chief of staff to the military governor of France. Young Hofacker introduced him to his commander, General von Stueplnagel, who was deeply involved in the conspiracy. Before long, both of Rommel's army commanders in France, Dollmann and von Salmuth, were privy to the secret and had pledged to obey Rommel's orders, even if they contradicted those issued by the Fuehrer. Geyr von Schweppenburg made a similar promise, and Lieutenant General Count Gerhard von Schwerin of the 116th Panzer and Lieutenant General Baron Heinrich von Luettwitz of the 2nd Panzer declared that their divisions were available for use against the regime.

By now, it seemed to the conspirators that the SS was likely to descend on them at any time. It was therefore imperative that Stauffenberg act quickly; and indeed, Eduard Wagner and General Franz Lindemann, the chief of the Artillery Directorate at OKH, were already pressing Stauffenberg to act.[38] So was Henning von Treschow. He sent word to Stauffenberg: "The assassination must take place *coute que coute*. Even if it does not succeed, the Berlin action must go forward. The point now is not whether the coup has any practical purpose, but to prove to the world and before history that German resistance is ready to stake its all. Compared to this, everything else is a side-issue."[39]

On July 11, Stauffenberg met with Hitler again on the Obersalzburg. He did not detonate the bomb, however, because Goering and Himmler were not present. On Saturday, July 15, the day after Hitler returned to the Wolf's Lair in East Prussia, Fromm and Stauffenberg boarded a Ju-52 and flew to Rastenburg, the latter with a bomb in his briefcase. The conference that day was cut short, however, before Stauffenberg could activate his explosives. At the next Fuehrer conference to which he was invited, however, Count von Stauffenberg resolved, he would actually detonate his bomb.

Monday, July 17, was another disastrous day on both the Eastern and Western Fronts, but it was especially disastrous for the conspirators. That was the day they lost Field Marshal Rommel.

The replacement of von Rundstedt by Hans von Kluge had not affected the conspiracy one way or the other. Rommel had tried to induce Rundstedt into joining the plot, but the aging marshal had merely replied: "You are young. The people know you and love you. You do it!" He had been as ambiguous toward the coup as Kluge. Rommel, however, intended to act. On July 15, he sent Hitler an ultimatum stating that the war could not be won militarily and concluding with the words: "The troops are everywhere fighting heroically, but the unequal struggle is approaching its end. It is urgently necessary for the proper conclusions to be drawn from this situation. As C-in-C of the army group I feel myself in duty bound to speak plainly on this point."[40]

"I have given him his last chance," the Desert Fox declared. "If he does not take it, we will act."[41]

On the morning of July 17, Rommel visited SS General "Sepp" Dietrich, the commander of the I SS Panzer Corps. Only a few hours before, the Desert Fox had again firmly committed himself to the conspiracy and pledged to General von Stuelpnagel, the military governor of France, that he would act "openly and unconditionally" with the rebels, no matter what his superior, Field Marshal von Kluge, decided to do.[42] Rommel told Dietrich of the ultimatum that he had sent to Adolf Hitler and asked him to commit himself: In case of a coup, would Dietrich back Hitler or Rommel? Dietrich was Hitler's former bodyguard, but he had become disillusioned with the Fuehrer's leadership and was sickened by the loss of so many fine young men in Russia and in Normandy. He extended his hand and declared: "You are the boss, Herr Field Marshal. I obey only you—whatever it is you're planning."[43]

With this pledge, the Waffen-SS on the Western Front was effectively neutralized, insofar as the conspirators were concerned. Their victory, however, was short-lived. About 4 P.M. that afternoon, Rommel was critically wounded. Hans von Kluge, the OB West, replaced him as commander of Army Group B. The situation in the West was now completely clouded, as far as the conspiracy was concerned. Rommel's word, after all, was worth something. If he said he would act, one could depend upon it absolutely. But Kluge? He had made promises before, but they had proven to be of doubtful value. In short, Rommel could be counted upon to put Germany first; Kluge could be counted upon to put his own self-interests first. There was no way of knowing how he would react in the event of a putsch.

Nevertheless, early in the morning of July 20, 1944, Stauffenberg boarded a Ju-52 transport and flew to Rastenburg, East Prussia (now

Ketrzyn, Poland). Hitler had relocated his headquarters here two days before, even though the Eastern Front was now only 60 miles away. At approximately 12:25 P.M., Stauffenberg primed his bomb to explode, pushed it under Hitler's conference table at such an angle that it would blow up between the Fuehrer's legs, and left the room. With iron nerve, he proceeded out of the compound and to the airstrip near the hamlet of Wilhelmsdorf, East Prussia, and boarded a Ju-52 back to Berlin.

Unfortunately, Stauffenberg had not been able to push his briefcase all the way under the table without leaning it against the heavy oak table support, which would deflect the force of the blast away from the Fuehrer. He therefore left it partially under the table and partially out. As he changed maps for his boss, Colonel Heinz Brandt, the principal assistant to General Heusinger, bumped into the briefcase with his foot. Since it was in the way, Brandt moved it behind a table support and pushed it all the way under the table. He thereby probably saved Hitler's life but not his own. Figure 2.1 shows the location of the bomb before and after Brandt moved it, as well as the approximate location of the conferees.

At approximately 12:35 P.M., back in the Fuehrer's hut, Heusinger was in the middle of his briefing. "The Russians are moving considerable forces northwards, west of the Dvina," he said. "Their leading troops are already southwest of Dvinaburg. If the army group [North] does not now withdraw from Lake Peipus, a catastrophe will—"

At that second the bomb went off. It was a powerful, deafening explosion with a yellow or blue flame, rupturing or damaging almost everyone's eardrums. "In a flash the map room became a scene of stampede and destruction," General Warlimont recalled. "At one moment there was to be seen a set of men and things which together formed a focal point of world events; at the next there was nothing but wounded men groaning, the acrid smell of burning, and charred fragments of maps and papers fluttering in the wind."[44] Everyone's trousers were torn to ribbons, and those near the windows were showered with glass. Almost everyone was knocked down. SS Lieutenant General Hermann Fegelein and SS Colonel Otto Guensche were thrown through the windows and lay unconscious on the ground outside. Both of recording secretary Dr. Heinrich Berger's legs were blown off, and he died later that afternoon. Colonel Brandt, an officer liked by everyone, who had once been a world-famous horse show rider and a member of Germany's Olympic teams in the late 1920s and early 1930s, had a leg shattered. He also lost an eye and died in the Rastenburg hospital two days later. General of Fliers Guenther Korten, the chief of the General Staff of the Luftwaffe, had been bending over the map table when the bomb exploded, and his abdomen was impaled by a large jagged remnant of the wooden table. It took him five days to die. Lieutenant General Rudolf Schmundt, Hitler's chief adjutant and chief of the Army Personnel Office, was blinded

Figure 2.1
The July 20 Assassination Attempt

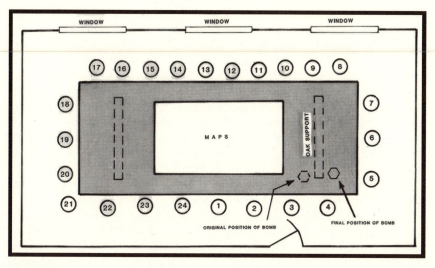

Key to Figure 5:
1. Hitler, wounded. **2.** General Heusinger, severely wounded. **3.** General Korten, mortally wounded. **4.** Colonel Brandt, mortally wounded. **5.** General Bodenschatz, liaison officer between Hermann Goering and FHQ (Fuehrer Headquarters), badly wounded in both legs. **6.** General Schmundt, mortally wounded. **7.** Colonel Borgmann, army adjutant to the Fuehrer, badly wounded. **8.** Rear Admiral von Puttkamer, naval adjutant to the Fuehrer, wounded. **9.** Dr. Heinrich Berger, stenographer, killed. **10.** Captain Assmann, naval adjutant to the Fuehrer and naval operations officer on OKW's Operations Staff. **11.** General Scherff, chief of the Historical Section of OKW, wounded. **12.** General Buhle, wounded. **13.** Vice Admiral Voss, naval liaison officer and deputy for the commander in chief of the navy. **14.** SS General Fegelein, representing Waffen-SS and FHQ, wounded. **15.** Colonel von Below, Luftwaffe adjutant to the Fuehrer. **16.** SS Major Guensche, SS adjutant to Hitler. **17.** Kurt Hagen. **18.** Lieutenant Colonel John, adjutant to Keitel. **19.** Major Beuchs, adjutant to Jodl. **20.** Lieutenant Colonel Waizenegger, OKW staff officer. **21.** Counselor von Sonnleithner, Foreign Officer representative. **22.** General Warlimont, wounded. **23.** General Jodl, wounded. **24.** Field Marshal Keitel.

After John W. Wheeler-Bennett, *The Nemesis of Power*, pp. 638–39.

by the explosion.[45] Generally regarded by the senior officers as a fundamentally decent man but not a very bright one, Schmundt hovered between life and death for weeks but finally succumbed to infection in the Rastenburg hospital on October 1, 1944. Hitler promoted him to general of infantry a month before his death. He was succeeded by Lieutenant General Wilhelm Burgdorf, a vicious and uncouth Nazi who became a close friend of the insidious Nazi Party chief, Martin Bormann.[46] Burgdorf would soon be involved in the purge of so many leaders that he would be nicknamed "the Gravedigger of the Officers' Corps." Generals

Buhle and Heusinger were also seriously wounded, and Heusinger, who was critical of National Socialism, was never reemployed. Alfred Jodl was temporarily disabled with a head injury. Luftwaffe General Karl Bosdenschatz was also severely wounded. Others suffered from moderate wounds, including Lieutenant Colonel Heinrich Borgmann, Hitler's OKH aide; Major General Walter Scherff, OKW historian; Captain Heinz Assmann, senior naval officer on the OKW Operations Staff; Rear Admiral Karl Jesko von Puttkamer, Hitler's naval aide; and Lieutenant Colonel Heinz Waizenegger, Jodl's senior staff officer. Warlimont staggered outside, then (ignoring the warnings of SS guards that there might be further explosions) returned to the map room to retrieve some documents; here he fainted and had to be carried out by his batman. Everyone except Hitler and Keitel suffered from concussion, and everyone except Keitel had their eardrums pierced.

At the moment of the explosion, Adolf Hitler was leaning over the table, propped on his right elbow, looking at a map. He was hurled to the floor and buried by debris. Both of his eardrums were ruptured, his legs and right arm were painfully injured, and his hair was burned. He later observed that he now had a "backside like a baboon."[47] He pulled himself to his feet and staggered through the smoke and fire, where he was grabbed by Field Marshal Keitel. "The Fuehrer is alive! The Fuehrer is alive!" Keitel cried as he half carried the wounded dictator out of the wreckage of the briefing hut.

Shortly after 4 P.M., Colonel Count von Stauffenberg arrived back at Replacement Army Headquarters and set Operation Valkyrie into motion. Colonel General Fritz Fromm, the commander in chief of the Replacement Army, telephoned Keitel, who assured him that Hitler was alive. "Keitel's lying, as usual," Stauffenberg snapped. Still the fat general—who, like too many others, was on both sides of the conspiracy—refused to act, so Stauffenberg and Olbricht arrested him. For a short time, the coup seemed to be progressing satisfactorily; then it fell apart, because the essential ingredient was missing: Adolf Hitler was not dead. Shortly before midnight the situation at the Bendlerstrasse had reversed itself: The complex had been taken over by the Grossdeutschland Guard Battalion, Fromm was back in charge, and Stauffenberg and his comrades were his prisoners.

When it was proven that Stauffenberg had detonated the bomb, Reichsfuehrer-SS Heinrich Himmler presented Hitler with a document, naming Himmler himself commander in chief of the Replacement Army. Adolf Hitler signed it on the spot. Unaware of this, Fritz Fromm disposed of the witnesses who knew too much about his ambivalent part in the conspiracy. He allowed Colonel General Ludwig Beck to shoot himself, but the former chief of the General Staff only succeeded in critically wounding himself. Fromm ordered a sergeant to finish him off. Then he informed Stauffenberg, General Olbricht, Lieutenant Werner von Haeften (Stauffenberg's aide),[48] and Colonel Mertz von Quirnheim that a court-martial had condemned them to death. The Guards then took the four officers downstairs and executed them shortly after 12:30 A.M. on July 21.

In the meantime, Hitler addressed the German people by radio. "I am speaking to you now so that you will hear my voice and know that I am unhurt, and so that you may know the details of a crime without equal in the history of the German people!" the Fuehrer began. He went on to denounce Stauffenberg and his fellow conspirators as "a very small clique of ambitious, unscrupulous, and at the same time criminally stupid officers" who had tried to stab the German Army in the back, just as the "November criminals" had done in 1918. In his eight-minute speech, Hitler promised that the conspirators of July 20 would be ruthlessly exterminated.

That was one promise Adolf Hitler kept.

One thing that did change immediately was Hitler's attitude toward his generals. Prior to July 20, 1944, officers like Model, Guderian, and Field Marshal Erich von Manstein could argue with him and occasionally get their way. No more. Now generals and field marshals were met with suspicion, paranoia, and outright hatred. Hitler now looked upon his army generals as his enemies, and he tolerated them only so long as they exhibited unquestioning obedience. Guderian (who was named acting chief of the General Staff on July 21) wrote of Hitler after July 20:

[T]he deep distrust [Hitler] already felt for mankind in general and for General Staff Corps officers and generals in particular, now became profound hatred. . . . [W]hat had been hardness became cruelty, while a tendency to bluff became plain dishonesty. He often lied without hesitation and assumed that others lied to him. He believed no one any more. It had already been difficult enough dealing with him; it now became a torture that grew steadily worse from month to month. He frequently lost all self-control and his language grew increasingly violent.[49]

THE COUP IN THE WEST

By 1944, Paris had become one of the major seats of the German Resistance. It was headed by General of Infantry Carl-Heinrich von Stuelpnagel, the military governor of France. Stuelpnagel, who was a longtime student of General Beck, had served as Halder's deputy chief of the General Staff and, unlike Halder, had never broken with the conspiracy. Basically a disappointment as a corps and army commander (he had commanded II Corps in France in 1940 and 17th Army in Russia), Stuelpnagel had been sacked and forced into retirement by Field Marshal von Brauchitsch in late 1941 but had been rescued from professional oblivion by Halder after Hitler fired Brauchitsch. Carl-Heinrich had succeeded his cousin, General of Infantry Otto von Stuelpnagel, as military governor of France on February 13, 1942.

Count Fritz-Dietlof von der Schulenburg had established the first links between the HQ of the military governor and the Beck-Goerdeler group in 1942, and Field Marshal von Witzleben's Headquarters, Army Group D (later Rundstedt's OB West) was already a nest of conspirators. The Commandant of Greater Paris and commander of the 325th Security Division, Lieutenant General Baron Hans von Boineburg-Lengsfeld, a thin, wiry Thueringen, had joined the conspiracy by the spring of 1942, when he was still commanding the 23rd Panzer Division on the Eastern Front. Boineburg's career in Russia had come to an abrupt end in late December 1942, when he was accidentally run over by a panzer, which seemed to break nearly every bone in his body; nevertheless, he returned to active duty in May 1943, when he became commandant. He was simultaneously commander of the 325th Security Division, which was the garrison unit of Paris. He placed himself unreservedly at Stuelpnagel's disposal in the summer of 1943, when he and his chief of staff, Colonel Karl von Unger, began detailed planning for the uprising in Paris.

The French capital was, of course, not yet an active theater of war, so Stuelpnagel's and Boineburg-Lengsfeld's headquarters could do their planning in relative calm, free from the constant pressure of the war. Their plans were therefore infinitely more thorough than those of Berlin.

Paris was alerted on the morning of July 20, when General Wagner, the Quartermaster General of the Army and the deputy chief of the General Staff in Zossen, telephoned Colonel Eberhard Finckh, the deputy chief of staff of OB West. Shortly after 4 P.M., Colonel von Stauffenberg telephoned his cousin, Caesar von Hofacker, at the Hotel Majestic in Paris (the headquarters of the military governor of France) and told him that Hitler was dead and the putsch was in progress. Hofacker informed his chief, Stuelpnagel, who acted immediately. All SS personnel in Paris were to be arrested at once, he commanded; anyone who resisted was to be shot.

Had the entire putsch gone as well as it did in Paris, Hitler would have died and the Nazi regime would have been overthrown. Most of the actual arrests were carried out by Reserve Lieutenant Colonel Kurt von Kraewel's 1st Security Regiment of Boineburg's division. Kraewel personally arrested SS Colonel Dr. Helmut Knochen, the senior SD officer in Paris (whom he had to have fetched out of a sleazy nightclub), and the Senior SS and Police Commander of Paris, SS Lieutenant General Carl-Albrecht Oberg, was personally arrested by Major General Walther Brehmer, a former Nazi who wore the "Blood Order" for his part in the Beer Hall Putsch of 1923. Brehmer had been a Nazi idealist but had lost his illusions long ago. He burst into Oberg's office with his pistol drawn. The SS man shot to his feet and demanded to know the meaning of this outrage, but Brehmer merely told him to shut up and hand over his pistol. Meanwhile, the SS, SD, and police barracks were rapidly surrounded in a flawless maneuver, during which only one shot was fired—by accident—and no one was hit. In all, 1,200 SS men and other Nazis were arrested; they were incarcerated in the Wehrmacht prison at Fresnes and in old Fort de l'Est. Oberg and the other senior SS and Gestapo officials were taken to the Hotel Continental, and preparations for their summary courts-martial were so far advanced that sandbags were piled up in the courtyard of the Ecole Militaire (the barracks of the 1st Security Regiment), where the executions were going to take place.

At 6:15 P.M., General von Stuelpnagel received a call from Field Marshal von Kluge, asking him and his chief of staff to come to la Roche Guyon for an important conference at 8 P.M. (Kluge had taken over Rommel's old headquarters in order to be closer to the front.) Stuelpnagel came, along with Colonel von Hofacker, Dr. Max Horst (General Speidel's brother-in-law), and his aide, but he left his chief of staff, Colonel Hans-Ottfried von Linstow, in charge in Paris.

Field Marshal Kluge had returned to his HQ from a tour on the front at 6 P.M., grabbed a quick snack, and immediately returned to work. He was briefed on military matters by General Speidel, his Army Group B chief of staff, who then told him about the assassination attempt. No one in France knew the true situation, but the radio said that the attempt had failed. Kluge received a telephone call from General Beck, who told him that Hitler was dead, a military state of emergency had been declared in the Reich, and asked, "Do you approve of our action and will you place yourself under my orders?" Kluge, hedging as usual, replied that he would think it over and would call back. "That's Kluge for you," Beck said contemptuously as he replaced the receiver. He knew that the field marshal would never call back.[50]

General Blumentritt, Kluge's chief of staff at OB West, arrived a few minutes later. He believed Hitler was dead, but the conspirators obviously did not control the radio stations—a sure indication that Valkyrie was not functioning properly, even though Blumentritt did not say so. Kluge therefore decided to telephone his friend General Stieff in Mauerwald, which was only a few miles from Rastenburg. He asked the "Poisonous Dwarf" if Hitler was really dead. No, Stieff replied; one of his staff officers had spoken with him an hour before. Kluge next telephoned the Bendlerstrasse, where his call was answered by Stauffenberg. The marshal asked to speak to Colonel General Fromm but was told that he was unavailable; Stauffenberg put him through to Colonel General Hoepner instead. Hoepner was telling Kluge that the radio reports were lies manufactured by the SS when they were disconnected. Kluge instructed his operator not to reconnect them. Then the marshal received a telephone call from General von Falkenhausen, the former military governor of Belgium and northern France, who had been sacked six days before. The senior commander on the Western Front told Falkenhausen that he did not believe Hitler was dead. Kluge was now on the side of the Nazis.

Shortly before 8 P.M., a Stauffenberg dispatch arrived at la Roche Guyon, forwarded by Colonel Bodo Zimmerman, Kluge's operations officer at St. Germain (OB West HQ in Paris). It announced the death of Hitler and the assumption of plenary powers by the Wehrmacht. All Waffen-SS units, Reich Labor Service (RAD) units, Organization Todt formations, and all officials and branches of the NSDAP were placed under army command. Kluge was impressed; he spoke of the historic significance of this moment and—just for a few minutes—was on the side of the conspirators. He decided that his first step would be to halt the V-1 attacks on London; they were only killing British civilians and had no effect on the military situation at all.

Then a teleprint arrived from Keitel, stating that Hitler was alive, Himmler was the new commander in chief of the Replacement Army, and all orders from Fromm, Witzleben, or Olbricht were to be ignored. Naturally, Kluge waived again. He ordered Blumentritt to get on the telephone and find out the truth. For Kluge, as with so many others, the decisive question was: "Was Adolf Hitler alive or not?"

By the time Stuelpnagel and his confederates arrived, Kluge was convinced that the assassination attempt had failed. He listened in silence as Hofacker spoke for 15 minutes. He described the plan, his own part in it, and what he thought the situation was at that moment. He ended with a passionate appeal for Kluge to break with the regime and assume leadership of the anti-Nazi movement in the West.

Kluge did not turn a hair. Then he announced that the attempt had failed and invited the four officers from Paris to join him for dinner. It was a candlelight-and-wine affair, held less than 60 miles from the Normandy battlefield, where hundreds of men were dying every day. Only Kluge seemed to be in a good mood. General Speidel later recalled that this meal was like dining in the house of the dead.

Before the meal was over, Stuelpnagel asked if he might speak to the field marshal privately. They adjourned into an adjoining room, where the military governor informed him that he already had the entire SS/SD establishment in Paris under lock and key. Kluge was shocked and then furious. Dinner resumed, but now Kluge's good mood was gone and there was no conversation at all.

After dinner, about 11 P.M., Kluge relieved Stuelpnagel of his duties as military governor of France. He walked him outside and gave him a personal piece of advice: Get into civilian clothes and disappear. Stuelpnagel, however, could not leave his fellow conspirators in the lurch; he intended to return to Paris instead.

"If only the swine were dead!" Kluge snapped.

"Herr Field Marshal, the fate of millions of Germans and the honor of the army lies in your hands," Hofacker declared, starting in on Kluge again.

"No!" the OB West cried.[51]

In the meantime, Colonel von Stauffenberg had telephoned from Berlin and informed Paris that the coup had failed. His executioners, he said, were at that moment beating on his door. Depression and loneliness gripped the hearts of the putschists in the French capital. For them, the bubble had burst very suddenly.

At 1:37 A.M. on July 21, Vice Admiral Theodor Krancke, the commander in chief of Naval Group West, telephoned for General Boineburg but could not reach him, so he spoke to Colonel von Unger.[52] He said that he knew what had happened in Paris, and if Oberg and the rest of the SS men were not released at once, he, Krancke, would march on the city with 1,000 marines. When Stuelpnagel learned this threat about 2 A.M., he ordered the revolt in Paris liquidated. It was of little use by itself anyway. Kluge had already named General Blumentritt his temporary successor, and Stueplnagel was not sure how much longer his troops would continue to obey him. Strangely, many of the SS men refused to leave their cells. We know the story; they told their jailers: shot while attempting to escape![53]

SS General Oberg was, of course, furious about being arrested, but Otto Abetz, the German ambassador to Vichy France, managed to calm him. A weird party was arranged at the Hotel Raphael, where the senior SS officers and leading putschists got drunk together and joked about their mutual experiences of July 20. Oberg actually smiled and shook hands with Stuelpnagel and lifted a glass of champagne in a toast to his host, who was as good as dead.[54]

Almost as soon as his uninvited guests departed, Field Marshal von Kluge sent a message to Hitler, calling the conspirators of July 20 "ruthless murderers" and assuring the Fuehrer of his own "unchangeable loyalty."[55] It was too late now, however, for Kluge to cover up his lukewarm support for the conspiracy, and he soon knew it. Colonel von Hofacker was one of the first people arrested by the Gestapo, and since his own "guilt" was easily proven, he took the path of least resistance and implicated both Rommel and Kluge. In the next few days, more than one of his former officers at Army Group Center committed suicide or went over to the Russians. From that point on, Kluge walked a tightrope. "After July 20," author John Keegan wrote, Kluge was forced "to play the super-loyalist for the sake of self-preservation."[56] He did not fail to notice that Hitler's dispatches to him became more and more insulting. There was now more at stake than just winning or losing the Battle of

Normandy—Kluge's very own life hung in the balance. He dared not fail or disappoint the Fuehrer again, no matter how irrational or out of touch with reality his orders seemed. This attitude characterized every move he made during the decisive battles of late July and August 1944, when disaster finally overtook the German armies on the Western Front.

NOTES

1. Guenther von Kluge Personnel Record, Air University Archives, Maxwell Air Force Base, Ala. (hereafter cited as "Kluge Personnel Record"); Keilig, p. 174; Telford Taylor, *Sword and Swastika: Generals and Nazis in the Third Reich* (New York: 1952; reprint ed., Chicago: 1969), p. 382 (hereafter cited as "Taylor, *Sword*"); Christopher Chant, Richard Humble, William Fowler, and Jenny Shaw, *Hitler's Generals and Their Battles* (New York: 1976), p. 86 (hereafter cited as "Chant et al."); Robert Wistrich, *Who's Who in Nazi Germany* (New York: 1982), p. 173 (hereafter cited as "Wistrich"); Louis L. Snyder, *Encyclopedia of the Third Reich* (New York: 1976), p. 197 (hereafter cited as "Snyder"); Robert J. O'Neill, *The German Army and the Nazi Party, 1933–1939* (New York: 1966), pp. 203, 211 (hereafter cited as "O'Neill").

2. Kluge Personnel Record; Taylor, p. 228; O'Neill, p. 217.

3. Baron Werner von Fritsch was born in 1880 and entered the service in 1898. Commissioned in the artillery at the turn of the century, he was a lifelong bachelor. An officer of the Old School, he nevertheless recognized the value of the panzer branch. Following his involuntarily retirement, he was named honorary colonel of the 12th Artillery Regiment. He used this rank to accompany this regiment to Poland in September 1939, where he apparently deliberately exposed himself to Polish fire. He was killed instantly.

4. Walther von Brauchitsch was promoted to field marshal on July 19, 1940. He was relieved of his command by Hitler on December 19, 1941, due to the failure of the German Army to capture Moscow. He was replaced by Hitler himself. He died of heart disease in British captivity in Hamburg in 1948. As part of his 1938 "deal" with the Nazis to become commander in chief of the army, Brauchitsch accepted the OKW-dominated command structure.

5. Wistrich, p. 173.

6. Werner von Blomberg was born in Stargard, Pomerania, on September 2, 1878. A romantic idealist, Blomberg was pro Hitler and very sympathetic to the NSDAP. As defense minister and later war minister from 1933 to 1938, he did much to further the Nazi Party's influence in the armed forces. He was promoted to field marshal on April 20, 1936. He was dismissed in late January 1938 for marrying a prostitute. Arrested at the end of the war, he died of cancer in American captivity in Nuremberg on March 14, 1946.

7. Kluge Personnel File; Taylor, *Sword*, p. 228.

8. David Irving, *Hitler's War* (New York: 1977), p. 5 (hereafter cited as "Irving, *Hitler's War*").

9. Ibid., p. 121

10. Heinz Guderian was born in East Prussia in 1888, the son of an officer who became a general. Heinz served in the signal corps and on the General Staff

during World War I and was an early advocate of the concept of mobile warfare. Commonly and correctly known as the "Father of the Blitzkrieg," he informally allied himself with Hitler and the Nazis to advance his military concepts. During the Hitler era, he led the 2nd Panzer Division (1935–38), XVI Panzer Corps (1938–39), XIX Panzer Corps (1939–40), Panzer Group Guderian (1940), and 2nd Panzer Group (later Army) (1940–41). After being relieved by Kluge, he was unemployed for more than a year. Recalled to duty in 1943, he was chief of the Panzer Inspectorate (with extraordinary powers) until July 21, 1944, when he became acting chief of the General Staff. His first act was to replace the traditional military salute with the Hitler salute throughout the armed forces. He was a much more pro-Nazi chief of the General Staff than his autobiography, *Panzer Leader* (New York: 1957; reprint ed., New York: 1967) suggests. Guderian was dismissed from his post on March 28, 1945, and surrendered to the Americans at the end of the war. He died on May 14, 1954.

During World War II, Hermann Hoth (born 1885) led the XV Motorized (later Panzer) Corps (1938–40), 3rd Panzer Group (1940–41), 17th Army (1941–42), and 4th Panzer Army (1942–43). Promoted to colonel general on July 19, 1940, he was sacked by Hitler on November 30, 1943, and was never reemployed. One of the outstanding armored commanders of the Eastern Front, he did not die until the 1980s.

11. *Kriegstagebuch des Oberkommando des Wehrmacht (Fuehrungsstab)* (Frankfurt-am-Main: 1961), Volume I, p. 1136; Irving, *Hitler's War*, p. 305; Albert Seaton, *The Battle for Moscow* (Briarcliff Manor, N.Y.: 1980; reprint ed., Chicago: 1981), pp. 43–45 (hereafter cited as "Seaton, *Moscow*").

12. Seaton, *Moscow*, pp. 169–70.

13. Fedor von Bock was born in Kuestrin in 1880. During World War II, he commanded Army Group North in Poland (1939), Army Group B in the Netherlands, Belgium and France (1940), and Army Group Center in Russia (1941). Relieved at his own request for reasons of health on December 19, 1941, he was nevertheless named commander in chief of Army Group South on January 16, 1942, replacing Walther von Reichenau, who had suffered a fatal heart attack. (Reichenau had replaced Rundstedt six weeks earlier.) A field marshal since July 19, 1940, Bock was sacked by Hitler on July 13, 1942, and never reemployed. In early May 1945, he was killed when his car was attacked by a fighter-bomber.

14. Seaton, *Moscow*, p. 245.

15. General of Mountain Troops Ludwig Kuebler (1889–1947) was demoted to the command of a corps and commanded at this level until the end of the war.

16. Friedrich Mieth (born 1888) was chief of staff of the 1st Army (1939) when he denounced the SS Einsatzgruppen for murdering Jews. Hitler dismissed him immediately. Mieth was rescued from professional oblivion by Franz Halder, the chief of the General Staff, who made him one of his deputies. Mieth later commanded the 112th Infantry Division (1940–42), battle groups and security troops in the Army Group Don sector, the ad hoc Corps Mieth, and IV Corps, all on the Eastern Front. A general of infantry since 1943, he fell in battle in Romania in September 1944.

17. Walter von Reichenau was a highly capable commander and a ruthless opportunist. He was Hitler's candidate for commander in chief of the army in 1934 and 1938 but was not selected due to the vehement opposition of the senior

generals. He commanded 10th Army in Poland and 6th Army in Belgium, France and Russia (1939–41). He succeeded Rundstedt as commander in chief of Army Group South on December 1, 1941, but suffered a fatal heart attack six weeks later, after returning from a six-mile run in temperatures of minus 20 degrees Fahrenheit.

Erwin von Witzleben was born in Berlin in 1881. He commanded Wehrkreis III (1938), 1st Army (1939–40), and Army Group D, which simultaneously became OB West in 1941 (1940–42). He was dismissed by Hitler on March 15, 1942, and never reemployed. Witzleben was hanged on August 8, 1944, for his part in the attempt to overthrow Hitler and the Nazi regime.

Ritter Wilhelm von Leeb was a decent man and defensive expert who commanded Army Group C in the West (1939–40) and Army Group North on the Russian Front (1941- 42). Fed up with Hitler's conduct of the war, he was relieved of his command at his own request in early 1942 and was never reemployed.

18. Franz Halder was born in Wuerzburg, Bavaria, in 1884. He entered the army in 1902 and spent most of his career in the artillery. He served as chief of staff of the 6th Infantry Division (1931–33), Artillery Commander VII (1933–35), commander of the 7th Infantry Division (1935–36), deputy chief of the General Staff (1936–38), and chief of the General Staff (1938–42). Promoted to colonel general on July 19, 1940, he was unceremoniously relieved by Hitler on September 24, 1942. He was discharged from the army in January 1945 and ended the war in a concentration camp.

19. Fabian von Schlabendorff, *Revolt against Hitler*, Gero v. S Gaevernitz, ed. (London: 1984), p. 127.

20. Dr. Carl Goerdeler, a former mayor and price control commissioner for the Third Reich, was captured by the Gestapo after the failure of the assassination attempt and told everything he knew, providing evidence that sent dozens of people to the hangman. Goerdeler himself was executed just before the end of the war.

21. Ludwig Beck was born in the Rhineland in 1880. He entered the service as a *Fahnenjunker* in the 15th Field Artillery Regiment in 1898. He became chief of the General Staff in 1933; he resigned in 1938 because he felt Hitler's Sudetenland policy would lead to a war that Germany could not win. He was promoted to colonel general (honorary) in November 1938 and was made honorary colonel of the 5th Artillery Regiment. Beck was a very cautious and conservative but very principled General Staff officer.

22. Baron Georg von Boeselager was killed in Poland in late August 1944 and was posthumously awarded the Knight's Cross with Oak Leaves and Swords.

23. Wilhelm Canaris was born in Aplerbek on New Year's Day in 1887. He entered the navy as a cadet in 1905 and became an ensign in 1908. He served primarily in torpedo boats and cruisers prior to World War I, and in 1915 he was interned in Chile as a spy. He escaped and made his way back to Germany, where he commanded a torpedo boat and later U-boats. He spent the 1920s and 1930s in a variety of fleet, shore installation, and General Staff assignments, commanding the battleship *Schlesien* (Silesia) (1932–34). He became chief of the Abwehr in 1935 and held the post until February 12, 1944, when he was relieved of his duties and sent into Fuehrer Reserve. After Hitler's anger over the intelligence failure at Anzio abated, he placed Canaris in charge of a special naval

transportation staff. He was arrested by the Gestapo on July 23, 1944, but the evidence connecting him with the July 20 plot was considered insufficient to bring him to trial, and he probably would never have been tried had he not kept a diary at work (including accounts of his part in the anti-Hitler plot) and left it there after his dismissal as chief of the Abwehr! This diary was discovered by pro-Nazi General of Infantry Walter Buhle in early 1945. He was executed at the Flossenbuerg concentration camp on April 9, 1945. Unlike most of the conspirators, Canaris's participation in the plot seems to have been something of an insurance policy, rather than having been motivated by genuine anti-Nazi feelings.

24. Hans Oster was Canaris's most fervently anti-Hitler deputy. He was born in Dresden in 1887 and joined the army as a *Fahnenjunker* in the artillery in 1907. Although he was selected for retention in the Reichsheer, Oster was only a major in 1933, when he was caught having an adulterous affair with the wife of a fellow officer. Cashiered from the service, he returned to active duty in 1935 as a reserve officer. He joined the Abwehr and rose to the rank of major general in 1942. He was cashiered again in January 1944 when the Gestapo caught him with incriminating documents. He implicated Canaris in the conspiracy and was executed with him on April 9, 1945.

25. Helmuth Stieff was born in Deutsch Eylau, East Prussia, in 1901. He entered the service as an officer-cadet in 1917 and was selected for the Reichsheer. He was commissioned into the artillery in 1922 and, by 1938, was a major on the General Staff. He spent the entire war in various OKH staff positions and was promoted to major general on February 1, 1944. He was hanged on August 8, 1944 (Keilig, p. 334).

26. Baron Rudolf-Christoph von Gersdorff was born in Lueben, Silesia, in 1905. He joined the Reichsheer as an officer-cadet in 1923 and was commissioned in the 7th Cavalry Regiment in late 1926. He was a major on the staff of the 14th Army when the war began. Later he was Ic of the XII Corps (1939–40), Ia of the 86th Infantry Division (1940–41), and on the supply staff of Army Group Center (1941–44) (Keilig, p. 106).

27. Joachim Kramarz, *Stauffenberg: The Architect of the Famous July 20th Conspiracy to Assassinate Hitler* (New York: 1967), p. 133 (cited hereafter as "Kramarz"); citing Hitler's Table Talk.

28. Ibid., p. 19.

29. Gerry S. Graber, *Stauffenberg* (New York: 1973), p 103.

30. Ibid., p. 116.

31. Kramarz, pp. 147–48.

32. Friedrich Olbricht was born in 1888 and joined the army as a *Fahnenjunker* in 1907. Commissioned in the infantry the following year, he rose to the command of the 24th Infantry Division in 1938. He led this unit until early 1940, when he became head of the General Army Office of the Home Army.

33. Kramarz, p. 170.

34. Fritz Fromm was born in Berlin in 1888. He joined the army as an artillery officer-cadet in 1906. His entire World War II service was as commander in chief of the Ersatz (Home or Replacement) Army and also chief of army equipment. Promoted to colonel general on July 19, 1940, he was arrested on the night of July 20–21, 1944, and was executed in March 1945.

35. Herbert Molloy Mason, *To Kill the Devil: Attempts on the Life of Adolf Hitler* (New York: 1978), p. 146 (hereafter cited as "Mason, *Devil*").

36. Kramarz, p. 173.

37. James Forman, *Code Name Valkyrie: Count von Stauffenberg and the Plot to Kill Hitler* (New York: 1975), p. 72.

38. Eduard Wagner was born in Kirchenlamitz in 1894 and joined the Bavarian Army as an officer-cadet in 1912. He served in World War I and in the Reichswehr and was a branch chief at OKH when the war began. He became quartermaster (chief supply officer) of the army on August 1, 1940, and held the post until July 23, 1944, when he placed a revolver against each temple and pulled the triggers.

Fritz Lindemann was born in Charlottenburg (near Berlin) in 1894. He joined the army as an officer-cadet in 1912 and served in the artillery. On the staff of the Home Army in 1938, he commanded the 138th Artillery Command (1939–42) and the 132nd Infantry Division (1942–43) before he was promoted to general of artillery and became chief of the Artillery Directorate in late 1943. He was discharged from the army by the so-called Court of Honor on August 5, 1944, and was hanged shortly thereafter (Keilig, p. 205).

39. Peter Hoffmann, *The History of the German Resistance, 1933–1945* (Cambridge, Mass.: 1977), p. 375 (hereafter cited as "Hoffmann"); Kramarz, p. 172.

40. Rommel, pp. 486–87.

41. Speidel, p. 111.

42. Mason, *Devil*, p. 153.

43. Irving, *Trail*, pp. 417–18.

44. Walter Warlimont, *Inside Hitler's Headquarters, 1939–1945*, R. H. Barry, trans. (Novato, Calif.: n.d.), p. 440 (hereafter cited as "Warlimont").

45. Rudolf Schmundt was born in Metz in 1896 and joined the army when World War I broke out. Commissioned in the 35th Fusilier Regiment in 1915, he remained in the Reichsheer and was named chief adjutant to the Fuehrer in late January 1938. He was rapidly promoted thereafter to lieutenant colonel (1938), colonel (1939), major general (1942), lieutenant general (1943), and general of infantry (1944). He became chief of the powerful Army Personnel Office in early October 1942, replacing Bodewin Keitel; however, he remained chief adjutant to Hitler. The army generals did not consider him very bright, but he was admired because of his hard work and fairness. His policies of favoring the combat officer were also looked upon positively by the generals (Keilig, p. 307).

46. Wilhelm Burgdorf was born at Fuerstenwalde on the Spree in 1895. He joined the army when World War I broke out and was commissioned in the infantry in 1915. After serving in the Reichsheer, he was adjutant of Wehrkreis IX and the IX Corps (1937–40), commander of the 529th Infantry Regiment (1940–42), branch chief in the Army Personnel Office (1942), and deputy chief of the Personnel Office (1942–44). Promoted to general of infantry on November 1, 1944, the brutal and uncouth Burgdorf committed suicide in the Fuehrer Bunker in Berlin in early May 1945 (Keilig, p. 57).

47. Hoffmann, pp. 404–5.

48. A reserve officer, the amiable 35-year-old Werner von Haeften had been severely wounded on the Eastern Front in 1942. He had carried a spare bomb

for von Stauffenberg in his briefcase on July 20. Ironically, his uncle was Field Marshal von Brauchitsch.

49. Anthony C. Brown, *Bodyguard of Lies* (New York: 1975), p. 771.

50. Mason, *Devil*, p. 169.

51. Ibid., p. 171.

52. Theodor Krancke was born in Magdeburg in 1893 and entered the Imperial Navy as a cadet (*Seekadett*) in 1912. Commissioned in 1913, he spent World War I serving in the torpedo boats. During World War II, he served as the captain of the surface raider ("pocket battleship") *Admiral Scheer* and sank 113,233 tons of Allied shipping from October 1940 to April 1941. In June 1941, he became chief of the Quartermaster Division of the naval staff, and in June 1942, he was named naval representative to the Fuehrer—a very difficult job indeed, even for the pro-Nazi Krancke. He was given command of Naval Group West in April 1943 and played an important role in suppressing the anti-Hitler revolt in Paris. He served as commander of Naval Group West until April 1945 and ended the war as commander of Naval Group Norway. Released from prison in 1947, he retired to Wentorf (near Hamburg), where he died in 1973. Krancke was promoted to rear admiral in 1941, vice admiral in 1942, and admiral on March 1, 1943.

53. Hoffmann, p. 478.

54. Carl-Heinrich von Stuelpnagel was summoned to Berlin on July 21 to explain why he had arrested the SS and Gestapo men in Paris the day before. That night, he drank heavily and had loud, irrational conversations with himself in his room. The next day he set out by car for Germany. At Verdun, where he distinguished himself as a young officer in World War I, he ordered his driver and aide to stop and proceed to the next village without him. He told them he wanted to revisit the battlefields of his youth. After they left, he ripped off his Nazi-era decorations, waded into the Meuse Canal, and shot himself. Both of his eyes were destroyed by the bullet, but he lived. His aide and driver, thinking he had been shot by partisans, pulled him out of the canal and carried him to the hospital. In delirium, and with Gestapo agents by his bed, he apparently called Rommel's name several times, implicating the Desert Fox. He was expelled from the army and hanged with piano wire shortly thereafter.

55. L. F. Ellis, *Victory in the West*, Volume I: *The Battle of Normandy* (London: 1962), p. 372 (hereafter cited as "Ellis").

56. John Keegan, *Six Armies in Normandy* (New York: 1982; reprinted ed., New York: 1983), p. 244 (hereafter cited as "Keegan").

CHAPTER III

THE BREAKOUT

THE FALL OF ST.-LÔ

As the Battle of Normandy unfolded, the Allies pushed doggedly south toward two objectives: The U.S. 1st Army on the right struggled for St.-Lô, while the British 2nd Army attempted to take Caen. Rommel deployed the 7th Army on his left against the Americans and Panzer Group West on his right, to protect Caen. He kept the bulk of his armor on the right for two reasons. First, if the left flank broke, he could still fall back toward Paris, the Seine, and eventually the Rhine. If his right flank collapsed, however, Montgomery would be in a position to cut the army group off from the Fatherland and destroy it. Second, the terrain south of the U.S. Army was still very defensible. If the Americans took St.-Lô, 7th Army would still be in hedgerow country. Not far south of Caen, on the other hand, lay the Falaise Plain—and tank country! Unfortunately, Hitler had sent a disproportionate number of panzer units to Normandy (ideal for infantry units), and they had suffered heavy losses, especially in tanks. Now there was little left with which to defend the rest of France except for infantry units. If the Allies ever pushed beyond the *bocage* in strength, there would be little left to stop them.

July 17, 1944, was a day of fierce combat on both the eastern and western sectors of the Normandy Front. In the east, the Anglo-Canadian forces railed against Panzer Group West south and east of Caen. In the west, the U.S. 1st Army closed in on St.-Lô. This center of the road network in western Normandy had a peacetime population of 11,000; now it was a mass of ruins. Since July 15, the fresh U.S. 35th Infantry Division had been trying to take the critical Hill 122 (just north of the town) from the burned-out remnants of Lieutenant General Dietrich Kraiss's 352nd Infantry Division, which had been in more or less constant combat since it was shattered on D-Day.[1] In the period July 15–17 alone, the 352nd calculated that it was attacked 40 times: twice in regimental strength, 12 in battalion strength, and 26 times in company strength. On July 17, General of Paratroopers Eugen Meindl, the arrogant but competent commander of the II Parachute Corps, reinforced Kraiss with his last remaining reserves: a few companies from the 266th Infantry Division and the remnants of the 30th Mobile Brigade (a bicycle unit of mediocre quality), which had held a sector west of the Vire and had just been relieved by the Panzer Lehr Division.[2] It was a case of too little, too late. Hill 122 fell that afternoon, and the shortage of troops and the nature of the terrain made it impossible for Meindl to reestablish his line north of the city.

In accordance with Hitler's "hold at all costs" policy, Kluge ordered SS Colonel General Paul Hausser, the commander of the 7th Army, to keep the Americans out of St.-Lô, but he had no reinforcements to give to Meindl and could offer nothing in the way of tangible help. Major General Gustav Wilke's 5th Parachute Division, which had recently come up from Brittany, had already been used to reinforce the Panzer Lehr,[3] and Lieutenant General Hans Schmidt's 275th Infantry Division, also coming up from Brittany, would not arrive in strength for another day or two.[4] In view of this situation, Kluge had no choice but to reluctantly rescind his order. Kraiss abandoned St.-Lô early the next morning (July 18). It was by no means a safe place for the Americans, however; the 352nd Infantry took up strong positions about a mile south of the ruined town, dug in, and continued to shell the ruins with mortars and its few remaining artillery batteries. Incidentally, the Anglo-Americans who were shelled by the *Nebelwerfer*—the six-barreled rocket mortar—considered themselves luckier than those subjected to regular German artillery fire. The *Nebelwerfer*, British Major General Essame recalled, "was a poor substitute [for regular artillery], really effective only against troops in the open. You could hear the rockets coming, and by flinging yourself in time on the ground you could dodge the fragments which, in any case, were very small. Its blast was admittedly terrific, but if in a slit trench, there was not much to fear."[5]

The rapid fall of St.-Lô embarrassed SS General Hausser, who ordered Meindl to have the 352nd Infantry retake the town. The paratroop general, in turn, asked Hausser to give him the vanguards of the 275th Infantry Division (just up from Brittany and moving in positions behind the Panzer Lehr) for the counterattack. Hausser refused, so the 352nd launched a weak counterattack, which came to nothing.

OPERATION GOODWOOD

Meanwhile, on the German right flank, General Montgomery ordered the British 2nd Army to launch a "massive stroke" in the Caen-Falaise area. It was codenamed Operation "Goodwood."

In their previous offensive, which had been launched on July 7, the British had been supported by 500 heavy bombers, which had dropped 2,560 tons of bombs on what was left of Caen, killing some 5,000 French civilians. They did not launch their main attack for another six hours, however, and when they did (at 4:20 A.M. on July 8), they were met by the 12th SS Panzer Division "Hitler Youth" and the 21st Panzer Division (minus Battle Group Luck—about one-third of the division—which was still holding a sector east of the Orne). Both were Kampfgruppen by now, however, and could not turn back the attacks of the fresh 59th (Staffordshire) Infantry Division, the British 3rd Infantry Division, the Canadian 3rd Infantry Division, the British 3rd Armoured Division, and two independent tank brigades. By dawn the next day, there was fighting in the northern suburbs.

Adolf Hitler ordered Caen to be defended to the last man. SS-Oberfuehrer Kurt "Panzer" Meyer, the divisional commander, ordered them to retreat anyway. "We were meant to die in Caen," he said later, "but one just couldn't watch those youngsters being sacrificed to a senseless order."[6] That night he abandoned that part of Caen that lay north of the Orne (i.e., most of the city). The two panzer grenadier regiments of the formerly elite Hitler Youth (Hitler Jugend, or HJ) division were now down to a strength of an infantry battalion, and the divisional anti-tank battalion had lost more than half of its guns.[7]

The British now held the northern two-thirds of Caen. South of the river, the Germans dug in, in the industrial suburbs of Colombelles and Faubourg de Vaucelles. It had taken Montgomery more than four weeks to advance 10 miles, and the British 2nd Army had suffered more casualties than its General Staff had projected for the entire balance of the war—and still the German line was intact.

The German soldiers, incidentally, generally got along well with their counterparts in the Waffen-SS. Lieutenant Martin Poeppel, a company commander in the 6th Parachute Regiment, was shot through the arm in the hedgerow fighting and found himself in the hospital with a number of SS men when the news arrived that a group of army officers had tried to overthrow Hitler. Even though some of them were SS officers, they all discussed the situation quite openly. (There was considerably more comradery between Waffen-SS officers and other ranks than existed in any other service.) Poeppel recalled that the men of the Waffen-SS "are front-line soldiers the same as us, not [like] the Black SS or the 'golden pheasants,' which is what we call the party bigwigs. . . . Even the SS men reckon that if we manage to win the war, the party will have to be dealt with afterwards," the paratrooper wrote in his diary. "Most of them don't agree with the assassination attempt, but the prevailing opinion is that the Generals are at fault for relinquishing the famed leadership qualities to the so-called 'Greatest Military Leader of all Time.' How did the poor buggers at the front, and the exhausted civilian population at home, deserve to be led so badly?"[8]

Operation "Goodwood" was designed to break the deadlock on the Allied left flank and push on to the Falaise Plain, where the British could at last use their strong armored units and superior mobility against Panzer Group West. Simultaneously, the American generals designed a similar plan, Operation "Cobra," in order to break the German left flank. Even if "Goodwood" failed, the British and Canadians would at least pin down most of the German panzer divisions, which would then not be available for immediate counterattacks against the U.S. "Cobra" forces.

Facing General Dempsey's British 2nd Army was Panzer Group West, whose line extended 70 miles. Its commander, Heinrich Eberbach, has generally been ignored by historians, but he was one of the best generals to ever fight on the Western Front. He was also a very handsome man except for his nose, about three-quarters of which had been shot off during World War I. Although considered pro-Nazi by Fuehrer Headquarters, he was in fact in contact with the anti-Hitler conspiracy, mainly because he saw no way this war was going to have a happy ending for Germany.

Eberbach deployed eight divisions (four corps) along the front, with five divisions in reserve. Since he assumed command on July 2, Eberbach had organized his defenses in considerable depth and was ready for the British offensive.

The diversionary attacks for Operation "Goodwood" started on the British right (western) flank on July 15, when the British XXX and newly committed XII Corps (Lieutenant General Sir Neil Ritchie)[9] advanced against the II SS Panzer and XXXXVII Panzer Corps, which were holding the high ground south of Villers-Bocage. They lost more than 3,500 men and gained very little ground, but they accomplished their real objective: They tied down the 10th SS Panzer and 2nd SS Panzer Divisions (which were being relieved by the 271st and 326th Infantry Divisions, respectively) and forced Eberbach to commit the 9th SS Panzer Division and part of SS Major General Teddy Wisch's 1st SS Panzer Division "Leibstandarte Adolf Hitler" to counterattacks.[10] Then Montgomery unleashed his main attack east of the Vire, out of the so-called airborne bridgehead that the British 6th Airborne Division had established on D-Day. His strike force included the 7th Armoured, 11th Armoured, and Guards Armoured Divisions, as well as five independent armored brigades, all under the British VIII Corps, which was led by Lieutenant General Sir Richard O'Connor, one of their best tank commanders.[11] All totaled, O'Connor had 2,250 medium and 400 light tanks.[12] The drive was supported by the Canadian II Corps on the right and the British I Corps on the left, as well as by 1,600 heavy bombers, 400 medium bombers and fighter-bombers, 720 artillery pieces, and naval gunfire. Its main objective was the Bourguebus Ridge, the commanding feature overlooking the Falaise Plain. The ridge was only 15 miles north of the city of Falaise.

As massive as this plan was, it had a number of serious flaws. First, despite every Allied effort, there was no surprise in it. The Germans still held Colombelles and its enormous steelworks. From its towers, the defenders could observe any major troop movement for miles around. Second, the terrain did not favor it. The area between Caen and Falaise was densely populated, with farming villages and hamlets throughout. Panzer Group West had converted each of these into a strongpoint. Two major railroad embankments also crossed the area and constituted dangerous obstacles for the British tanks. Third, the bridgehead east of the Orne was too constricted. It was already held by the British 6th Airborne and 51st Highland Divisions and was simply not large enough to hold a force of this size. Accordingly, O'Connor decided to advance with his divisions in file (i.e., one behind the other), with the 11th Armoured in the lead. Fourth, the road network was inadequate to accommodate more than one armored division's advance at a time. Each British armored division contained more than 2,700 vehicles. This not only meant that the British could only deploy one-third of their armor initially—it meant that their artillery could not follow and they would quickly outrun their artillery support. Also, due to the road network, the plan called for three armored divisions to advance down a corridor, the size of which would have been normal for a single armored brigade. This would give the British very little room to maneuver. Finally, to maintain secrecy, the 51st Highland Division was not told about the offensive until almost the last minute. Only on July 16 was it discovered that the 51st had laid a minefield directly across VIII Corps' axis of advance. This minefield had been put down hastily the month before and had not been properly mapped. Now it was overgrown, and it would take five or six days to remove it—if the work was done during daylight hours—a move that would surely tip off the Germans that something was afoot. (They did not realize that the Germans already knew.) All the British could do was delay the main attack until July 18 and open a few narrow lanes through the minefield; then they would have to push three armored divisions through them!

British intelligence also badly underestimated the depth of the German defense and estimated that they would encounter no more than three divisions and 120 tanks. "The next day was to demonstrate yet again the seemingly endless habit of the Allies to underestimate the tenacity of their opponent," Colonel Carlo D'Este wrote later.[13]

The main attack began at 5:30 A.M. on July 18, when Allied bombers dropped 6,000 tons of bombs on German lines. The smoke and dust were so thick from this bombardment that when the medium bombers of the U.S. 8th and 9th Air Forces began arriving over their targets at 7 A.M., the battlefield was still so obscure that some of them had to return to base without dropping their bombs; however, another wave from the 8th U.S.A.F. did drop nearly 13,000 one-hundred-pound and 76,000 twenty-pound fragmentation bombs on Bourguebus Ridge.

"Among the thunder of the explosions, we could hear the wounded scream and the insane howling of men who had been driven mad," Captain Baron Richard von Rosen, the commander of the 3rd Company, 503rd Heavy Tank Battalion, recalled. The blasts were strong enough to turn one of his 60-ton Tigers upside down. Half of Rosen's tanks were knocked out.[14] Many of the infantrymen of the 16th Luftwaffe Field Division were captured by the British and Canadians, who found them so shaken by the bombardment that they could not coordinate their limbs. Many had to be allowed to sit beside the roads until they had recovered sufficiently to walk.[15] Many of the prisoners were so stunned that they could not be interrogated for 24 hours.[16] "The land laid waste by the bombers seemed like a piece of devastated territory which could scarcely conceal a living thing," one historian wrote later. "Trees were uprooted, fields pitted and littered with dead cattle, and theoretically nothing could be left alive on this lunar landscape."[17]

The air attacks destroyed much of Major Becker's 200th Assault Gun Battalion of the 21st Panzer Division, which was directly in the path of the main advance. The I/125th Panzer Grenadier Regiment also suffered heavy casualties. The bombing, however, failed to destroy the artillery behind the ridge or all of the antitank guns in several of the hamlets situated along the flanks of the corridor down which the British 11th Armoured Division now advanced.

The well-trained 11th Armoured was considered by many to be the best British armored division to fight in Europe. It was well led by Major General G.P.B. "Pip" Roberts, who was the youngest and one of the best divisional commanders in the Empire.[18] He was not happy, however, when his corps commander ordered him to capture the villages of Cuverville and Demouville to his front, thinking it would divert too much of his infantry, which he would need at Bourguebus Ridge. He felt that he should bypass them and let the Highlanders deal with them, since they were holding a trench line only two miles away and were not engaged in an attack, but he was overruled by O'Connor. (Roberts did not learn until after the war that Montgomery had, in an excessively cautious order, decreed that the 51st was to remain in its trenches, in case the Germans counterattacked.) O'Connor did agree, however, to let Roberts only mask the strongly defended village of Cagny until the Guards Armoured Division arrived; then they would take Cagny. Reluctantly, Roberts ordered the 159th Infantry Brigade to Cuverville and Demouville.

Both taking Cuverville and Demouville and masking Cagny were mistakes. All that was in Cagny were four 88mm guns from the 16th Luftwaffe Field Division, which was now under the operational control of the 21st Panzer Division. This particular sector was under the command of Colonel Baron Hans von Luck, the leader of the 125th Panzer Grenadier Regiment. By some miracle, the 88s were not destroyed in the aerial bombardment despite the fact that Allied bombers had dropped 650 tons of bombs in the Cagny area alone.[19] Colonel von Luck, who had just returned from a three-day pass in Paris, arrived at his headquarters just in time to witness the aerial bombardment. He went forward to see what had survived and was surprised to see a panzer, an 88mm antitank gun, and the four 88s; however, the Luftwaffe guns were pointed skyward, just as the vanguard of the 11th Armoured—about 100 tanks—passed by. Luck ordered the battery commander to let them continue unmolested toward the railroad embankment and the ridge but to open fire on the second echelon. The air force officer refused, on the absurd grounds that his mission was air defense, not to shoot up tanks. Luck had no time to argue. He drew his pistol, pointed it at the officer, and asked if he preferred to obey orders or to be shot. He chose the first alternative.

The 11th Armoured Division was spearheaded by the 29th Armoured Brigade. Its vanguard, the 3rd Battalion, Royal Tank Regiment, and most of the 2nd Fife and Forfar Yeomanry, had just passed Cagny. The second echelon, a squadron of the 2nd Fife and Forfar, had been ordered by Roberts to mask Cagny. When the deadly 88s opened up, it lost 16 tanks in a matter of a minute or so. More important, the little battle group at Cagny held up most of the units following the 3rd Tank through the narrow corridor, including part of the Guards Armoured Division. The rest of the Guards were tied up in the minefield or in the monumental traffic jams behind it. Only the 23rd Hussars with one infantry battalion in support (8th/The Rifle Brigade) followed the 3rd Tank and 2nd Fife toward Bourguebus Ridge. Here, at noon, they were stopped cold.

The British had attacked into the zones of the LXXXVI and I SS Panzer Corps. In was here that General Eberbach—who had been anticipating the offensive for days—had constructed the best defensive infrastructure in Normandy. It was almost 10 miles deep and included four belts plus a mobile reserve. The first belt was manned by the 346th Infantry and 16th Luftwaffe Field Divisions. The second belt was defended by the 125th and 192nd Panzer Grenadier Regiments of the 21st Panzer Division, which were liberally augmented with tanks, assault guns, flak, and antitank guns. The third belt included a series of fortified villages and hamlets, defended by infantry and antitank guns and backed by 270 *Nebelwerfers* (six-barreled mortars), whose fire also supported the second belt. Belt number four extended from Bourguebus Ridge in the west to Troarn in the east. The ridge itself was defended by the 220th Panzer Engineer Battalion and the 21st Reconnaissance Battalion, both of the 21st Panzer Division. Behind them lay three intact artillery battalions. Finally, Eberbach's mobile reserves consisted of mixed Panther/PzKw IV battalion of the 1st SS Panzer Division (46 tanks), plus two battle groups of panzer grenadiers and what was left of the Tiger battalion of the 12th SS: around 15 tanks. They were led into battle by SS General Sepp Dietrich.

The Battle of Bourguebus Ridge was the largest tank action of the entire campaign. Although outnumbered, the Panther and Tigers were technologically much superior to the Shermans and Cromwells, outgunning them in both range and power. Had it not been for the rocket-firing Typhoons from the RAF, the 29th Armoured Brigade would probably have been destroyed.

The Germans also took a battering. The nearby tank workshop at Foret de Cinglais did such a magnificent job of quickly patching up damaged tanks and sending them back into battle that Dietrich later made it a point to personally decorate every man in the shop with the Iron Cross, 2nd Class, a medal very rarely given to people not directly in combat.

By the end of the day, the 29th Armoured Brigade had lost 126 tanks. Two of its three regiments had only 20 tanks left. Normally they had around 90. The Guards Division had lost 60 tanks, most of them in front of Cagny and Emieville. (As was the case with the Germans, many of these were recovered and soon repaired.) German casualties had also been heavy. Between them, the 1st and 12th SS had lost 109 tanks.[20]

During the night of July 18, Panzer Group West rushed further reinforcements into the Bourguebus Ridge sector and further strengthened its right flank as well. The battle resumed the next day, with casualties increasing on both sides. Elements of the 7th Armoured Division—which had at last made their way through the minefield—managed to occupy part of the ridge but could not hold it. The next day, July 20, the British attacked again and lost another 1,000 men and 68 tanks at Bourguebus Ridge. That afternoon it began to rain; it soon became a cloudburst and the battlefield became a quagmire. The British tanks, which had little room to maneuver anyway, lacked the traction of the Panthers and Tigers; they called off the battle and retreated a short distance. The Germans did not pursue.

The British lost 5,500 men during Operation "Goodwood" and more than 400 tanks: 36% of all British armor on the mainland of Europe.[21]

Only the secondary operation had been successful. While the Battle of Bourguebus Ridge was in full swing, the II Canadian Corps had secured the last of the Caen suburbs, although they had lost more than 100 tanks in the process.

Guenther von Kluge had already drawn the appropriate conclusions. As early as July 12, he signaled Fuehrer Headquarters that he was no pessimist, but "the situation couldn't be grimmer."[22] He watched the Battle of Bourguebus Ridge with growing apprehension. Now he knew the truth beyond a shadow of a doubt: The problems in the West were due to a lot more than poor generalship, and good generalship alone would not solve them. In the long run, the front would not hold. Now all he could do was to hold on desperately, hoping for a miracle that, his calculating brain told him, was not going to happen. Now that Stauffenberg had failed, his own head was on the block. On July 21, he wrote Hitler and tried to prepare him for the coming disaster. He said:

In the face of the enemy's complete command of the air, there is no possibility of our finding a strategy which will counterbalance its truly annihilating effect, unless we give up the field of battle. . . . [T]he moment is fast approaching when this overtaxed front line is bound to break.[23]

He was certainly right about that, but he had no idea the moment he foresaw would occur in less than 72 hours.

OPERATION COBRA: THE BREAKOUT

On the other flank, the latest U.S. offensive came to an end on July 19. Although they had captured St.-Lô, the American generals were by no means satisfied. With a dozen divisions, they had only advanced a maximum of seven miles in 17 days and had suffered 40,000 casualties—90% of them infantry—in the process. General Bradley had 15 divisions (counting 3 just down from Cherbourg) with more on the way from England. Hausser's 7th Army opposed him with 9 divisions, more than half of which were Kampfgruppen, and the Americans outnumbered the Germans 750 to 110 in tanks. Bradley was not fighting in tank country, however, and, against German troops, odds of 3 to 1 in favor of the attacker were necessary to ensure victory. In the *bocage* country, however, this ratio changed to 5 or 6 to 1.

The most pressing problem the Americans faced was the need to break out of hedgerow country. Only then would they be able to bring their superior firepower and mobility fully to bare against the Wehrmacht; however, they first had to find a solution to the Germans' delaying tactics. The *Feldgrau* were conducting an active defensive, featuring frequent local counterattacks with infantry, often supported by a few panzers and/or assault guns. As their infantry strength declined, they made increasing use of artillery, which usually fired heavy concentrations for a short duration against a few key targets. (This tactic of all guns firing at once and then all going silent at the same time made it difficult for the Allied spotter airplanes and fighter-bombers to locate many artillery positions.) When they were forced to retreat, the main German body broke contact during the hours of darkness and fell back to easily defensible positions (of which there were hundreds in hedgerow country), leaving behind scattered minefields and strong rearguards, which were equipped with large numbers of automatic weapons. They forced the Americans to deploy and bring up reinforcements; the Germans then fell back to their next delaying line, while a security force in a nearby breaking position provided covering fire. The rearguard thus fell back from delaying position to delaying position, until it reached the next main line of resistance (MLR). Because of these tactics, the Allies had already suffered more than 100,000 casualties and were still stuck in *bocage* territory, despite their overwhelming superiority in every material area of classification. General Omar Bradley, the commander of the U.S. 1st Army, however, conceived of an idea to defeat these tactics and break the deadlock in Normandy. His plan was called Operation "Cobra," and it involved using massive formations of strategic bombers to blast a hole in the German line; then he would commit his armor through the gap, in an effort to penetrate beyond hedgerow country before the Germans could recover. While plans for this operation proceeded at full pace, a lull descended over most of the western sector of the Normandy Front.

Field Marshal von Kluge and his subordinates were also having their problems. Due to the total Allied domination of the air, supplies could be brought in during the nights, which were only about nine hours long during the summer in France. The result could be seen in every meaningful category. In addition, Hitler, as usual, was obsessed with new divisions, and the old units in Normandy were bled white. Replacements, both men and material, were slow in being sent and slow in arriving. From D-Day until July 11, German losses totaled almost 2,000 officers and 85,000 men. Only 5,210 replacements (6% of the losses) had arrived, although 7,500 more had been promised, and some were actually on the way. Naturally, losses were heaviest in the combat units, in the infantry battalions of the infantry divisions and in the panzer and panzer grenadier regiments. By July 11, for example, the 243rd Infantry Division had lost more than 8,000 men, the 352nd Infantry had lost almost 8,000 (more than half of its pre-invasion strength), and the 716th Infantry (in the Caen sector) had lost more than 6,000 men—about two-thirds of its pre-invasion strength. The panzer grenadier regiments of the 12th SS Panzer Division were down the strength of one infantry battalion, and both the 21st Panzer and Panzer Lehr Divisions had lost more than 3,000 men—

most of them from their grenadier regiments. By July 17, German losses were near the 100,000 mark; replacements (including those promised or en route) equaled only 12% of the casualties.[24] A week later, on July 24, Kluge reported that he had received only 10,000 replacements, but German losses to date included 113,000 men and more than 2,000 panzers, as well as 340 airplanes. Although he still believed that the Allies had 52 divisions in the United Kingdom, he now doubted that there would be another invasion, implying (but not too forcefully) that some of the 19 divisions of the 15th Army could safely be transferred to Normandy. OKW ignored the suggestion.[25]

The situation was similar in all categories. In tanks, Army Group B had lost 150 Mark IVs, 85 Panthers, 15 Tigers, and 167 75mm assault guns. Only 17 of these had been replaced. The artillery batteries had also suffered heavy material losses, and those that could still fire were low in ammunition. In the Caen sector on July 10, for example, the British 2nd Army shot an estimated 80,000 artillery rounds at German positions, but the Germans could only fire 4,500 shells in return. All of this, naturally, was beginning to affect the fighting spirit of the German soldier. Although morale still remained remarkably good, some of the senior German commanders were becoming concerned that the old aggressiveness was declining, especially in the panzer divisions. Rommel voiced this conclusion in reports dated July 10 and 16. On July 11, General of Panzer Troops Heinrich Eberbach, the commander of Panzer Group West, clearly implied that the Reich was nearing operational bankruptcy in terms of manpower reserves when he signaled Rommel that it was time to close most of the Wehrmacht's specialist schools and to send the students to the front. Field Marshal von Kluge agreed that the situation was developing into an "ungeheures Kladderadatsch"—an awful mess—and informed Jodl that Germany could no longer afford the Fuehrer's inflexible methods of defense because of the heavy casualties that resulted. Because he did not believe the infantry could hold out much longer, he told Jodl, he wanted more tanks to act as "corset stays" behind the depleted rifle platoons. His reserves were inadequate and the situation was "very serious," he told the OKW chief of operations and asked him to relay his comments to Hitler.[26]

The Fuehrer's response was categorical. Kluge was to "stand fast" ("Starre Verteidigung!"). He did not elucidate as to how the OB West was to do so. On July 22, however, he sent an order that was even more explicit: "Anyone who gives up an inch of ground will be shot." Later that day, he sent a dispatch that read: "Anyone who speaks to me of peace without victory will lose his head, no matter who he is or what his position."[27]

These orders had the desired affect on Field Marshal Guenther von Kluge, who had been on both sides of the July 20 conspiracy. He was fully aware that the Gestapo was investigating every aspect of the assassination attempt, and Kluge was desperately anxious to prove that he was *Fuehrertreu*—completely loyal to the Fuehrer. His own head depended upon it, as Hitler's dispatch of July 22 clearly indicated. This attitude would color his entire conduct of operations during the next three and a half weeks of the Battle of Normandy and would be a significant contributing factor to the debacle that followed.

Despite the heavy German losses and the growing odds against them, it was by no means a foregone conclusion that the Allies would win the battle. The Normandy bloodbath—naturally—was affecting them as well. Combat fatigue and physical and mental exhaustion were taking their tolls on both sides. The U.S. 90th Infantry Division, for example, had been fighting in France only six weeks, but its enlisted infantry replacements amounted to more than 100% of its authorized infantry strength, and infantry officer replacements totaled almost 150% of its authorized number. Its new troops were both "green" and, for the moment at least, undependable. (Before the war ended, the 90th Infantry was one of the best divisions in the American army, but, at this moment, it was having its problems.) On July 22, in a pre-Cobra operation, it attacked elements of the 2nd SS Panzer Division and captured St. Germain-sur-Seves, a hamlet located on a muddy piece of low ground just south of the Seves. Casualties in the assault units were heavy, however—50% in the lead battalion. Efforts to reinforce the bridgehead with tanks and tank destroyers failed, because German artillery fire and the wet terrain prevented the American engineers from building a bridge over the river. There were, however, an adequate number of antitank guns in the bridgehead to deal with a counterattack on a moderate scale. That night, however, stragglers began to drift to the rear, away from the battlefield, individually and in small groups. Some disguised themselves as messengers, others faked wounds, and others pretended to be helping evacuate the wounded. The following morning, four German assault guns, supported by about 30 infantrymen, attacked the U.S. battalion on the southern bank. Suddenly, panic broke out in American ranks, and about 200 men threw down their weapons and surrendered to the surprised Germans, who were outnumbered 6 to 1. The rest of the battalion fled into a nearby swamp and eventually reached friendly lines.[28] The 90th Division's commander was held responsible for the debacle at St. Germain and was relieved of his command.

Although this rout was an isolated incident, it did indicate that exhaustion and battle fatigue were beginning to tell on the Americans, who had been slugging it out in hedgerow country for weeks now, without even a hint of a decisive breakthrough. And the 90th was certainly not the only Allied unit with problems. Even the performance of the British 7th

Armoured Division—the famous "Desert Rats"—was not living up to expectations; in fact, it had performed so poorly that Dempsey sacked its commanding officer, Major General Sir W.E.J. Erskine. Lieutenant General G. C. Bucknell, the commander of the XXX Corps, was also relieved of his command. The veteran 51st Highland Division was not doing as well as the 7th Armoured. Montgomery cabled Field Marshal Sir Alan Brooke, the chief of the Imperial General Staff (CIGS), that it was not fighting with any determination at all and was not battleworthy. He replaced its commander (Major General D. C. Bullen-Smith) with Major General T. G. Rennie (a more forceful officer) and even considered sending the division back to England for retraining.[29]

It was the same problem up and down the line. The veteran 50th (Northumbrian) Division, for example, did not encounter the same problems as the 7th Armoured and 51st Highland (or at least not to the same degree), but it was also exhibiting timidity in the attack. As a result, junior officers were assuming greater and greater burdens and were being lost at an appalling rate. The situation was so bad that Brigadier James Hargest, the former commander of the 5th New Zealand Brigade in Crete and North Africa, was sent to investigate. A veteran infantry officer, Hargest had fought in 20 major engagements in World War I and had risen from second lieutenant to lieutenant colonel in four years. He reported that due to the nature of the terrain in Normandy the men tended to lie down and stay there, safe from German snipers. They could only be persuaded to move forward by the urging and the personal example of their officers, who thus had to expose themselves. In this manner, the 9th Durham Light Infantry Battalion lost all four of its company commanders in one day (June 14). Hargest reported that the men often lost heart when officers were not present. This led to the serious problem of bunching—men clustering together in combat. This practice gave them a sense of not being alone and a false sense of security, but it also increased their casualties significantly. Hargest reported that a single German mortar round killed or wounded 8 soldiers on June 8, so tightly were they bunched. On June 22, 30 men gathered around a Bren carrier to get food. Obviously they were spotted by a German forward observer. The Germans fired three mortar rounds into them, killing or wounding 22. Hargest concluded, "The morale of the infantry officer and soldier is not high. This applies to new troops as well as veterans. . . . Even senior officers grumble. . . . The troops have not that spirit essential to Victory."[30]

It was no different in the newer units. The 6th Battalion, the Duke of Wellington Regiment (6th DWR) of the 49th West Riding Division, for example, entered the battle on June 13. By the end of the month, it had lost 23 of its original 35 officers and 350 other ranks. Every original company commander was dead or in a hospital. Unit morale was scattered, and there were numerous cases of shell shock or hysteria every time the Germans shelled them, and there were several cases of self-inflicted wounds. The situation was so bad that the 6th DWR had to be disbanded in early July.

With a few exceptions, it was the same story all across the Allied front. The strain of fighting in a constricted bridgehead in hedgerow country was taking its toll. The hard fact is that neither the British nor Americans were prepared for the kind of battle they were facing in Normandy. The Allied generals had done an outstanding job in planning for D-Day and had their men well prepared for it, but they had done an inadequate job in planning for operations beyond the beach; their men were not prepared for what they were facing. The Allied leaders had not appreciated how difficult it would be to break out of Normandy, nor had they understood what it would be like to fight in hedgerow country against a determined and experienced enemy. The troops, therefore, had not been adequately indoctrinated or trained for this kind of fighting. The mental strain also led to drinking—Calvados was produced here and was readily available—a fact that further undermined discipline.

The Allies were also fundamentally unprepared for the combat philosophy of the Germans. Unlike the Americans, the Germans had for centuries been imbued with a tradition of responding to leadership—whatever the source. The sergeants understood that they were expected to provide aggressive leadership if their officers were absent or became casualties, and they did so as a matter of course. If the sergeant fell, the corporal knew that he was expected to provide bold and forceful leadership, and this is usually what he did. The men in the ranks—trained from childhood to respond to authority with unquestioning obedience—usually remained true to their upbringing and followed their new leader without question. This concept of leadership permeated German military society (and society as a whole) from top to bottom. As a result, Allied leaders were frequently amazed at how rapidly German units recovered, even after a devastating defeat, and how rapidly they reorganized. In addition, the British in particular were surprised to learn that to the German the word *defense* was an active word; it by no means implied passivity. To the German, it implied counterattack. It is a well-known and universally accepted military maxim that the enemy is weakest just after he has captured an objective—and that is the best moment to counterattack. Unlike the case with the armies of many countries, however, the Germans actually launched these counterattacks. "The basic [German] defensive tactic," Brigadier Bidwell wrote later, "was a counter-attack. British troops were to learn quickly, albeit painfully, that their fight only started after they had thankfully reached their objective."[31]

The Allies were also slow in appreciating what the layout was of a typical German defense and thus were slow in adapting their tactics to it. Almost without exception, they laid a heavy (and, in the case of the Americans, lavish) artillery bombardment on the German front line and followed it with a tank attack. The Germans, however, were always prepared to sacrifice their forward line, which was defended just strongly enough to require a proper attack. The Allied artillery bombardment warned the Germans that an attack was coming and tipped them off as to what the probable objective was of the Allied attack but did not destroy their tanks, self-propelled antitank guns, and assault guns, most of which were some distance to the rear. By the time the Allies broke through the German front line (which was something of a combat outpost line), the Germans had reinforced their main line of resistance with enough antitank (AT) firepower to inflict heavy losses on the attackers and stop them short of their objectives. Often the German MLR was not touched by the preliminary bombardment. Also, the Germans—many of whom had fought on the Eastern Front—were past masters of separating enemy tanks from their infantry. A tank without infantry support was vulnerable, especially in hedgerow country. Early in the campaign, the British and Canadians were particularly bad about sending their tanks charging forward while the infantry lagged behind to deal with some isolated strong point or bunker. As a result, their armored units were often slaughtered by German panzer and AT units, especially those equipped with 88s. By the end of June, all of this had introduced an element of timidity into many armored units, which often failed to grasp real opportunities when they presented themselves, out of a fear of running into another German ambush. The undeniable talent the German infantrymen had for shooting a tank in the rear (where the armor was thinnest) with a *Panzerfaust* further exacerbated this tendency toward timidity.

On the other side of the hedgerow, the success of the invasion to date had lowered German morale somewhat, but not to the degree that it constituted a threat to the overall defense of Normandy. The rank and file overall still had faith in Hitler, in the rightness of their cause, and in the opinion that, even now, everything would somehow work out all right. All they had to do was check the Anglo-Americans here in Normandy until the "miracle weapons" were ready. What did they think of the success of the invasion to date? "The one emotion which gripped them all was incredulity," Milton Shulman observed later. "They had not yet begun to despair."[32]

The Germans—soldiers and civilians—were heavily influenced by the media, which lied with great frequency. "Having been duped so long by propaganda, the effects did not easily wear off," Shulman wrote later. "Much more time and much more suffering was needed before the German soldier finally awoke to the reality of events about him."[33]

Goebbels, the master propagandist, realized that the crushing defeats on the Eastern Front, the devastating bombing of the Fatherland, and the increasing pressure on the Western defenses might shake the Germans' faith in ultimate victory. To prevent this from happening, he launched a major propaganda campaign, which included multiple tales of successes achieved by pilotless aircraft and V-1 flying bombs, along with fervent promises of more and better secret weapons that had nearly been perfected and were about to go into production. There was, of course, a grain of truth in these stories, which were all the more believable to the soldiers in Normandy, who occasionally spotted a ghostly V-1 on its way to England. German morale, therefore, held up relatively well in Normandy. On the other hand, the growing reluctance of British and American combat units to advance into the *bocage*, coupled with the rout of a significant part of the U.S. 90th Infantry Division at St. Germain, certainly did not bode well for Operation "Cobra," but it did demonstrate how necessary it was for the Allies to break out of Normandy before the situation deteriorated any further.

General Bradley's plan called for a massive commitment of Allied airpower, including all of the heavy bombers of the 8th U.S. Air Force, all of the medium bombers of the 9th U.S.A.F., the fighters and fighter-bombers of the 8th U.S.A.F., the 2nd Tactical Air Force of the RAF, and the U.S. IX Tactical Air Command: about 2,500 airplanes in all. Their mission was to obliterate all German units and positions in a 7,000-yard-wide and 2,500-yard-deep rectangular target area due south of the Periers–St.-Lô Highway. According to the plan, the aerial bombardment would begin 80 minutes before the ground assault, when the German positions would be attacked by 350 fighter-bombers. They would be immediately followed by 1,800 heavy bombers, which would attack in wave after wave for an hour. Following the carpet bombing, 350 fighter-bombers would strafe and bomb the target area from low altitudes for another 20 minutes. Then 400 medium bombers would attack the southern half of the rectangle for 45 minutes, while the American infantry advanced. All this time, some 500 fighters would provide air cover further south, in the unlikely event that the Luftwaffe tried to intervene. In all, the aerial bombardment would last two hours and 25 minutes and would deposit almost 5,000 tons of high explosives, napalm (jellied gasoline), white phosphorous, and thousands of 100-pound and 260-pound fragmentation bombs on a target area of only six square miles. It was to be the most concentrated application of strategic bombers in support of ground forces in the history of the world up until that point.

The aerial attack would be supplemented by an artillery bombardment of more than 1,000 guns, including nine battalions of heavy artillery on loan from 1st Army Headquarters. These guns would fire 125,000 rounds in support of the breakout.[34]

In the ground phase of the battle, Lieutenant General J. Lawson Collins's VII Corps was to lead the breakthrough, so Bradley reduced his corps' frontage to 4 5 miles. The U.S. 9th and 30th Infantry Divisions were to seize the towns of Marigny and St. Gilles on the flanks of the breakthrough; then through this 3-mile gap, Collins would commit the U.S. 2nd and 3rd Armored Divisions and the motorized 1st Infantry Division. Because Collins was concerned about the exhaustion of the 9th and 30th Infantries, Bradley gave him the 4th Infantry Division for the initial breakthrough as well. According to American estimates, their ground forces alone would outnumber the Germans 5 to 1, even before the air attacks began.

As an additional advantage, three of every five U.S. tanks were equipped with "Rhinoceroses" or "Rhinos." This new device, invented by U.S. Sergeant Curtis G. Culin, consisted of several heavy steel prongs welded to the front of the tank. They looked like horizontal tusks and allowed a Sherman to slice through a hedgerow without exposing its belly to a German antitank gunner.

The plan called for the Allied air forces to tear a gap in the German line by annihilating the Panzer Lehr Division. Collins would then attack through the gap and drive about 15 miles to the southwest, capturing the city of Coutances—a move that would cut off Lieutenant General Dietrich von Choltitz's LXXXIV Corps and unhinge the entire German Front in Normandy. Meanwhile, Middleton's VIII U.S. Corps (79th, 8th, 90th, and 83rd Infantry and 4th and 6th Armored Divisions) would launch frontal attacks against Choltitz, to pin down the LXXXIV Corps and prevent it from escaping. The final American objective was Avranches, a city at the base of the Cotentin peninsula. If the Americans could capture this place, they would be in a position to break out and overrun France. The offensive was slated to begin on July 24.

Meanwhile, Field Marshal von Kluge took advantage of the relative lull to shore up his line and even create some reserves. Rastenburg (as Hitler's Headquarters in East Prussia was called) had at last come to the conclusion that the Normandy landings might be the real main invasion after all and begrudgingly began to reinforce Army Group B with troops from the 15th Army. In all, between July 10 and 22, Kluge was given four infantry divisions from southern France and the Pas de Calais sector, and more were promised to him. He used the 277th Infantry Division to replace the 9th SS Panzer Division in the front line, the 272nd Infantry to relieve the 1st SS and 12th SS Panzers, the 271st Infantry to replace the 10th SS Panzer, and the 326th Infantry to relieve the 2nd Panzer

Division. Unfortunately, Montgomery's Operation "Goodwood" forced him to recommit almost all of his panzer reserves to front-line combat. He would have very few tanks available in reserve when "Cobra" struck, and they were not in the St.-Lô sector. Kluge was also dissatisfied with the dispositions of SS General Hausser, the commander of the 7th Army and his old classmate from Gross Lichterfelde, the German equivalent of West Point.[35] He suggested that Hausser replace the Panzer Lehr Division with the 275th Infantry, and the 2nd SS Panzer with the 353rd Infantry. The SS general, however, did no such thing; in fact, as Martin Blumenson wrote, he "did little more than clamor for battlefield replacements, additional artillery and supplies, and the sight of air cover."[36] Hausser was, in fact, an excellent divisional commander, but he was a mediocre corps commander and was clearly "over his head" as an army commander in Normandy, as the events of the next few weeks would clearly demonstrate.

On July 24, 7th Army had two corps: Choltitz's LXXXIV on the left (along the coast) and Meindl's II Parachute on the right. Left to right, the LXXXIV controlled the remnants of the 243rd Infantry Division, defending along the coast; the 91st Air Landing Division (including the remnants of the 77th Infantry Division and an exhausted and depleted battle group from the 265th Infantry); much of the still battleworthy 2nd SS Panzer Division, which also controlled the 6th Parachute Regiment; the remnants of the 17th SS Panzer Grenadier Division, holding the Periers sector; the 5th Parachute Division (now down to a single infantry regiment); and the Panzer Lehr Division, on the extreme right flank of the corps. Choltitz's only reserve was the depleted 353rd Infantry Division, resting a few miles south of Periers.

On Choltitz's right flank lay the II Parachute Corps, which only controlled two divisions: the burned-out 352nd Infantry, which was still holding south of St.-Lô, and the 3rd Parachute (with a regiment of the 5th Parachute Division attached) on its right, which linked up with the 326th Infantry Division of Panzer Group West near Caumont. General Kraiss's 352nd had absorbed the main blow on D-Day and had slaughtered the Americans on Omaha Beach.[37] Now, however, after six weeks of constant fighting, it was down to a strength of 650 combat troops. To help it hold its positions, Hausser and Meindl had reinforced it with elements of the 275th, 343rd, and 353rd Infantry Divisions, plus a battle group from the 266th Infantry. General Meindl had no reserves worth mentioning. Seventh Army had only two reserve formations: a battle group from the 2nd SS Panzer Division (two tank and two infantry companies) and the 275th Infantry Division, just arriving from Brittany. It controlled two infantry regiments and was posted just behind the Panzer Lehr Division.

Lieutenant General Bayerlein's Panzer Lehr lay entirely within the rectangle that Bradley planned to bomb out of existence. It controlled 2,200 combat effectives from its own regiments, plus 450 combat troops from the badly damaged Kampfgruppe Heinz (of the 275th Infantry Division), a parachute regiment from the 5th Parachute Division, and a few elements of the 2nd SS Panzer Division—a total of about 3,200 combat effectives. When the Battle of Normandy began, it had almost 15,000 men (including just over 7,000 combat troops) and more than 200 tanks and armored vehicles. As of July 23, only about 45 of these were still running.

The Luftwaffe could do nothing against "Cobra." Although 3rd Air Fleet had been reinforced with almost 800 fighters during the first two weeks of the invasion, it was never able to mount a single serious challenge to the Allied domination of the air. By the time these *Gruppen* began to arrive, the carefully prepared and well-provisioned airfields in the sector had been destroyed by the Allied fighter-bombers, and the fighters had to use hastily constructed dirt landings strips, which lacked signal equipment and navigational facilities. These strips were also poorly camouflaged, and they acted like magnets for the ubiquitous Allied fighter-bombers. By June 21, the new groups were already smashed and down to an operational strength of 2 or 3 airplanes each. Most of them had an average of about 35 airplanes when they departed for Normandy. More than half of the reinforcing fighters had been destroyed in the first two weeks of the campaign.[38] Eight groups had to be withdrawn to the Reich to rebuild.

Goering had only sent the new wings to France on the assumption that the Allies would not launch many significant large-scale raids against German industry during the early stages of the invasion. In mid-June, however, the 8th U.S. Air Force launched a major series of attacks against the German synthetic oil plants, from which the Luftwaffe obtained 95% of its fuel. During May alone the American bombers had reduced the daily output of German synthetic aviation fuel from 5,850 to 2,800 tons per day, mainly by blasting the two major refineries at Leuna and Poelitz. Within two weeks after D-Day they had returned to the attack and (in cooperation with nighttime raids by the RAF) had knocked out the Reich's third largest synthetic oil plant at Gelsenkirchen. By June 22, the total German output of aviation fuel was down to 632 tons a day. Total production for June 1944 dropped to 53,000 tons, as opposed to 175,000 in April; that same month, the Luftwaffe consumed 124,000 tons of fuel, making considerable inroads into its central reserve, which had stood at 400,000 tons in May.[39] To meet the threat on the "oil front," the Luftwaffe had to limit the flow of reinforcements and fighter replacements to the west. The eight battered groups that had returned to Germany to refit Goering transferred to Air Fleet Reich and committed to the defense of Germany. This ended any thin chance the 3rd Air Fleet might have had to challenge the Allied air forces in Normandy. Through-out the zone of Army Group B, Allied fighter-bombers roamed virtually unmolested, blasting German tanks, artillery emplacements, transport columns, supply installations, and bridges. The German air force never did become a combat factor on the Western Front.

No thanks to the Luftwaffe, Operation "Cobra" failed on the first attempt. July 24 was characterized by thick, overcast clouds and low visibility. British Air Chief Marshal Leigh-Mallory ordered a postponement of the aerial bombardment, but his orders did not reach every unit, several of which were already airborne. A number of formations dropped their loads on German lines; others dropped theirs on American positions, killing 25 and wounding 131 men, mainly members of the 30th Infantry Division. Several newspapermen were also killed or wounded. The most prominent victim was Lieutenant General Leslie J. McNair, who had recently succeeded Patton as commander of the 1st Army Group, which had done such a fine job of deceiving the Germans into thinking that the Normandy landings were not the main invasion. As chief of Army Ground Forces, the 61-year-old McNair had been the organizational genius largely responsible (after General Marshall) for expanding the U.S. Army from a force slightly smaller than the Portuguese Army into a global force of several million men. When he arrived in London, he expected to be given a real field command, and he and Eisenhower had exchanged harsh words when McNair learned the true nature of his assignment. One of the unsung heroes of the American war effort, he had gone forward to observe the bombardment, and his body was found by the side of a dirt road. He had apparently been thrown quite a distance by a bomb blast; he could only be identified by one of his shoulder patches, which had three silver stars on it. He was secretly buried that night and replaced by Lieutenant General John L. DeWitt. For reasons of security (and the need to continue to deceive Berlin), news of McNair's death was not released for some time.

The surviving American generals feared that the abortive attacks might have alerted the Germans and compromised the security of "Cobra"; nevertheless, they decided to try again at 11 A.M. the next day. Fortunately for the Allies, only Dietrich von Choltitz, the commander of the LXXXIV Corps, correctly interpreted the signs and recognized that there as a major concentration of American armor north of the St.-Lô–Periers road; however, when he suggested that this might be the prelude to a major offensive, 7th Army sent back a message that began with the word "Nonsense."[40] Hausser expected the Allies to launch a major attack in the Caen sector, as did Kluge, who concluded that the American aerial attacks of July 24 were just a feint. Even General Fritz Bayerlein was completely convinced that the Allies would strike in the Caen sector.[41]

He was even more convinced on the morning of July 25, when the American infantry north of the St.-Lô–Periers road began withdrawing. It did not occur to him that they might be retreating to put a further measure of safety between them and the Panzer Lehr Division, which was about to be pulverized by a bomber stream that was 100 miles long.

On the morning of July 25, more than 2,200 heavy and medium bombers deposited more than 60,000 bombs on a 3.5-mile by 1.5-mile rectangle, most of which was held by the 5,000 men of the Panzer Lehr Division and the adjoining 13th and 15th Parachute Regiments. This amounted to 12 bombs for each German combat soldier in the rectangle. Once again, however, a number of bombs fell short, killing 111 American troops and wounding 490. That was nothing, however, compared to what the aerial bombardment did to the Panzer Lehr Division. Of its perhaps 3,200 combat effectives, at least 1,000 were killed or critically wounded, and most of the rest were wounded or dazed. Quite a few were deaf for the next 24 hours. Bayerlein reported 70% casualties and three battalion command posts were wiped out. The 901st Panzer Grenadier Regiment and the 15th Parachute Regiment (which was attached to the division) were virtually annihilated and ceased to exist as effective combat forces. The headquarters of the 901st vanished in flame and smoke, never to be seen again. Panzers were thrown through the air like so many plastic toys, and entire companies were buried alive and completely wiped out. The bombs rained out on Panzer Lehr again and again, until its sector resembled the surface of the moon. General Bayerlein only survived because he was visiting a regimental command post that was situated in an old Norman château whose walls were 10 feet thick. He recalled:

The planes kept coming over, as if on a conveyor belt, and the bomb carpets unrolled. . . . My flak had hardly opened its mouth, when the batteries received direct hits which knocked out half the guns and silenced the rest. After an hour I had no communication with anybody, even by radio. By noon nothing was visible but dust and smoke. My front lines looked like the face of the moon. . . . All my forward tanks were knocked out, and the roads were practically impassable.[42]

Shortly after the war, he wrote:

Again and again the bomb carpets rolled toward us, most of them passing only a few yards away. The ground shuddered. Quick glimpses outside showed the whole area shrouded by a pall of dust, with fountains of earth spewing high in the air. For many hours we were unable to leave the cellar and it was afternoon before I was able to get out of the chateau and ride back on my motorcycle to Division H.Q. (I had long since learned to prefer a motorcycle to a car, having had six cars shot up during the invasion battle and several drivers killed.) We were repeatedly troubled by fighter-bombers on the way back.

When I arrived at Division Headquarters the first reports were just coming in of enemy infiltrations into the bombed area. Resistance was offered by the surviving detachments of my division, but most of these groups were wiped out. . . . Some weak reserves from other sectors tried to halt the avalanche by counterattacks, but their attempts were smashed by the enemy artillery and air force in the forming up stage and came to nothing. By the following morning, the American breakthrough was complete.[43]

Bayerlein estimated that at least 70% of his men were killed, wounded, driven crazy, or just stunned by the bombardment.[44]

In Panzer Lehr's sector, the only battalion-sized unit still capable of offering effective resistance was Kampfgruppe Heinz of the 275th Infantry Division, on Lehr's right flank, but it could do little against the entire U.S. 9th Infantry Division. It made its last stand near Hebecrevon. By the end of the day, it also had ceased to exist.

In reserve behind Panzer Lehr, the bulk of the 275th Infantry Division was also attacked by the bombers and fighter-bombers. Although elements were able to push forward and join the survivors of the Panzer Lehr, the 275th Infantry was, for the most part, also smashed.

At the front, the Germans, led by aggressive noncommissioned officers (NCOs) and junior officers, put up a deceptively strong resistance against the American spearheads. That night, a great gloom hung over Eisenhower's headquarters. Delayed by stubborn German resistance and the huge craters caused by their own bombs, as well as by a natural caution bred by weeks of hedgerow fighting, the forward American assault battalions had gained less than three miles; nowhere had they captured their objectives for the day, and the Germans still held the vital crossroads towns of Marigny and St.-Gilles, less than three miles south of the St.-Lô–Periers road. Bradley was afraid that the offensive had failed, and Eisenhower vowed that he would never again use strategic bombers in support of ground troops.

Only General Collins suspected the truth: The Germans had been damaged far more than anyone in the Allied headquarters realized, and the stubborn German Resistance was being put up by isolated squads, patrols, platoons, and companies that had survived the aerial onslaught. If this thin crust was broken, he thought, he could pour through the gap with his tanks and achieve the decisive breakthrough. That night, he decided to commit his armor the next morning.

It was the decisive moment of the campaign.

Meanwhile, on the other side of the hill, Generals von Choltitz and Hausser reacted swiftly on July 25. Choltitz immediately committed about half of his reserve—a regimental-sized battle group from the 353rd Infantry Division—to the Chapelle-en-Juger sector in an effort to seal off the penetration, and Hausser committed a regiment of the 275th Infantry

Division to the same sector from the opposite direction. Neither move met with the slightest success. The regiment from the 275th was blown apart by American fighter-bombers near Canisy, and the regiment sent by Choltitz was too weak to have much of an impact on the battle. The U.S. 4th Infantry Division took la Chapelle-en-Juger early on the morning of July 26, confirming to Collins that his order committing his armor was the correct one. By nightfall on July 26, the U.S. 2nd Armored Division had taken St.-Gilles, the 4th Infantry Division was seven miles south of the St.-Lô–Periers road, and the 30th Infantry Division was fanning out to the southeast and had already captured two bridges over the Vive, in the rear of the 352nd Infantry Division. The Americans had achieved their decisive breakout. To make matters worse, as far as the Germans were concerned, Field Marshal von Kluge was slow in recognizing this fact. On July 26, he sent a lieutenant colonel as a messenger to Bayerlein's headquarters, ordering him to hold his positions. "Out in the front everyone is holding out, Herr Oberstleutnant," Bayerlein replied to the envoy with the greatest bitterness. "Everyone. My grenadiers and my engineers and my tank crews—they're all holding their ground. Not a single man is leaving his post. Not one! They're lying in their foxholes mute and silent, for they are dead. Dead! Do you understand? You may report to the Field Marshal that the Panzer Lehr Division is annihilated."[45]

At almost the same moment, Brigadier General Maurice Rose's Combat Command A (CCA) of the 2nd U.S. Armored Division was barreling through the gap opened by the heavy bombers and pushing into the rear of the 352nd Infantry Division. The following morning (unknown to Rose) it came within a mile of Lieutenant General Kraiss's command post. The commander of the 352nd Infantry only just managed to escape. On the right flank of the American breakthrough, the U.S. 3rd Armored Division finally took the vital crossroads town of Marigny from Colonel Count Frido von Schulenberg's 13th Parachute Regiment, and the 5th Parachute Division was outflanked. Combat Command B (CCB) of the 3rd Armored and the U.S. 1st Infantry Division pushed forward, down the excellent road to Coutances, meeting only scattered opposition. They did, however, capture a great many dispatch riders on motorcycles, staff officers in Volkswagens, ambulances, and other rear-area personnel who had no idea that the Americans were running free in the rear of the German 7th Army.

Field Marshal von Kluge still failed to recognize that the situation on his left flank was catastrophic. For some inexplicable reason, he spent July 27 inspecting Panzer Group West (i.e., the Caen sector). That night, he signaled Bayerlein that he was sending him an SS panzer battalion of 60 tanks. When it arrived, it had 5 panzers, not 60. It brought Bayerlein's total armored strength to 14—hardly enough to check an entire U.S. corps of three armored and three motorized infantry divisions. In addition, Kluge belatedly ordered the 2nd Panzer Division from the Orne River sector to the Vire, but there was no way it could possibly arrive in time to restore the German line. It was also heavily attacked by fighter-bombers en route. Kluge also pulled General of Panzer Troops Baron Hans von Funck's veteran XXXXVII Panzer Corps Headquarters out of the line and ordered it to take control of the 2nd Panzer, as well as the 2nd SS Panzer, Panzer Lehr, and 352nd Infantry Divisions, which were already at the front.[46] The XXXXVII Panzer's old sector, which was relatively quiet, Kluge assigned to General of Panzer Troops Walter Krueger's newly arrived and relatively inexperienced LVIII Panzer Corps.[47]

Despite his concern about the breach in the front of the 7th Army, Kluge was even more concerned about the situation in the zone of Panzer Group West, which he still judged to be the target of main Allied effort. The II Canadian Corps had launched two more major thrusts south of Caen (in the direction of Falaise) on July 25 and 27. Although these attacks were checked by the 9th SS Panzer Division, they nevertheless diverted Kluge's attention from the really vital area for three critical days.

Meanwhile, on July 27, the Americans had pushed to within 10 miles of Coutances, against scattered resistance. If they took this city, they would cut off the entire LXXXIV Corps. All Hausser could throw against them was a four-company battle group from the 2nd SS Panzer Division. Meanwhile, with the "Rhino," the Americans were able to literally drive through the hedgerows with little loss of speed. It gave them an entirely new mobility, allowing them to bypass mined roads and roadblocks, instead of having to deploy and fight. Overhead, the American tank and motorized columns were covered by Thunderbolts, which were in constant radio contact with the ground force commander. They flew standing patrols and served as airborne artillery, blasting German positions and roadblocks on call. Coutances was only saved because General von Choltitz reacted very swiftly, pulled strong mobile groups from the 2nd SS Panzer and 17th SS Panzer Grenadier Divisions, which, along with the 6th Parachute Regiment, temporarily halted the Americans west of Coutances and the sea. It was clear that the 30,000-man-strong LXXXIV Corps was in a rapidly forming trap, however, and it was high time to pull it back south of Coutances and the Soulle River—if it was not too late already.

On the morning of July 28, the 2nd SS, 17th SS and 6th Parachute halted the Americans two miles west of Coutances. Meanwhile, the majority of LXXXIV Corps disintegrated in a headlong retreat to the south, trying to escape encirclement. Kluge signaled Choltitz and ordered him to reestablish his positions. This dispatch did not reach the corps commander for hours. In the meantime, the 7th Army's Command Post was cut off by the rapid American advance. SS General Hausser was fired at by an American armored car; he only avoided serious injury or death by hurling himself into a muddy ditch. He and his operations staff then escaped to the south by infiltrating overland, recrossing the roads between the serials of American tanks and trucks like so many fugitives. SS Colonel Christian Tychsen, the stocky, scar-faced 34-year-old commander of the 2nd SS Panzer Division, was not so lucky: He was killed near Coutances in a firefight with an American patrol.[48]

New reports, meanwhile, gave Field Marshal von Kluge a more accurate idea of the extent of the disaster that had befallen LXXXIV Corps. Realizing that the 2nd Panzer Division would not be enough to restore the situation, he sent the 116th Panzer Division to join the XXXXVII Panzer Corps as well. Again, however, it would take this unit days, not hours, to reach its assembly areas. Meanwhile, the U.S. 4th and 6th Armored Divisions joined the U.S. 3rd Armored and 1st Infantry Divisions and pushed to the outskirts of Coutances after some hard fighting, virtually cutting off LXXXIV Corps and most of the 17th SS and 2nd SS Divisions in the process. It was obvious that LXXXIV Corps' last escape route would soon be cut. Meanwhile, to the north, the U.S. 2nd Armored Division hastily set up a series of roadblocks along the corridor to prevent the Germans from breaking out in that direction. This led to a series of wild melees and perhaps the hardest fighting that took place during "Cobra," but the 2nd Armored kept LXXXIV Corps "in the bag."

Late that afternoon, SS Lieutenant Colonel Otto Baum, the commander of the 17th SS Panzer Grenadier Division, took charge of the 2nd SS Panzer as well.[49] (Three days later, SS Colonel Otto Binge assumed permanent command of the 17th SS Panzer Grenadier.)[50] Baum was joined at his headquarters by Colonel Friedrich von Criegern, the corps chief of staff.[51] Together they decided to break out to the south, in the direction of Roncey and Percy. Meanwhile, orders from Hausser arrived at LXXXIV Corps Headquarters: The corps was to escape to the south and rally in the vicinity of Roncey, about four miles southeast of Coutances. Choltitz protested immediately, because this move would virtually strip the west coast of the Cotentin peninsula of defenders, but Hausser refused to rescind his order.

During the night of July 28–29, the rear guards of the LXXXIV Corps pulled out of Coutances, abandoning several thousand of their foot soldiers north of the city. Some of these men eventually escaped, but not many. The U.S. 2nd Armored Division alone took 4,000 prisoners during Operation "Cobra," and Middleton's VIII Corps took more than 8,300 in two days. All totaled, the U.S. 1st Army took 28,000 prisoners in the month of July; 20,000 of these were taken in the last six days of the month, and most of them were taken when Choltitz's corps was smashed. When the Americans occupied the area two days later, they counted 66 tanks, 204 vehicles, and 11 guns destroyed and 56 tanks and 55 vehicles damaged or simply abandoned.[52] Cut off from their supplies and under the pressure of massive U.S. air attacks, many of LXXXIV Corps' regiments disintegrated altogether on July 29 and 30, while the U.S. VII Corps widened the area of the breakout and the U.S. VIII Corps, spurred on by U.S. Lieutenant General George S. Patton, drove along the coast toward Avranches, at the base of the Cotentin.

Meanwhile, due to the orders of Baum, von Criegern, and Hausser, a huge German traffic jam developed along the road to Roncey, about four miles south of Coutances. German horse-drawn and motorized vehicles were stacked up for two miles—three abreast in places. They were pounced upon by the American fighter-bombers, which attacked virtually nonstop for six hours, destroying hundreds of them, including 100 tanks and 250 motorized vehicles. This slaughter soon became known as the "Roncey Massacre." By the end of the day, several veteran German divisions had been reduced to remnants or Kampfgruppe strength, including the 91st Air Landing, 243rd Infantry, 77th Infantry, 17th SS Panzer Grenadier, 5th Parachute, 353rd Infantry, 275th Infantry, and of course, the Panzer Lehr. The 2nd SS Panzer was also severely damaged. That same day, July 28, Kluge made a quick inspection of the 7th Army area. He clearly (and, to a large extent, correctly) held Hausser responsible for the disaster and stated that 7th Army's performance was "farcical, a complete mess, the whole army [is] putting up a poor show."[53] He either did not have the authority to relieve the SS general of his command, however, or (more likely) he did not dare to do so. Kluge also had (or was purported to have) a low opinion of Hausser's chief of staff, Major General Max Pemsel, and had less reluctance in acting against army officers.[54] He was also good at political maneuvering and finding scapegoats, as he had proven beyond a shadow of a doubt on the Eastern Front. Kluge sacked Pemsel on the evening of July 28 and replaced him with his former chief intelligence officer, Colonel von Gersdorff. (It is ironic that this would-be "human bomb" who once tried to assassinate Adolf Hitler in a suicide mission [see Chapter II] should end up working for an SS officer.)[55] Kluge also sacked General von Choltitz and replaced him with Lieutenant General Otto Elfeldt.[56] That same day, he attached his son, Lieutenant Colonel Guenther von Kluge, as OB West's permanent representative to Headquarters, 7th Army—a clear indication of Kluge's mistrust of Hausser.

Meanwhile, the British 2nd Army and the U.S. XIX Corps (east of the "Cobra" gap) continued to attack, pinning down Panzer Group West, Meindl's II Parachute Corps, and most of Kluge's reserves. The U.S. 30th Infantry Division almost broke through the XXXXVII Panzer Corps front, and the 2nd Panzer Division had to be committed near Troisgots to prevent the capture of the town and the collapse of the German line. It would not be available for a counterattack to the west for some time. Kluge's plan had been spoiled. Simultaneously, Patton pushed the U.S.

VIII Corps along the coast toward Avranches, an ancient town of 7,000 citizens. He struck through the gap between the German flank and the sea; the U.S. 4th Armored Division advanced 25 miles in 36 hours, reaching Avranches at nightfall on July 30. By the following night it had fanned out to the south and west and established a bridgehead over the River Selune at Pontaubault. The German left flank had collapsed, and the U.S. Army was in Brittany.

Ironically, the American columns had passed within 200 yards of a farmhouse that sheltered SS General Hausser and von Gersdorff. Once again Hausser was on the run and had to infiltrate between American armored columns. He and his staff officers eventually reached German lines, commandeered some vehicles, and reestablished a command post at Mortain. Hausser stated in a private letter written at this time that as many as 10 of his divisions had disintegrated, leaving small bands of leaderless and demoralized men roaming about the countryside, living off the land. Quite a few, he suspected, had been murdered by French terrorists. The paratroopers, he noted, were especially hated by the French.[57]

Meanwhile, with his divisions in western Normandy in total disarray and 7th Army Headquarters temporarily hors de combat, Kluge realized that Avranches had to be recaptured via immediate counterattack, or the Americans might never be contained. Only one unit was in the area and immediately available for this counterattack: Colonel of Reserves Rudolf Bacherer's 77th Infantry, which was in remnants. (In late June, the 77th had been cut off and its original commander, Major General Rudolf Stegmann, had been killed by an American fighter-bomber. Bacherer had infiltrated through American lines and led what was left of the division to safety.) At midnight on July 30–31, Bacherer nevertheless received the following order from General of Artillery Wilhelm Fahrmbacher, the commander of the XXV Corps in Brittany: "Avranches is to be taken and held at all costs. It is the keystone of our defense. On it hinges the decision in the West."[58]

Bacherer was a tough, determined, energetic, and resolute officer who quickly assembled every man and gun he could get his hands on, including 14 self-propelled assault guns and several decimated elements of the 5th Parachute Division. He struck at dawn on July 31, took the Americans by surprise, and promptly overran the critical bridge at Pontaubault. By full daylight, the skies were overcast and there was a drizzle. Visibility was so low that the American fighter-bombers were grounded, and Bacherer pushed into the southern edge of Avranches and began the house-to-house struggle for the town. It appeared that he might pull off a miracle and recapture Avranches, when, at noon, the skies cleared. Within an hour, American Thunderbolts and Mustangs had destroyed all 14 of Bacherer's assault guns; then the Americans counterattacked with their Shermans. The German infantry was powerless to stop them and was soon routed. By nightfall, as the U.S. tanks approached his command post, Colonel Bacherer slipped away, down a dirt road, with all the troops he had left: one lieutenant and two privates. The American army had not seen the last of this tough and determined commander, however.

By now, the Third Reich was running out of manpower. On June 22, the Red Army launched its largest offensive to date. It hurled 2.5 million men, supported by 4,000 tanks, 24,400 guns and mortars, and 5,300 aircraft, against Army Group Center. The Germans met the onslaught with only 700,000 men and were overwhelmed. Within 10 days, the Russians had ripped a 250-mile hole in the German Front, and 28 divisions no longer existed. Army Group Center lost 300,000 men, 215 tanks, and more than 1,500 guns. Hitler replaced the army group commander, Field Marshal Ernst Busch, with his top troubleshooter, Field Marshal Walter Model, "the Fuehrer's fireman." Model managed to save at least part of the command and stopped the Soviets in front of Warsaw, but only barely. By the time this drive was halted, the Russians were on the Memel and the Vistula—on the very borders of the Reich itself.[59]

Against a loss of 300,000 men in days, the Home Army was supplying the field armies with only 60,000 new men (mostly draftees) each month. Himmler would quadruple this figure[60] by drafting boys and old men, eliminating most deferments (including armaments workers), and lowering the medical standards even further, but little would be available in terms of new divisions until fall. Hitler therefore tried another desperate measure to stabilize the Eastern, Western, and Italian Fronts, all of which were in a state of near collapse. Unlike the Russian, British, and American armies, where men went for years without leave, the German soldiers generally enjoyed a rather liberal furlough policy. At least 10,000 of these men passed through the leave centers each day, and each carried his own weapon with him. According to Hitler, these men could be used to create 20 new divisions. He ordered the creation of 56 furlough battalions (mainly in the East) as well as five static divisions from the cadres of the "Shadow Divisions" at the Wahn, Neuhammer, Wildflecken, and Bohemia maneuver areas. In this manner, the 59th, 64th, and 226th Infantry Divisions ("Wave 27") were formed and hurried to the Western Front, whereas the 232nd and 237th Infantry Divisions were sent to Genoa and Trieste, Italy, respectively.[61]

The results of this idea were disastrous. The new battalions consisted only of men with rifles: They lacked signal and medical equipment, medium and heavy machine guns, artillery, transport, motorized vehicles, antitank guns, supply columns, and support services of all types. The men did not know their officers, their NCOs, or each other. They distrusted each other and quickly and loudly voiced their displeasure at being in the new battalions. Morale in the new units was low at the outset and never improved. Some of the men deserted, but most of those who left simply returned to their old regiments, where they were greeted as old friends. The new battalions were depleted, often before they met the enemy, and few of them lasted very long.

NOTES

1. Dietrich Kraiss was born in Stuttgart in 1889. He attended various cadet schools and was commissioned directly into the 126th Infantry Regiment in 1909. He fought in World War I, served in the Reichsheer, and was commander of the 90th Infantry Regiment (1937–41) when World War II began. In 1941 he was promoted to major general and given command of the 168th Infantry Division. Later he led the 355th Infantry Division (1943) and took command of the 352nd on November 6, 1943. He had been promoted to lieutenant general on October 1, 1942. General Kraiss was mortally wounded near St.-Lô on August 2 and died four days later (Keilig, p. 183).

2. The 30th Mobile Brigade was a bicycle unit that had been virtually destroyed during the first week of the invasion.

3. Gustav Wilke was born in Deutsch-Eylau, East Prussia, on March 6, 1898. He joined the 4th Grenadier Regiment as an officer-cadet in 1916 and fought in World War I. Discharged in 1920, he reentered the army in 1925 as a second lieutenant. In 1935, as a captain, he switched over to the Luftwaffe, successively commanding a bomber squadron and a basic training regiment. He became a group (battalion) commander in the 1st Glider Wing in 1940, and he was assigned to work with Messerschmitt corporation in 1942 to develop large gliders. In May 1942, as a colonel, he commanded a Luftwaffe Field regiment on the Eastern Front, and in December 1943, he became acting commander of the 2nd Parachute Division when General Ramcke fell ill.

A major general in 1943, Wilke was named commander of the new 5th Parachute Division in the spring of 1944 and was promoted to lieutenant general on May 1. He led the 5th until late 1944, when he was ordered to organize the 9th Parachute Division. In April 1945, he was sent to form a new 10th Parachute Division but had barely started the job when he was captured by the Americans. He was released in 1947 and died on March 14, 1977. Florian Berberich, "Gustav Wilke," in Chandler and Collins, p. 596; Absolon, p. 42.

4. Lieutenant General Hans Schmidt (born 1895) was a big man who was known for his imperturbability. He was born in Bayreuth on March 14, 1895, and entered the army as a cadet in August 1914. He fought on the Western Front in World War I and remained in the army. A major when Hitler came to power, he commanded III/41st Infantry Regiment (1935–38), the 46th Replacement Training Regiment in Bayreuth (1938–40), and the 245th Infantry Regiment (1940–43), both in France and on the Eastern Front. As a colonel, he assumed command of the 68th Infantry Division in early 1943. Promoted rapidly to major general

and lieutenant general in 1943, Schmidt was an excellent divisional commander, but he could not prevent his unit from being smashed in Russia. Named commander of the 275th Infantry Division in late 1943, he sent the motorized third of his new unit to Normandy as Kampfgruppe Heinz. He was severely wounded in Huertgen Forest, where he distinguished himself. He was leading the 275th in Czechoslovakia when the war ended.

5. H. Essame, "Normandy Revisited," *Military Review*, Volume XLIII, No. 12 (December 1963), pp. 76–77.

6. Carell, pp. 215–16.

7. Tony Foster, *Meeting of the Generals* (Toronto: 1986), p. 338 (hereafter cited as "Foster").

8. Martin Poeppel, *Heaven and Hell: The War Diary of a German Paratrooper*, Louise Willmot, trans. (London: 1988), p. 221.

9. Sir Neil Ritchie had previously commanded the British 8th Army in the desert (1941–42). Relieved of his command following the fall of Tobruk and the German invasion of Egypt, he had accepted a demotion to divisional commander in 1943 in order to return to active duty.

10. Bernard Law Montgomery, *The Viscount of Alamein, Normandy to the Baltic* (London: 1958), p. 78; Ellis, Volume I, p. 334.

11. Carlo D'Este, *Decision in Normandy*, reprint ed. (New York: 1983), p. 354 (hereafter cited as "D'Este"); Ellis, Volume I, Appendix IV.

12. Sir Richard O'Connor had previously commanded the XIII Corps in the desert. He led it with great distinction until 1941, when he was captured during Rommel's first drive on Tobruk. Sent to a prisoner-of-war camp in Italy, he escaped in 1943.

13. D'Este, pp. 367–68.

14. Keegan, p. 201.

15. Ibid.

16. David Mason, *Breakout: The Drive to the Seine* (New York: 1969), p. 35 (hereafter cited as "Mason, *Breakout*").

17. Keegan, p. 207.

18. "Pip" Roberts had led the 22nd Armoured Brigade at Alam Halfa Ridge during the El Alamein campaign. Later he was acting commander of the 7th Armoured Division. He commanded the 56th Armoured Brigade of the 6th Armoured Division before assuming command of the 11th Armoured Division. He was 37 years old in 1944. D'Este, pp. 372–73.

19. Blumenson, *Liberation*, p. 48.

20. Ibid., pp. 50–51.

21. Ibid., p. 51.

22. Keegan, p. 240.

23. Ibid., p. 219.

24. Martin Blumenson, *Breakout and Pursuit. United States Army in World War II. The European Theater of Operations* (Washington, D.C.: 1961), pp. 177–81 (hereafter cited as "Blumenson, *Breakout and Pursuit*").

25. Seaton, *Fortress*, p. 119.

26. Blumenson, *Breakout and Pursuit*, pp. 177–81.

27. Ibid.

28. William B. Breuer, *Death of a Nazi Army: The Falaise Pocket* (New York: 1985), p. 42 (cited hereafter as "Brever, *Death*").

29. D'Este, pp. 273–74. Rennie had commanded the 3rd Infantry Division on D-Day but was wounded in action shortly thereafter. He quickly improved the performance of the 51st. Rennie was killed crossing the Rhine in 1945. Bucknell was replaced by Lieutenant General Sir Brian Horrocks. Erskine was replaced by Major General G. L. Verney, who failed to improve the 7th Armoured's performance enough to satisfy Dempsey or Montgomery. He was relieved and replaced in November by Major General L. O. Lyne, the former commander of the 59th Infantry Division, which had since been disbanded.

30. Ibid., pp. 278–82.

31. S. Bidwell and D. Graham, *Firepower: British Weapons and Theories of War, 1904–1945* (London: 1982), pp 215–16.

32. Milton Shulman, *Defeat in the West* (London: 1947; revised ed., New York: 1968), p. 157 (hereafter cited as "Shulman").

33. Ibid.

34. Russell F. Weigley, *Eisenhower's Lieutenants* (Bloomington, Ill.: 1981), p. 151 (hereafter cited as "Weigley").

35. Hausser and Kluge graduated from Gross Lichterfelde in 1899. Kluge, of course, had a much more distinguished army career than Hausser, which may have provoked Hausser's jealousy.

36. Blumenson, *Breakout and Pursuit*, p. 226.

37. Specifically, Colonel Goth's 916th Grenadier Regiment had fought at Omaha Beach. By July 23, it had virtually ceased to exist.

38. Chester Wilmot, *The Struggle for Europe* (New York: 1952), pp. 383–84 (hereafter cited as "Wilmot").

39. See Samuel W. Mitcham, Jr., *Men of the Luftwaffe* (Novato, Calif.: 1988) (hereafter cited as "Mitcham").

40. Breuer, *Death*, p. 47.

41. Fritz Bayerlein was born in Wuerzburg in 1899 and entered the army as a *Fahnenjunker* in 1917. He joined the Reichsheer as an enlisted man in the early 1920s and was commissioned in the 21st Cavalry Regiment in 1922. He served as Guderian's Ia in the Polish and French campaigns and became chief of staff of the Afrika Korps in 1941. After General Gause was wounded in the Gazala Line battles, he became chief of staff of the Afrika Korps and temporarily commanded the corps in late 1942, after General Ritter Wilhelm von Thoma was captured. He was chief of staff of the 1st Italian-German Panzer Army in Tunisia in early 1943 but was wounded and evacuated back to Europe shortly thereafter. He led the 3rd Panzer Division on the Eastern Front (October 1943 to early January 1944) before his old friend, Heinz Guderian, now the chief of the Panzer Inspectorate, arranged for him to be given command of the newly formed Panzer Lehr Division.

After the Normandy campaign, Bayerlein led Panzer Lehr in the Siegfried Line battles and in the Battle of the Bulge, where his performance left much to be desired. He was nevertheless named acting commander of the LIII Corps in February 1945 and was captured in the Ruhr Pocket in April. He died in Wuerzburg of kidney disease on January 30, 1970.

42. Mason, *Breakout*, p. 45.

43. Rommel, pp. 489–90.
44. Mason, *Breakout*, p. 45.
45. Carell, p. 235.
46. Baron Hans von Funck was born on his family's estate on December 23, 1891. He volunteered for active duty when World War I broke out and was commissioned *Leutnant* in 1915. He spent most of the war with the cavalry on the Eastern Front. One of the pioneers in mechanized warfare, he commanded a motorized machine gun company as early as 1919. He worked closely with Oswald Lutz, the first general of panzer troops, and Guderian in the 1920s and 1930s. Funck was military attaché to Portugal when the war broke out. Later he led 5th Panzer Regiment in France (1940), briefly commanded the 3rd Panzer Brigade and 5th Light Division (1940–41), and the 7th Panzer Division on the Eastern Front (1941–43). He was acting commander of the XXIII Corps in late 1943 and became commander of the XXXXVII Panzer Corps on March 5, 1944. Despite the fact that he did an excellent job as a corps commander in Normandy, Hitler sacked Funck on September 1, 1944. The panzer baron held a minor post in Wehrkreis XII from October 1944 to January 1945 (commander of Reserve Panzer Command XII in Wiesbaden), when he was forced into retirement and dismissed from the army by Wilhelm Burghoff, the chief of the Army Personnel Office. Funck was captured by the Russians at the end of the war and spent 10 years in Soviet prisons. He died in West Germany on February 14, 1979 (Stauffenberg MS).

47. Walter Krueger was born in Zeitz in 1892. He joined the army as an officer-cadet in the infantry in 1910 but soon transferred to the cavalry. He commanded the 10th Cavalry Regiment (1937–39) and the 171th Infantry Regiment (1939) before transferring to the mobile branch. He led the 1st Rifle Brigade (1940–41) and the 1st Panzer Division (1941–43) before assuming command of the LVIII Panzer Corps on January 1, 1944. Promoted to general of panzer troops on February 1, 1944, he was relieved of his command on March 25, 1945. On April 10, he assumed command of Wehrkreis IV (Keilig, p. 189).

48. Christian Tychsen was born on December 3, 1910, in Flensburg, Schleswig-Holstein, the son of a master carpenter. He joined the SS in 1935 and earned both the Knight's Cross and the Oak Leaves in 1943, as commander of the II Battalion, 2nd SS Panzer Regiment. He was badly wounded and his face badly scarred in the process. A lieutenant colonel in 1944, Tychsen succeeded to command of the division but was killed in action by American soldiers on July 28, 1944 (E. G. Kraetschmer, *Die Ritterkreuztraeger der Waffen-SS*, 3rd ed. [Preussisch Oldendorf: 1982] pp. 452–55 [hereafter cited as "Kraetschmer"]). The 2nd SS Panzer lost two-thirds of its men during the Normandy fighting. Max Hastings, *Das Reich* (New York: 1981), pp. 217–18 (hereafter cited as "Hastings").

49. SS Colonel Otto Baum was born in Stettin bei Hechingen, Hohenzollern, on November 15, 1911, the son of a merchant. After attending an agricultural school in Stuttgart, he matriculated in 1934 and promptly joined the SS. He attended the Junker School at Braunschweig (Brunswick) in 1935 and was commander in 1936. He became a company commander in 1938 and fought in Poland. Eventually transferred to the 3rd Totenkopf ("Death's Head") Infantry Regiment, he rose to the command of the III Battalion by 1942 when, as a major, he was awarded the Knight's Cross during the Battle of Demyansk on the Eastern

Front. By 1943 he was an SS lieutenant colonel, commanding the 5th Panzer Grenadier Regiment of the 3rd SS Panzer Division "Totenkopf." After the death of Colonel Tychsen, he briefly commanded the 2nd SS Panzer Division and was awarded the Swords to the Knight's Cross with Oak Leaves. Later he commanded the 16th SS Panzer Grenadier Division "Reichsfuehrer SS" in Italy and Hungary. He surrendered his command to the British at the end of the war (Kraetschmer, pp. 304–17).

50. Binge had served as commander of the 17th SS Panzer Grenadier Division during its formation phase (October, 1943–January 1944). He was replaced by SS Oberfuehrer (later SS Major General) Werner Ostendorff, who was wounded on June 15. Binge took charge of the division from June 16 to 18, when he was replaced by Baum. Roger James Bender and Hugh P. Taylor, *Uniforms, Organization and History of the Waffen-SS* (Mountain View, Calif.: 1971), Volume IV, p. 152 (hereafter cited as "Bender and Taylor").

51. Colonel Friedrich von Criegern had previously served as Ia of the 35th Infantry Division on the Eastern Front (1943).

52. Weigley, p. 160.

53. Seaton, *Fortress*, p. 121.

54. Max Pemsel was born in Regensburg on January 15, 1897, and entered the army as a *Fahnenjunker* (officer-cadet) in the 11th Bavarian Infantry Regiment in 1916. A member of the mountain troops' branch, he was Ia of the 1st Mountain Division when World War II broke out. He became chief of staff of the XVIII Mountain Corps in late 1940 and held this post until joining the 7th Army as its chief of staff in May 1943.

Even though he was relieved of his post by Hans von Kluge in late July, Pemsel was given command of the 6th Mountain Division in Norway in late August. He was promoted to lieutenant general in November and was earmarked to be commandant of Berlin in the last weeks of the war. Fortunately for him, weather grounded his airplane. By the time he arrived in the capital of the Reich, another commander had been appointed—much to Pemsel's relief. General Jodl named him chief of staff of the Ligurian Army in northern Italy instead. Here he narrowly avoided being killed by partisans before he managed to surrender to U.S. forces. By 1958, he was commanding the II Corps of the West German Army, headquartered in Ulm (Keilig, p. 253).

55. Gersdorff had been transferred to the West in February 1944 as chief of staff of LXXXII Corps. Somewhat remarkably, his role in the anti-Hitler conspiracy was never discovered. He was promoted to major general on January 30, 1945, and was chief of staff of 7th Army until Final Victory. Since his native Silesia was now under Soviet occupation, he relocated to Cologne, where he was still living in the late 1950s (Keilig, p. 106).

56. Otto Elfeldt was born in Mecklenburg in 1895 and joined the army as an artillery cadet in 1914. He was commander of II/56th Artillery Regiment (1935–39), commander of the 619th Artillery Regiment (1939), on the staff of Army Group A (1939–40), chief of staff to the general of artillery at OKH (1940–42), and commander of the 302nd and 47th Infantry Divisions (1942–44). He became acting commander of the LXXXIV Corps after Kluge fired Choltitz (Keilig, p. 81).

57. Seaton, *Fortress*, p. 121.

58. Breuer, *Death*, p. 123. Also see Blumenson, *Breakout and Pursuit*, p. 398.

59. Earl F. Ziemke, *Stalingrad to Berlin: The German Defeat in the East* (Washington, D.C.: 1966), pp. 314–15 (hereafter cited as "Ziemke"); Albert Seaton, *The Russo-German War* (New York: 1971), p. 442 (hereafter cited as "Seaton, *Russo-German War*"); Christopher Chant, ed., *The Marshall Cavendish Illustrated Encyclopedia of World War II* (New York: 1972), Volume 6, p. 1653 (hereafter cited as "Chant").

60. Keegan, p. 238.

61. Seaton, *Fortress*, pp. 229–30; Tessin, Volume 1, p. 78.

CHAPTER IV

THE CONQUEST OF BRITTANY

On August 1, the U.S. 3rd Army under General Patton was officially activated. The colorful and eccentric general had almost ruined his career in Sicily by slapping a pair of soldiers who were suffering from combat fatigue, and he had been in the official doghouse ever since. (Berlin and Rastenburg, perhaps reasonably, did not believe the Americans would even consider forcibly retiring the man who was arguably their best tactical commander for such a minor infraction, but Berlin and Rastenburg were wrong.) Patton's name, however, still had value, so he was given command of the bogus 1st Army Group in southeastern England with 45 divisions—all fictitious. Although he hated his assigment, Patton nevertheless played a significant role in the success of the invasion by helping tie down the 19 divisions of the 15th Army. Now, however, OKW had finally awakened to the fact that the Normandy landings might be the real invasion after all, as evidenced by the fact that the 326th and 363rd Infantry Divisions from the 15th Army had arrived in the zone of the 5th Panzer Army during the last week of July. Although Eisenhower still wanted to hide the fact that Patton was now in France, there was really no further need to maintain pretenses. In any case, once he took charge of operations, Patton was not the kind of general one could hide.

Initially, Patton assumed control over the U.S. VIII, XII, XV, and XX Corps. The VIII was already in action, the XV was just coming up, and the XII and XX were scheduled to be committed within a matter of days. At the same time, Headquarters, U.S. 12th Army Group was activated under the command of General Omar Bradley (controlling the 3rd and 1st Armies), and Lieutenant General Courtney Hodges assumed command of the U.S. 1st Army (V, VII, and XIX Corps). In all, Bradley now had 21 divisions in France (more than 900,000 men), with more coming ashore daily.[1] Simultaneously, the Headquarters, British 21st Army

Group was activated under Montgomery. It included the British 2nd Army (Sir Miles Dempsey) and the Canadian 1st Army (Lieutenant General Henry D. G. Crerar). Together, Monty's armies had five corps, 16 divisions (6 of them armored), and several independent armored brigades. Monty retained overall ground command until Eisenhower superceded him on September 1.

Patton was a dashing and charismatic leader of great daring who thought that nothing was impossible. Considered by many to be the best ground commander the United States produced in World War II, he inaugurated his tenure as leader of the 3rd Army with the first of many incredible feats: He pushed seven divisions (more than 100,000 men, complete with tens of thousands of armored and nonarmored vehicles, guns, supplies, and equipment) down a single, narrow road, through Avranches, and over the Pontaubault Bridge in only three days. The Germans—who had a great capacity for making quick tactical recoveries—had absolutely no time to regain their balance. Almost as soon as his headquarters was activated, Patton was attacking three directions at once: to the south and west (to get behind Army Group B and to force it to abandon Normandy) and to the east, to capture Brittany. The occupation of this peninsula would liberate a vast portion of France and open up important ports for the Allies.

Patton planned to capture Brittany by driving southwest from Avranches through Rennes to Quiberon Bay, to cut the peninsula off from the rest of France and isolate the battlefield. Then he would unleash strong armored columns that would rapidly overrun the region. Specifically, he assigned the 4th Armored and 8th Infantry Divisions the job of capturing Rennes in the center of the peninsula and advancing on to Quiberon Bay, while the 6th Armored and 79th Infantry Divisions pushed 200 miles to the west, taking Brest in one smashing drive. Initially, Patton kept the 5th Armored, 83rd Infantry, and 90th Infantry Divisions in reserve.[2] Overall supervision of the Brittany campaign fell to Middleton's U.S. VIII Corps. General Middleton was a good corps commander but a man who was much more methodical and meticulous (and therefore much slower) than Patton himself. His armored division commanders, however, thought more like Patton than Middleton. Figure 4.1 shows the conquest of Brittany.

The task of defending the peninsula devolved on Fahrmbacher's XXV Corps, which had already sent most of its combat troops to Normandy. Of the 100,000 troops available on June 6, less than one-third remained at the end of July, excluding the 319th Infantry Division, which garrisoned the Channel Islands. Although technically a part of the XXV Corps, Hitler would not allow Kluge and Fahrmbacher to use this strong division—it had some 30,000 men and was larger than many German corps in 1944—for the defense of Brittany, and it would still be on the

Figure 4.1
The Conquest of Brittany

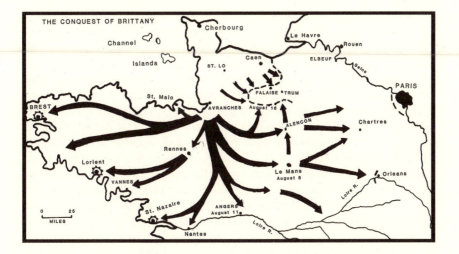

islands when the war ended. To defend Brittany, Fahrmbacher had only two full-strength divisions: the 2nd Parachute and 343rd Infantry, both camped near Brest.[3] He also had the remnants of the 77th Infantry and 91st Air Landing Divisions (which had been pushed out of Normandy) and weak elements of the 265th and 266th Infantries, but the bulk of these divisions had already been sent to the front. The 266th was located near Morlaix, and the 265th garrisoned Lorient, St. Nazaire, and Nantes. To defend all of Brittany, therefore, Fahrmbacher had only 10 reliable infantry battalions, 4 unreliable "Eastern" battalions, and about 50,000 immobile noncombat troops (including sailors and Luftwaffe service personnel), mostly concentrated in the ports. Four of these—St. Malo, Brest, Lorient, and St. Nazaire—had already been designated "fortresses" by the Fuehrer. As soon as Patton crossed from Normandy into Brittany, Fahrmbacher sent the remnants of the 91st Air Landing Division to defend Rennes, a commercial city of 80,000 that linked Brittany to the rest of France. Thought by some to be the ugliest city in the nation, the Breton capital was also a transportation hub. No fewer than 10 major highways converged on the city. After virtually destroying the 77th Infantry Division south of Avranches, the spearheads of Major General John S. Wood's 4th Armored Division raced 40 miles to the southwest and reached the northern suburbs of Rennes on the afternoon of August 1. They were met by two Luftwaffe 88mm batteries, supported by perhaps 100 infantrymen with a handful of machine guns and *Panzerfausts*. This little ad hoc force put up a surprisingly stiff resistance, however, and checked the American advance. The U.S. vanguard halted, regrouped, and awaited reinforcements. While they waited, two German Army replacement-training battalions (about 1,900 men) reached Rennes from le Mans. They were quickly issued machine guns and *Panzerfausts* (shoulder-fired, single-shot, disposable antitank weapons) and sent to the front lines. They had arrived in the nick of time. That night, Combat Command A (CCA) of the 4th Armored Division launched a prepared attack on the city but was beaten back after two hours of heavy fighting. Eleven Sherman tanks were knocked out in the process.

The defense of Rennes was conducted by Colonel (later Lieutenant General) Eugen Koenig, who had commanded the 91st Air Landing Division since June 10 (four days after its original commander, Lieutenant General Wilhelm Falley, was killed in a firefight with American paratroopers).[4] Like most of the German divisional commanders, Koenig was a competent tactician. So was his counterpart, General Wood, who saw no reason to involve his armored division in a protracted battle in an urban area. For the next two days, Wood awaited the arrival of the bulk of his division (which was strung out along the 50 miles of highway between Avranches and Rennes), as well as supplies, ammunition, gasoline, and a task force from the 8th Infantry Division. With his tanks, Wood bypassed Rennes, only to be recalled by General Middleton, who ordered both divisions be committed to the capture of the city. By August 3, the 4th Armored and 8th Infantry Divisions were closing in on the place, which was partially surrounded. At 11 P.M. that night, however, Hausser gave Koenig permission to break out. After burning his excess supplies and German military installations, Koenig slipped out of Rennes with 2,000 men at about 3 A.M. on the morning of August 4. Moving cross country and over back roads, Koenig was able to avoid the rapidly moving Americans, who were operating almost exclusively on the major highways. As a result, he was able to reach the fortress of St. Nazaire and safety on August 9.

General Wood, meanwhile, jumped off for Quiberon Bay at 2 P.M. on August 5 and severed the peninsula at Vannes seven hours later, meeting almost no opposition. He pushed on to the outskirts of Lorient on August 7 but decided not to attack it because the defenses were thought to be too strong, and neither Wood nor Middleton wanted to involve an armored division in operations against a fortress, which would better be left to the infantry. Inside the city lay Headquarters, XXV Corps. General Fahrmbacher, who commanded the defenses of Lorient, later stated that the fortress would probably have fallen if Wood had attacked that day. Entire sectors of the defense had not yet been organized, many of the troops were untrained, and Fahrmbacher only had 197 guns, instead of the 500 the Americans thought he had. As a result, the 25,000 men of the Lorient garrison remained isolated in the fortress until the end of the war. Fahrmbacher finally surrendered to the U.S. 66th Infantry Division on May 10, 1945.

Meanwhile, U.S. Major General Robert W. Grow's 6th Armored Division overran the northern and central portion of the Brittany plateau and continued almost nonstop in its headlong dash for Brest. The 6th Armored was delayed by occasional German rearguards and by one halt order from General Middleton, which Patton countermanded as soon as he learned of it. During the advance, the American tankers overran the rearguard of the 266th Infantry Division on August 8 and captured its commander, Lieutenant General Karl Spang, and several members of his staff. Spang had contributed units to the Dinard and St. Malo garrisons and was trying to retreat into Brest with the rest of his men when he was taken prisoner.[5] Another static German division had ceased to exist. By now, an estimated 32,000 armed Bretons had joined in the battle against the Germans, and another 50,000 were acting as couriers or guides or assisting the Americans in other capacities. Many Germans were relieved at being able to surrender to the Americans instead of the maquis (guerrilla fighters in the French underground). The fast-moving tankers, however, promptly turned most of these prisoners-of-war over to the French Maquis, and many of them were never seen again. Elements of the 6th Armored reached the outskirts of the city of Brest on August 7 but could not take the city by coup de main. The next day, General Grow issued a surrender ultimatum, but it was rejected by Colonel Hans von der Mosel, the fortress commandant. The Americans launched a full-scale assault on the fortress on August 9, but the German line held. Meanwhile, the 2nd Parachute Division, which had been bypassed by the rapid American advance, slipped into Brest from the south on August 9, bringing the strength of the garrison to 35,000 men. The leader of the 2nd Parachute was Lieutenant General Hermann Ramcke, a strong Nazi who could be counted on to obey Hitler's orders and fight to the last round.[6] On August 12, Ramcke was named fortress commander, and von der Mosel became his chief of staff. At this point, Grow was ordered not to launch a major offensive against the city; the 6th Armored was simply to keep it isolated, for the time being.

Meanwhile, on August 4, the rapid American advance isolated the fortress/port of St. Malo and the port of Dinard, which lay just across the Rance River The U.S. 83rd Infantry Division was given the task of reducing the twin ports. St. Malo was well prepared for a siege. Like Dinard, it was supported by the heavy artillery emplacements on the island of Cezembre, about three miles offshore. The fortress of St. Malo had been under construction by the Organization Todt for more than two years, and OB West considered it the most advanced of any fortress in France. In addition, the nearby Channel islands of Jersey, Guernsey, and Alderney could furnish the fortress with supplies, replacements, and hospital facilities. The commandant of St. Malo was Colonel Andreas von Aulock, a veteran of Stalingrad, who had received his orders directly from Hitler. "You will fight to the last man," Hitler demanded.[7]

Aulock promised to make St. Malo "another Stalingrad." He said: "I was placed in command of this fortress. I did not request it. I will execute the orders I have received and, doing my duty as a soldier, I will fight to the last stone." On August 3, as the Americans approached, he ordered the French population out of the city. He informed the city officials that they were fine fellows but that he preferred to have them "in front of me rather than behind my back." The Americans reached the outer perimeter on August 4, and most of the civilian population entered American lines the next day. Dinard was defended by Colonel Bacherer, the commander of the 77th Infantry Division—or at least of the tiny remnant that was left of it. Still a tough and resourceful commander, Bacherer replied defiantly to the American demand that he surrender. "Every house must become a fortress, every stone a hiding place, and for every stone we shall fight."[8]

Fight he did. Bacherer forced Major General Robert C. Macon, the commander of the U.S. 83rd Infantry Division, to commit most of his unit, and still the fighting lasted a week. Colonel Bacherer was finally forced to surrender on August 14, and another 4,000 Germans were captured. Then Macon turned his attention toward St. Malo, which held out in protacted fighting until the afternoon of August 17. Aulock only surrendered because troop morale had deteriorated to the point that further resistance was senseless. Another 6,000 German soldiers marched off to the prisoner-of-war camps. In the meantime, however, German engineers had rendered the port useless to the victors. They did such a thorough job that, on November 21, when the U.S. engineers handed it over to the French civilian administration, its harbor was still not operational. The Americans gave it up as not being worth the effort it would take to clear it. In addition, by tying down an entire American division for two weeks, Colonels Bacherer and von Aulock had prevented Middleton from using it at Brest or Lorient, and Ramcke and Fahrmbacher had been given invaluable time to organize the defenses of their fortresses. Meanwhile, elements of the U.S. 4th Armored Division took Nantes (just down the Loire River from St. Nazaire) on August 13. The garrison on the island of Cezembre (320 men) surrendered on September 2. All of the German forces in Brittany had now either been destroyed, isolated, or forced to surrender; however, despite the elimination of another whole German combat corps, the Brittany campaign had been a sideshow from the American point of view—and an expensive and frustrating one at that. It had not accomplished the basic strategic objectives for which it had been launched, for the Americans had not captured a single usable port.

Both St. Malo and Nantes had been demolished beyond the hope of immediate repair, and Brest, Lorient, and St. Nazaire were still being held by the Germans. To make matters worse, all three were now fully fortified and would be very difficult to capture. The conquest of Brittany had not helped the Allies' supply situation one bit; in fact, the opposite was true. This fact did not seem important to the Allies in the second week of August; however, it would be one of overwhelming significance before the month of September was out.

NOTES

1. Robert A. Miller, *August 1944* (Novato, Calif.: 1988; reprint ed., New York: 1989), p. 12 (hereafter cited as "Miller").

2. Keegan, pp. 236–37.

3. Wilhelm Fahrmbacher was born in Zwiebruecken in 1888 and joined the 4th Bavarian Field Artillery Regiment as a *Fahnenjunker* in 1907. He fought in World War I, served in the Reichsheer, and commanded the 35th Artillery Command (Arko 35) in 1938, 5th Infantry Division (1938–40), VII Corps (1940–42) on the Russian Front, and XXV Corps (1942–45). He surrendered the surviving German forces in Brittany at the end of the war and died on April 27, 1970.

4. Eugen Koenig was born in Trier on September 19, 1896. He joined the Imperial Army as a war volunteer in 1915 and was commissioned reserve second lieutenant in 1917. Discharged in 1920, he reentered the service in 1936 as a reserve first lieutenant. Nine years later he was a lieutenant general. After the 91st Air Landing Division had suffered so many casualties that it had to be disbanded, Koenig led the 272nd Volksgrenadier Division until it was forced to surrender at the end of the Battle of the Ruhr Pocket in April 1945. Koenig settled in Bitburg after the war (Keilig, p. 178).

5. Karl Spang was born in 1886 in Mergentheim and joined the Imperial Army as a *Fahnenjunker* in 1905. He was commissioned in the artillery in 1907, fought in World War I, served in the Reichsheer, and was commander of Arko 7 in 1937. He commanded an ad hoc division on the Western Front in 1939–40, served on the staff of the 1st Army, and led the 337th Infantry Division (1940–41). He commanded a rear area unit in the Crimea and the 502d Rear Area Command (Korueck) in 1941–42 and led a battle group at Stalingrad. Flown out of the pocket in late December, he was in charge of the Rear Area Command Don until early 1943, when his health gave way. After a recovery period of almost six months, he assumed command of 266th Infantry Division on June 1, 1943. He was promoted to major general in 1938 and to lieutenant general in 1940.

6. Hermann Ramcke was born on January 24, 1889 and served in the naval infantry (marines) in World War I. Later commissioned into the Luftwaffe, he was in his late forties when he went to parachute school and did the entire physically demanding course—not a VIP (very important person) course. He fought in the Battle of Crete and trained the Italian Folgore Parachute Division for an air assault on Malta—an invasion that Hitler canceled. Ramcke was then named commander of the 2nd Parachute Brigade and fought in the Battle of El Alamein. Isolated in the desert, cut off by the British, and written off by High

Command, Ramcke nevertheless hijacked a British convoy and escaped, finally reaching friendly lines with his entire command. A hero of Nazi Germany, he was promoted to lieutenant general and given command of the 2nd Parachute Division. During the Battle of Brest, he was promoted to general of paratroopers and decorated with one of Germany's highest decorations—the Knight's Cross with Oak Leaves, Swords and Diamonds. He died on July 7, 1968.

7. Blumenson, *Breakout and Pursuit*, p. 401.

8. Ibid.

CHAPTER V

HITLER PUTS HIS HEAD INTO THE LION'S MOUTH

Although the loss of Brittany was undoubtedly a defeat for the Germans, it was by no means a decisive one. The threat posed by Patton's other corps, the XV, was potentially much more dangerous. Controlling two mobile infantry divisions and the U.S. 5th Armored Division, it was beyond the left flank of the 7th Army and was threatening to break into the rear of Army Group B—a development that could have the most severe consequences. Kluge telephoned Jodl from 7th Army Headquarters and admitted that his commanders had completely lost control of the battle. "It's a madhouse here!" he cried, then described the situation as a *Riesensauerei*—roughly translatable as "one hell of a mess."

Since Kluge had no reserves to deal with the forces that were turning his flank, he would very much have preferred to retreat. Such a withdrawal would mean the evacuation of France, however, since the next strong, short defensible position in the west was the Siegfried Line on the German border. On July 31, Jodl brought up this possibility to Hitler, who (surprisingly) reacted favorably to the idea. The OKW chief of operations then called General Blumentritt, the chief of staff of OB West, and told him to be ready to receive an order for a withdrawal to the West Wall.[1] Then, on August 1, Jodl's deputy, General Walter Warlimont, was ordered to France as OKW's liaison officer to OB West.[2] He was called into the Fuehrer's presence, expecting to receive instructions concerning the mass withdrawal. Hitler's orders were far different: "Tell Field Marshal von Kluge that his job is to look forward to the enemy, not backward!" the dictator snapped angrily.[3] He had changed his mind. Instead of retreating, Army Group B was to counterattack and restore the Avranches–St.-Lô front. To replace the shattered forces of 7th Army, Hitler agreed that OB West could take control of certain Luftwaffe and naval ground units until the emergency had passed, but the very strong 319th

Infantry Division on the Channel Islands was to remain where it was. Also, the dictator ordered Kluge to mass at least four panzer divisions in the Mortain sector (on the west flank of 7th Army), break through the right flank of the U.S. 1st Army, and drive to the sea, cutting off Patton's 3rd Army in the process. Then, according to Hitler, "We must wheel north like lightning and turn the entire enemy front from the rear."[4] Hitler's plan was designated Operation *Luettich* (Liege).

Early on the morning of August 2, a Ju-52 transport carried Warlimont from East Prussia to France. The tri-engine aircraft never flew above 3,000 feet because the general was still suffering from the effects of a brain concussion he sustained on July 20. The airplane landed at the Strasbourg airport in western Germany (now eastern France), which was deemed as far west as it could safely go without taking the risk of blundering into Allied fighters. (Warlimont was unaware that he was also under suspicion as being a conspirator simply because he was a General Staff officer who had had professional contact with some of the would-be assassins and was not himself a rabid Nazi. "He's off to the West to arrange with Kluge for a fresh attempt on my life!" the paranoid Fuehrer exclaimed to Jodl moments after Warlimont departed.[5] This, of course, was nonsense, especially when one considers that Warlimont was in the briefing room when the bomb went off. Had he known what Stauffenberg had in his briefcase, he would have been nowhere near the place.) After landing at Strasbourg, the 49-year-old general of artillery got into an armored car, which carried him to Kluge's OB West Headquarters at St.-Germain, just outside Paris. Here he presented Hitler's plan to the tall chief of staff. Normally an amiable man who got along with "the powers that be," General Blumentritt grew very angry as his listened. When Warlimont finished, he bluntly told the deputy chief of operations that *Luettich* was totally at odds with reality. He pointed out that OB West had 1,400 tanks on D-Day and had lost 750; in addition, 7th Army had lost 160,000 men killed, wounded, or captured out of 450,000 men engaged since June 6. "You don't know the true situation," Blumentritt said.

"My orders are to put you on guard against any retreat," the OKW officer replied. "You must hold with fanatical determination."

As Warlimont left to give Kluge the detailed instructions for the counterattack, Blumentritt felt as though the death warrant for the German armies in France had already been signed.[6]

In the meantime, Hausser's 7th Army recovered rapidly. Helped by the excellent defensive terrain, it rallied and checked Leonard Gerow's U.S. V Corps and Peter Corlett's U.S. XIX Corps 5 to 10 miles outside of Vire, an important crossroads town that was defended by the tough 3rd Parachute Division. Further to the east, the three divisions of the II SS Panzer Corps checked a major British thrust against Caumont. Only in the Avranches sector and in Brittany was German resistance weak. Taking advantage of this situation, Collins's VII Corps (now part of Hodges's 1st Army) launched an offensive to expand the Avranches corridor, which was only 8 miles long. Their objective was Mortain, a medieval town of 2,000 that boasted a 12th-century convent. More important, it was a communications center: Seven roads radiated out of the place. It was located 19 miles east of Avranches, in the zone of the U.S. 1st Army. Despite the fact that they were fighting in good defensive terrain in the hedgerow country, the U.S. 1st Infantry Division, supported by CCA of the 3rd Armored Division, overran and destroyed elements of Lieutenant General Hans Schmidt's 275th Infantry Division and captured the town at 3:15 P.M. on August 2. Collins's forces also took the high ground east of the town—excellent defensive terrain that would further safeguard Patton's rear, in case of a German counterattack. This would prove to be an excellent move in the near future.

Every senior German commander in Normandy except Hausser opposed Operation *Luettich*, including Kluge and Eberbach. Sepp Dietrich, the commander of the I SS Panzer Corps, was especially outspoken.[7] For more than a month, his corps had held off Montgomery outside of Caen; now it had the British and Canadians stalemated south of the city. Hitler's plan would dismantle this barrier to the interior of France and simultaneously send the bulk of the irreplaceable panzer divisions into the jaws of a nutcracker. "It's madness, sheer madness!" the SS general yelled at General Warlimont. "We shall run into a trap!"[8]

He was right.

Dietrich did not let the matter drop but instead took it directly to the OB West. He later recalled: "I protested with von Kluge for over an hour about the impracticability of such an operation. I used every argument in the book. . . . To each of my arguments, von Kluge had only one reply, 'It is Hitler's orders,' and there was nothing more that could be done. I gave him what he wanted."[9]

On the evening of August 3, following the capture of Mortain, Kluge warned Warlimont that the Avranches gap could not be closed. The only rational move remaining was to retreat to the Seine, using his best mobile units to delay the Americans, while the infantry carried out a deliberate withdrawal.

The next morning, Hitler replied with a categorical order. Kluge was to launch a counteroffensive from the Vire-Mortain area to Avranches and the coast. Eight of the nine panzer and panzer grenadier divisions in Normandy were to take part in the attack, supported by a thousand planes from the Luftwaffe. Furthermore, he was not to attack "until every tank, gun and plane was assembled."[10] Kluge did not dare wait this long, because Patton was already around his left flank; in fact, Haislip's spearheads covered 30 miles on August 6 and hardly saw a German.

Besides, Montgomery and Hodges were continuing their attacks in the Vire and Caen sectors, pinning down several panzer and panzer grenadier units and making it impossible for them to disengage. Kluge signaled Hitler that he could not guarantee that his battered infantry divisions north of the attack forces' assembly areas would be able to hold their positions against Allied tank attacks. "I must attack as soon as possible," he concluded.[11] He and his generals wanted to strike during the night of August 6–7, and Hitler gave his begrudging consent. By August 6, Patton's tanks were approaching Le Mans, and Kluge diverted the 9th Panzer Division, just coming up from southern France, to this sector to halt his drive to the east. Le Mans was to be defended by the General of Panzer Troops Adolf Kuntzen's LXXXI Corps, which controlled the 708th Infantry and 9th Panzer Divisions (Major General Edgar Arndt and Lieutenant General Erwin Jolasse, respectively).[12] Patton struck at it with fast-moving General Wade Haislip's XV Corps, which was spearheaded by the 79th and 90th Infantry Divisions and the 5th Armored Division.

Meanwhile, with its eyes wide open, the Wehrmacht rushed into the lion's den at Mortain. Warlimont signaled Rastenburg that all the generals were confident and enthusiastic about the Fuehrer's plan—an out-and-out lie. The *Luettich* attack was to be directed by General Baron von Funck's XXXXVII Panzer Corps. Instead of the eight panzer divisions stipulated by Hitler, von Funck only had four: the 116th Panzer, the 2nd Panzer, the 1st SS Panzer, and the 2nd SS Panzer, which had about 250 tanks between them. Due to the British and Canadian attacks in the Caumont sector, it had been impossible to withdraw the 9th and 10th SS Panzer in time; also, the 9th and 11th Panzer Divisions, which had been earmarked for Army Group B, had not yet arrived. The 11th Panzer, in fact, never even departed. It was desperately needed to cover the retreat of Army Group G, and General Blaskowitz simply could not afford to let it go. Table 5.1 shows the German Order of Battle on August 6. It is, however, somewhat deceptive, as virtually every division was greatly understrength, and several were in remnants. As of the end of July, Hausser listed the following divisions as practically destroyed during that month alone: Panzer Lehr, 5th Parachute, 17th SS Panzer Grenadier, 91st Air Landing, and 352nd, 275th, 243rd, and 77th Infantry Divisions. In addition, the 16th Luftwaffe Field had been annihilated near Caen, and the 326th Infantry Division had been destroyed at Caumont.[13] In addition, the divisions trapped in Brittany—the 2nd Parachute, 343rd Infantry, and much of the 265th and 266th Infantries—were write-offs, as far as Army Group B was concerned. Finally, the 319th Infantry Division (about 30,000 men) was hopelessly cut off on the Channel Islands, and several divisions still fighting in Normandy had been reduced to Kampfgruppen size. Despite these handicaps, and the continued Allied domination of the air, the skillful German commanders pulled a minor

Table 5.1
Order of Battle, Army Group B, August 6, 1944

5th Panzer Army[1]

    LXXXVI Corps
        346th Infantry Division
        272nd Infantry Division (+)
        711th Infantry Division (−)

    I SS Panzer Corps
        89th Infantry Division[2]
        271st Infantry Division
        12th SS Panzer Division

    LXXIV Corps
        277th Infantry Division
        276th Infantry Division
        326th Infantry Division

    II SS Panzer Corps
        21st Panzer Division
        9th SS Panzer Division
        10th SS Panzer Division (−)

    85th Infantry Division[3]

7th Army

    II Parachute Corps
        3rd Parachute Division
        363rd Infantry Division
        Elements, 10th SS Panzer Division

    LXXXIV Corps
        353rd Infantry Division[4]
        243rd Infantry Division[4]
        275th Infantry Division[4]
        84th Infantry Division[2]

    XXXXVII Panzer Corps
        116th Panzer Division
        2nd Panzer Division
        2nd SS Panzer Division
        1st SS Panzer Division
        17th SS Panzer Grenadier Division[4]

    LXXXI Corps[5]
        9th Panzer Division (−)[6]
        708th Infantry Division (−)[6]
        Elements, 5th Parachute Division
        Elements, 13th Flak Division

115

Table 5.1 (*continued*)

7th Army

Headquarters, LVIII Panzer Corps[7]

XXV Corps[8]
2nd Parachute Division
343rd Infantry Division
77th Infantry Division[4]
91st Air Landing Division[4]
265th Infantry Division (−)
266th Infantry Division (−)
319th Infantry Division (+)[9]
331st Infantry Division[10]

Notes:

[1]Formerly Panzer Group West; upgraded to 5th Panzer Army on August 6, 1944.
[2]Just arrived from 15th Army.
[3]En route from 15th Army to 5th Panzer Army; its leading elements were south of Rouen on August 6.
[4]Kampfgruppe.
[5]Recently transferred from 15th Army.
[6]Transferred from Army Group G.
[7]Transferred from Army Group G. Assumed command of 271st and 276th Infantry Divisions on August 2; reassigned to 7th Army, August 6.
[8]In Brittany; directly subordinate to Army Group B.
[9]On garrison duty in the Channel Islands.
[10]En route from 15th Army to 7th Army. Its leading elements were near Briouze on August 6.

Source: Martin Blumenson, *Breakout and Pursuit. United States Army in World War II. The European Theater of Operations* (Washington, D.C.: 1961), ff. 748.

tactical miracle by disengaging as many panzer divisions as they did, without being detected by Allied reconnaissance airplanes.

During the evening of August 6, the British Ultra codebreakers at Bletchley Park outside London intercepted shocking dispatches: The German Army in France, thought to be on its last legs, was planning to launch a major offensive against Avranches in just a few hours. Before long, they had deciphered the entire plan, including the timing of the attack, the dispositions of the assault forces, and the strengths of the four panzer divisions that would spearhead the assault. The news was quickly relayed to General Bradley.

Fortunately, Bradley had anticipated the German attack days before. In recent years, certain authors have, in my view, overstated the impact of radio intercepts and codebreakers upon the war—most especially their influence on individual battles and operational and tactical situations.

While the use of Ultra intercepts was often of extremely great value at the strategic level, they had little or no influence on vitally important tactical operations. The Battle of Avranches is an excellent case in point. Bradley received the Ultra intercepts only four hours before the storm broke. That gave him time to send a warning order to his forward units that the Germans were about to attack (a warning that had no impact on the battle, as we shall see) but left him with insufficient time to make any significant changes in his tactical dispositions. Fortunately for the Allies, however, Bradley's positioning of the American divisions was already excellent.

The task of keeping the 20-mile-wide Avranches corridor open had already been assigned to Collins's VII U.S. Corps, which included the 30th, 1st, 9th, and 4th Infantry Divisions, as well as strong elements of the 2nd and 3rd Armored Divisions. Just in case a crisis developed, however, Bradley had already recalled Major General Paul Baade's 35th Infantry Division from Fougeres in Brittany and ordered Patton to halt the three divisions of the XX Corps (the U.S. 35th and 80th Infantry and French 2nd Armored) in the vicinity of St.-Hilaire, much to the disgust of "Old Blood and Guts." Meanwhile, as soon as Bradley realized that Army Group B was not going to retreat, he devised a plan to trap both of its field armies in a vast encirclement. While Collins absorbed the German blow, he ordered Patton to drive into France south of Army Group B, dash east, and then turn north, behind the 5th Panzer and 7th Armies. Meanwhile, Montgomery's 21st Army Group would push south, linking up with the Americans in the vicinity of Falaise, encircling Kluge's entire army group. With Hitler's main armies thus destroyed, nothing could prevent the prompt liberation of all of France; in fact, the end of the war itself might well be in sight. Eisenhower and Montgomery (who was still the Allied ground forces commander in France) quickly approved the plan.

On the eve of *Luettich*, Hausser issued this order to his corps and divisional commanders:

The Fuehrer has ordered the execution of a breakthrough to the coast to create the basis for the decisive operation against the Allied invasion front. For this purpose, further forces are being brought up to the Army.

On the successful execution of the operation the Fuehrer has ordered depends the decision of the War in the West, and with it perhaps the decision of the war itself. Commanders of all ranks must be absolutely clear about the enormous significance of this fact. I expect all corps commanders to take good care that all officers are aware of the unique significance of the whole situation. Only one thing counts, unceasing effort and determined will to victory.

For Fuehrer, Volk and Reich,
Hausser[14]

Baron von Funck, a veteran of a hundred battles, planned to attack with the 116th Panzer on the north, the 2nd Panzer in the center, and the 2nd SS Panzer on the right (against Mortain itself). The 1st SS Panzer he held in reserve, as an exploitation force. To gain the element of surprise, Funck planned to attack without a preliminary artillery bombardment. The baron knew his chances of success were slim, but he did have a chance if he could jump off by midnight and gain at least half the distance to Avranches (10 to 11 miles) by daybreak, before the American fighter-bombers appeared. Unfortunately, Lieutenant General Count Gerhard von Schwerin did not disengage his 116th Panzer Division quickly enough and was slow, lethargic, and even insubordinate. Funck soon had enough of him.[15] About 4 A.M., he asked Hausser's permission to relieve him of his command. "Schwerin's messed up the situation!" the veteran panzer corps commander cried. "He'll be delayed by several hours in getting the attack started."[16] Hausser agreed that Schwerin was performing poorly but did not think it wise to sack him just before the attack. Figure 5.1 shows the battle as it actually developed.

To the south, Lieutenant General Baron Heinrich von Luettwitz, the rotund, monocled commander of the 2nd Panzer Division, was also having problems in the darkness.[17] He was supposed to advance in two columns, roll through St. Barthelemy and Mesnil-Adelee, and push to the sea. At midnight, however, his left column was still not formed up; nevertheless, Luettwitz struck with his right (the reinforced 304th Panzer Grenadier Regiment under Major Hans Schneider-Kostalsky) and achieved total surprise all along the line. The American infantry, who had received Bradley's warning that a major attack was to take place only an hour before, was not alarmed by the dispatch. There were no special alerts, and the frontline units had generally ignored the warning. There had been so many false alarms of this nature in recent days that they understandably failed to take this one seriously, and it cost them heavily. The fact that the panzers struck without the usual preliminary artillery barrage further heightened the surprise and consternation of the American infantry. By dawn, the 304th Panzer Grenadier had gained about eight miles. Unfortunately its commander, the brave Major Schneider-Kostalsky, had been killed when his command vehicle ran over a mine. Luettwitz's left-hand column did not jump off until dawn (six hours late), but it was lucky: Dense fog grounded the "Jabos," and it was able to overrun the surprised American defenders at Bellefontaine with little trouble. At the village of St. Barthelemy, however, the Americans rallied and had to be systematically attacked. The village was taken, along with more than 100 prisoners, but a short distance beyond the 2nd Panzer was met by strong elements of the U.S. 3rd Armored Division, which checked it in heavy fighting. On the German left (southern) flank, SS Colonel Otto Baum's 2nd SS Panzer Division "Das Reich"

Figure 5.1
The Battle of Mortain, August 6–7, 1944

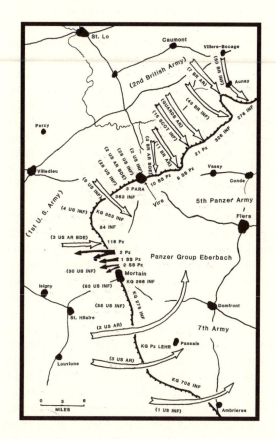

surged forward exactly on schedule, achieved complete surprise, broke the lines of the U.S. 30th Infantry Division, stormed Mortain at a full gallop, and captured the command post of the 2nd Battalion of the 120th Infantry Regiment inside the Hôtel de la Croix-Blanche.

Most of the American battalion, however, was dug in on Hill 317, a dominating position east of town. Here Captain Reynold Erichson took charge and held out, despite repeated attacks by the SS. Since Hill 317 commanded the road over which Baum's supplies had to pass, he surrounded the position and continued to attack it and shell it with his artillery. The 17th SS Panzer Grenadier Division (now hardly the size of a reinforced battalion) also joined the effort to reduce Hill 317. Meanwhile, Baum's spearheads advanced four miles behind the front of the 30th Infantry Division, took the villages of Fontenay and Milly, and threatened the town of St.-Hilaire. Due to the absence of Allied airplanes,

Funck's attack did cause some uneasy moments in Allied higher head-quarters, because it seemed as if he might actually pull it off and split the U.S. 1st and 3rd Armies, despite the odds against him. Later in the morning, however, the fog burned off. Hitler had promised to commit his entire Luftwaffe fighter reserve—a thousand airplanes—to support this attack. This reserve turned out to be 300 airplanes, grouped in the fields around Paris under the command of Lieutenant General Alfred Buelowius.[18] On the morning of August 7, there was no fog in the neighborhood of the French capital, and wave after wave of British and American fighter-bombers pounded the German airfields. Allied fighters quickly intercepted the German fighters that actually managed to take off, and dozens of spectacular dogfights took place over and around France's primate city. Not one German airplane, however, reached the battle zone around Mortain and Avranches, and only 110 German fighters were still operational the next day.

Meanwhile, hundreds of American Thunderbolts, Mustangs, and Lightnings, supported by 10 squadrons of rocket-firing British Typhoons, blasted von Funck's tanks. The U.S. Air Force had gotten a bit of a spotty reputation during the Normandy campaign because of a tendency they had not to confine their attacks to just German targets. A joke made the rounds that when the RAF bombs, the Germans take cover; when the Luftwaffe bombs, the British take cover; and when the Americans bomb, everybody takes cover. No one was laughing this day, however, and the U.S. pilots were right on target. Each Allied fighter-bomber had a pair of 500-pound wing bombs, and the 1st SS, 2nd, and 2nd SS Panzer Divisions were subjected to three hours of uninterrupted hell. The Typhoons fired salvos of 60-pound rockets and concentrated against the 2nd Panzer Division, north of Mortain, where they knocked out half of their remaining 60 tanks and destroyed dozens of other vehicles. When it was over, the roads toward Avranches and the nearby fields were littered with the bodies of dead German soldiers. In all, the Allied airplanes destroyed 81 Tigers, Panthers, and PzKw IVs. Another 54 panzers were damaged, and 26 were simply abandoned—the crews got out of their metal coffins before the Allied aviators could finish them off. Hundreds of trucks were also destroyed, along with uncounted armored cars, Volkswagens, artillery pieces, antitank guns, supply wagons, and assault guns. Luettwitz's 2nd Panzer Division also suffered heavy losses due to American artillery, which would not have been there had the 116th Panzer Division attacked, as it had been supposed to do.

From his command post at Alençon, Kluge closely followed the success of the attack and the ensuing disaster. Looking over his shoulder was the chief of OKW's Army Staff and Hitler's personal spy, General of Infantry Walter Buhle (now partially recovered from the wounds he suffered on July 20), who had been sent from Wolfsschanze to "observe" the battle.[19] (Hitler had recalled Warlimont, the deputy chief of operations at OKW, because he suspected the general was involved in the July 20 plot. Warlimont went on sick leave three weeks later—ironically because of wounds he suffered on July 20—and was never reemployed.) Despite the depressing reports, an urgent signal arrived from Rastenburg that afternoon: Continue the attack, Hitler ordered, "recklessly to the sea, regardless of the risk. . . . The greatest daring, determination and imagination must give wings to all echelons of command. Each and every man must believe in victory. Cleaning up in rear area . . . can wait until later."[20]

Hitler was unaware of how badly the panzer divisions had been beaten. Nevertheless, Baron von Funck immediately began to prepare another attack. In the process, he found out that General Count von Schwerin, the commander of the 116th Panzer Division (the "Greyhounds") and one of Germany's most decorated officers, had lost faith in victory to the point that he had not just failed to attack—he had deliberately withheld Funck's orders from his subordinates and had even withheld a tank battalion from the 2nd Panzer Division, despite the fact it was available for employment. When Hausser learned this, he withdrew his protection from Schwerin and allowed Funck to sack him. He was temporarily replaced by Colonel Walter Reinhard, the chief of staff of the XXXXVII Panzer Corps. This began one of the strangest incidents in the history of the German Army. Reinhard was soon succeeded by Colonel Gerhard Mueller, who was earmarked to be Schwerin's permanent replacement.[21] The officers and men of the 116th Panzer, however, refused to obey the orders of the one-armed colonel, whom they regarded as incompetent. By this time, Hitler had replaced von Funck, and Eberbach restored Schwerin to commander of the division. But he would soon be sacked again, during the Battle of Aachen, when his defeatism again led him to foul up on a grand scale.

The Mortain offensive cost XXXXVII Panzer Corps almost 100 tanks. Inconclusive fighting continued on August 8, but Funck's second attack was never delivered. It was overtaken by events to the south, north, and east as the Allied armies began to close in on Army Group B.

In the meantime, to the south, the XV Corps of Patton's 3rd Army moved too rapidly for General Kuntzen, the commander of the LXXXI Corps, and struck his vanguards before his divisions could arrive and deploy. Instead of giving ground and assembling his units in some defensible position east of Le Mans, Kuntzen committed each regiment piecemeal, as far forward as possible, as soon as it arrived. As a result, each unit was swamped individually, and Kuntzen was unable to even significantly slow down the American advance. About half of the 708th Infantry Division was destroyed, most of the 9th Panzer Division's reconnaissance battalion was lost, and the motorized 79th U.S. Infantry Division took the city of 75,000 by nightfall on August 8. Paul Hausser's Headquarters, 7th Army, had already withdrawn. The general himself had been among the last to leave, skulking out of town in a lone armored car with only his orderly and driver. Bradley now ordered Patton to turn XV Corps north, toward Alençon and Argentan (Figure 6.1). The Battle of the Falaise Pocket—as the encirclement of the 5th Panzer and 7th Armies was called—was beginning to take shape.

By now, Patton had 12 divisions south of the Avranches. In the meantime, General Montgomery's 21st Army Group began its drive to the south, toward Falaise. Excited by the success of Operation "Cobra," Monty and General Henry D. G. Crerar, the commander of the 1st Canadian Army, planned Operation "Totalize," which was to be preceded by a massive employment of strategic bombers. The ground attack was to be directed by Lieutenant General Guy G. Simonds, the competent but ambitious and ruthless commander of the II Canadian Corps. Its target was the 89th Infantry Division.

Lieutenant General Conrad-Oskar Heinrichs 89th Infantry ("Horseshoe") Division had been formed in Norway in early 1944 and had led a relatively easy existence until August 2, when it was suddenly rushed on to ships, transported to Holland, and hurriedly trucked to Normandy, where it replaced the 1st SS Panzer Division at the front near Caen on the night of August 4–5.[22] It had been in the line less than 72 hours when it was attacked by 1,020 Halifax and Lancaster heavy bombers shortly before midnight on August 7. It was pounded for more than an hour; then it was shelled by 360 guns; finally, the 2nd Canadian Infantry and 51st British Highland Divisions advanced along a narrow six-mile sector between the villages of St.-Martin and Soliers, supported by hundreds of Cromwell tanks and other armored vehicles. This was more than the green German division could stand; its men panicked and fled, some of them throwing away their rifles as they ran. General Eberbach had stationed the veteran 272nd Infantry Division behind the 89th, but it was too depleted to halt the British and Canadians and so soon gave way as well.

Fortunately for the Germans, SS Oberfuehrer Kurt Meyer was nearby with his 12th SS ("Hitler Youth") Panzer Division.[23] (The SS rank Oberfuehrer lay between colonel and *Generalmajor* [major general]; it has no English equivalent.) It was also very much understrength; of the 214 tanks it had on D-Day, only 48 were still operational. The 34-year-old SS general walked out into the middle of the road and, with a cigar in mouth, personally rallied many of the fleeing infantrymen, temporarily checking the Allied advance. On the morning of August 8, however, Meyer still did not have nearly enough firepower to halt the entire II Canadian Corps. But the expected major attack did not come. Meyer was puzzled. Except for his two badly understrength battle groups and 48 tanks, the road to Falaise was open. Why did the Canadians not resume their attack? he wondered. He had no way of knowing that the inexperienced Allied tank commanders were exhibiting excessive caution because they were not sure of themselves. In any case, Meyer decided not to wait. A veteran of two years on the Russian Front, he realized that the entire sector was on the verge of collapse, and his best chance of keeping it intact was to launch a spoiling attack of his own. The Hitler Youth went forward at 12:30 P.M.

On the Allied side of the line, General Simonds was preparing to commit the Canadian 4th Armored and Polish 1st Armored Divisions through the Canadian 2nd Infantry and British 51st Highland Divisions when Meyer struck. On the left, one battle group (8 sixty-two-ton Tigers and 14 forty-five-ton Panthers) drove toward Cintheaux; on the right, 20 Tigers advanced along the road toward St.-Aignan-de-Cramesnil. As they attacked, 492 Flying Fortresses from the 8th U.S. Air Force appeared and blasted the area around the area from whence the 12th SS had just left. Had they not attacked, the Hitler Youth battle groups would have been slaughtered, and the road to Falaise would have been wide open. Although elements of the division were hit by stray American bombs, it had been very lucky.

The Polish and Canadian armored divisions, which were also struck by errant bombs, did not feel so lucky. In addition to losing several dozen soldiers, they lost one of their best loved commanders, Major General R.F.L. Keller, the leader of the 3rd Canadian Infantry Division. Nicknamed "Captain Blood" by his men because of his red hair, the 44-year-old Keller had not lived up to the expectations of his commanders (Simonds, Crocker, and Montgomery) but was very popular with the rank and file. Keller's headquarters was one of the places mistakenly attacked by the American bombers. Keller himself was in a coma for a week and had to be invalided out of the service.[24]

After being bombed by the Americans, the Canadians and Poles were hit by the SS panzers. Meyer's left-hand column burst into Cintheaux and took the town from the Canadians. The right-hand battle group plowed into General Waldimar Maczek's 1st Polish Armored Division, which destroyed 6 of its 20 panzers. The SS gunners, however, knocked out 26 Polish Shermans. Meyer's counterattack was halted in fierce fighting, but Montgomery's advance was, for the moment, also completely derailed.

The cost on the German side had also been heavy. Among those listed as missing in action was SS Lieutenant Michael Wittmann, the leading tank ace of World War II. When last seen, he was being attacked from three sides by five or six Shermans. Wittmann had destroyed 141 enemy tanks and 132 antitank guns. He remained missing until 1987, when a

French road construction crew accidentally discovered his body and those of his crewmen. Despite this damaging loss, however, "Panzer" Meyer had achieved his objective. That evening, the British, Poles, and Canadians dug in, 11 miles short of their goal. Falaise remained in German hands.

NOTES

1. Albert Jodl was born in Wuerzburg in 1890 and joined the Bavarian Army as a *Faehnrich* (senior officer cadet) in 1910. Commissioned in 1912, he fought in World War I, served in the Reichsheer, and became chief of operations of OKW in 1938. On October 1, 1938, Jodl began a tour of troop duty when he became commanding officer of the 44th Artillery Command. He was recalled to OKW as chief of operations and held this position throughout the war. Hitler's chief military adviser, Jodl was promoted to major general (April 1, 1939), general of artillery (July 19, 1940), and colonel general (January 30, 1944). He skipped the rank of lieutenant general altogether. Albert Jodl was hanged at Nuremburg as a war criminal in October 1946. He was later cleared by a West German court. His younger brother Ferdinand (born 1896) rose to general of mountain troops and commanded XIX Mountain Corps and Army Detachment Narvik.

2. Walter Warlimont was born in Osnabrueck in 1894 and joined the Imperial Army in 1913 as an 18-year-old officer cadet in the 10th (Lower Saxony) Foot Artillery Regiment at Strasburg, Alsace. He attended the War School at Danzig (1913–14) and was commissioned in 1914. During World War I he served as a battery officer, an adjutant (battalion, regiment, and brigade), and battery commander on the Western and Italian Fronts. He was a 1st lieutenant in the Maercker Freikorps, which was accepted into the Reichsheer in its entirety. Warlimont underwent clandestine General Staff training (1922–26) and, as a captain, was named second assistant to the chief of the General Staff in 1926. Later he served in the economics section of the Defense Ministry and in the foreign armies intelligence section. He spent a year attached to the U.S. Army to study industrial mobilization (1929–30). After spending a year as a battery commander in the 1st Artillery Regiment in Allenstein, he was promoted to major on the staff of the industrial mobilization section of the Defense Ministry. He became section chief in 1935.

Lieutenant Colonel Warlimont was Reich military plenipotentiary to General Franco (1936–37) and commanded the II Battalion/34th Artillery Regiment at Trier and the 26th Artillery Regiment at Duesseldorf (1937–38). In 1938, he was named chief of the national defense section of the General Staff in OKW and (during Jodl's tour of troop duty) was chief of operations at OKW (1938–39). From September 1939 to September 1944, Warlimont was deputy chief of operations at OKW and was successively promoted to major general (1940), lieutenant general (1942), and general of artillery (April 1, 1944). He was placed in Fuehrer Reserve in September 1944 and was never reemployed. After the war, he was sentenced to 25 years' imprisonment as a war criminal. His sentence was later commuted, and he retired to Rottach-Egern.

3. Warlimont, p. 446.

4. Keegan, p. 241.

5. Warlimont, p. 447. Conversely, Colonel General Kurt Zeitzler, the chief of the General Staff, was sacked on July 21, in part because he was not in the briefing hut on July 20. His deputy, Heusinger, was convinced that Zeitzler "must have known" about the plot and never forgave him for leaving him in the room with Stauffenberg's bomb.

6. Breuer, *Death*, pp. 145–46.

7. Josef "Sepp" Dietrich was born in Hawangen, Swabia, on May 28, 1892, the son of a master meatpacker. He dropped out of school at age 14 and became an agricultural driver. Later he was an apprentice in the hotel trade. He served in the Royal Bavarian Army in 1911 and was recalled to active duty when World War I broke out. He served in the artillery and was wounded by shrapnel in the lower leg and by a lance thrust above his left eye. He served on the Western Front throughout the war, was wounded a third time, and ended up in one of Germany's few tank units. After the war, he fought with the Freikorps and joined the Bavarian Landespolizei (provincial police) and the Nazi Party. He took part in the Beer Hall Putsch of 1923 on the side of the Nazis, which no doubt accounts for his sudden dismissal from the police. He worked at various jobs in Munich from 1924 to 1929 and in the meantime joined the SS. He became Hitler's bodyguard and one of his favorites at this time. He became a member of the Reichstag in 1930 and an SS-Gruppenfuehrer (major general) in 1931.

In March 1933, Dietrich organized the Leibstandarte Adolf Hitler (Adolf Hitler Bodyguard) unit. It eventually grew from 117 men into the 1st SS Panzer Division, with a strength of 21,000 men. Dietrich commanded it for 10 years, fighting in Poland (1939), the West (1940), and Russia (1941–43). In July 1943, Dietrich became the commander of the I SS Panzer Corps. Later he led the 5th Panzer, 6th Panzer, and 6th SS Panzer Armies, rising to the rank of SS colonel general.

After the war, Dietrich was sentenced to 25 years' imprisonment for the Malmedy massacre, despite the fact he was nowhere near the place. After passions died down somewhat, he was paroled in 1955, but in 1958 he was sentenced to 18 months' imprisonment by a West German court for his part in Hitler's Blood Purge of the Storm Troopers (1934). Released after only five months due to health problems, he retired to Ludwigsburg, where he died in bed on April 21, 1966, at the age of 73.

8. Breuer, *Death*, p. 157.

9. Shulman, p. 195.

10. Wilmot, p. 400.

11. Keegan, p. 246.

12. Adolf Kuntzen was born in Magdeburg in 1889 and joined the 1st Hussars Regiment as an officer cadet in 1909. He fought in World War I, served in the Reichsheer, and was commander of the 3rd Light Division in 1938. He led this division in Poland and France and oversaw its conversion into the 8th Panzer Division in the winter of 1939–40. Kuntzen led the LVII Panzer Corps in Russia (1941–42) and took charge of the XXXII Corps Command in 1942. This headquarters was later upgraded to LXXXI Corps. Relieved of his command on September 4, 1944, he was never reemployed. He was promoted to general of panzer troops in 1941.

Edgar Arndt was born in Lissa in 1892. He joined the army as a *Fahnenjunker* in 1911 and retired as a major in 1932. Recalled to duty as a reserve officer in late 1933, Arndt was a "retread." He was promoted to lieutenant colonel of reserves in August 1939, to colonel in 1940, and to major general on July 1, 1943. He commanded 337th Infantry Regiment (1939–40) and the schools of the 1st Army (1942), was on special assignment to the commander of 1st Army (1942–43), and was acting commander of the 158th Reserve Division (May 1943). He assumed command of the 708th Infantry on July 30, 1943, and was killed in action during the retreat from France, reportedly on August 24.

General Erwin Jolasse was born in Hamburg in 1892. He entered the service as a *Fahnenjunker* in 1911 and was commissioned in the infantry. Discharged after World War I, he became an instructor pilot for the clandestine German air forces. In 1934, however, he rejoined the army as a captain. He was a commander of the II Battalion, 39th Infantry Regiment, when the war broke out. He successively commanded the 52nd Infantry Regiment (1940–42), the 18th Panzer Brigade (1942–43), and the 9th Panzer Division. Severely wounded on September 16, 1944, he did not return to active duty until January 1945, commanding a battle group north of Breslau. He assumed command of the 344th Infantry Division on the Eastern Front in March 1945 but managed to surrender to the Western Allies at the end of the war. He was promoted to lieutenant general on April 20, 1945 (Keilig, p. 159).

13. Blumenson, *Breakout and Pursuit*, p. 442.

14. Rohmer, p. 181.

15. Count Gerhard von Schwerin, a holder of the Knight's Cross with Oak Leaves and Swords, was born in Hanover in 1899. He joined the army as a *Faehnrich* (senior officer cadet) in the elite 2nd Guard Regiment of Foot when World War I broke out and was discharged as a lieutenant in 1920. He reentered the service in 1922 and was on the staff of OKH when the next world war broke out. Count von Schwerin commanded the I Battalion of the elite Grossdeutschland Motorized Infantry Regiment, the 86th Rifle Regiment, the Grossdeutschland Regiment itself, and the 200th Special Purposes Regiment (1939–41), before taking charge of the 76th Infantry Regiment (1941–42). After briefly serving as deputy commander of the 254th Infantry Division (1942), he was acting commander of the 8th Jaeger Division (1942) and commander of the 16th Panzer Grenadier Division (1944), which was upgraded to the 116th Panzer Division in the spring of 1944. Sacked during the Battle of Aachen, his friends on the General Staff saved his career and secured for him the command of the 90th Panzer Grenadier Division in Italy (December 1944). From April 1 to 25, 1945, Schwerin commanded the LXXVI Panzer Corps in Italy and surrendered it to the Western Allies. He was living in Bonn at last report (Keilig, p. 319).

16. Breuer, *Death*, p. 179.

17. Baron Heinrich von Luettwitz was born on the family estate at Krumpach, East Prussia, on December 6, 1896. His military ancestors dated back to the 1340s. Unable to secure his father's permission to enter the service, however, Heinrich joined the army as a private in 1914 and went to the Western Front at age 17. His mother, Klara von Luettwitz nee von Unruh, also came from a military family and used her influence to have Heinrich brevetted second lieutenant two days before his eighteenth birthday. Luettwitz distinguished himself in the trench

fighting in France in 1917, during which he was severely wounded. He ended the war commanding a troop of the 1st Uhlan Regiment.

Luettwitz was accepted into the Reichsheer as a cavalry officer but was converted to the concept of motorized warfare in 1929 and commanded the 3rd Motorized Battalion in 1936–37. In 1936, he was also leader of the German Olympic Equestrian Team. Because it did not win the Gold Medal, Luettwitz's career suffered, and he served in backwater posts until the invasion of the Soviet Union. (He was not sent to the front in Poland until the campaign was decided, and even then, he was unlucky enough to be severely wounded. He was on garrison duty in Poland during the French campaign of 1940.) Finally, Major General Walter Nehring (future commander of the Afrika Korps and the 1st Panzer Army) rescued Luettwitz from professional exile and gave him command of the 101st Motorized Infantry Regiment in his own 18th Panzer Division. He was abruptly relieved on orders from Berlin in January 1941. Nehring strongly protested, as did Guderian and Hoepner. This led to Luettwitz being given command of the 59th Rifle Regiment of the 20th Panzer Division, which he led in Russia (1941–42). After Stalin's winter offensive was checked, Luettwitz commanded the 20th Rifle Brigade (1942), the 13th Panzer Division (1942–43), and the 2nd Panzer Division (1944). He led the XXXXVII Panzer Corps after Funck was unjustly placed in Fuehrer Reserve in September 1944. He was a very good divisional commander but was less successful commanding a corps, especially in the Battle of the Bulge, where he received the answer "Nuts" from American commander of Bastogne, whose surrender he had demanded. Luettwitz surrendered the XXXXVII Panzer Corps at the end of the Battle of the Ruhr Pocket and retired to Neuberg in Bavaria, where he again cultivated his horsemanship and acquired a stable from funds saved from his old estates, which were now lost. He died at Neuburg on October 9, 1969. He was promoted to lieutenant general on June 1, 1943, and to general of panzer troops on November 1, 1944.

18. Alfred Buelowius was born on January 14, 1892, and joined the Prussian Army in 1912 but was discharged as a captain at the end of World War I. He joined the secret Luftwaffe in 1933 and served primarily with bomber and dive-bomber schools until 1942, when he joined the VIII Corps in Russia. Named commander of Luftwaffe Command North in September 1942, he led the 1st Air Division in Russia (1942–43). He commanded the German fighter forces in Sicily and Italy (1943) and II Air Corps during the Normandy campaign. After this failure, Buelowius commanded various air administrative areas from December 1944 until the end of the war. His last command was Luftgau III in Dresden. Promoted to general of fliers on December 1, 1944, Buelowius died in August 1968 (Absolon, p. 30; Buelowius Personnel File, Air University Archives, Maxwell Air Force Base, Montgomery, Alabama, n.d.).

19. Walter Buhle was born in Heilbronn, Wuerttemberg, on October 26, 1894. He joined the Imperial Army as a *Fahnenjunker* on July 10, 1913, received his commission when World War I broke out, and served with the infantry during the war. He alternated between infantry, cavalry, and General Staff assignments in the 1920s and 1930s and, as a lieutenant colonel, became chief of operations of Wehrkreis V in 1937. A promotion to colonel followed. Recognized as a hard worker, an expert on armaments, and a convinced Nazi, Buhle was summoned to Berlin in 1939 and named chief of the Organizations Section of OKH. (Ironi-

cally, his principal assistant in this post was Colonel Count von Stauffenberg.) Buhle established a personal relationship with Adolf Hitler while at Fuehrer Headquarters and was named chief of the Army Staff at OKW in early 1942. He was promoted to major general (1940), lieutenant general (1942), and general of infantry (April 1, 1944). Buhle was Hitler's first choice to succeed Zeitzler as chief of the General Staff, but it took Buhle weeks to recover from his July 20 wounds, so the appointment went to Guderian. In early 1945, Hitler named Buhle to replace Himmler in one of his many posts—chief of armaments for the army. General Buhle survived the war and subsequent trials and retired to Stuttgart, where he was still living in the late 1950s.

20. Breuer, *Death*, p. 187.

21. Gerhard Mueller was born in Breslau in 1896 and joined the army in 1915 as an officer cadet. Commissioned the following year, he fought in World War I but was not selected for retention in the Reichsheer. He served in the police for the next 15 years and rejoined the army as a captain in 1935. He commanded the 33rd Anti-Tank Battalion (1938–40), the I Battalion, 33rd Panzer Regiment (1941), and the 5th Panzer Regiment (1942). He fought in Poland and France and lost an arm in North Africa. A branch chief in OKH (1942–44), he was given command of the 116th Panzer Division and was promoted to major general on September 1, 1944, but was relieved shortly thereafter because his staff revolted. He never held another significant post, ending the war as deputy commandant of Pilsen. He retired to Landau (Keilig, p. 232).

22. Conrad-Oskar Heinrichs was born Wallstawe in 1890 and joined the Imperial Army in 1911. Commissioned in the infantry in 1913, he fought in World War I, served in the Reichsheer, and was on the staff of the 59th Infantry Regiment when World War II began. He was named commander of the 24th Infantry Regiment in late 1939. Heinrichs commanded the 290th Infantry Division (1942–44) on the Eastern Front before assuming command of the 89th Infantry Division on February 10, 1944. He was promoted to lieutenant general on February 1, 1943, and was killed in action on September 8, 1944 (Keilig, p. 133).

23. Kurt "Panzer" Meyer was born in 1910, the son of a laborer. He worked as a miner and as a policeman before joining the Nazi Party in 1930. He became an officer in the SS in 1932 and transferred to the Leibstandarte, Hitler's personal bodyguard, in early 1934. He commanded the Leibstandarte Adolf Hitler (LAH) antitank company in Poland and led a motorcycle company in France. He led the Leibstandarte's reconnaissance battalion in Greece (1941) and Russia (1941–43), earning the Knight's Cross and the Oak Leaves in the process.

In July 1943, Meyer was transferred to the 12th SS Panzer Division as commander of a panzer grenadier regiment. He succeeded to divisional command when General Witt was killed. The youngest divisional commander in the entire Wehrmacht, he was captured in September 1944. Tried for murdering Canadian prisoners, Meyer was sentenced to death in December 1945, but his sentence was reduced to life imprisonment and he was released in 1954. An unreconstructed Nazi until the end, he died on his birthday in 1961.

24. Born in England in 1900, Keller emigrated to British Columbia with his family as a child. He graduated from the Royal Military College of Canada in

1920 and served primarily in the light infantry. He died in London following a heart attack he suffered in Caen in 1954, during the tenth anniversary of the Battle of Normandy. John A. English, "R.F.L. Keller," in Chandler and Collins, pp. 328–29.

Field Marshals Erwin Rommel and Gerd von Rundstedt at the latter's head-quarters, St.-Germain, Paris.

Field Marshal Walter Model, the commander-in-chief of Army Group B and OB West.

Field Marshal Model, speaking with one of his soldiers. Although he was often quite harsh when dealing with his officers, "the Fuehrer's Fireman" always treated his enlisted men with courtesy and respect (U.S. Army Institute for Military History).

Field Marshal Hans von Kluge, the OB West from July 2 until August 15, 1944, and commander-in-chief of Army Group B from July 17 to August 15, 1944. Implicated in the plot to assassinate Hitler, Kluge committed suicide on August 18 (U.S. Army Institute for Military History).

Colonel General Hans von Salmuth, commander of the 15th Army; Field Marshal Erwin Rommel, the commander-in-chief of Army Group B; and Field Marshal Gerd von Rundstedt, the OB West (U.S. Army Institute for Military History).

Colonel General Alfred Jodl, chief of operations of the High Command of the Armed Forces, 1938–1945. When this photo was taken in May 1945, Jodl was on his way to surrender to General Eisenhower. Jodl was later tried as a war criminal and executed in 1946.

Field Marshal Sir Bernard Law Montgomery as he appeared in 1955. From June 6 until September 1, 1944, Monty was the overall commander of Allied ground forces in France (courtesy, Col. Dr. Edmond Marino).

A German panzer lieutenant briefs his crew, Normandy, 1944 (Bundesarchiv, Kolbenz).

A German sniper takes aim, Normandy, 1944. He has two "potato-masher" grenades by his right arm (Bundesarchiv, Kolbenz).

A spotter keeps an eye out for Allied airplanes, Normandy, 1944. The "German glance" was a fugitive look over one's shoulder for enemy airplanes. Everyone from field marshal to private had it after a few days at the front (Bundesarchiv, Kolbenz).

Caen, 1944, after it had been struck by Allied bombers. The British and Canadians finally captured the ruins of the former university town after six weeks of bitter fighting (Bundesarchiv, Kolbenz).

A German antitank gunner, dug in at the foot of a hedgerow, waits for an Allied tank to come down the road, Normandy, 1944 (Bundesarchiv, Kolbenz).

Field Marshal Erwin Rommel, the "Desert Fox," inspecting a panzer artillery unit in France, 1944 (Bundesarchiv, Kolbenz).

A formal photograph of Field Marshal Gerd von Rundstedt, OB West, 1944. Rundstedt is wearing the uniform of a colonel. When he retired in 1938 (the first of four times!), Rundstedt was named honorary colonel of the 18th Infantry Regiment. This was a signal honor in the German Army and Rundstedt was very proud of it; thereafter, he wore his colonel's uniform more frequently than that of a general or field marshal. On the rare occasions when he left his headquarters, junior officers and enlisted men often mistakenly addressed him as a colonel. Rundstedt thought this was highly amusing and rarely corrected the person in question. (Photo provided by Colonel Dr. Edmond D. Marino, who received it from Rundstedt's daughter-in-law, Dr. Editha von Rundstedt).

The commander of a panzer engineer battalion presents a corporal with a special award for destroying an Allied tank in Normandy, 1944. The corporal already wears both grades of the Iron Cross, the Close Combat Badge, the Wounded Badge, and the Eastern Front campaign medal (U.S. Army Photo).

A German tank platoon, hiding in the hay.

The port of Cherbourg, 1944. The destruction was so thorough that Hitler awarded Admiral Hennecke the Knight's Cross, even though he was in captivity (U.S. Army Photo).

Field Marshal Erwin von Witzleben, the OB West, 1940–1942.

Colonel General Heinz Guderian, the "father" of the blitzkrieg and commander of the 2nd Panzer Army on the Eastern Front. Later he was inspector of panzer troops (1943–1944) and chief of the General Staff of the Army (1944–1945).

Sepp Dietrich, commander of the I SS Panzer Corps and 5th Panzer Army in France, 1944 (U.S. National Archives).

On July 20, 1944, a wounded Colonel General Alfred Jodl discusses his experience with Joseph Goebbels, the minister of propaganda (U.S. National Archives).

General of Panzer Troops Heinrich Eberbach, the commander of the 5th Panzer Army and Panzer Group Eberbach during the Normandy campaign. An excellent commander, Eberbach was captured by the British on September 1, 1944.

Utah Beach a day or two after the initial invasion landings (U.S. Army Institute for Military History).

American combat troops on parade in Paris, August 26, 1944, the day after the city was liberated. These troops were given no time to celebrate. They marched through the city and were in combat again by nightfall (U.S. Army Institute for Military History).

CHAPTER VI

THE FALAISE POCKET: ARMY GROUP B IS SLAUGHTERED

On August 9, as the 2nd Battalion of the U.S. 120th Infantry Regiment (now dubbed the "Lost Battalion") clung stubbornly to the wooded slopes of Hill 317, despite the repeated attempts of the 17th SS Division to dislodge it, Omar Bradley held a briefing for a VIP delegation from Washington, led by U.S. Secretary of the Treasury Henry Morganthau. "This is an opportunity that comes to a commander not once in a century," he said. "We are about to destroy an entire hostile army. If the other fellow will only press his attacks here at Mortain for another 48 hours, he'll give us time to close at Argentan and there completely destroy him.... We'll go all the way to the German border."[1]

Bradley would have been pleased indeed to learn that Hitler intended to give them the time he needed—and more. At Fuehrer Headquarters in East Prussia, Hitler flew into a fine rage on the morning of August 8. He ranted that Operation *Luettich* had failed because Field Marshal von Kluge lacked the courage to wait until all of the panzer divisions were in position to attack. If he had waited, as Hitler had ordered, the attack would have been successful. "The attack failed because Field Marshal Kluge *wanted* it to fail!" the dictator charged. Later, he repeatedly referred back to this attack, implying that Kluge's lack of nerve had cost him victory in the West. The attack, he said, was launched "too early and too weak when the weather was favorable to the enemy air force."[2] Hitler ordered the attack to resume on August 11, using six panzer divisions (two more than on August 7); furthermore, the *Schwerpunkt* (main point of attack) was to be farther to the south. In addition, he replaced General von Funck. This panzer baron was a former staff officer of Colonel General Baron Werner von Fritsch, the non-Nazi commander in chief of the army in the 1930s whom Hitler, for a time, considered a threat to the Nazi regime. Hitler hated Fritsch and never liked the aristocratic Funck; he felt Funck looked down on him as something of an upstart peasant—and with some justification. He replaced Funck as assault commander with Heinz Eberbach, although Funck remained in command of the XXXXVII Panzer Corps, for the moment at least. Eberbach was instructed to form an ad hoc Panzer Group Eberbach, and SS General Sepp Dietrich became acting commander of the 5th Panzer Army—much to the disgust of General Eberbach. "Dietrich is totally unqualified for the job," he cried in anguish to his aides.[3] Dietrich's order from Rastenburg was to disengage the 10th SS Panzer Division and to send it to Mortain; furthermore, Kuntzen was to detach the 9th Panzer Division from LXXXI Corps and to rush it north, so that it could also take part in Eberbach's drive to the sea. The Ultra interceptors promptly passed this critical intelligence on to Generals Eisenhower, Bradley, and Montgomery.

Eberbach's small staff included the field marshal's son, Lieutenant Colonel Guenther von Kluge, as chief of staff and Major Arthur von Eckesparre, Rommel's former chief supply officer, as chief of operations. The panzer general was unenthusiastic about his new assignment and doubted that it had the slightest chance of success. Eberbach was a highly capable officer and a longtime veteran of tank battles on the Eastern Front. He had been advocating a withdrawal to the Seine since he arrived in Normandy in July. He really became depressed when he learned that his assault divisions had only about 125 operational tanks left. Furthermore, he knew that, due to enemy aerial superiority, his attacks would have to be concluded by 10 A.M. This meant that a daytime attack was out of the question, and a night attack would require some light from the moon. The moonlight he needed would not be available until August 20, so he asked Kluge for a delay. The field marshal relayed the request to Fuehrer Headquarters, although he knew what the answer would be. Sure enough, Rastenburg ordered Eberbach to attack on August 11, as the Fuehrer had instructed. That same day, August 9, George Patton reinforced Haislip with the French 2nd Armored Division and sent the U.S. 80th Infantry Division to cover the 25-mile gap between him and the 1st Army. The next day, the U.S. XV Corps began its drive to the north with two armored and two motorized infantry divisions. Its objective was the town of Argentan, 14 miles south of Falaise; here it was to link up with Montgomery's 1st Canadian Army, which was advancing on Argentan from the north to complete the encirclement of Army Group B. The distance between the two forces was 60 miles. Haislip made good progress on the first day, despite the efforts of the 9th Panzer Division to slow him down. (The 708th Infantry Division—a low-quality unit to begin with—had ceased to be battleworthy by this time.) By the end of the day, the French 2nd and U.S. 5th Armored Divisions had gained 15 miles, or about half the distance to Alençon.

To the north, however, the Canadians were having serious problems. The British Columbia Regiment moved forward too rapidly and was quickly surrounded by the Hitler Youths. They knocked out 47 tanks and virtually destroyed the regiment. Two supporting infantry companies from the Algonquin Regiment were also slaughtered. Also, they ran into a number of 88mm batteries belonging to the III Flak Corps. All totalled, the Canadians lost more than 150 Sherman tanks in the wheatfields north of the Liaison River on August 8 and 9.[4]

Meanwhile, Hans von Kluge hesitated. Eberbach had predicted just exactly the operation as Bradley had planned and had recommended the only possible countermeasure: an immediate retreat behind the Seine. Kluge knew he was right; he had been involved in enough double envelopments on the Eastern Front to recognize what was happening. He also knew, however, that he was under suspicion for complicity in the conspiracy of July 20, he knew that the Gestapo was on his trail, and he dared not provoke the wrath of the Fuehrer any further, so he hesitated. Some of the generals tried to persuade Hitler's former bodyguard, SS General Sepp Dietrich, to intercede and personally tell the Fuehrer the truth. "If I want to get shot, that's a good way to do it!" Dietrich snapped. He was already convinced that Hitler was crazy and had even called him "a madman" a few weeks before, during a discussion with Field Marshal Rommel. He refused to put his head into the noose, so to speak. Finally, late on August 10, Kluge mustered up his courage, signaled Jodl, and suggested the panzer divisions in the Mortain sector first attack to the southeast, against the advancing Americans, before advancing to the sea. This recommendation brought a flurry of questions from Rastenburg, but Kluge quickly informed Hitler and OKW that all three of his senior commanders—Dietrich, Hausser, and Eberbach—agreed with him on the issue. The Fuehrer, as often was the case, could not bring himself to make a decision involving a retreat.

Finally, around 6 P.M. on August 11, the field marshal decided that he could wait no longer. Taking measures into his own hands, he issued the order that became known as the "Alençon Plan." Panzer Group Eberbach was instructed to hand responsibility for the Mortain sector over to General of Panzer Troops Walter Krueger's LVIII Panzer Corps (recently up from southern France) and take charge of the XXXXVII Panzer and LXXXI Corps. They would regroup in the vicinity of Carrouges and, spearheaded by the 1st SS, 2nd, and 116th Panzer Divisions, would be prepared to attack in the direction of Alençon. In the meantime, Hausser's 7th Army would take charge of the southern jaw of the developing salient, while 5th Panzer Army retired in stages across the Orne and then the Touques Rivers, covering the army group from the north. Several hours later, Hitler approved the plan but emphasized that he had not given up the idea of the Mortain offensive; as far as he was concerned, it was only being temporarily delayed. Eberbach pulled out with the 116th, 1st SS, and 2nd SS Panzer Divisions along the three roads still open in the pocket. His withdrawal from the Montain sector enabled the Americans to rescue the "Lost Battalion" on Hill 317. Of the original 800 men, fewer than 300 survived, and many of them were wounded, and all were weak due to lack of food. Some had had nothing to eat for 92 hours except green apples.

Meanwhile, to the north, the Canadians had pushed to within six miles of Falaise, or about 20 miles north of Argentan, while the Americans were fighting in the vicinity of Alençon, 27 miles south of Argentan. The Canadians, however, seemed to be stalled, while the Americans had already advanced 30 miles since they took Le Mans—hence, Kluge's decision to send the panzers to the south, against Patton and Haislip. But the German tanks were still 50 miles to the west, the American spearheads were gaining ground rapidly, and the morale of their soldiers had improved markedly, now that they were out of the *bocage* territory. On August 12, the U.S. XV Corps neared the Forêt d'Ecouves, a dense, hilly forest that covered 60 square miles between Alençon and Argentan. Aware of the defensive potential of this area, Haislip decided to bypass it by sending the 5th Armored around to the right (east) of the forest and the French 2nd Armored to the left (west). The American tank division's objective was Argentan, and the French were ordered to take Ecouché, 5 miles west of Argentan. These towns lay on the boundary line between the Allied 21st and 12th Army Groups, as drawn by Montgomery a few days before.

U.S. Major General Lunsford E. Oliver's 5th Armored Division barreled rapidly past crumbling German resistance on August 12, and one of his columns advanced down the Sees-Argentan Road to within 5 miles of the town. There, however, it ran out of gasoline and had to wait six critical hours, almost within sight of its objective, while its tanker trucks were stalled behind French troops. The commander of the 2nd French Armored Division, Major General Philippe Leclerc, had disobeyed orders and deliberately sent one of his units down a road reserved for the Americans![5] By the time the mess was straightened out, Eberbach had reached Argentan with the vanguard of the 116th Panzer Division. The town, which was virtually defenseless during the morning of August 12, would not fall for more than a week. General Eberbach set up a command post in the village of Chendeouit (12 miles west of Argentan) and rushed reinforcements into the sector. On August 13, the decimated remnants of the 708th Infantry Division were taken out of the battle, except for the still extant 728th Grenadier Regiment, while the 116th Panzer Division (with the 728th attached) continued to arrive and checked the American advance up the Sees-Argentan Road, and the 2nd Panzer Division contained Leclerc just north of Ecouché. The 1st SS Panzer Division entered

Figure 6.1
The Falaise Pocket, August 13, 1944

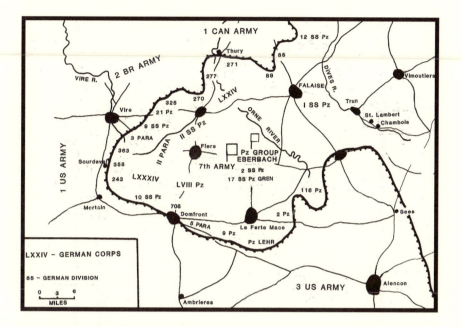

the battle south of Ecouché, where it clashed with elements of the U.S. 90th Infantry Division. However, since his three panzer divisions had only 73 tanks and assault guns between them (29 in the 2nd Panzer, 15 in the 116th Panzer, and 29 in the 1st SS Panzer), Eberbach's position was still far from enviable.[6] Before the day was out, his command post was attacked by fighter-bombers and most of his headquarters vehicles were destroyed; then the CP was shelled by American artillery; and finally it was fired upon by U.S. infantry. All Eberbach had to counter this threat was a company of bakers. He pulled out; the Alençon attack was never launched. In the meantime, elements of the French 2nd Armored managed to break through and capture the center of Argentan, but they were promptly driven out by elements of the 116th Panzer Division. In the meantime, the 1st Infantry and 3rd Armored Divisions of Collins's VII Corps closed up on Haislip's left. Except for the gap north of Argentan, Army Group B was now completely encircled.[7] Figure 6.1 shows the situation inside the pocket, whereas Figure 6.2 shows the situation along the entire front, where, south of Army Group B, Patton was advancing unchecked toward the Loire and the Seine.

Back at La Roche Guyon, Hitler continued to harass Kluge with dispatches that grew progressively more unrealistic. He wanted Panzer Group Eberbach to avoid becoming decisively engaged, he wanted 9th

Figure 6.2
The Normandy Sector, August 7–11, 1944

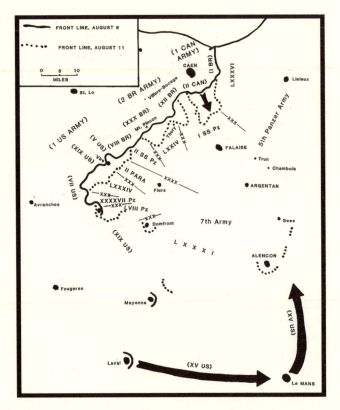

and 10th SS Panzer and 21st Panzer to attack the Americans, and he informed Kluge that his primary mission was now to destroy the U.S. forces near Alençon. Panzer Group Eberbach was, of course, fighting for its life, the 9th and 10th SS and 21st Panzers were straining every muscle and had committed their last reserves against the Canadians around Falaise, and Kluge could no longer even supply his army, much less destroy two American corps near Alençon.

On August 14, the 1st Canadian Army launched Operation "Tractable," Montgomery's latest effort to break through the 5th Panzer Army. In contrast to their usual pattern, the Allies struck at noon, to gain the element of surprise, using heavy concentrations of smoke instead of darkness to cover their advance. They were also supported by a tremendous application of air power: more than 800 heavy bombers, which dropped 3,700 tons of bombs just south of the Allied lines. They blasted the weak and poor-quality 85th and 89th Infantry Divisions but also had a number of "shorts," which killed 150 Canadian soldiers.

General Simonds's II Canadian Corps launched the main attack, which was supposed to swing east of the Falaise Road, cross the Laison River, outflank the Germans defending Falaise, and capture the town. Simultaneously, a diversionary attack was to be launched along the Caen-Falaise Road, to pin down the German reserves. Unfortunately, the night before, a Canadian scout car, with a copy of General Simonds's plans in it, had blundered into German lines, and "Panzer" Meyer already knew the timing and location of the main attack. When the Polish 1st Armored and Canadian 3rd Infantry and 4th Armored Divisions jumped off, they ran straight into the 12th SS Panzer Division, and Brigadier E. L. Booth, the commander of the Canadian 4th Armoured Brigade, was killed by an antitank round as he tried to cross the river. German 88s blasted Canadian and Polish Shermans and Churchills, which soon littered the battlefield. Despite the heavy losses and serious delays he inflicted on these two divisions, however, Meyer's burned-out unit had only 500 grenadiers left: not enough to halt two full-strength tank divisions indefinitely. The Poles and Canadians slowly pushed the Hitler Youth back, until they were reinforced by the 21st Panzer Division—itself a Kampfgruppe. The remnants of the 501st SS Heavy Panzer Battalion—Wittmann's old unit—also joined the battle, even though it had to drive half of its tanks directly from the battalion maintenance workshops, which were now scarcely a mile behind the front lines. Ominously several of the tanks dropped out of formation before they reached the line because they were out of fuel. Due to the constricted nature of that part of the road network still under German control, their supply system was failing. By nightfall, the Canadians had crossed the Laison and were within three miles of Falaise.

To the south, the French and Americans were stalled in heavy fighting. By now, the 9th Panzer Division was down to a strength of 260 men, a dozen tanks, and a few pieces of artillery. The 1st SS Panzer Division could field only 352 men and 29 tanks and assault guns. Compared to them, the 2nd Panzer Division was in relatively good shape: It had 2,230 men, 12 tanks, and five assault guns. These three units and a handful of other burned-out commands were facing an American corps of 70,000 men and 650 tanks.[8]

Meanwhile, due to the effects of defeat, doubts of Wehrmacht invincibility began to surface in the minds of the German frontline soldiers—the first crack in their morale. In addition, untrue rumors began to circulate about July 20, the losses on the Eastern Front, and the damage to essential industries caused by Allied bombings. (The truth was bad enough!) It was even rumored that Field Marshal Busch, the former commander in chief of Army Group Center, had defected to the Russians! The German generals reacted quickly to crush these rumors and to stop new ones from spreading. ("Latrine rumors" of this kind are the bane of all armies, especially defeated ones.) Lieutenant General Kurt Badinski, the commander of the 276th Infantry Division, issued an order, stating, "I condemn this irresponsible chatter as sabotage of the worst sort. It is punishable by death." He ordered all such rumors be investigated.[9] Lieutenant General Richard Schimpf, commander of the 3rd Parachute Division, commented, "Foul rumors are the same as bad odors, both originate from the rear." He also condemned the rumors and ordered that his men were to slap anyone across the face who spoke defeatism.[10]

On August 14, despite the deteriorating situation in the Falaise area, Field Marshal von Kluge traveled to his OB West Headquarters, in the Saint-Germain section of Paris. Here he met with his OB West chief of staff, General Blumentritt, and General Dietrich von Choltitz, whom Hitler had recently appointed commandant of Paris, just a few days after Kluge had sacked him as commander of the LXXXIV Corps in Normandy. They discussed a Fuehrer Order concerning the defense of the city and the destruction of the bridges, public buildings, and all industrial plants and utilities. All present were in apparent agreement: If its capture seemed imminent, Paris must be destroyed. Kluge then drove toward the front, along "roads clogged with traffic and dispirited troops."[11] He met with Sepp Dietrich at the latter's headquarters at Fontaine l'Abbe, near the town of Bernay. Dietrich described how the 12th SS Panzer was slowing the latest Canadian offensive but that it could not check it all by itself. For that reason, Dietrich had diverted the 21st Panzer (which was scheduled to join Panzer Group Eberbach in the Alençon offensive) to the northern sector of the front, to stabilize the situation around Falaise. Even with these reinforcements, Dietrich said, he was not confident that he could hold Falaise or prevent a breakthrough in the zone of 5th Panzer Army. Satisfied with Dietrich's arrangements but far from happy, Hans von Kluge left Fontaine l'Abbe early the next morning, August 15, heading for a 10 A.M. meeting with Hausser and Eberbach at the village square in Nécy, 4 miles south of Falaise and 40 miles from Dietrich's command post. Then he disappeared. Eberbach and Hausser waited for von Kluge for three hours. Then, deciding that they could wait no longer, they returned to their respective command posts, which were very close to each other. When Eberbach arrived at his CP, there was a message from Fuehrer Headquarters, demanding to know where Kluge was. It further instructed him to find out and to report the results of his investigations hourly.

Hans von Kluge finally turned up at Eberbach's CP at 9:00 that night, shaken and disheveled. What had happened to him was not unusual. He had set out in his Horch, the German equivalent of the jeep, accompanied by his son, Lieutenant Colonel Guenther von Kluge, and his aide, Lieutenant Karl Tangermann. They were preceded by a motorcycle with sidecar and followed by the marshal's communications truck. The dis-

astrous state of the road system had slowed him down, and Jabos destroyed his radio truck, killing all four occupants. Then the
fighter-bombers had forced the marshal and his party to take cover,
where they had remained all day, completely cut off from the outside
world. When nightfall approached, the enemy airplanes had returned to
base, but Kluge's little group got lost in the darkness and confusion.
When he finally arrived at the panzer group CP, he had been missing
for 12 full hours.

Hitler, meanwhile, suffered a major attack of paranoia. He had already
received indications from Himmler that Kluge had been aware of the
July 20 conspiracy, had done nothing to thwart it, and may have been
directly involved. Now Hitler convinced himself that the missing field
marshal must be secretly negotiating with the Western Allies. This "fact"
was reinforced by a dispatch von Kluge sent to Jodl at 2 A.M. on August
16, in which he stated that the troops in the pocket simply were not
strong enough to defeat the enemy, and it would be a fatal mistake to
cling to the hope that they would be successful. After a long consultation
with Hausser and Eberbach, he described the deteriorating situation in
the pocket: "roads virtually impassable, tanks repeatedly immobilized
for lack of fuel, ammunition supplies erratic, troops hungry and exhausted, communications almost non-existent."[12] He recommended that
the 5th Panzer and 7th Armies be withdrawn through the ever-
narrowing gap between Falaise and Argentan as rapidly as possible,
while there was still time for them to escape. This recommendation had
the full support of Eberbach, Hausser, and Dietrich, the marshal quickly
pointed out. As always, Kluge liked to lace unpleasant messages with
endorsements from SS generals and officers perceived as pro-Nazi. It did
him no good this time, however; Adolf Hitler had already fired von
Kluge.

At 7:30 P.M. on August 15, on the recommendation of General Jodl, he
named SS General Hausser acting commander of Army Group B. By this
time, he had narrowed the choice for the new OB West to Albert Kesselring or Walter Model. (Jodl apparently recommended Hausser as a
permanent appointment, but Hitler had always distrusted him because
of his beady eyes. The fact that he had lost one of them in the Fuehrer's
service apparently did not count very much; besides, he was not "pure"
SS, having been a member of the General Staff and having retired from
the army as a lieutenant general, and he had once retreated against orders at Kharkov.) Hitler finally decided on Model because he felt that
Kesselring was indispensable in Italy. For the moment, however, he did
not inform Kluge that he was about to be replaced. He merely signaled
that Kluge was forbidden to go back inside the pocket.

Hans von Kluge spent the morning of August 16 at Fontaine l'Abbe,
agonizing. Why had he heard nothing from Fuehrer Headquarters, other

than an order from Hitler, instructing him to leave the pocket immediately and to direct operations from outside the cauldron? Had he not made it clear that speed was of the essence? Early in the afternoon he telephoned Jodl, who expressed sympathy for Kluge's position and promised that authorization to withdraw would be coming shortly. After a telephone conversation with General Speidel, he instructed his subordinates to start preparing for the withdrawal immediately. He had already authorized Hausser, Dietrich and Eberbach to send their non-essential administrative personnel out of the cauldron.

The Falaise pocket was now 35 miles long (east to west) and 15 miles wide (north to south). Its eastern end was essentially defined by the Dives River, which ran generally southeast to northwest and was located about 5 miles east of the Falaise-Argentan highway. To reach safety, the Germans would have to reach the eastern bank of the Dives. Kluge's plan called for the 7th Army (at the western extremity of the pocket) to conduct a phased withdrawal across the Orne River on the nights of August 16 and 17. Part of the army would then be used to reinforce the 5th Panzer Army, while the rest headed across the Dives to safety. Then the 5th Panzer Army and Panzer Group Eberbach would conduct their own phased withdrawal across the Dives. Table 6.1 shows the Order of Battle of Army Group B on August 15, along with OKW and OB West units in Army Group B's zone of operations. Panzer Group Eberbach was not reported separately.

Although it was probably the best one that anyone could have come up with, this plan was full of danger. The German forces would have to cross two sizable rivers (the Orne, then the Dives) under pressure from three Allied armies. To make things immeasurably more difficult, the terrain of central Normandy was hilly and the road network was poor (especially east to west), virtually every foot of the pocket was within range of Allied artillery, and their fighter-bombers seemed to be everywhere. To complicate the problem even further, there was a severe shortage of fuel, supplies, and ammunition within the pocket. (Fortunately for the Germans, Normandy was a rich agricultural region, and German troops were able—to a certain extent—to live off of the land.) Since traffic control was absolutely essential, Kluge stripped the LVIII Panzer Corps of its troops and placed it in charge of policing traffic.[13]

The German withdrawal from the Falaise pocket began on the night of August 16–17. There was no panic, at least for the moment, although morale was falling and there were incidents of desertion. Kluge had set up a rigid timetable, and his commanders followed it exactly; the moment when German organization and discipline dissolved had not yet arrived, despite the deteriorating situation. The roads were clogged with vehicles of every description and were under constant artillery fire. Many supply units had already been evacuated, and those that remained

Table 6.1
Order of Battle, Army Group B, August 15, 1944

Armed Forces Netherlands

    347th Infantry Division
    719th Infantry Division

15th Army

    LXXXIX CORPS
        70th Infantry Division
        165th Reserve Division
        712th Infantry Division

    LXXXII CORPS
        47th Infantry Division
        18th Luftwaffe Field Division[1]
        49th Infantry Division[1]
        182nd Reserve Division

5th Panzer Army

    LXVII CORPS
        348th Infantry Division
        245th Infantry Division
        226th Infantry Division
        5th Security Regiment

    LXXXVI CORPS
        711th Infantry Division
        346th Infantry Division
        272nd Infantry Division
        Elements, 710th Infantry Division

    I SS PANZER CORPS
        85th Infantry Division
        12th SS Panzer Division
        89th Infantry Division

    LXXIV CORPS
        271st Infantry Division
        277th Infantry Division
        276th Infantry Division
        Elements, 21st Panzer Division
        326th Infantry Division

    II SS PANZER CORPS
        21st Panzer Division (−)
        9th SS Panzer Division
        3rd Parachute Division

    5th Panzer Army Reserve
        136th Special Purposes Division (z.b.B.)

Table 6.1 (*continued*)

7th Army

II PARACHUTE CORPS
Kampfgruppe, Panzer Lehr Division
353 Infantry Division + Elements, 1st SS Panzer Division
Kampfgruppe, 363rd Infantry Division + Elements, 331st Infantry Division

LXXXIV CORPS
Kampfgruppe, 243rd Infantry Division
84th Infantry Division
Kampfgruppe, 17th SS Panzer Grenadier Division
Kampfgruppe, 275th Infantry Division
10th SS Panzer Division

LVIII PANZER CORPS
708th Infantry Division
Remnants, 5th Parachute Division
Elements, 9th Panzer Division
Kampfgruppe, 2nd SS Panzer Division

XXXXVII PANZER CORPS
116th Panzer Division
Elements, 9th Panzer Division
2nd Panzer Division
Remnants, Panzer Lehr Division
1st SS Panzer Division
Kampfgruppe, 9th Panzer Division

Directly Under OKW

Staff, 1st Parachute Army
319th Infantry Division
Fortress St. Malo
    Remnants, 77th Infantry Division
    Remnants, 91st Air Landing Division
    Elements, 5th Parachute Division

Fortress Brest
    343rd Infantry Division (−)
    2nd Parachute Division
    Remnants, 266th Infantry Division

Fortress Lorient
    XXV Corps
    Elements, 265th Infantry Division

Fortress St. Nazaire
    Elements, 265th Infantry Division

Table 6.1 (*continued*)

OB West

  Military Governor, Belgium, Northern France
  Military Governor, France
  Staff, LXXX Corps
  Staff, LXVI Corps

Note:
[1] In transit.

Source: Kurt Mehner, ed., *Die Geheimen Tagesberichte der deutschen Wehrmachtfuehrung im Zweiten Weltkrieg, 1939–1945* (Osnabrueck: 1985), Volume 10, pp. 507–8.

often could not reach their destinations due to the roads, which were jammed with weapons, heavy equipment, and vehicles, many of which were burning. Already self-propelled guns and tanks (which consumed three gallons of fuel per mile traveled) were falling out, due to dry fuel tanks. Many had to be destroyed or abandoned.

While Kluge's evacuation began, the Canadians continued their relentless attacks. Kurt Meyer slowly withdrew his battered 12th SS Panzer Division back to Hill 159, a mile north of Falaise. He had done a brilliant job of keeping Montgomery out of the town, but this was the last defensive position, and Simonds already had two armored divisions across the Laison River. As the Canadian artillery began shelling the hill, Meyer fell backwards: A shell fragment had struck him in the head, and blood was pouring down his face. His men managed to get him back to an aid station, where medics inserted several stitches in his head. By the time he returned to the front, the Canadians had overrun Hill 159, and the remnants of the Hitler Youth Division were falling back into Falaise itself. With a heavy heart, Meyer gave the order to retreat, leaving behind a rear guard of 60 men and two Tiger tanks, which took up final defensive positions in and around the École Supérieure. They were being sacrificed, and they knew it.

After a three-hour battle, the École Supérieure was finally stormed about midnight by the Royal Fusiliers, supported by tanks and mortar fire. Fifty-four of the Germans were killed, and of the six who surrendered, four were wounded. The birthplace of William the Conqueror was finally in Allied hands, although Falaise was by now mostly rubble.[14]

Hans von Kluge's military career came to an end on the evening of August 17, when Field Marshal Walter Model arrived at La Roche Guyon, less than 48 hours after he had received his first telephone call from the Fuehrer concerning the possibility of assuming command in the

West. Like Kluge, "the Fuehrer's Fireman" was commander in chief of both Army Group B and OB West. His new Army Group B chief of staff, Lieutenant General Dr. Hans Speidel, wrote of him:

Model was short of stature, somewhat uncouth, extra-ordinarily active of mind and body. He hardly knew what sleep was and was fearless in the heat of battle. But his keen tactical eye was not balanced by an instinct for the possible. He thought too highly of his own ability, was erratic, and lacked a sense of moderation. . . . His unstable temperament made him susceptible to the ideology of Hitler, often against his better knowledge.[15]

General of Panzer Troops Baron Hasso von Manteuffel, whom Model had threatened to court-martial during a disagreement on the Eastern Front in the winter of 1941–42, and who later commanded the 5th Panzer Army under him during the Battle of the Bulge, said of him:

Model was a very good tactician, and better in defence than in the attack. . . . His manner was rough, and his methods were not always acceptable in the higher quarters of the German Army, but they were both to the Fuehrer's liking. Model stood up to Hitler in a way that hardly anyone else dared to do, and even refused to carry out orders with which he disagreed.[16]

There was much in Model's background to recommend itself to Hitler. He was not of the aristocracy or of the Prussian *Junker* class; rather, he was the son of a Lutheran schoolteacher. Like Hitler, therefore, he had a middle-class background. There was no military tradition in his antecedents, and he owed his rank to individual effort and achievement, rather than to family connections. Also like Hitler, he had fought in the trenches in World War I and had earned the same important decorations: the Iron Cross, 1st Class; the Iron Cross, 2nd Class; and the Wounded Badge (both had been wounded twice). Unlike Hitler, Model had undergone officer training before the war (1910) and had been recommended for General Staff training by his division commander, who was none other than Oskar, the son of the kaiser and prince of Prussia. After an abbreviated General Staff course, Model had ended the war as a captain.

Model's career was characterized by extreme energy, almost incredible physical courage, hard work, aloofness, and a reputation for being a harsh and demanding superior and an outspoken and uncomfortable subordinate. He had no close friends. Very ambitious and very good at his job, especially in a crisis situation, he pushed both himself and his men ruthlessly, and he was utterly lacking in either fear or tact. He was nevertheless respected within the army as an efficient and forward-thinking officer; he never stooped to looking for scapegoats or relieving other officers to save himself, unlike Kluge and Brauchitsch. Model had reached the rank of lieutenant colonel by the time the Nazis came to power in 1933.

Walter Model was an early advocate of mobile and armored warfare and was an early convert to the blitzkrieg theories of Heinz Guderian. He was also a Nazi sympathizer who impressed Hitler as early as 1938. He advanced rapidly during the Nazi era, serving as an infantry battalion commander (1933–34), commander of the 2nd Infantry Regiment (1934–35), chief of the technical and doctrine section of the General Staff (1935–38), chief of staff of IV Corps (1938–39), chief of staff of 16th Army (1939–40), commander of the 3rd Panzer Division (1940–41), and commander of XXXXI Panzer Corps (1941–January 1942). During this process, he fought in Poland, Belgium, France, and Russia and was promoted to colonel (1934), major general (1938), lieutenant general (1940), general of panzer troops (1941), and colonel general (February 1942). It was as commander of the 9th Army on the Eastern Front, however, that he came into his own. The battered 9th was nearly surrounded at Rzhev during the Soviet winter offensive of 1941–42, and its commander, Colonel General Adolf Strauss, could not stand up under the strain. He was replaced by Model, who rallied the army and checked the Red advance, largely on the force of his own live-wire personality. The incredibly energetic and optimistic general was likely to show up at any place and at any time, often in the thick of the fighting, and his utter disregard for his own safety especially endeared him to his men, who felt he would not ask them to do anything he would not do himself. With renewed courage and determination, 9th Army successfully beat back every Soviet attack, despite being outnumbered at least 4 to 1.

At one point during the battle, Model and Hitler had their only confrontation. Another major Soviet offensive aimed at destroying the Rzhev salient was obviously about to begin, so the general visited Fuehrer Headquarters and asked for reinforcements. Hitler agreed to give him a panzer corps but also told him where it was to be employed—i.e., where Hitler and OKW expected the main blow to strike. This interference Model refused to accept. After a brief argument, Model screwed his monocle into his right eye, coldly looked down on Hitler as if he were still a corporal, and asked: "Fuehrer, who commands 9th Army—you or I?" Hitler's mouth fell open—he was not accustomed to people speaking to him in that manner. Before the surprised and befuddled dictator could regain his composure and respond, the general—in the manner of a pure-bred Prussian—informed him that he (Model) knew much more about the local tactical situation than did anyone at Fuehrer Headquarters—including Hitler—and that he insisted upon being allowed to conduct the battle as he saw fit. The flabbergasted Fuehrer, for once, backed down. "Did you see that eye?" Hitler later asked a member of his entourage. "I trust that man to do it. But I wouldn't want to serve under him!"

Shortly thereafter, the Russians attacked just exactly where Model said they would and were slaughtered by the recently arrived panzer corps. Hitler never again doubted Model's ability or judgment. Again and again staffs were amazed, as Hitler sacked a commander for disagreeing with him or for wanting to retreat. Then Model would take charge. He would sometimes offer the same proposals as the previous commander, and Hitler would approve them without a word of protest. If Model wanted to retreat, Adolf Hitler reasoned, then retreat was, without doubt, the right thing to do.

Walter Model unquestionably saved the 9th Army and the Rzhev salient in 1942. After commanding 9th Army on the Eastern Front for more than a year, he was given a number of challenging assignments in rapid succession, including commander in chief of Army Groups North, South, North Ukraine, and Center, earning him a promotion to field marshal (March 1, 1944) and the reputation throughout the Reich as "the Fuehrer's fireman." He was only given the most difficult and dangerous assignments. It should not have surprised anybody that he turned up in France in August 1944, just as the Western Front collapsed.

After meeting his new staff, the astonishingly energetic and humorless Model was up early on the morning of August 18, heading for the combat zone. He scheduled a 9 A.M. meeting with Dietrich, Hausser, and Eberbach at Fontaine l'Abbe, but Hausser decided that the situation in 7th Army's zone was too critical for him to leave his CP, so he sent his chief of staff, Colonel von Gersdorff, instead. Eberbach, who had to travel further, was delayed by fighter-bombers. It took him six hours to cover 45 miles, and he did not arrive until after 11 A.M. In an angry mood, Eberbach bluntly informed Model that the morale of the German soldiers in the West was now poor. "The Atlantic Wall has been represented to the German soldier as impregnable for too long. The invasion has been represented as a certain defeat for the invader. We have been promised in vain new armies, new air forces, and new submarines. And here we are waging a poor man's war." Eberbach went on to state that the morale of the troops had collapsed.

"These are opinions, not facts," Model retorted.

"Well, here are the facts, Herr Feldmarschall," Eberbach continued. "For the first time in the history of this war our deserters are no longer conscripted Alsatians or Poles, but [native] Germans. Serviceable tanks are found on the terrain, deserted by their crews, brand-new rifles clutter up the ditches, and trucks are abandoned. There are laggards everywhere. Posts for arresting deserters behind the lines have been formed."

Not even the SS divisions were fighting with their former enthusiasm, he concluded.[17]

Hausser's appreciation of the situation, presented by Colonel von Gersdorff, was not this negative, but it was also pessimistic. (Eberbach's situation report was probably overly pessimistic. The morale of the German soldier had not yet collapsed, but Eberbach saw it coming.) After listening to their reports, Model issued his orders for the evacuation of the pocket and the withdrawal behind the Seine. Dietrich was instructed to pull out his Headquarters, 5th Panzer Army, and to take charge of the forces east of the pocket. Hausser was placed in overall command in the cauldron, and Eberbach was given the responsibility (under Hausser) of keeping the gap open until 7th Army could escape. The II SS Panzer Corps was to keep the northern shoulder open, while the XXXXVII Panzer performed the same task to the south.

Model completed a brief inspection of the front and returned to his Army Group B Headquarters without incident. He was, however, extremely and uncharacteristically depressed. He slumped into a chair and told General Speidel that the situation was far worse than he excepted and rivaled anything he saw on the Eastern Front. Eberbach and von Gersdorff were not so lucky. It took the panzer group commander almost seven hours to reach his destination (the Headquarters of the II SS Panzer Corps, which was only 20 miles away), and he had several brushes with death in the form of fighter-bombers. Gersdorff was even less fortunate. His car was struck by lightning near Chambois, and he was painfully injured. He did not arrive back at 7th Army HQ (located in a rock quarry near Villedieu, a village 2 miles south of Trun) until late that night.

Upon returning to La Roche Guyon, Model contacted Jodl and told him of his plans. He hoped to have all of his troops west of the Falaise-Argentan road by sunset; by nightfall on August 20, he hoped to be across the Touques River (20 miles further east). By this time, he hoped to have several panzer divisions back on the Seine, while Meindl's II Parachute Corps covered the retreat of the rest of the army group. After the retreat was finished, his line would be defended (north to south) by the 7th Army, 5th Panzer Army (again under Eberbach), and the 1st Army, whose staff was now coming up from southwestern France. Hitler naturally wanted Model to hold Paris. The field marshal knew that this would be impossible, once the Battle of the Falaise pocket was over, so he presented OKW with a long list of reinforcements he would require in order to successfully defend the city. It included 20 replacement battalions (4 of them for the panzer divisions and 6 for the SS panzer divisions), 5 army engineer battalions, at least 270 tanks or assault guns, 9 artillery battalions (to replace only the guns lost by the panzer divisions), plus huge numbers of trucks and motorized vehicles. He also asked for the six new panzer brigades, then being formed in Germany.[18] Since he knew that Hitler could not meet all of these requirements, Model left Paris out of his calculations and accepted the loss of the French capital as a matter of long-term policy.

Meanwhile, the U.S. 3rd Army added considerably to Model's problems. On August 13, while the XV Corps clashed with Panzer Group Eberbach in and around Argentan, Patton assembled his XX and XII Corps (each with one infantry and one armored division) in the Le Mans area. General Bradley was not sure what to do with these divisions, but Patton had less trouble making up his mind. Instead of sending the XX Corps north, to support the XV Corps at Argentan, he proposed sending it on a wide swing to the Seine via Dreux, 60 miles to the northeast. Meanwhile, the XII would drive for Chartres, with the long-range mission of reaching the Seine upriver from Paris. The dynamic 3rd Army commander convinced Bradley, who then went one step further. He suggested taking the XV Corps (controlling the 5th Armored and 79th Infantry Divisions) out of the line and sending it toward Dreux. The XX Corps (Major General Walton Walker) could then advance on Chartres, and the XII Corps (Major General Gilbert Cook) could take an even wider flanking movement to the southwest, toward Orleans and the Loire River. Meanwhile, the 2nd French and 90th Infantry Divisions at Argentan would be handed over to 1st Army, which would direct the American side of the battle at Falaise. Patton eagerly accepted this proposal. In effect, the 3rd Army surged out for the Seine, with corps objectives located along a 100-mile stretch of the river, both above and below the French capital city, with a secondary thrust toward the southwest, threatening the lines of communication of Army G (lst and 19th Armies). Patton began his advance at 10:30 P.M. on August 14. By the evening of August 15, the vanguards of the 7th Armored Division had gained 60 miles and were on the outskirts of Chartres, just 50 miles from Paris. Here the remnants of two German regiments were able to make a stand, but the city fell after the U.S. 5th Infantry Division joined the battle on August 16, and 2,000 more Germans were captured. That same afternoon, the U.S. XX Corps reached the Seine at Mantes, 30 miles downriver. German armies were beginning to collapse all over France.

It could have been much worse for Army Group B. On August 14, thinking that the Germans must be streaming east by now, instead of just holding fast (as was the case), General Bradley acted very conservatively (lost his nerve?) and halted the American spearheads just north of Argentan, on the pretext that it would be improper for him to cross an interallied boundary line drawn by Montgomery some days before. Bradley should have signaled Monty and asked him to move the boundary line to the north, so that Patton could link up with Dempsey's spearheads and encircle the 7th and 5th Panzer Armies, but he did not.

Eisenhower later backed Bradley's decision, stating that he also did not want to run the risk of accidentally causing a collision and a bloody battle between Americans and the British. Presumably, however, even if there had been cases of friendly fire, both sides would have stopped firing when they discovered at whom they were shooting. And as tragic as it would have been for a few dozen Allied soldiers to have been accidentally killed by friends, would not the complete destruction of the entire 5th Panzer and 7th Armies been worth the loss? Patton, on the other hand, was furious at the halt order. He blamed Montgomery (as usual) and wanted to continue his drive to the north—even if it meant throwing the British Army back into the sea for another Dunkirk. Of course, he was speaking in jest when he said that. I think.

No doubt Patton's attitude was a factor in Bradley's decision to turn the southern wing of the encirclement over to Lieutenant General Courtney Hodges's 1st U.S. Army. Patton was given the task of continuing his advance through the Orleans Gap and beyond the Seine. This mission was more to his liking, and he happily set off, swamping the German 1st Army's defensive lines before that army could man them.

Friday, August 18, was another disastrous day for the Wehrmacht on the Western Front. When dawn broke, 11 of the 20 divisions trapped in the Falaise pocket were still operating as divisions: 1st SS Panzer, 10th SS Panzer, 12th SS Panzer, 2nd Panzer, 116th Panzer, 3rd Parachute, and the 84th, 276th, 277th, 326th and 353rd Infantry. Allied air attacks, however, were relentless, and Army Group B had already ordered the flak batteries to leave the rapidly forming pocket during the night of August 14–15. For the last three days there had been nothing to protect the defending infantry. By morning, the Canadian 4th Armored Division pushed to within 10 miles of Trun and 15 miles of Chambois—the two key bridges along the Dives between which all German escape efforts were directed. To the south, Gerow's U.S. V Corps advanced northward with the French 2nd Armored and U.S. 80th and 90th Infantry Divisions to try to sever the last line of retreat. By nightfall, Trun had fallen to the Canadians, and the American infantry had gained 2 to 3 miles against desperate resistance from the 116th Panzer Division and the 728th Grenadier Regiment (of the 708th Infantry Division) and were on the outskirts of Chambois. The last hard surface road to the east was cut when Thun fell. The gap between the British and American army groups along the Dives was now less than 5 miles. The Germans, meanwhile, stabilized the northern flank of the Falaise pocket near Mont Ormel, although Hill 262, a key position 3 miles north of Chambois, remained in Polish hands. The escape route to the east was still open for the 7th Army, however, because the Allies failed to capture the stone bridge at St. Lambert.

At this point, Model's own headquarters was temporarily eliminated from the battle. An American detachment arrived on the Seine, just across the river from La Roche Guyon, and began shelling the HQ with mortars. There was considerable confusion as Army Group B evacuated the château and headed for Margival, a town 5 miles north of the Soissons and 60 miles west of Paris, where it resumed operations the next day. One of the last to leave was Field Marshal Guenther Hans von Kluge, who bid an emotional farewell to the members of his former staff. Kluge was in no hurry to return to Germany, for he knew that the Gestapo would soon be after him, if it was not already. He finally headed back, by car, on August 19. He was under no illusions as to what his fate would be if he completed the journey. He ordered his driver to halt in a peaceful place near Metz, the scene of some of his World War I battles, not far from the place where General von Stuelpnagel had shot and blinded himself in an unsuccessful suicide attempt a few days before. Kluge spread a blanket and asked to be left alone. Then he quietly bit down on a cyanide capsule. His farewell letter to Hitler read:

When you receive these lines I shall be no more. I cannot bear the accusation that I sealed the fate of the West by taking the wrong measures . . . I have never feared death. Life for me, who am already included on the list of war criminals to be surrendered, has no more meaning. . . .

Both Rommel and I, and probably all the leaders here in the West, who have experienced the struggle with the English and Americans and [witnessed] their wealth in material, foresaw the development that has now appeared. . . . Our views were not dictated by pessimism but by sober recognition of the facts.

I do not know if Field Marshal Model, who has proven himself in all respects, will be capable of mastering the situation. I hope so with all my heart. If that is not to be the case and if the new weapons—especially air weapons, which you are so eagerly awaiting, are not to bring you success, then, my Fuehrer, make up your mind to finish the war. The German people have endured such unspeakable sufferings that the time has come to put an end to their terrors. There must be ways to arrive at this conclusion and, above all, to prevent the Reich from being condemned to the hell of Bolshevism. . . . I have always admired your greatness and your iron will to maintain yourself and National Socialism. If your destiny overcomes your will and your genius, it will be because Providence has willed it so. You have fought a good and honorable fight. History will bear witness to this. If it ever becomes necessary, show yourself great enough to put an end to a struggle which has become hopeless.

I depart from you, my Fuehrer, as one who stood nearer to you than you perhaps realize, in the consciousness that I did my duty to the utmost.

Hitler read the letter without comment. Then he canceled Kluge's state funeral (Rundstedt was to deliver the eulogy) and ordered that he be buried quietly, on the grounds of his estate, with military pallbearers but without military honors. The propaganda ministry announced that he had died of a cerebral hemorrhage.

Two weeks later, on August 31, Hitler commented to Generals Hans Krebs and Siegfried Westphal: "I myself twice promoted him [Kluge]. I gave him a big gratuity so that he should have no worries and I gave him a big supplement to his pay as field marshal. So for me this [betrayal] is the bitterest and most disappointing thing which could happen."[19]

Saturday, August 19, dawned clear and sunny. With it appeared swarms of Jabos and Allied bombers, which destroyed hundreds of stalled and trapped German vehicles. The pocket was now about six miles long and six miles wide and was crammed full of German units. "It was almost impossible to fire an artillery shell or drop a bomb into the pocket without hitting German troops or their vehicles," Breuer wrote later.[20] As usual, the Luftwaffe was nowhere to be seen. The *Feldgrau* joked to their buddies that it was easy to identify the nationality of airplanes above you in Normandy. If they were camouflaged, they were British. If they were silver, they were American. And if they were not there at all, they were Luftwaffe. The Allies' complete domination of the air made it impossible for the *Soldaten* on the ground to counter Allied moves in anything that remotely resembled a timely manner. As a result, the Allied armies completed the encirclement of the 5th Panzer and 7th Armies about 6 P.M. on August 19, when the Poles joined hands with elements of the U.S. 90th Infantry Division at Chambois. Like all such encirclements, however, this one was loose at the moment it was completed. Along the five-mile stretch of the Dives from Trun to Chambois, the Allied hold was weak. For part of the distance, the Poles could not establish a continuous line or even cover the gap with patrols; they had to depend on weapons fire only, and that was not enough. It was still possible for the Germans to get out of the pocket by crossing the Dives over the stone bridge at St. Lambert. In the meantime, General Bradley was anxious to complete a wider encirclement, to trap the German forces between the Falaise pocket and the Seine. Haislip's XV U.S. Corps had already made a good start, and now Bradley decided to commit the XIX Corps (of the 1st Army), with its 2nd Armored and 28th and 30th Infantry Divisions. The problem, however, was that the rapid American advances were outpacing their ability to supply their forward divisions.

Inside the cauldron, the pocket continued to contract, but it did not collapse. The rear guard, Meindl's II Parachute Corps skillfully withdrew to positions around La Londe, a few miles south of Trun and the Dives River. Meindl's corps included the 3rd Parachute Division and 353rd

Figure 6.3
The Closing Pocket, August 18, 1944

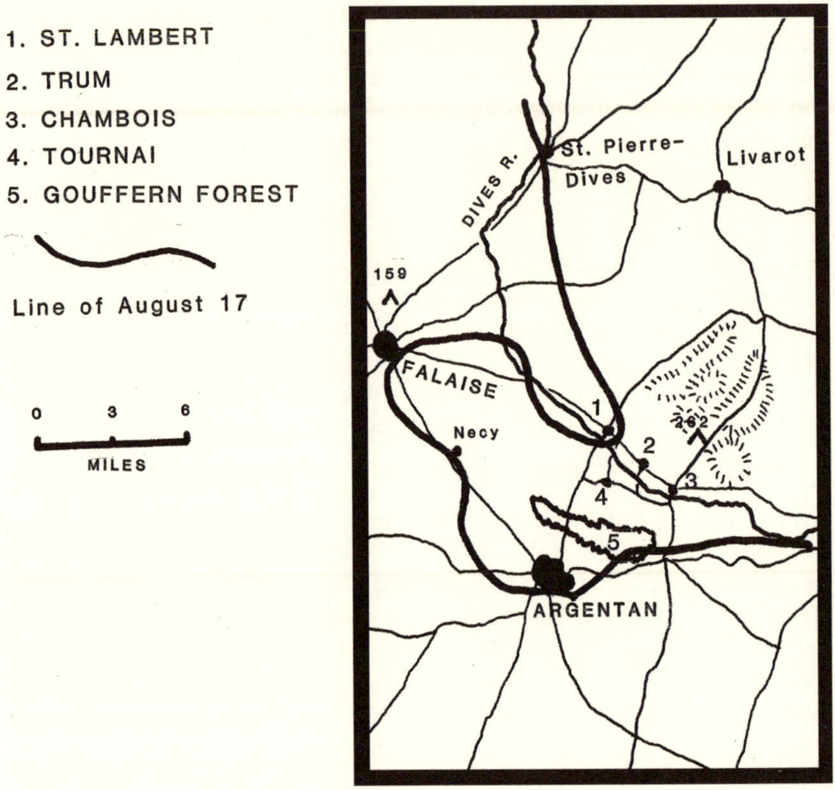
1. ST. LAMBERT
2. TRUM
3. CHAMBOIS
4. TOURNAI
5. GOUFFERN FOREST
Line of August 17
0
3
6
MILES
St. Pierre-
Dives
Livarot
DIVES R.
159
FALAISE
Necy
262
1
2
3
4
5
ARGENTAN

Infantry Division, which was well led by the highly capable and imperturbable Lieutenant General Paul Mahlmann.[21]

Knowing that the pocket was about to close, Meindl was ready with a breakout plan. During the day, his artillery fired all of its remaining shells; that night, he planned to assemble his troops in a wooded area, abandon his guns, and head for Hill 262. (Figure 6.3 shows the area east of Falaise.) He planned to infiltrate out of the pocket single file, in two columns, bypassing all obstacles and resistance. One column would be commanded by Colonel Hermann Blauensteiner, his chief of staff; Meindl would lead the other himself. Their men would only be permitted to fire when they reached the Hill 262 area. Hausser (who was still in the pocket) immediately approved the plan and told Meindl that he could expect help from the 2nd SS Panzer and 9th SS Panzer Divisions, which were already east of the Dives. They would attack to the west and try to link up with the II Parachute Corps. Hausser did not tell Meindl that the two divisions had less than 30 tanks between them.

During the day, Meindl's troops huddled in the woods, ate what little food they had left, and prepared for the breakout. Some of them even managed to get a little sleep. Morale was surprisingly good as they set out in the rain at 10:30 P.M. They carefully avoided several enemy tanks and reached the Dives two hours later. There were several firefights in the dark, and Major Eric Stephan, the commander of the 9th Parachute Regiment, was killed in action. Another casualty was Lieutenant General Richard Schimpf, the commander of the 3rd Parachute Division, who was painfully wounded by a bullet in the leg.[22] He was carried out of the pocket by his aides. Meindl personally assumed command of the 3rd Parachute Division.

The rain ended about dawn, just as Meindl came within sight of Hill 262. He was bitterly disappointed to find that the 2nd SS Panzer Division had not recaptured the position during the night—it was still strongly occupied by the Poles. Some of his men were on the point of launching a direct, frontal attack on the hill when Meindl arrived and ordered them to work their way to the north, in an effort to avoid the Polish division. Later that morning, Meindl met with General Hausser. This conference was not held in a luxurious French château, as in the past, but in a bomb crater, about a mile south of the hill. Hausser told Meindl that the 2nd SS Panzer was moving south and would attack the northern end of Hill 262 that afternoon. He asked Meindl to organize an attack from the south. By nightfall, much of the 1st Polish Armored Division was surrounded in the area of Hill 262. Although the Germans were not able to break their perimeter, the Poles were no longer able to control all of the terrain between the parachute corps and the SS panzer division and were soon low in ammunition. News of this gap in the Allied line spread like wildfire, and thousands of German soldiers escaped during the night.

General Meindl remained behind inside the pocket. His foremost concern was his wounded. How was he going to get them out? The only available route was the Coudehard Road, and it was controlled by Polish guns. Meindl organized several large Red Cross flags and put the wounded in whatever vehicles were available. At 6:30 P.M. on August 20, he stopped all traffic on the road for 30 minutes. Then he sent the first column of wounded down the road. The Poles did not fire. A half an hour later, he sent the second column. Again the gallant Poles—who had plenty of reason to hate the Germans—held their fire. This process continued until all of the wounded had been evacuated. "Not a shot was fired at them," the normally arrogant and egotistical Meindl commented later, "and I recognized, with thankfulness in my heart, the chivalrous attitude of the enemy. . . . After the ugly scenes I had witnessed that day, the nobility of our enemies made me forget for a moment the nastiness of it all and I offered thanks in my heart in the name of the wounded."[23]

In the meantime, SS General Hausser directed the bulk of his panzer units into the narrow area of the Dives River between Chambois and the hamlet of Saint-Lambert. Here he attempted to break out through the Canadian 4th Armored and 90th Infantry Divisions with his 1st SS, 2nd Panzer, 12th SS, and 116th Panzer Divisions—or what was left of them. Once the pride of the Wehrmacht, they were now in remnants, almost completely disorganized, disheveled, dirty, unshaven, and near exhaustion—looking as much like outlaws on the run as soldiers. The German combat formations began to collapse on August 20. Communications broke down completely, and the entire battlefield was littered with burning and abandoned German vehicles, tanks, guns, and destroyed equipment. Dead horses lay everywhere, and travel on the roads was impossible. The horror was intensified by the ubiquitous Allied fighter-bomber and the fact that every foot of the pocket was within range of Allied artillery, and their guns never stopped firing. The German artillery, on the other hand, was silent. All of their guns had already been abandoned or destroyed, and the German field artillery units had ceased to exist. Thousands of men who had once been the Fuehrer's elite were now stragglers, desperately seeking a way out of the hell that was Falaise—little more than fugitives. Only junior officers and NCOs, in command of small bands, maintained what discipline remained within the pocket. They were the only hope Hausser had left of extracting even part of the 7th Army from the cauldron.

True to a promise he made to Meindl, Hausser did not launch his armored breakout attempt until after midnight on Sunday, August 20. Colonel Baron von Gersdorff, the chief of staff of the 7th Army, led one of the first battle groups (from the 1st SS Panzer Division), which crossed the Dives between Chambers and Saint-Lambert, and surprised and captured part of the U.S. 90th Infantry Division. Gersdorff disarmed his prisoners and turned them loose: He was only interested in moving east as fast as he could, and he would not do anything to slow his escape. After all, dawn, as he knew, would bring the fighter-bombers.

At the same time, Lieutenant General Otto Elfeldt and "Panzer" Meyer led the remnants of the 12th SS Panzer, 84th Infantry, and 363rd Infantry Divisions and a battle group of the 1st SS, as well as the staff company of the LXXXIV Corps, in a breakout attempt south of Chambois. During a fierce battle in the darkness, they were checked by the Americans. Since it was clear that they could not escape as a unit, Elfeldt and Meyer ordered their men to split up and escape into the night in small groups. It was virtually an "every man for himself" order. Individually and in small bands, they attempted to cross the river between Chambois and Saint-Lambert. Oberfuehrer Meyer was successful in crossing the stream and in infiltrating Allied lines northeast of Hill 262, where he was rescued by elements of the 2nd SS Panzer Division. General Elfeldt was not so lucky. In the darkness, he and the remnants of his staff blundered into an Allied tank battalion, which captured them all. The LXXXIV Corps ceased to exist.

Nearby, Germany lost two other excellent commanders: 36-year-old SS Brigadier Theodor Wisch and 30-year-old SS Colonel Max Wuensche. "Teddy" Wisch had joined the SS as a private in 1933 and had succeeded Sepp Dietrich as commander of the elite 1st SS Panzer Division "Leibstandarte Adolf Hitler" in early 1944. On August 20, he was so severely wounded in both legs that he was never reemployed.[24]

Max Wuensche was blond and strikingly handsome in his black SS tanker's uniform. He could easily have been the model for an SS or Hitler Youth recruiting poster. Wuensche had joined the Black Corps as a private in 1934 and was assigned to the Leibstandarte. He had been transferred to the 12th SS Panzer Division "Hitler Jugend" in early 1944 and had commanded the 12th SS Panzer Regiment with considerable distinction. He had been awarded the Oak Leaves on August 11. (He had earned the Knight's Cross in Russia.) He was severely wounded during the breakout but was carried out of the pocket by his men. Although he succeeded in escaping Falaise, he was too badly wounded to make his way across the Seine and was taken prisoner by British pursuit forces on August 24.[25]

Shortly after daybreak, the 2nd Panzer Division—which was down to its last 15 tanks—overran Saint-Lambert and captured the bridge across the Dives. Its commander, Lieutenant General Baron Heinrich von Luettwitz, ignored his wounds and personally led the attack. "The crossing of the Dives bridge was particularly horrible," Luettwitz recalled later, because of "the bodies of killed men, dead horses, vehicles, and other equipment having been hurled from the bridge into the river to form there a gruesome tangled mass."[26] Why no one on the Allied side thought of blowing up this small, stone structure is one of the minor mysteries of the campaign. The remnants of the 2nd Panzer pushed on to the northeast and made good its escape, even though it had lost 90% of its armor in the Normandy cauldron. Half of the 116th Panzer Division followed Luettwitz and made good its escape. The other half of the division—including its last 10 tanks—tried to break out near Trun but was smashed and destroyed.

General Hausser also escaped during the night of August 20–21, but not in the manner in which he envisioned. He joined a battle group of the 1st SS Panzer Division and was marching forward on foot with a machine pistol draped around his neck when an Allied shell exploded in front of him, and a piece of shrapnel hit him in the face. Some SS troops placed him on the stern of a panzer and eventually got the seriously wounded officer back to German lines after a number of narrow escapes in the darkness. He was carried to the Luftwaffe hospital at Greifswald, where he slowly began to recover. Meanwhile, Baron Hans von Funck took temporary command of the 7th Army.

It began to rain again that night, but the Germans continued to exit the pocket until dawn, when the last blocking units made their escape to the northeast. The last organized unit to get away was the covering force, General of Infantry Erich Straube's LXXIV Corps, which included the 276th, 277th, 326th, 84th, and 363rd Infantry Divisions. It was a chaotic escape, as communications were completely disrupted and overall control was impossible. Colonel Wilhelm Viebig, the commander of the 277th Infantry, could not get in touch with anybody in authority and broke out northwest of Saint-Lambert on his own responsibility during the night of August 20–21. A few days later, he was able to assemble a "division" of 2,500 men, 1,000 of which were combat troops.[27] Lieutenant General Kurt Badinski's 276th Infantry Division was not so fortunate: Even before Viebig launched his breakout, it had been overrun by Allied tanks, and only a few stragglers managed to escape. Badinski was among those taken prisoner. The remnants of the 326th Infantry Division made good their escape, but most of Lieutenant General Irwin Menny's 84th Infantry Division was captured, including the general himself. Lieutenant General Augustus Dettling, the commander of the 363rd Infantry Division, organized his command into three battle groups and ordered them to break out at 10 P.M. on August 20. About 2,500 escaped; the 363rd Infantry lost all of its artillery, most of its heavy weapons, and almost all of its vehicles. General Straube, the corps commander, got away in the darkness. The Americans and Canadians closed the last escape route about 6 A.M. on August 21, although a few stragglers made their way out as the day wore on. General Meindl's 3rd Parachute Division was one of the last to escape. It was down to a strength of 2,500 to 3,500 men, of which only 600 were combat troops. Meindl himself had been seriously wounded by a shell splinter in the last phase of the breakout but had been carried out by his men.[28] The next day, Luftwaffe Major General Walter Wadehn arrived and took charge of what was left of the division.

Except for mopping up operations, which continued until August 22, the Battle of the Falaise Pocket was over. It had not been the overwhelming Allied victory it might have been, but from the perspective of the Wehrmacht, it was disastrous enough. Of the 100,000 men encircled in the pocket, 10,000 were killed and 40,000 to 50,000 were captured or missing. Fewer than 50,000 escaped, and a high percentage of these were service and supply troops. In terms of material, Army Group B was a wreck. A partial inventory of the battlefield indicated that the 5th Panzer and 7th Armies had lost 220 tanks, 160 assault guns or pieces of self-propelled artillery, 700 towed artillery pieces, 130 anti-aircraft guns, 130 half-tracks, 5,000 motorized vehicles, and 2,000 wagons. At least 1,800 horses had been killed in the pocket, and another 1,000 were captured by the U.S. 90th Infantry Division alone. Between them, seven panzer divisions escaped with only 62 tanks and 26 guns.[29] They had lost 1,300 tanks. Panzer Lehr, 10th SS Panzer, and 9th Panzer Divisions had no "runners" left at all. The infantry and parachute units were also in very bad condition. Both the 5th Panzer and 7th Armies had been smashed. Since D-Day, they had lost at least 50,000 men killed and more than 200,000 captured.[30] Tens of thousands of others were isolated on the Channel Islands or in Hitler's "fortresses," from which they would never return. To make matters worse, Paris was doomed. Model had dispatched the 17th Luftwaffe Field and 344th Infantry Divisions to hold the Paris–Orleans Gap, between the Loire and the Seine, but they had little chance against Patton's rampaging 3rd Army and were quickly smashed. On August 20, as the Battle of the Falaise Pocket reached its climax, elements of the U.S. 79th Infantry Division reached Mantes, about 35 miles downriver from Paris, and found the city undefended. They also found a small footbridge across the Seine, which the Germans had failed to destroy. By afternoon, the 79th had established a foothold across the river, and its engineers were building a traffic bridge. By nightfall, the entire division was on the north bank—the first Allied division to cross France's Seine. As a result, Model would not be able to make a prolonged stand on the Seine. The German grip on France was broken. The only major questions that remained were: Could Model rally before OB West was completely destroyed? Could he ever stop the Anglo-Saxons? If so, when and where? And how much of the German Wehrmacht in the West could he bring out of the rapidly deteriorating debacle in France?

NOTES

1. Omar N. Bradley, *A Soldier's Story* (New York: 1951), pp. 375–76 (hereafter cited as "Bradley").

2. Seaton, *Fortress*, p. 122.

3. Breuer, *Death*, pp. 236–37.

4. Shulman, p. 200.

5. Leclerc's real name was Philippe, Vicomte de Hauteclocque. He had assumed a nom de guerre to protect his family, which was in German-held territory.

6. On August 13, the 1st SS Panzer Division had 14 PzKw IVs, seven Panthers, and eight self-propelled guns. James Lucas and Matthew Cooper, *Hitler's Elite Leibstandarte SS, 1933–1945* (London: 1975), p. 126 (hereafter cited as "Lucas and Cooper").

7. It was at this point that General Patton wanted to ignore the boundary

lines between the army groups and cross into British territory, in order to complete the encirclement. He was sternly overruled by General Bradley, creating a controversy that rages until this day. It seems clear to this author, however, that had Patton been given his head, the Falaise encirclement could have been complete several days earlier than was the case, and very little of Army Group B would have escaped.

8. Breuer, *Death*, pp. 260–61.

9. Kurt Badinski was born in Grebenstein, Kurhessen, in 1890. He joined the army in 1910 and was commissioned into the 9th Jaeger Battalion in 1911. He fought in World War I, served in the Reichsheer, and was commander of the I Battalion, 16th Infantry Regiment when World War II began. Later he commanded the 489th Infantry Regiment (1939–42), the 23rd Infantry Division (1942), the 269th Infantry Division (1942–43), and the 276th Infantry (1943–44). After being released from the prisoner-of-war camps, Badinski settled in Oldenburg.

10. Shulman, pp. 207–8.

11. Keegan, p. 257.

12. Ibid., p. 259.

13. Formerly LVIII Reserve Panzer Corps, it was upgraded on July 6. It was commanded by General of Panzer Troops Walter Krueger.

14. Eddy Florentin, *The Battle of the Falaise Gap*, Mervyn Savill, trans. (New York: 1969), p. 187 (hereafter cited as "Florentin").

15. Miller, pp. 149–50, citing Speidel, p. 144.

16. Hart, *Hill*, pp. 101–2.

17. Ibid., p. 188.

18. Blumenson, *Breakout and Pursuit*, p. 533.

19. See Warlimont, p. 454.

20. Breuer, *Death*, p. 287.

21. Paul Mahlmann was born in Gispersieben in 1892 and, after attending various cadet schools, entered the service as a second lieutenant in the 98th Infantry Regiment in 1914. He fought in World War I, served in the Reichsheer, and assumed command of the 181st Infantry Regiment upon mobilization. He was acting commander of the 137th Infantry Division in 1942 and, after a brief tour of staff duty in Germany, assumed command of the 147th Reserve Division (1942–43). He also commanded the 39th Infantry Division (1943) before assuming command of the 353rd, which he led until February 15, 1945. Meanwhile, he distinguished himself in the Battle of the Huertgen Forest. Mahlmann was either wounded or reported ill on that date; in any case, he held no further appointments. His division was destroyed in the Ruhr Pocket two months later. He lived in Munich after the war (Keilig, p. 215).

22. Richard Schimpf was born in 1897 in Eggenfelden, Bavaria. He joined the Bavarian Army as a cadet in 1915 and was commissioned a year later. After joining the Reichsheer, he trained as a civilian pilot in 1925 and then underwent clandestine General Staff training. He also attended secret air force training courses in the Soviet Union. In 1930, he enrolled in the Berlin Technical University and graduated as an engineer. He transferred to the Luftwaffe in 1935. He initially commanded a reconnaissance squadron and, as a lieutenant colonel, served with the Condor Legion during the Spanish Civil War.

When World War II began, Schimpf was Ia of the 3rd Air Fleet in the West.

He became chief of staff of 4th Air Fleet in late 1940, and from February 1941 to September 1942, he was chief of staff of several Luftwaffe territorial commands in the East. In September 1942, he was given command of the 21st Luftwaffe Field Division. He was in Fuehrer Reserve from October 1943 to February 1944. The records do not indicate whether he was wounded or ill. In any case, he was given command of the 3rd Parachute Division in February 1944 and was seriously wounded on August 20. His men carried him off the field on a repaired armored personnel carrier. Upon recovery, he resumed command of his division, which had been rebuilt in the Netherlands. During the Battle of the Ruhr Pocket, he surrendered Bad Godesberg and the remnants of his division, to prevent further senseless destruction. Released from an American prison-of-war (POW) camp in late 1947, he worked as a civilian engineer until 1957, when he joined the Bundeswehr as a major general (equivalent to a *Generalleutnant* in 1944). Schimpf retired from the service in 1962 and taught military technical affairs at the Technical University of Aachen. He died on December 30, 1972. "Richard Schimpf," in Chandler and Collins, pp. 481–82; Absolon, p. 41.

23. Miller, p. 168, citing General Eugen Meindl, interview with Major Kenneth Hechler, January 1946, U.S. Military History Institute, Carlisle Barracks, Pa., p. 26.

24. Kraetschmer, pp. 190–94. Theodor Wisch was born in Wesselburener Koog, Schleswig-Holstein, on December 13, 1907, the son of a builder. After studying agriculture at a trade school, Wisch joined the SS and was a second lieutenant in Poland. By 1941, he was an SS major, commanding the II Battalion of the Leibstandarte Adolf Hitler, which was then a motorized infantry regiment. He assumed command of the division on February 12, 1944. Eight days after he was wounded, he was awarded the Knight's Cross with Oak Leaves and Swords.

25. Max Wuensche was born on April 20, 1914, in Kittlitz, Loebau, the son of a forester. He joined the SS-Verfuegungstruppe (combat SS, the forerunner of the Waffen-SS) in 1934. Sent to the SS Junkerschule (Officers' Training School) at Bad Toelz in 1936, he was commissioned and sent to the LAH in Berlin. Wuensche fought in Poland, Belgium, France, Greece, and Russia, where he led a panzer battalion (I/1st SS Panzer Regiment). In early 1944, he was given command of the panzer regiment of the Hitler Youth Division. He was released from prison in 1948 and was still alive in the 1980s. Kraetschmer, pp. 378–81.

26. Blumenson, *Breakout and Pursuit*, p. 549; Heinrich von Luettwitz, "Avranches," Foreign Military Studies *MS # A-904*, Office of the Chief of Military History, Washington, D.C.

27. Wilhelm Viebig, "277th Infantry Division (13 Aug–8 Sep 1944)", Foreign Military Studies *MS # B-610*, Office of the Chief of Military History, Washington, D.C.

28. Eugen Meindl was born in 1892 in Donaueschingen, Baden. His father was a forestry official for the prince of Fuerstenberg. After school, Meindl joined the 67th Field Artillery Regiment in Hagenau, then in German Alsace. During World War II, he was a platoon and battery commander and a regimental adjutant on the Western Front. He was retained in the Reichsheer and, in 1935, was a major, commanding a battalion in the 5th Artillery Regiment. In 1938, he was given command of the 112th Mountain Artillery Regiment, which he led in Poland. In 1940, he made a parachute jump at Narvik, even though he had no parachute

training. Later that year, he transferred to the Luftwaffe, commanding the Airborne Storm Regiment, which he led at Crete, where he was seriously wounded.

During the winter of 1941–42, Meindl created the first Luftwaffe Field division, which was initially called Group Meindl. In October 1942, he was named commander of the XIII Air Corps, the headquarters responsible for creating and organizing 22 Luftwaffe Field divisions. In November 1943, Meindl was given command of the II Parachute Corps, which was then in Italy. He was promoted to general of parachute troops on April 1, 1944.

After Falaise, II Parachute fought the British at Cleve and Nijmegen. In 1945, Meindl fought at Venlo and defended the Wesel bridgehead on the lower Rhine. He surrendered his corps to the British in Schleswig-Holstein. Released from prison in 1947, he died in Munich on January 24, 1951. Reinhard Stumpf, "Eugen Meindl," in Chandler and Collins, pp. 360–61; Absolon, p. 28; Ernst Martin Winterstein and Hans Jacobs, *General Meindl und seine Fallschirmjaeger: Vom Sturmregiment zum II. Fallschirmjaegerkorps, 1940–1945* (Braunschweig: 1976).

29. Blumenson, *Breakout and Pursuit*, p. 558.

30. Keegan, p. 283.

CHAPTER VII

THE INVASION OF SOUTHERN FRANCE

On August 15, while the 5th Panzer and 7th Armies were fighting for their lives in the Falaise pocket, the U.S. 7th Army landed east of Toulon, and the invasion of southern France began.

Southern and central France—indeed, two-thirds of the country—was defended by Colonel General Johannes Blaskowitz's Army Group G, which was a motley collection of third- and fourth-rate reserve and "Eastern" units. Most of its men suffered from low morale and were poorly trained. OB West had already tapped its mobile reserves and virtually stripped it of first-class and armored units for the Battle of Normandy. The only really good division it had left was the 11th Panzer, which was well led by Major General Wend von Wietersheim. It had approximately 11,000 men but only 25 PzKw IVs and 50 Panthers—about half of its authorized tank strength. Table 7.1 shows the Order of Battle of Army Group G on August 15.

Johannes Blaskowitz was a veteran Prussian officer with haunting eyes. Born in Peterswalde, East Prussia, on July 10, 1883, he had joined the Imperial Army as an officer-cadet (*Fahnenjunker*) in 1901. Commissioned second lieutenant in the 18th Infantry Regiment the following year, he commanded a company and later a battalion of infantry during World War I. Remaining on duty during the Reichswehr period (1919–33), he was a major general before Hitler came to power. He had commanded the 8th Army during the invasion of Poland (1939) and ended his chances of ever being promoted to field marshal during the winter of 1939–40 when, as commander of German occupation troops in Poland, he had tried unsuccessfully to stop Himmler's Einsatzgruppen (murder squads), which were committing atrocities against Jews, Polish intellectuals, mental patients, and others in the East. During the 1940–44 period, he served only in backwater posts and saw more than a dozen officers

Table 7.1
Order of Battle, Army Group G, August 15, 1944

ARMY GROUP G: Colonel General Blaskowitz

1st Army: General of Infantry Kurt von der Chevallerie
    LXXX Corps: General of Artillery Gallenkamp
        16th Infantry Division[1]
        331st Infantry Division (−)
        Kampfgruppe, 5th Parachute Division
        Remnants, 352nd Infantry Division

    LXIV Corps: General of Engineers Sach
        159th Reserve Division
        950th Infantry Regiment[2]

19th Army: General of Infantry Wiese

    IV Luftwaffe Field Corps: General of Fliers Petersen
        716th Infantry Division[3]
        198th Infantry Division (−)
        189th Reserve Division (−)

    LXXXV Corps: General of Infantry Kniess
        Elements, 198th Infantry Division
        Elements, 189th Reserve Division
        244th Infantry Division

    LXII Corps: General of Infantry Neuling
        242nd Infantry Division
        148th Reserve Division

    Army Reserve:
        11th Panzer Division
        157th Reserve Mountain Division
        338th Infantry Division[3]

    Army Group Reserve:
        Volunteer Depot Division "East"

Notes:
[1]Recently formed by combining the 158th Reserve Division and the 16th Luftwaffe Field Division.
[2]An independent regiment.
[3]In transit.

Source: Kurt Mehner, ed., *Die Geheimen Tagesberichte der deutschen Wehrmachtfuehrung im Zweiten Weltkrieg, 1939–1945* (Osnabrueck: 1985), Volume 10, p. 508.

junior to him in rank promoted over his head. Blaskowitz, meanwhile, commanded the 9th Army in France (1940) and served briefly as military governor of northern France (June 9–26, 1940) before Hitler sent him into involuntary retirement. Recalled to active duty in October 1940, he was named commander of the 1st Army in occupied France and continued to hold this thankless post until May 5, 1944, when he officially assumed command of Army Group G.[1]

Lieutenant Colonel Bodo Zimmermann, Rundstedt's chief of operations, recalled that Blaskowitz had "a strong spiritual and religious turn of mind. . . . [H]e always remained the straightforward soldier who wanted to do his duty simply for the sake of his Fatherland and his people."[2] A solid and competent officer, but not a brilliant one, the strait-laced Blaskowitz despised the Nazis and was thoroughly hated by Adolf Hitler. He owed his appointment to army group command in 1944 solely to the influence of his friend and fellow Prussian aristocrat, Gerd von Rundstedt, who saw him as a potential counterweight to the more dynamite Erwin Rommel, who was then commander in chief of Army Group B.

Blaskowitz controlled two armies: General of Infantry Kurt von der Chevallerie's 1st and General of Infantry Friedrich Wiese's 19th. The 1st Army, which was responsible for defending southwest France and the Bay of Biscay area, directed three infantry divisions (one in remnants, one understrength, and one recently formed), two reserve divisions, and what was left of the 5th Parachute Division, which had been pushed south of the Loire by Patton's 3rd Army. It had very little combat strength. In all, von der Chevallerie had perhaps 100,000 men, but very few were first-rate combat soldiers. Most of them were garrison, security, or coastal defense troops, fit only for occupation duties, antipartisan operations, or limited defensive missions.

Southeastern France was defended by the 19th Army, which had approximately 210,000 men and was responsible for defending 400 miles of Mediterranean coastline between the Italian and Spanish borders. To perform this task, it had 10 infantry and reserve divisions: 1 division for each 40 miles. As usual, there were too few men to defend too much space; obviously both 1st and 19th Armies had impossible missions.

The story of the defense of southern France began on November 8, 1942, when three Allied tasks forces invaded French North Africa. To the surprise and anger of Adolf Hitler, the armed forces of Vichy France (as the unoccupied zone of France was called) offered no more than token resistance. Three days later, at 7 A.M. on November 11, the German Army invaded the unoccupied zone. Three divisions under the command of 1st Army—the 7th Panzer, 327th Infantry, and 3rd SS Panzer—moved in from the west, while Armeegruppe Felber (the former XIII

Corps under General of Infantry Hans Felber) crossed the demarcation line from the north with the 10th Panzer, 328th Infantry, and 335th Infantry Divisions.[3] The 100,000-man army of Vichy France did not resist, and by evening, the 7th Panzer had reached Toulouse, 160 miles from its jump-off point. The next day German infantry (moving via rail) occupied Marseilles and towns west of the Rhone River, while other units pushed as far south as the Pyrennes and the Spanish border. Shortly after noon on November 11, four divisions of General Vercellino's 4th Italian Army advanced west along the coast of the French Riviera and into the mountains east of the Rhone, while two other Italian divisions sailed from Genoa and Sardinia toward Corsica, which they occupied the next day (November 12). By November 13, all of Vichy France was in German or Italian hands except the vital naval fortress of Toulon. Here lay the French fleet, which consisted of 80 ships in various states of repair, including 3 battleships, 7 cruisers, 29 destroyers, 20 submarines, and a seaplane carrier. The fleet reaffirmed its desire to remain neutral, and an uneasy truce ensued until November 17, when Hitler declared that the Toulon sector was a Vichy France in miniature and must be occupied. He assigned the task of seizing it to SS General Paul Hausser, who set up a planning staff at Aix-en-Provence. Among other forces, Hausser controlled the 7th Panzer and 1st SS Panzer Divisions.

Hausser and his staff realized that their chances of capturing the fleet intact were slim at best, but at least they could force the French to scuttle it and thus could prevent this formidable force from falling into Allied hands. Hausser called his plan Operation, "Lila," and it began when the German tanks roared out of their assembly areas in the predawn darkness of November 27. The French, however, were not taken by surprise, and by the time the German spearhead arrived in the dock area, the sailors were already sinking their ships, and the SS Panzertruppen could only watch helplessly as ship after ship went down. By 8:30 A.M., only 12 ships remained afloat (four destroyers, two submarines, and six minesweepers). The Axis nevertheless considered the operation a success. Only four submarines escaped to join the Western Allies, and over the next few months, the Italians raised more than 30 vessels.

Despite the lack of opposition and the elimination of the French fleet, the German occupation of Vichy France was a distinct negative for the German Wehrmacht. Already spread too thin, it was now responsible for defending another 275 miles of coastline from possible Allied invasion—excluding 125 miles occupied by the Italians. Over the next few months, the best and most mobile divisions of 1st Army and Armeegruppe Felber (later redesignated 19th Army)—including the 7th Panzer, 10th Panzer, 3rd SS Panzer, and 1st SS Panzer—were sent to more dangerous sectors, and they were replaced by units suitable for coastal defense missions only—including the 326th, 338th, and 356th Infantry Divisions. By July 1943, the Germans had 57,818 men defending the coasts of southern France.

The German defensive mission in the south of France became more difficult after July 24, 1943, when the Fascist Grand Council voted no confidence in Mussolini by a margin of 19 to 9. The next day, the Duce was deposed and replaced by Marshal Pietro Badoglio, whose government was devoted to the task of pulling Italy out of the war. As part of that policy, the Italian 4th Army began to hand over the French Riviera to General of Infantry Georg von Sodenstern's 19th Army on August 29.[4] By the time Italy defected from the Axis on September 8, this process was well advanced. That evening, the Wehrmacht began disarming Italian forces. The 356th Infantry occupied the coastline in and around Toulon, whereas the 715th Infantry took the sector from Cavalaire-sur-Mer to east of Cannes, and the 60th Panzer Grenadier Division "Feldherrnhalle" seized the mountain passes on the Franco-Italian border. In all, 41,057 Italians were captured in southeastern France. About 1,400 volunteered for German combat units, and about 29,500 agreed to serve in the German armed forces as noncombatants; the rest were interned and sent to the Reich or to the East, to work in the armaments industry or in labor battalions.

Meanwhile, the Allies landed at Salerno on September 8. Kesselring's Army Group C quickly occupied southern Italy, whereas Rommel's Army Group B did the same in the north. Both were in desperate need of reinforcements, and the French Mediterranean was the closest reservoir. Soon the 356th Infantry and "Feldherrnhalle" divisions were on their way, to be replaced by three mediocre divisions and several battalions of Osttruppen—Russians, Azerbaijanis, Turkomans, and others. By November 20, 10,000 of the 48,000 German soldiers in southeast France were "Eastern Troops." Many of the rest were over 37 or under 19 years of age.

The German defensive position in southern France involved only very gradually. By December 1943, the Wehrmacht had five divisions there (under two corps headquarters), and they were responsible for defending 400 miles of coastline—which meant that the average divisional sector was about 80 miles long. Six months later, Sodernstern had seven divisions along the coast, with the 9th and 2nd SS Panzer Divisions in reserve. The quality of the coastal divisions, however, had declined again. The 326th Infantry Division had been sent to northern France in January, and the 715th Infantry had been sent to Italy after the Allies landed at Anzio. Of those remaining, the 242nd and 244th Infantry and 148th Reserve Divisions had only recently been formed and the 338th was short of troops. New reinforcements, in the form of the 271st, 272nd, and 277th Infantry Divisions, began to arrive in January 1944, but they were also recently formed units, short of infantrymen, equipment, and vehicles of every kind.

In mid-May 1944, Field Marshal Erwin Rommel visited the region. Although his command prerogatives were limited to Army Group B, the Desert Fox had the additional duty of inspecting all of the Atlantic Wall, as well as the "South Wall"—the German coastal defenses on the Mediterranean. The problem was, as Rommel discovered, the South Wall did not exist. Mediterranean France was virtually devoid of defensive positions of any kind. Rommel was furious and gave Blaskowitz and von Sodenstern a fierce dressing down. The talkative Sodenstern (who was a known anti-Nazi) eventually saw the merits in Rommel's defensive theory—that the Allies would have to be defeated on the invasion beaches by repulsing the landings, if they were to be defeated at all— and began to improve the coastal defenses of southeastern France. He had only just started, however, when he was involuntarily retired and replaced by General of Infantry Friedrich Wiese.[5]

Wiese was born in Nordhastedt on December 5, 1892, and was three weeks younger than Field Marshal Rommel. He entered the service as a war volunteer in August 1914, when World War I broke out, and received his commission in the 147th Infantry Regiment as a second lieutenant of reserves in 1915. Discharged in 1919, he became a police officer in Hamburg. He was recalled to active duty as a major in 1935 and was named commander of the I Battalion, 116th Infantry Regiment, in 1936. When World War II began, Friedrich Wiese was a lieutenant colonel, commanding the same battalion. Later he led the 39th Infantry Regiment (1940–42), the 26th Infantry Division (1942–43), and the XXV Corps (August 1943–June 1944). He served in France (1940) and spent the last three years on the Eastern Front, fighting at Leningrad, Orel, Bryansk, Gomel, and Bobruisk, where he mastered a number of crises. He was a cool, imperturbable officer who was noted for his tactical skill. When he was assigned to command the 19th Army, Wiese paid the normal visit to Fuehrer Headquarters, where he received his orders from Hitler himself. It was a stern warning. "There will be no withdrawal," the dictator snapped. "If anything happens along the Riviera, you will fight to the last man and the last bullet! Do you fully understand, Herr General?"

Wiese understood. Blaskowitz's orders to him were also stern. "Go all-out to strengthen the South Wall," he commanded, "—beginning immediately!"

Work did began immediately and around the clock. Capably assisted by his chief of staff, Major General Walter Botsch,[6] Wiese concentrated on the 100-mile sector between Nice and Marseilles. At his disposal, he had 14,000 workers from the Organization Todt (many of them conscripted Frenchmen), as well as hundreds of army and navy engineers. They constructed almost 600 casemates, each protecting a coastal defense gun or field piece. Wiese also became convinced that the Allies would land paratroopers and gliders in his rear, so he installed thousands of sharp stakes in open fields in the interior. They could not be seen by aerial reconnaissance flights, but they could (and did) impale paratroopers.

The German defenses of southeastern France took two major blows after the Allies landed in northern France on June 6. With the permission of OKW, OB West transferred the 9th Panzer Division from Avignon to Normandy; the 2nd SS Panzer Division "Das Reich" was also sent to the front. The 271st, 272nd, and 708th Infantry Divisions, as well as Headquarters, LVIII Panzer Corps, were also sent to reinforce the 7th Army and Panzer Group West/5th Panzer Army in Normandy, leaving General Wiese with practically no mobile reserves when the Anglo-Saxons landed in southeastern France. These first- and second-class divisions were replaced by the 716th Infantry, 198th Infantry, and 189th Reserve Divisions. The 716th had been one of the two divisions to receive the full shock of the Allied attack on D-Day. On June 6 alone it lost five of its six infantry battalions, and when it was sent to the rear a few days later, it was a division in name only. The 198th had suffered a similar fate on the Eastern Front, and the 189th Reserve was a training command. To make matters worse, 19th Army was forced to send four motorized artillery battalions, as well as a number of anti-aircraft, antitank, and assault guns, to the hedgerows in July. Kluge even demanded the 242nd Infantry—one of Wiese's best remaining divisions—but OKW turned down this request.[7]

By this time, Army Group G did not have nearly the manpower necessary to control the interior of France, and the French Resistance Army (the Forces Françaises de l'Intérieur—Free Forces of the Interior, or FFI) revolted after it became obvious that the Allied invasion had succeeded in establishing a foothold on the Continent. By July, the Germans were reporting that, outside the cities, travel in southern France was possible only with a heavy escort. Travel by rail was virtually impossible. The line between Toulouse and Saint-Gaudens, for example, was only 60 miles long but had been cut in 38 places. On July 28, Blaskowitz reported to OB West that partisan activity had gradually increased to the point that "control over a greater part of the area can no longer be referred to. Only where German troops are in evidence can peace and order be preserved."[8]

The maquis in the Vercors plateau area southwest of Grenoble revolted and proclaimed the "Free Republic of Vercors" in late June. This was an open provocation that General Wiese could not ignore, so he sent the 157th Reserve Mountain Division to put down the rebellion. French resistance, however, was not broken until July 21, when an elite SS unit launched a daring and successful glider attack on the guerrilla headquarters. Elsewhere, however, the French partisans continued to run wild and became bolder and bolder; there were simply not enough German troops to deal with them all.

Wiese headquartered at Avignon, a beautiful and historic city that was the home of the papacy in the fourteenth century (the so-called Avignon Captivity). To this point, it had been spared the rigors of war, and because it lay in a prosperous agricultural region, its rations were much better than in Paris, where the people were on a near-starvation diet. All of this began to change on July 17, when a flight of U.S. heavy bombers blasted the city. Their target was the Hôtel Dominion, where the 19th Army's headquarters was located, and Wiese and his staff had to flee for their lives. After the raid, Wiese moved his HQ to a château outside the city, but the Allied raids continued—and not just on Avignon. They pounded Nice, Cannes, Saint-Tropez, Toulon, Marseilles, and dozens of other targets along the French Riviera, including bridges, radio and radar stations, gun positions, barracks, troop assembly areas, and other military installations. By the first week in August, the entire Côte d'Azur (the 100-mile stretch of French coast east of the Rhone River) was under more or less continuous aerial bombardment. This led Wiese to deduce that the Allies intended to invade southern France and would land in the Côte d'Azur sector. Kesselring, the OB South (*Oberbefehlshaber Sued*, the German commander in chief, Italian Front) agreed, although he felt that an attack against Genoa could not be entirely ruled out. (Kesselring had, of course, noticed that all four Free French divisions had disappeared from opposite his front lines in Italy and that three of the best American divisions had vanished as well.) Blaskowitz agreed with Wiese and asked the Fuehrer's permission to move the 11th Panzer Division from the Bordeaux sector to positions behind the Côte d'Azur zone. However, the XX Committee (nicknamed the Double Cross Committee), a British secret service organization, had fed the Abwehr (OKW's military intelligence and secret service agency) a steady diet of "disinformation," which convinced it that the Allies intended an invasion of southwestern France. (German military intelligence did not function any better under the SS Reich Central Security Office than it had under Admiral Wilhelm Canaris, who had been sacked for his incompetence in February.)[9] Hitler, however, accepted the Central Security Office's recommendation and kept the 11th Panzer Division at Bordeaux, about 400 miles west-northwest of the invasion beaches.

This erroneous conclusion on the part of German intelligence is especially curious when one considers that Operation "Anvil" (as the invasion was codenamed) was one of the worst-kept secrets of the war. In fact, the Allies had to change its codename to "Dragoon" because of multiple security violations. This change did no good at all: Everyone in

Italy from priests to hookers seemed to know the plan and the approximate destination of the invasion. In Sunday Mass, one Catholic priest prayed for the American boys who would soon be landing in southern France. A prostitute in a Naples brothel bid farewell to one of her "regulars": She knew that his unit was earmarked for the invasion. Enterprising Italian merchants were even selling maps of the French Riviera to American GIs on the streets. Even "Axis Sally," also known as "the Berlin Bitch"—the German radio announcer employed by the Propaganda Ministry to undermine the morale of enemy soldiers—shocked the American paratroopers by correctly telling them where they would soon land and informing them in her coy, sexy voice that they would not need their parachutes, because the flak would be so thick they could simply walk down on it.[10] (Fortunately, she was wrong about the second part of her prediction.) German intelligence must have known much of this, as they had left behind agents in Allied-occupied Italy, and Mussolini's rump Fascist Republic had its spies as well. Even so, despite the overwhelming evidence pointing to an invasion of Mediterranean France, Himmler's intelligence agency clung to the Bay of Biscay theory, as did Hitler, who refused to allow Blaskowitz to move the 11th Panzer from near the Atlantic seaboard to the Mediterranean sector until August 12. Since a road march from Bordeaux to the coast east of the Rhone normally took eight days, Hitler's decision to release the 11th Panzer came too late to be of any help at all.

The German Navy and Luftwaffe would also be of little help in defending southern France. As of the first of August, Vice Admiral Paul Wever, the German Naval Commander, Mediterranean, had only five destroyers, 28 torpedo boats, nine submarines, and 15 patrol craft, mostly concentrated in and around Marseilles and Toulon.[11] On August 6, an air strike against Toulon put four of the submarines out of commission, and by August 15, the German Navy had only one operational destroyer (anchored in Genoa), three submarines, seven escort vessels, 30 patrol boats, and approximately 30 auxiliary vessels (such as minesweepers) in the Mediterranean.[12] It also had a new commander. Admiral Wever died of a heart attack on August 11 and was temporarily succeeded by Rear Admiral Heinrich Ruhfus.[13] Wever's permanent replacement, Vice Admiral Ernst Scheurlen, would not arrive at Aix-en-Provence until August 17.[14]

Like the navy, the Luftwaffe in southern France was on the verge of operational bankruptcy in August 1944. It had only 186 airplanes, and many of these were inoperative. They included about 30 Me-109 fighters, 65 Ju-88 bombers, 35 reconnaissance airplanes of various types, 15 unreliable (and dangerous) He-177s, and about 30 obsolete Do-217 bombers, all under the control of the 2nd Air Division. Another 50 fighters in northern Italy were available for transfer on short notice. They were opposed by General Ira Eaker's 15th U.S. Air Force, which had 4,056 aircraft, including 1,271 heavy bombers. Even if its inoperative airplanes were included, the Luftwaffe in southern France was outnumbered 20 to 1.[15]

West of the Rhone, General Wiese posted the 189th Reserve, 198th Infantry, and 716th Infantry Divisions. Around the mouth of the river, he stationed the 338th Infantry Division, minus one regimental-size battle group, which had been sent to Normandy. His main concentration lay east of the Rhone, in the Côte d'Azur sector, where he posted Lieutenant General Hans Schaefer's 244th Infantry Division (in the Marseilles sector), Major General Johannes Baessler's 242nd Infantry Division (in the Toulon sector), and Major General Otto Fretter-Pico's 148th Reserve Division, with only two infantry regiments, which defended Wiese's left flank from Agay to the Maritime Alps.[16] All three divisions were under the command of General of Infantry Ferdinand Neuling's LXII Corps. The 157th Reserve Division Wiese had already committed to antipartisan operations in the mountains to the north, around Grenoble, and it constituted his only major reserve, other than the 338th Infantry Division, which was in transit to Army Group B.

The three divisions that Wiese had assigned to the defense of the Côte d'Azur were the best in 19th Army—but they were not very good. They included too many "Eastern" battalions, made up of Poles, Ukrainians, Azerbaijanians, Georgians, and others. Many of them could not even pronounce the German passwords, and their loyalty to the Third Reich was questionable at best. To make matters worse, they knew there was very little in reserve behind them. Although he had done the best that he could (and probably as well as anyone could have done under the circumstances), General Wiese was under no illusions: He would not be able to halt the coming avalanche. Even if the 11th Panzer Division had been handled in the theoretically best possible manner, "Dragoon" would still have succeeded, although American casualties would undoubtedly have been higher and their inland progress slower.

The Allied plan called for a preinvasion parachute attack by Brigadier General Robert Frederick's 1st Airborne Task Force ("Rugby Force"), which included the U.S. 517th Parachute Infantry Regiment, 509th and 551st Parachute Infantry Battalions, 550th Glider Infantry Battalion, 460th Parachute Field Artillery Battalion, and the British 2nd Independent Parachute Brigade. Rugby Force, which commanded 9,000 highly trained men, was to secure the exits from the invasion beaches, especially the key hamlet of Le Muys, 12 miles from the sea, which commanded one of the few valleys that cut through the high ridge running along the coast between Nice and Marseilles.

General Lucian Truscott's U.S. VI Corps (3rd, 45th, and 36th Infantry Divisions) was scheduled to make the initial amphibious landing. It would be followed by the General Jean-Marie de Lattre de Tassigny's

French II Corps, which would mop up German resistance and liberate the port cities of Toulon and Marseilles. All of these forces were under the command of Lieutenant General Alexander M. "Sandy" Patch, Jr., the soft-spoken and highly capable commander of the U.S. 7th Army. In all, the Allied landing forces did not badly outnumber the 19th Army (250,000 to 210,000 men), but the quality of their divisions was much higher, they were much better equipped and more mobile, and they were a massive superiority at sea and in the air.

The huge Allied naval armada of 880 ships and 1,370 smaller vessels (mostly landing craft) began to assemble on D minus 6, sailing from Naples, Taranto, Salerno, Malta, Sardinia, Corsica, Sicily, and ports in North Africa. Their goals were five beaches along a 45-mile stretch of coast between Cavalaire and La Calanque d'Antheor. From traitors and double agents in the French underground, General Wiese learned that the probable invasion date was August 15—Napoleon's birthday. An uprising that began on August 14 confirmed his fears. As the Allied landing forces approached, Wiese placed 19th Army on full alert, and Blaskowitz unilaterally halted the transfer of the 338th Infantry Division, which OB West had summoned to the north. Even so, when the Allies landed on August 15, resistance was weak, thanks primarily to a massive preliminary aerial bombardment by 1,300 Allied heavy bombers and 700 other combat aircraft, which began at 5:50 A.M. Figure 7.1 shows the battlefield of southern France.

"All up and down the thirty miles of beaches and for several miles inland, the ground shook and shivered and thrashed about under the enormous pounding," Breuer wrote later.

Gigantic orange balls of fire and gushers of earth shot into the air. Countless forest fires broke out. Wooded buildings were turned into splinters and stone structures into powder.

German soldiers in pillboxes, nearly driven out of their minds by the drumfire of explosives, bled profusely from the nose, mouth, and eyes from the concussion of blockbuster bombs hitting on or near their thick-ceilinged concrete structures.[17]

The raid lasted for 90 minutes. Then came the fighters and fighter-bombers: Thunderbirds, Mustangs, Spitfires, and Lightnings. They flew 4,200 missions in direct support of the amphibious assaults and thousands of others in indirect support. They were followed by a massive bombardment from 400 naval guns, which fired 16,000 shells at German positions in 19 minutes. "How can anything live under such a bombardment?" General Truscott exclaimed to Admiral Andre Lemonnier, the chief of staff of the French Navy.[18] The naval gunfire was followed by commando attacks against key points.

The French and Americans landed at 8 A.M. along a 45-mile stretch of

Figure 7.1
Southern France, 1944

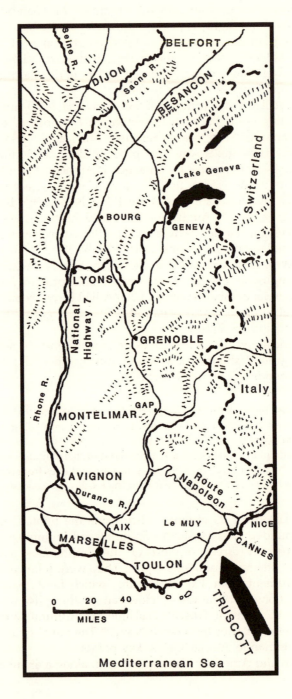

coastline between the small resort village of Cavalaire-sur-Mer and Agay. The 242nd Infantry Division, which was responsible for the entire sector between Toulon and Agay, was stretched too thin to defend anything except unconnected strong points, and many of these were neutralized by the Allied air and naval bombardments. In all, there were about 6,000 German troops in the entire 45-mile-long invasion sector—and many of these were Osttruppen. When the Allies landed, resistance was weak to nonexistent in most sectors. By nightfall, they had 94,000 men and 6,000 vehicles ashore, at the cost of only 320 killed. They had also taken 2,041 prisoners—many of them Russians and Armenians.[19] The most important position to hold out was Le Muy. Like the Allies, General Wiese had recognized its importance and had stationed a two-regiment Kampfgruppe under Major General Richard von Schwerin to defend it.[20]

Meanwhile, to the east, General von Wietersheim had mercilessly pushed his 11th Panzer Division forward almost without rest for 58 hours.[21] Realizing that speed was of the essence, Wietersheim quickly loaded his division onto 33 trains and headed east, but his men were soon forced to abandon the railroad and proceed via highway. The young general ordered his columns to proceed down the major highways instead of the secondary roads, thus ignoring the threat of Allied fighter-bombers. His risk paid off; in one day and two nights, the 11th Panzer covered the 150 miles from Carcassone to the Rhone River east of Avignon. Now, however, Wietersheim learned that he had lost the race: The Allies had already landed. Even so, it was essential that his panzers reach the threatened sector before the Americans fought their way through the coastal mountain ranges and completely destroyed the LXII Corps. The problem now was crossing the Rhone. Allied bombers and fighter-bombers had destroyed every bridge south of Avignon, all the way to the coast, which was 90 miles away. Wietersheim, however, heard that the bridge at Pont-Saint-Esprit, 25 miles to the north, was still intact, so he sent his tanks toward it at maximum speed. They had only gone a few miles, however, when his reconnaissance unit reported that this bridge had been destroyed by Allied bombers that very morning. If Hitler's order releasing the division had come just 12 hours earlier, the 11th Panzer could have crossed the river. Now, however, Wietersheim had no choice but to try to cross the Rhone via barge, ferry, or whatever other means he could find. This would not be quick, easy, or without loss, since the Jabos were already making their presence felt.

Like General Wiese, General Neuling, the commander of the LXII Corps, was a cool, imperturbable officer and an accomplished tactician.[22] He refused to panic, despite the overwhelming firepower that had already reduced his 242nd Infantry Division to a Kampfgruppe. He tried to organize a counterattack against the Allied landings, but his communications failed, and this proved to be impossible. (Most of the German telephone lines had been cut by Allied paratroopers or members of the resistance, and many of their radios had been knocked out by Jabos.) Neuling then turned his attention to defensive measures in a futile effort to prevent the Allies from reaching the Rhone River Valley. Although he did what he could, Neuling, like Wiese, realized that the situation was hopeless from the beginning.

Late that morning, at his headquarters at Rouffiac, near Toulouse, Colonel General Blaskowitz's telephone line to 19th Army went dead, apparently cut by the French Resistance or an Allied paratrooper. Blaskowitz, however, had enough information to realize that the main Allied invasion of southern France had begun and that Eisenhower's strategy was obvious. He felt sure that the Americans intended to thrust northward up the Rhone Valley and link up with the forces of Bradley and Patton, which were now roaring almost unchecked across the countryside of Normandy, Brittany, and western France. He also realized that there was little to prevent this link-up and, that if it occurred, 1st Army and his own headquarters would be cut off in southwestern France. At 11 A.M., he ordered his staff to move the army group headquarters to Avignon, beginning at once.

Meanwhile, on the Rhone east of Avignon, General von Wietersheim attempted to cross the river in daylight, using barges and locally acquired vessels, in spite of the Jabos circling overhead. His divisional anti-aircraft guns and flak artillery were not strong enough to prevent the fighter-bombers from attacking both sides of the river and the barges in midstream, and the 11th Panzer Division suffered heavy losses in tanks, trucks, Volkswagens, and guns. Wietersheim almost cried with frustration. It would be four days before his division could complete its crossing of the Rhone and re-form on the east bank: far too late to have any impact at all on the fighting on the Riviera.

While Wietersheim was struggling to get across the wide Rhone, Adolf Hitler was in Rastenburg, listening to one report of woe after another. Army Group Center had collapsed, the Red Army was sweeping across Poland, Army Group North was cut off, Montgomery and Bradley were about to encircle Group B in the Falaise pocket, Middleton had overrun most of Brittany, and Patton's forces were galloping unchecked across western France, heading for the Seine. On top of all of this, Field Marshal von Kluge, who the Gestapo had just reported as being implicated in the July 20 plot, was missing, 19th Army was being smashed, and 1st Army was in danger of being trapped as well. Hitler sat, hunched in his chair, as Jodl read him a report describing the latest disaster in southern France. Everyone expected Hitler to throw one of his famous tantrums about his "cowardly and incompetent" generals, but, to their surprise, he remained impassive. "This has been the worst day of my life!" was all he said.[23]

To the astonishment of Jodl, Keitel, and the other members of the Fuehrer's entourage, who were accustomed to tirades on days like this one, Hitler remained calm in the face of adversity, for a change. At the end of the conference, he astonished them even further by announcing that he was ready to consider whatever measures were necessary if the situation in France continued to worsen. After months of demanding that every piece of soil be held at all costs, he had suddenly reversed himself—he was ready to evacuate France and pull the entire Wehrmacht back to the Siegfried Line—on the very borders of the Fatherland itself. OKW quickly relayed word of this decision to the 1st and 19th Armies, which at once began to prepare to evacuate southern France.

The next day, August 16, the German 1st Army began to withdraw from the Atlantic coast of southwestern France. General von der Chevallerie had about 100,000 men, but very few of them had any combat value and most were without motorized vehicles. Of his two corps, Chevallerie had already sent the LXXX north, to guard the Loire River crossing against a possible thrust into the army group's rear by Patton's 3rd Army. (Patton had no intention of doing this, but, given the available information and the tactical situation, Chevallerie's reaction was certainly a sensible one.) This left 1st Army with only General of Engineers Karl Sachs's LXIV Corps (the 159th Reserve Division and a few miscellaneous battle groups) on the Bay of Biscay.[24] They set out on foot to the northeast, harassed by the FFI, hoping to reach the Seine before Eisenhower could bar the door. Failing that, they hoped to fall into American hands and not those of the French partisans.

Meanwhile, on D-Day, General Frederick's 1st Airborne Task Force lost about 450 men killed or captured and 300 wounded in their airborne operations. In addition, another 300 had been injured, mostly in the glider assaults, which had run into the sturdy wooden poles known as "Rommel's asparagus" (*Rommelspargel*). Of the 404 Waco gliders involved in the glider landings, only 45 were salvageable. As high as these casualties may sound, they were rather light for an airborne operation, and Frederick's men had captured all of their objectives except the major two: The British 2nd Independent Parachute Brigade had failed to take Le Muy, the vital village and road junction 12 miles from Truscott's beaches, and the 551st Parachute Infantry Battalion had not yet captured Draguignan, a beautiful town of 10,000, which served as the headquarters of Neuling's LXII Corps and Major General Ludwig Bieringer's 800th Field Administrative Headquarters.[25]

Bieringer was a haughty, arrogant Prussian, complete with monocle, who was determined to hold Draguignan as long as possible, despite the fact that he had little with which to defend it. His 700-odd troops were of indifferent quality, and many of them merely wanted to surrender to the Americans, rather than to the French. Bieringer nevertheless held off the elite U.S. paratroopers and French partisans until the afternoon of August 16, when he was finally captured by the Americans. General Neuling and his staff only barely managed to escape. They were captured on the morning of August 18 by Lieutenant Colonel Charles J. Hodge, the commander of the cavalry reconnaissance squadron of the "Texas Army" (the U.S. 36th Infantry Division). The LXII Corps had ceased to exist. In the meantime, the 198th and 338th Infantry Divisions began their retreat up the Rhone River Valley, where they were joined by the 11th Panzer Division. These three divisions, which took up defensive positions southeast of Avignon, formed the screen behind which the bulk of the 1st Army and more than half of the 19th Army made good their escape. At the same time, as previously planned, the men of the static 244th Infantry Division retreated into Marseilles, and the remnants of the 242nd Infantry fell back into Toulon, to prepare for the inevitable siege of the French naval fortresses. Both of these divisions knew that they had been "written off" when Wiese retreated up the Rhone valley, but a hard core of them were determined to deny the ports to the Allies as long as possible, just as the Fuehrer commanded.

Le Muy was finally captured on the afternoon of August 16 by the U.S. 550th Glider Infantry Battalion. Truscott promptly pushed through the rough coastal ridges toward the Rhone, in pursuit of Wiese, and simultaneously sent a strong detachment to the east, to seize Cannes and Nice, two world-renowned resort cities whose capture would have a severe psychological effect on the German Wehrmacht and a worldwide negative impact on Hitler's prestige. This American force, however, was checked by the 148th and 157th Reserve Divisions, which had fallen back to the east, toward the Italian border. (They were now part of Kesselring's OB South.) At the same time, von Schwerin put up stiff resistance at Brignoles and held off the U.S. 3rd Infantry Division until August 19, but the remnants of the LXII Corps were unable to prevent the French 1st Combat Command from reaching Highway 7 and driving west, toward Aix-en-Provence.

Meanwhile, in Berlin, Joseph Goebbels's propaganda ministry announced the latest disasters to the German people and tried to prepare them for even more. "We must be prepared for a German withdrawal from France," Radio Berlin announced. "We must expect the loss of places with world-famous names."[26]

Famous indeed. The next major city to fall was named Paris.

NOTES

1. Keilig, p. 36. After the fall of France, Blaskowitz was placed in Fuehrer Reserve on September 21, 1944. He was recalled to active duty and led Army

Group G again from December 24, 1944, to January 28, 1945. He led Army Group H in the Netherlands from January 28 to April 7, 1945, and was commander in chief of OB Netherlands when Germany surrendered. Arrested as a war criminal because he had blown up some Dutch dikes to delay the Allied advance (a militarily prudent act), he was broken in spirit and committed suicide in Nuremberg on February 5, 1948.

2. Bodo Zimmermann, "OB West: Command Relationships," Foreign Military Studies *MS # B-308*, Office of the Chief of Military History, Washington, D.C.; Alan F. Wilt, *Riviera Campaign*, p. 40.

3. Hans Felber was born in Wiesbaden in 1889. He was chief of staff of 8th Army (1939), chief of staff of 2nd Army (1939–40), chief of staff of Army Group C (1940), commander of XIII Corps (1940–42), commander of XXXXV Corps Command (later LXXXIII Corps) (1942), and commander of Armeegruppe Felber (1942–43). Later he was Military Commander Southeast (1943–43), commander of Army Detachment Serbia (1944), and Corps Felber (later XIII Corps) (1944–45). He commanded 7th Army from February 22 to March 25, 1945. Placed in Fuehrer Reserve, he was not reemployed. He retired to Frankfurt. Felber was promoted to general of infantry on August 1, 1940 (Keilig, p. 88). He was considered a mediocre field commander at best (Friedrich von Stauffenberg, personal comments).

4. Georg von Sodenstern was born in Kassel in 1889 and entered the army in 1909. As a general of infantry, he served as chief of staff of Army Group A (later South) until August 13, 1943, when he was given command of the 19th Army. He was relieved of his command a few days before D-Day and was never reemployed. An anti-Hitler conspirator as early as 1938, his activities were never discovered by the Gestapo, and he survived the war. He died in Frankfurt/Main in 1955.

5. Friedrich Wiese led the 19th Army until December 19, 1944, when he was sacked by Heinrich Himmler, who had recently been appointed OB Upper Rhine and thus become his superior. Despite his talent, Wiese was never reemployed. He retired to Launsbach/Giessen.

6. Promoted to lieutenant general on September 1, 1944, Botsch, a 47-year-old Wuerttemberger, was an infantryman and a veteran General Staff officer, having served on the staff of OKW (1938–39), as chief of operations and chief of staff of the XXX Corps (1939–43), and as chief of staff of XIII Corps and Armeegruppe Felber (1943). Later he was commander of the 18th Volksgrenadier Division (1945) and acting commander of LIII Corps (1945). In this last position he narrowly avoided execution, because Remagen bridge—the first bridge over the Rhine captured intact by the Allies—was in his sector.

7. Alan F. Wilt, *The Riviera Campaign of August 1944* (Carbondale: 1981), p. 42 (hereafter cited as "Wilt").

8. Ibid., p. 43.

9. After its disastrous intelligence failure concerning Anzio—the most recent in a long string of intelligence failures—the Abwehr was transferred from OKW control to the Reich Central Security Office (Reichssicherheitshauptamt) of the SS.

10. William B. Breuer, *Operation Dragoon* (Novato, Calif., 1987; reprint ed., New York, 1988), pp. 22–23 (hereafter cited as "Breuer, *Dragoon*").

11. Paul Wever was born in Langenberg, Rhineland, on January 28, 1893. He

entered the naval as a cadet (*Seekadett*) in 1912 and became an ensign in 1913. He spent the first three years of World War I aboard light cruisers but volunteered for U-boat service in 1917. He survived the war and was selected for retention in the Reichswehr, serving on the staff of the Admiral, Baltic Sea. He spent most of the 1920s and 1930s in the surface fleet and was naval attaché to Paris and Madrid (1933–36). He was first officer on the *Graf Spee* (1936–37) and commander of the cruiser *Emden* (1938–39). Wever was promoted to captain (1937), rear Admiral (1941), and vice admiral (October 1, 1943). He spent the war as chief of staff of Naval Group West (1939), in staff assignments at the High Command of the Navy (OKM) (1940), and on the Franco-German Armistice Commission (1940–43). Named Admiral, French Southern Coast, on September 2, 1943, he died in Aix-en-Provence, southern France, on August 11, 1944. Hildebrand and Henriot, Volume 3, pp. 542–43.

12. Wilt, p. 45.

13. Heinrich Ruhfus was born in Berlin-Charlottenburg in 1895. He entered the Imperial Navy as a cadet in 1913 and was promoted to ensign in 1915. He served on cruisers until mid-1915, when he transferred to torpedo boats. After 1916, he was with the destroyer flotilla off the coast of Flanders. Following the war, Ruhfus's career was marked by slow but steady progress, mainly in base and school commands. He was promoted to captain in 1938 and to rear admiral on September 1, 1942. He was a prisoner of war until June, 1947. He died in Flensburg-Muerwik (the site of a naval school that he had commanded) on May 26, 1955. Hildebrand and Henriot, Volume 3, pp. 168–69.

14. Ernst Scheurlen was born in Strassburg, Alsace, in 1894. He joined the navy as a cadet in 1912 and was commissioned ensign in 1915. During World War I, he worked aboard a coastal tanker, a heavy cruiser, and a minelayer. Kept in the Reichsmarine, he specialized in coastal artillery and naval gunnery. When the war broke out, he was a captain, commanding the light cruiser *Koenigsberg*. Later he was in charge of naval artillery on the Pomeranian coast. He was earmarked to command a transport fleet during Operation "Sea Lion," the invasion of England, but this operation was cancelled. He served on the naval staff in the Crimea and the Kerch peninsula (1942–43), before becoming coastal commander on the German Bight. He was commanding admiral, French Southern Coast, until September 6, 1944, when he again became commanding admiral, German Bight. Admiral Scheurlen was named commander of the 2nd Marine Division on February 11, 1945, and was killed in action near Gross-Eilsdorf on the Lueneburger Heide on April 8, 1945. He was promoted to captain in 1938, rear admiral (April 1, 1942), and vice admiral (August 1, 1944). Hildebrand and Henriot, Volume 3, pp. 215–16.

15. Otto Fretter-Pico was born in Karlsruhe in 1893 and joined the army as a cadet in 1914. Commissioned in the artillery in 1915, he remained in the service between the wars and commanded a forward observer battalion in 1939–40. Later he led 297th Artillery Regiment (1940–42), 102nd Artillery Command (1942), and the 57th Infantry Division (1943) before assuming command of the 148th Infantry Division on September 25, 1943. He led this division for the rest of the war. Otto Fretter-Pico retired to Freiburg, Brunswick, after the war. His older brother was Maximilian Fretter-Pico, who commanded the 6th Army in 1944.

16. Wilt, p. 71. These figures included attached aircraft (i.e., airplanes not or-

ganic to the 15th U.S. Air Force. but under its control) and 412 troop-carrying aircraft.

17. Breuer, *Dragoon*, p. 160.

18. Ibid., p. 161.

19. Wilt, p. 105.

20. Richard von Schwerin was born in Peitschendorfswerder, East Prussia, in 1892. He was educated in various cadet schools, entered the army as a senior officer cadet in 1913, received his commission in the 2nd Grenadier Regiment in 1914, fought in World War I, and served in the Reichsheer. He was commander, I Battalion, 87th Infantry Regiment (1936–39); commander, 212th Infantry Regiment (1939–42); commander, 79th Infantry Division (early 1942–1943); commander, 189th Reserve Division (1943–September 25, 1944); and commander, 172nd Reserve Division (November 24, 1944) and 172nd Division Staff for Special Purposes (February 1, 1945–end). He died in Dobrock in 1951. Keilig, p. 319.

21. Wend von Wietersheim was born in Neuland, Loewenberg, in 1900. A cadet in 1918, he was commissioned *Leutnant* in the 4th Hussars in 1919. He transferred to the panzer arm in the 1930s and was a major and adjutant of the 3rd Panzer Division (1938–39) when World War II began. He rose rapidly in rank, being promoted to lieutenant colonel (1941), colonel (1942), major general (November 1, 1943), and lieutenant general (July 1, 1944). In the process, he commanded the 1st Motorcycle Battalion (1940–41), the 113th Panzer Grenadier Regiment (1941–43), and the 11th Panzer Division (1943–45). He lived in Bad Godesberg after the war. Keilig, p. 370.

22. Ferdinand Neuling was born in Bautzen in 1885 and joined the service as a *Fahnenjunker* in 1905. He became an infantry second lieutenant in 1906. After serving in World War I and in the Reichswehr, Neuling was a Landwehr commander in Oppeln in 1939. When the war broke out, he was given command of the 239th Infantry Division, which he led until 1942. He assumed command of the LXII Corps on September 15, 1942.

23. Breuer, *Dragoon*, p. 199.

24. Karl Sachs was born in 1886 at Crossen/Oder and was educated in various cadet schools. He began his military career as a senior officer cadet in the 1st Railroad Battalion in 1905. After serving in World War I, he was not selected for the Reichsheer and was discharged as a major in 1919. He promptly joined the police and was a police colonel in 1934. He rejoined the army in Hitler's expansion of 1935 as a colonel in the engineers. Sachs was promoted to major general in 1937, to lieutenant general in early 1939, and to general of engineers in 1942. He was engineer general for Army Group B in Poland and France (1939–41), commander of the 257th Infantry Division (1941–42), and commander of the 159th Mobilization Division (1942). He assumed command of the LXIV Corps on September 20, 1942, but was relieved of his command on September 2, 1944. Never reemployed, he was arrested by the Russians at the end of the war and died in a Soviet prison in the winter of 1952–53. Keilig, p. 290.

25. Ludwig Bieringer was born in Metz (then a part of Germany) in 1892. He joined the army in 1914 in the 8th Trains Battalion and spent virtually his entire career in the supply service, rising to major general in 1943. He was sent to France later that year; he was given command of the 800th Field Administrative Command on May 12, 1944. He retired to Hanover after the war. Keilig, p. 35.

26. Breuer, *Dragoon*, p. 236.

CHAPTER VIII

THE RETREAT BEHIND THE SEINE

While the Franco-American forces were "hitting the beaches" on the Côte d'Azur on August 15, the U.S. XV Corps in Normandy left part of its forces at Argentan and began a wider envelopment of the Seine, while other elements of the U.S. 3rd Army drove for the Paris-Orleans gap— the next objective of Patton's legions. At the same time, however, Bradley gave Patton one additional mission: Protect the Allies' southern flank along the Loire River from German incursions. This Patton was already in the process of accomplishing, and it was easily done. All General von der Chevallerie had to defend the Loire River line with was General of Artillery Curt Gallenkamp's LXXX Corps, which consisted of the 16th Infantry Division, the remnants of the 331st Infantry, 352nd Infantry, and 5th Parachute Divisions (all of which had been pushed out of Normandy and into the zone of the 1st Army by the Americans), and the 708th Infantry Division, which had performed poorly in Normandy and had been sent to the rear to reorganize and rebuild.[1] The 16th Infantry—the mainstay of Gallenkamp's forces—had only been formed a few weeks before, when the 158th Reserve and 16th Luftwaffe Field Divisions were consolidated. It was originally intended to provide reinforcements for the Normandy Front, but on August 8, it was charged with the task of covering the Loire River line, in order to prevent Patton from launching attacks to the south. Eventually it was given responsibility for the entire Loire line from Nantes (on the coast) to Orleans.

The 16th Infantry was deficient in equipment, but it was well trained and well led by Lieutenant General Ernst Haeckel and his subordinates.[2] Again, however, there was too much space to defend with too few men. On August 7, the U.S. 5th Infantry Division attacked part of the division at Angers, a city of 95,000. The Germans put up a determined resistance, and the city did not fall until August 11, but the Americans took another

2,000 German prisoners. Nantes, meanwhile, was captured by the U.S. VIII Corps on August 6. In the meantime, General Gallenkamp organized the defense of Orleans and Châteaudun with remnants of the 708th Infantry Division and a few hastily assembled security and rear guard units but had so few combat troops that it was almost a perfunctorly resistance. The U.S. XII Corps (4th Armored and 35th Infantry Divisions) advanced rapidly and seized Orleans on the morning of August 16, and Châteaudun was captured (along with several hundred German prisoners) the following afternoon.

The fall of Orleans accelerated the general withdrawal of the 1st Army from the Bay of Biscay to Dijon. Simultaneously, General Haeckel blew up all of the Loire River bridges not already in American hands, in an effort to keep Patton from advancing south, to cut off and destroy Army Group G.

He need not have worried. The Allied generals in Normandy were not looking to the south. They were hatching plans to cut off and destroy Army Group B—which was vastly more important than Army Group G—to push over the borders of the Reich itself and seize the Ruhr industrial area, without which Hitler could no longer make war. They had in mind nothing less than defeating Nazi Germany by Christmas.

Meanwhile, on August 20, Adolf Hitler ordered Field Marshal Walter Model to establish a defensive line at the Touques River. If this line could not be held, he authorized the OB West to withdraw behind the Seine. Hitler was right when he guessed that the Allies would try to destroy Army Group B between Argentan and the lower Seine (i.e., the downstream from Paris), but he did not appreciate how weak and disorganized the German forces were. Model and Dietrich, meanwhile, organized the sector for defense. On August 20, the field marshal subordinated 7th Army to 5th Panzer Army, giving Dietrich command of the entire area between the coast and the boundary of the 1st Army, which ran from Chartres to the northwestern outskirts of Paris. (This decision seems to indicate that Model had more confidence in Dietrich than Hausser. He almost certainly did not yet know that the 7th Army commander had been wounded.) Dietrich, in turn, ordered the panzer units that were now escaping the Falaise pocket but that were unfit for combat to proceed to the Beauvais-Senlis area, for rehabilitation under the direction of the LVIII Panzer Corps. The nonarmored units were sent to other places to rebuild or were put to work constructing fortifications or preparing the west bank of the Seine for defense.

Dietrich organized his remaining combat forces into three corps: Obstfelder's LXXXVI on the coast, Bittrich's II SS Panzer in the center, and Kuntzen's LXXXI on the left. He also created an armored reserve (of sorts) in the Evreux area, under the command of SS General Georg Keppler's I SS Panzer Corps.[3] This HQ controlled the remnants of several panzer divisions, and it appeared quite strong—on paper. In reality, it was very weak. The 10th SS Panzer Division, for example, controlled only one half-strength infantry battalion (around 300 men) and had no tanks and no artillery. The 12th SS Panzer had 300 men, 10 tanks, and no artillery; the 2nd SS Panzer mustered 450 men, 15 panzers, and 6 guns; the 9th SS Panzer deployed 460 men, 20 to 25 tanks, and 20 guns; and the 116th Panzer Division had between 500 and 600 men, 12 tanks, and no artillery. On August 28, after another week of fighting, the combat strength of all of Model's armored divisions totaled only 1,300 men, 24 tanks, and 60 guns.[4] Model sent the formerly elite 1st SS Panzer Division "Leibstandarte Adolf Hitler" and the 2nd Panzer Division off the field and behind the Seine to rehabilitate on August 20.

The defense of Paris had initially been assigned to General of Fliers Karl Kitzinger, who had succeeded Stuelpnagel as military governor of France. Kitzinger, however, chose to headquarter in Nancy, leaving General Baron von Boineburg-Lengsfeld in charge in the city. This did not suit Hitler, who, on August 7, directed OKH to establish a special command in Paris, directly subordinate to OB West. On the Fuehrer's orders, this job fell to General Dietrich von Choltitz, the military commander of Greater Paris. He was selected, according to one OKW officer, because he "never questioned an order, no matter how harsh it was." Choltitz's appointment may have also sent a message to Kluge, who had relieved him of his command only a week before.

Choltitz was a tough customer, a fact belied by his short, fat body. (He appeared to be almost as wide as he was tall.) He had, in fact, spent almost three years on the Eastern Front. His regiment, the 16th Infantry, had been largely responsible for capturing the Soviet Black Sea naval fortress of Sevastopol on the Crimea, which fell in July 1942 after some of the bloodiest and most intense fighting in the war. When the shooting finally stopped, only 347 of its original 4,000 men were still standing.[5] Choltitz himself had been wounded in the arm but remained at his post. He was awarded the Knight's Cross and given command of the 260th Infantry Division. Later, he was deputy commander of the XXXXVIII Panzer Corps, acting commander of the XVII Corps, and commander of the 11th Panzer Division.[6] He was promoted to major general in 1942 and to lieutenant general in 1943. "Since Sevastopol," he later observed, "it has been my fate to cover the retreat of our armies and destroy the cities behind them."[7]

General von Choltitz was summoned to Rastenburg and met with Hitler on the day of his appointment. He was treated to a fierce tirade from the pathological dictator. Hitler began calmly, wandering down memory lane, describing how he had founded the Nazi Party and formed it into the perfect instrument to guide the German people and their fighting spirit. Then, abruptly, his voice rose and he described the victories he was about to win with his miracle weapons. Suddenly he changed topics again and, with his face only inches from Choltitz's, began shrieking. "Since the 20th of July, Herr General," he raged, "dozens of generals—yes, dozens—have bounced at the end of a rope because they wanted to prevent me, Adolf Hitler, from continuing my work, from fulfilling my destiny of leading the German people." But nothing would stop him, he screamed, until he had led the Third Reich to Final Victory! On and on he raged, his whole body shaking. Apparently forgetting who he was talking to (or perhaps not caring), he stormed at "the clique of Prussian generals" who had tried to kill him and described the tortures they would endure before they died. Finally, he slumped back in his chair. After a long pause, he spoke again, this time barely above a whisper. He ordered Choltitz to turn Paris into a "frontline city" and to "stamp out without pity" any civilian uprising. He promised the general his full support. Then he fell silent again.

Sensing that the interview was over, Choltitz saluted and walked out. It seemed to him that Hitler's eyes were burning into his back.

Choltitz's previous confidence in the Fuehrer was completely shattered by this interview. He left Rastenburg convinced that his Supreme Commander was insane.

For the general, things got worse on the trip back. On the train, he ran into Robert Ley, a cabinet-level labor official, whom he had set next to at lunch. Sensing that the general was depressed, Ley offered to share a bottle of prewar Bordeaux with him. Choltitz felt he needed a drink. As they consumed the Bordeaux, Ley told him that he had been called to Fuehrer Headquarters to draft a new law: *Sippenhaft*, or collective family responsibility. If a soldier plotted against the Fuehrer or surrendered too easily, his family would be held responsible for his failure, even if it entailed the death penalty.

This news sickened Choltitz, a family man. He declared that if Germany starting using methods like this, it was returning to the Dark Ages.

Ley admitted that the measure was extreme and muttered something about these being exceptional times. The conversation died, and shortly thereafter, Ley left General von Choltitz alone with his thoughts.[8] A few hours later, the train stopped in Berlin, where he received a cable from General Burgdorf, the new chief of the Army Personnel Office, informing Choltitz that, by special order of the Fuehrer, he had been promoted to general of infantry. The Prussian general was not as happy about his advancement as he would have been even two weeks before.

The new commandant of Paris stopped the next day at Baden-Baden, where he briefly visited his wife and three children, ages 14 to four months. He held the baby, his only son, for what would be the last time for three years. Then he proceeded to the capital of France.[9]

Choltitz did what he could to prepare the city for defense. He used his special powers as Wehrmacht commander to send all superfluous units out of the city. He also sent virtually all of his able-bodied men to the front lines and began to restore discipline among troops who were not used to it, owing to years of luxurious living in the City of Light.

Choltitz's predecessor, General Baron von Boineburg-Lengsfeld, had already established an "obstacle line" west and southwest of Paris, which he felt was defensible. Choltitz agreed and sent most of the 325th Security Division—25,000 to 30,000 men under Boineburg—to man it. The defenses of Paris soon profited from Hitler's desire to hold the city. To defend the approaches to the city from the east and west, Army Group B received antitank units from Army Group G, and the 6th Parachute, 48th Infantry, and 338th Infantry Divisions, as well as individual AT guns and dozens of *Panzerfaeuste*. Colonel Hermann Oehmichen, an antitank expert, was sent from the Home Army, along with a cadre of instructors, to teach antitank defense techniques and demolitions to the defenders, many of whom had little or no combat experience.

As the Americans neared the city, new units joined the defenses, including the remnants of the 352nd Infantry Division, 20 batteries of 88mm guns, and smaller units. The perimeter defense (about 20,000 men of somewhat low quality) was placed under the command of Lieutenant Colonel Hubertus von Aulock, the brother of the defender of St. Malo, who received a special promotion to major general.[10] Choltitz remained inside Paris with about 5,000 men, 50 artillery pieces, and about 60 airplanes. Despite this appearance of strength, however, Choltitz was under no illusions: If he was heavily attacked, he could not hold Paris for any length of time.

Hitler must have known it, too. On August 15, he authorized the SS, Gestapo, the SD, and the area's administrative staffs to evacuate the city. They left quickly, but with the most astonishing collection of loot, including furniture, art treasures, Baccarat goblets, wine by the case, and even herds of pigs. Luftwaffe Field Marshal Sperrle evacuated his headquarters, the Palais du Luxembourg—which had once housed Louis XVI and Napoleon—on August 16. Like much of the Luftwaffe in the west, he took to his heels. Two days later, he was replaced by Colonel General Otto Dessloch.[11]

On August 15, on the orders of Field Marshal von Kluge, Choltitz had seized the armories and disarmed all the policemen of Paris. The next day, the police went on strike. They were soon joined by other workers, including those who ran the railroads.

It was the beginning of an insurrection.

THE FALL OF PARIS

The official commander of the Free Forces of the Interior—the military arm of the French Resistance—was General Pierre Koenig, a supporter of and former chief of staff to Charles de Gaulle, who headquartered in

London.[12] Part of Koenig's job was to coordinate Resistance activities with the movement of the Allied armies. In July, as the Allies began to threaten Paris and there was unrest in the city, Koenig ordered an immediate cessation of any activities that might provoke civil disorder and German retaliation. Koenig knew something the Parisians did not: Eisenhower had no intention of liberating Paris immediately. He planned to bypass the city, partially because he did not want it to become a battleground and partially because he did not want to have to feed it. Providing provisions for Paris, which had 3.5 million people and was (is) the largest city on the European mainland, would require as much food, fuel, medical supplies, transport, and other necessities as supplying eight divisions. The loss of this amount of supplies would require Eisenhower to halt one of his two major drives: the continuing effort to destroy the 5th Panzer and 7th Armies or Patton's surge toward Lorraine and the Siegfried Line. Accordingly, Montgomery issued orders that Paris was not to be taken until there was a militarily sound reason to do so. Eisenhower and Bradley heartily agreed.

Not all of the French partisans, Resistance leaders, or FFI listened to Generals Eisenhower, Montgomery, or Koenig, however, because not all of them liked the idea of a liberated France under a government headed by Charles de Gaulle. Henri Tanguy (who was better known by his nom de guerre, Colonel Rol) was the leader of the Communist underground in Paris and the de facto leader of the FFI in the French capital as well. A veteran Communist and union organizer, he fought in the Spanish Civil War and had joined the French Resistance in 1940. By 1944, Rol commanded the strongest force in the capital. By August 18, as the Americans neared Paris, excitement gripped the city. The collaborationist Petain government disintegrated, Premier Pierre Laval fled the city, Petain was already in Germany, more than half of the railroad workers went on strike, almost every policeman in the city disappeared, government workers refused to answer their telephones, there were frequent anti-German demonstrations, and armed FFI units moved openly through the streets. German reaction to all of this was quite feeble, and Colonel Rol saw his chance. On August 19, he instigated an uprising in Paris, which had two objectives: (1) to force the Germans out of the city and (2) to seize power in Paris (and thus possibly all of France as well) for the Communist Party. Rol knew that such an uprising would be very costly in terms of damage to the city and in human blood, but he was willing to pay the price. "Paris is worth 200,000 dead," he declared.[13]

By midmorning, the rebellion was well under way. Large parts of the city were in Communist hands, isolated groups of German soldiers were being attacked, and the city's telephone exchange had been sabotaged. Alexandre Parodi, the chief of the Gaullist resistance faction in Paris, had a very different worldview than Rol; he and his followers looked upon the insurrection as little more than a Communist attempt to seize control of the country from its rightful heirs, the supporters of General de Gaulle. When he learned what Rol was up to, Parodi reasoned that he and his forces could not sit idly by while the Reds took control. As a result, he began an insurrection of his own and (with considerable help from the police themselves) took over the Prefecture of Police—an important symbol of civil authority and (arguably) the most important public building in Paris. By the end of the day, various FFI factions, acting without central direction, had seized local police stations, national ministries, newspaper buildings, the city hall, and the Hôtel de Ville. The Gaullists, however, were beginning to doubt the wisdom of their actions by 8 A.M., when panzers appeared in the square between the Prefecture and the Cathedral of Notre Dame. They did not attack, however. General von Choltitz, who was surprised and angry at this development, nevertheless had no desire to turn Paris into a battleground, since this would inevitably lead to the deaths of thousands of people and the destruction of large sections of one of the world's most important cities and cultural centers.

There is little doubt but what Choltitz could have put down the rebellion at this point if he had been willing to unleash his men with their tanks, machine guns, and artillery. The Resistance leaders seemed to realize this as well. Fortunately for them, they had secured the assistance of Raoul Nordling, the Swedish consul general, who had already succeeded in talking Choltitz into releasing several thousand political prisoners, instead of deporting them to Germany, where they would probably have been executed. On behalf of the Resistance, Nordling met with Choltitz at his headquarters, the luxurious Hôtel Meurice, near the Palace de la Concorde and the Tuileries, and negotiated another deal with the general. He agreed to regard certain vaguely defined sections of Paris as FFI territory and to treat captured Resistance members as regular soldiers. In return, the Resistance leaders agreed to regard parts of the city as free for German use; in these areas, German troops would have unimpeded right of passage. An uneasy truce ensued, although it began to break down almost immediately in certain areas because Colonel Rol refused to honor it. In other sectors, however, it held—at least for the moment. Already, by nightfall on August 20, the rebellion had cost the lives of 125 French people and 50 members of the Wehrmacht.[14]

Since 1944, the reasons behind Choltitz's willingness to negotiate have been the subject of debate. Did he wish to spare the lives of innocent women and children, or was he afraid that he no longer had the strength to crush the Resistance? Choltitz later said both were true. There were other reasons as well. Some Resistance factions feared other French factions as much as the Wehrmacht, and the Gaullists were especially wary of the Communists, who wanted to take advantage of the situation to seize control of France for themselves. One reason, for which he is not commonly given credit, is that Dietrich von Choltitz appreciated the cultural and aesthetic significance of Paris. "Prussian general" and "a person who appreciates cultural sites" are not terms often used together, but neither are they mutually exclusive. In his youth, Choltitz had been a page to the queen of Saxony in Dresden, the cultural center of the region and the seat of the Wittenburgers, the Saxon royal family, who had modeled it after Paris. Hitler probably did not know this when he sent the general to France's primate city. (Unfortunately, the Allies would not have as much respect for Dresden in 1945 as Choltitz had for Paris in 1944.) Also, it seems quite likely that Choltitz was hoping to pit one resistance group against the other, and this strategy might well have worked, had not events raced so rapidly to their conclusion.[15] In addition, Choltitz used the truce to discreetly bring up reinforcements, including a tank company from the Panzer Lehr Division. At the same time, Model dispatched the 348th Infantry Division to Paris, even though he doubted it would arrive in time to do any good. He also ordered the incompletely formed 26th and 27th SS Panzer Divisions from the Troyes sector to the city. These units, the former 49th and 51st SS Panzer Grenadier Brigades, respectively, did not amount to more than a regiment each. They had been formed as SS Kampfgruppen 1 and 3, respectively, from emergency battalions from SS schools and replacement units and from the SS NCO School in Lauenberg, Pomerania. They had been sent to Denmark to replace the 363rd Infantry Division when it was sent to Normandy. The two SS battle groups were upgraded to brigades on June 18. The 49th had three grenadier battalions and the 51st had two. Both had an artillery battalion and an engineer company. On August 4, the 51st SS was sent by rail to Troyes (in the Champagne region), followed nine days later by the 49th. Their mission was to reinforce the 1st Army. Led by SS Lieutenant Colonel Walter Joeckel, the 51st had fewer than 3,000 men, and the 49th did not have many more. Both units were nevertheless upgraded to the status of SS panzer divisions of August 10, with no increase in their strengths. Neither had any tanks.

Two authors have made much of the fact that Model did not inform Choltitz that these two "panzer divisions" were en route to Paris and suggest that Choltitz might have behaved differently, had he known. Model did not tell Choltitz that the 26th and 27th SS were on their way to Paris because they were not on their way to Paris. When Model issued his orders, the 27th SS was already decisively engaged in combat against Patton's armored divisions near Troyes, where it would be largely destroyed. (In his letters, General Patton spoke highly of the 27th [nee 51st] SS.) It also proved impossible for the 1st Army to disengage the 26th SS.

These two authors also state that the two SS panzer divisions were expected to arrive in Paris on August 25 or 26. Perhaps this is true, but they do not state who expected them to arrive on these dates. Certainly no one who knew anything about the true situation expected them.

The authors also suggest that Choltitz might have behaved differently, had he known the two divisions were coming. He would not have. Even if they had shown up as early as August 20, they would have increased the size of the forces defending Paris from 30,000 to 37,000 at the very most. Seven thousand ill-equipped men—even those of SS—would have made no difference in the long run. It is, of course, possible that the authors took the orders at face value and assumed that the 26th SS and 27th SS were real, full-strength, German SS panzer divisions. If so, they would be right. Had Choltitz been reinforced with two divisions, each with 20,000 determined SS men, each backed by 200 Panthers and Tigers—not to mention assault guns, AFVs, and self-propelled artillery— he would have behaved differently. He would have quite possibly checked the Allied advance and held Paris. But, after Falaise, there was no way OB West could have provided reinforcements with this kind of armored punch, even if it had sent Choltitz the entire 5th Panzer Army. OB West was, in fact, operationally bankrupt.

Paris, Field Marshal Model had already correctly decided, could not be held against a combined internal insurrection and an external Allied attack. He therefore signaled OKW that he had ordered an alternate line of defense reconnoitered north of the city. This provoked a reaction from Hitler, who had already ordered that "Fortress Paris" be defended to the last. His newest order, dated 11 A.M. on August 23, read:

In history the loss of Paris always means the loss of France. Therefore the Fuehrer repeats his order to hold the defense zone in advance of the city. . . .

Within the city every sign of incipient revolt must be countered by the sharpest means . . . [including] public execution of ringleaders. . . .

The Seine bridges will be prepared for demolition. Paris must not fall into the hands of the enemy except as field of ruins.[16]

Choltitz, meanwhile, continued to deliberately understate the extent of the FFI rebellion. A man of the Eastern Front, he was fully aware that the sometimes harsh Model had an unpredictable bad temper. He did not want the field marshal's wrath to descend on Paris. In addition, he turned down an offer of assistance from Otto Dessloch, the commander in chief of the 3rd Air Fleet. Specifically, Dessloch had 150 bombers at Le Bourget airport, seven miles away. He wanted to conduct a terror bombing raid on the city. With their bases so close and no Allied fighters to impede them, Dessloch's bombers could make 10 sorties each in a single night, raze the northeastern part of Paris, and create a "little Hamburg."[17] Besides, there were plenty of bombs at Le Bourget, and the Luftwaffe could neither use them nor carry them away. Choltitz said he would consider the matter but never got back in touch with Dessloch's liaison officer.[18]

While Choltitz tried to "keep the lid on" in Paris, Model tried to make a stand south of the Seine, as Hitler had ordered. The quality of the resistance varied considerably. On his own initiative, for example, SS Captain Kurt Wahl of the 38th SS Panzer Grenadier Regiment organized a battle group from elements of the 2nd SS, 9th SS, and 2nd Panzer Divisions and placed them in positions to defend the Seine crossings. He was reinforced with elements of the 1st SS Panzer Division and was superseded in command by SS Colonel Wilhelm Mohnke, a harsh and disliked man even by SS standards.[19] This ad hoc Battle Group Mohnke was attacked by the strong U.S. 5th Armored Division on August 19, but because of the Germans' skillful use of terrain and *Panzerfausts*, it took the Americans five days of heavy fighting to gain 20 miles and take Louviers (on the Seine, 30 miles north of Mantes). On the other hand, the U.S. 28th Infantry and 2nd Armored Divisions attacked the 344th Infantry, 331st Infantry, and 17th Luftwaffe Field Divisions at the same time, and the German opposition "just melted away."[20] A counterattack by the LXXXI Corps (with elements of four panzer divisions) could not restore the situation, and the American divisions neared Elbeuf on August 23. Seeing that the Americans were threatening to cut off his retreat to the Seine crossings, Sepp Dietrich committed elements of eight panzer divisions near Elbeuf, between the Seine and Risle Rivers, on August 24 but could not stop the U.S. XIX Corps from taking the town on August 26. Meanwhile, the Canadians came up from the west, replaced the Americans at Elbeuf, and threatened the Seine crossings near Rouen. Figure 8.1 shows the Allied drive to the Seine.

While the British, Canadians, and Americans were clashing with German rear guards south of the Seine, the rest of the Wehrmacht was trying to escape across the river. Once again the Germans demonstrated a remarkable ability to improvise. Between August 20 and 24, they put more than 20 ferries and a pontoon bridge into operation in the area of Rouen alone. During the day, they hid the ferries and pontoons along the river bank and operated only at night. Small French-owned boats were captured and put into operation, while some troops actually cut down trees and constructed their own rafts. Others seized French wine barrels, emptied them, tied them together with ropes, and nailed planks on top, forming excellent rafts. Between August 20 and 24, the Germans managed to get 25,000 vehicles and 75,000 to 100,000 men across to the east bank. Thousands of other vehicles, however, were destroyed by Allied fighter-bombers and artillery. The carnage was particularly bloody at the entrances to the river crossing points, where German units jammed together and offered especially inviting targets for Anglo-Saxons. Dietrich, who was in overall charge of the operation, later stated that the

Figure 8.1
The Allied Drive to the Seine

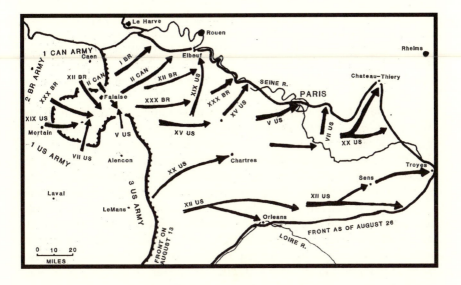

Germans lost almost as many vehicles crossing the Seine as in the Falaise pocket.

On August 25, Model ordered Dietrich to withdraw his units across the Aisle River that night, then to pull all of his forces behind the Seine the following night. The II Parachute Corps was then to proceed to Nancy, where it was to be rebuilt under the control of the 1st Parachute Army. The 7th Army (now under Eberbach) was to fall back to the rear, where it was to reconstruct 11 divisions that were no longer battleworthy: the 84th, 85th, 89th, 243rd, 272nd, 276th, 277th, 326th, 363rd, and 708th Infantry Divisions and the 3rd Parachute Division. This left 5th Panzer Army with 18,000 infantrymen, 314 guns, and 42 tanks and assault guns to face more than 190,000 Allied infantrymen, supported by 2,400 guns and 3,900 tanks. Fortunately for Dietrich, the Allies did not push as hard as they might have on August 26 and 27, and at the same time, their air forces were negligent in attacking the Seine crossing sights. As a result, Dietrich and the 5th Panzer Army managed to escape, despite some disorder and even panic in the ranks. Unfortunately for Nazi Germany, however, the panzer army did not escape in any condition to defend the Seine. The U.S. 79th Infantry Division had already established a bridgehead at Mantes, and Dietrich had no hope of eliminating it; he, therefore, had no hope of successfully defending the Seine. The retreat would have to continue, although (naturally) it would take the Fuehrer several days to draw the same conclusion.

South of Paris, meanwhile, the Americans under General Patton were forging ahead at full speed. On August 21, the U.S. XX and XII Corps (with one armored and two motorized infantry divisions each) advanced abreast, with the objective of carrying the Paris-Orleans gap. They were opposed by the 1st Army, now under the command of General of Panzer Troops Otto von Knobelsdorff.[21] Despite the fact that he was in no way responsible for the disasters in the west, General Kurt von der Chevallerie was abruptly sacked and never reemployed. (After the war, he was kidnapped and murdered by the Russians.)

Knobelsdorff tried desperately to assemble enough forces to delay the Americans and simultaneously defend the upper Seine: an impossible mission, since he had only a few security troops, flak detachments, and stragglers from all kinds of units. His only intact combat divisions were the 48th and 338th Infantries. The 48th was inexperienced, poorly trained, and deficient in all types of equipment. The 338th was equipped with captured French transport—and not enough of that. Knobelsdorff also had what was left of the poor-quality 708th Infantry Division. He had been promised the 348th Infantry and 17th Luftwaffe Field Divisions, but they were diverted to positions north of the Seine. About all he received was the 26th SS and 27th SS Panzer Divisions (see above), which amounted to about two peacetime regiments.

The U.S. XII Corps (now under Major General Manton C. Eddy) moved out rapidly. Patton had reluctantly replaced Major General Gilbert R. Cook (whom he trusted) with Eddy because Cook had a circulatory illness, but he had strong reservations that the infantry general was too conservative to command a corps in the 3rd Army—and told Eddy so to his face. The new corps commander, therefore, had something to prove when he began his advance on August 21, and he proved himself very quickly. On the first day, the XII Corps pushed forward from Orleans to Sens, an advance of more than 70 miles. Its drive was so rapid that its vanguard captured a party of German officers who were visiting the twelfth-century cathedral as tourists. Within three days Eddy's men had pushed all the way to Troyes (an advance of 120 miles), where they ran into significant resistance.

Troyes was defended by the 26th and 27th SS Panzer Divisions, which were the former 49th and 51st SS Panzer Grenadier Brigades. They had been upgraded on August 10 but had received no additional reinforcements or equipment, other than the I Battalion, 199th Army Security Regiment (I/199th), which only had three understrength companies, and a few naval infantry detachments. The 27th SS had a two-battalion panzer grenadier regiment, an engineer company, a flak company, a reconnaissance company, an artillery battalion, and a staff company. Its recon unit was probably a bicycle company, although it did have some modern transport. The records do not mention a signal company, but it probably had one. The structure of the 26th SS was the same as that of the 27th, except that its panzer grenadier regiment (the 49th) had a III Battalion.[22] Neither German nor U.S. records mention any panzer units or any tanks, however, so they could not have been very impressive if they did exist, which apparently they did not. It is interesting that the German Wehrmacht in 1944 was forming panzer divisions that did not have any panzers.

The 27th SS first met Patton's spearheads on August 23 but arrived too late to prevent the capture of Sens. The 27th fell back into bridgehead positions on the west bank of the Seine. SS Lieutenant Colonel Walter Joeckel, the division commander, set up his headquarters in a bank in Troyes, on the other side of the river.

The next day, the FFI revolted—one day too early. Since the SS men were not yet decisively engaged against the rapidly approaching U.S. 4th Armored Division, they turned on the FFI and routed it, crushing the revolt in the process.

On August 25, Eddy's men struck with Sherman tanks. They expected a demoralized enemy and an early capitulation. They got their first real battle since Brittany, and the defenders even earned the admiration of General Patton. The 51st SS Engineer Company was particularly good. On the west side of the river, however, most of the I Battalion/51st SS Panzer Grenadier Regiment was destroyed, and on the east bank, the rest of the 27th SS was gradually pushed back in house-to-house fighting. One by one, the SS lost their positions. Finally, on the morning of August 26, Colonel Joeckel ordered his "division" to break out. Unfortunately, most of his transport had already been overrun. He and his staff escaped Troyes but were captured by an American reconnaissance unit on August 28, before they could reach the German border. Seeing no escape, the I/199th Army Security Regiment turned and fought it out with the Americans. (This was not normal behavior for a weak security unit in the fifth year of the war, at least on the Western Front.) It was destroyed at Vogesen, and its commander, Captain Kropf, was killed. The remnants of the 27th SS (a little more than the battered II/51st SS Panzer Grenadier Regiment) finally reached German lines at the end of the month. They were absorbed by their sister unit, the 26th SS Panzer Division, which was itself absorbed by the rebuilding 17th SS Panzer Grenadier Division "Goetz von Berlichengen" at Metz a few days later. The 26th SS Division became the 37th SS Panzer Grenadier Regiment, whereas the survivors of the 27th were used to form the 38th SS Panzer Grenadier Regiment.[23]

After the fall of Troyes, the U.S. 4th Armored Division was just 100 miles from Nancy, but an ominous development took place in Eddy's rear: His corps was consuming gasoline at a rate of 200,000 to 300,000 gallons per 50 miles, and now his supply officers reported that they had only 31,000 gallons in reserve. If higher headquarters could not provide the corps with more fuel very quickly, the rapid advance would come to an end.

Meanwhile, the U.S. 5th Infantry Division (of the XX Corps) smashed Lieutenant General Karl Casper's 48th Infantry Division, took Montereau on August 24, and pushed across to the east bank of the Seine that evening. At the same time, the U.S. 7th Armored Division crossed the Seine at Melum, 10 miles north of Fontainebleau and 25 miles south of Paris. By August 25, Patton's 3rd Army had four bridgeheads across the upper Seine, south of Paris, between Melun and Troyes. Like Dietrich, Knobelsdorff found it impossible to rally his battered forces in time to defend the river.

Meanwhile, for General von Choltitz at Paris, time had run out.

On August 21, French General d'Armee Alphonse Juin visited SHAEF, armed with a letter from Charles de Gaulle, and personally appealed to General Eisenhower to reconsider his decision to delay the liberation of Paris.[24] The visit from the highly respected Juin had its effect, and when Eisenhower met with Bradley the next day, they reversed their previous strategy and decided to capture the French capital as quickly as possible. In accordance with an earlier promise Eisenhower made to de Gaulle, Leclerc's French 2nd Armored Division would be given the honor of entering Paris first.

Meanwhile, within the city, General von Choltitz had done everything he could to avoid executing Hitler's "field of ruins" order. After his visit to Fuehrer Headquarters on August 7, Choltitz had already drawn the only possible conclusion: "the man was mad."[25] And Dietrich von Choltitz did not want to destroy the cultural center of the Western world for a madman.

On August 17, his last day in command, Kluge had ordered Choltitz to start destroying the industries of the French capital, but the commandant had ignored him. Jodl issued synonymous orders later, but Choltitz had ignored him as well. He also avoided contact with Model, for fear that he would give similar instructions. He did speak with General Speidel, the chief of staff of Army Group B, which was now headquartered at Margival, near Soissons, in the complex originally constructed in 1940 as a command post from which Hitler would direct the conquest of the United Kingdom. Speidel instructed Choltitz to obey the orders to destroy Paris—perhaps because he, even more so than Kluge, was implicated in the unsuccessful coup of July 20—but Speidel spoke with a notable lack of enthusiasm. Jodl, meanwhile, issued further orders for Choltitz to destroy the 70-plus bridges in the French capital, but Choltitz did not wire a single one for demolition. He also did nothing to destroy the 200 industrial plants in Paris, although he did blow up the communications center.

General Leclerc attacked Choltitz's perimeter on August 24 but made little progress against stiff resistance and lost more than 300 men, 35 tanks, and six self-propelled guns in the process. Eisenhower and Bradley, however, suspected that Leclerc had not made a strong enough effort, so they ordered the U.S. 4th Infantry Division to strike for Paris as well. During the night, however, Choltitz ordered General Aulock to withdraw behind the Seine. The following day, the French 2nd Armored liberated western Paris, while the U.S. 4th Infantry took the eastern half of the city, including Notre Dame. A few German detachments made last-ditch stands in public buildings, including the Quai d'Orsay (the French foreign ministry building), the Luxembourg, Palais Bourbon, the Hôtel des Invalides, and the École Militaire. About 2,600 German soldiers also held out in the Bois de Boulogne.

Choltitz naturally remained behind. His headquarters (the Hôtel Meurice) was surrounded by French tanks shortly after noon, and a young French officer burst into Choltitz's room.

"Do you speak German?" he shouted.

"Probably better than you," Choltitz retorted coldly. He was then taken prisoner and forced to formally capitulate to General Leclerc at the Prefecture of Police building later that afternoon. Paris had been captured—and at very little cost. The Americans, for example, lost only 628 killed, whereas 3,000 Germans were killed and approximately 10,000 taken prisoner.[26] De Gaulle, accompanied by Koenig and Leclerc, staged a victory parade down the Champs-Elysees the following day, much to the disgust of General Gerow, the American corps commander, who wanted to use the French 2nd Armored Division to pursue the Germans. The parade was extremely premature in any case; not all of the German pockets of resistance had been eliminated, and there was scattered shooting. Fortunately for everyone, the German battle group at Bois de Boulogne opted to surrender, instead of shelling the parade route, as it easily might have done.

Hitler was also disgusted. "Is Paris Burning?!" was the question he roared at General Jodl, who immediately instructed a staff officer to telephone General Speidel. When he was informed that Paris was not burning, the raving dictator ordered Army Group B to fire heavy artillery and V-weapons into the city. Speidel ignored the order. That night, however, Dessloch finally got to launch his terror attack on Paris, although by now 3rd Air Fleet was too far away to employ shuttle bombing, which meant the French capital was only subjected to 150 sorties, not 1,500. Dessloch's bombers were unopposed, however; the Allied fighters had not yet moved up, and there were no Allied anti-aircraft guns in the city. In the largest air raid Paris suffered during the war, the Luftwaffe killed 213 people, wounded 914 more, and damaged or destroyed 597 buildings.

Retreat to the Reich

Three days later, Field Marshal Model asked the president of the Reich Military Tribunal to open criminal charges against General von Choltitz.

The capture of Paris was a huge psychological and propaganda blow to the Third Reich. It was also a huge logistical blow to the Allies. The supply officers at SHAEF calculated that Paris and its 3.5 million people would need 5,500 tons of supplies per day. To transport this tonnage would require 3,000 trucks and another 300 assorted heavy vehicles. The effort would also require 1 million gallons of gasoline every two weeks. For George Patton especially, this was terribly frustrating. He was only 100 miles from the Rhine with little to bar his path—but he was running out of gasoline. Doubly frustrating to Patton was the fact that he knew the window of opportunity was closing. The German General Staff was rushing reinforcements to the endangered sector. "My men can eat their belts, but my tanks have gotta have gas!" he cried in dismay. This was all that could stop him at the moment, but stop him it did. By the time Patton received enough fuel to make another significant advance, the German 1st Army had been reinforced with the veteran 3rd and 15th Panzer Grenadier Divisions from Italy, among others, the 17th SS Panzer Grenadier Division had been rebuilt, and the 462nd Volksgrenadier Division had been formed. This unit included the elite Officers' Training Regiment, probably the best regiment to fight in the European Theater of Operations in World War II. It had no privates. Most of its men had earned their commissions on the battlefields of the Eastern Front. The combination of fuel shortages and a reinforced 1st Army checked Patton's advance in front of Metz. The U.S. 3rd Army would not cross the Rhine until March 22, 1945.

NOTES

1. Curt Gallenkamp was born in Wessel in 1890. He entered the army in 1909 and was commissioned into the field artillery the following year. He fought in World War I and served in the Reichsheer. During the World War II era, he commanded Arko 16 (1937–39), was chief of staff of III Corps (1939), commanded the 78th Infantry Division (late 1939–42), and LXXX Corps (1942–44). On August 8, 1944, he was placed in Fuehrer Reserve and never reemployed. Gallenkamp's replacement was Dr. Franz Beyer, who had served in the navy in World War I. Not selected for the Reichswehr, he joined the police and entered the army in 1935 as a lieutenant colonel. Beyer had previously commanded the 131st Infantry Regiment (1939–41) and the 331st Infantry Division (1941–43) and, as acting commander only, had led XVII Corps, LVII Panzer Corps, V Corps, and XXXXIX Mountain Corps (1944). The LXXX Corps was a permanent assignment and he held it until the end of the war. Keilig, p. 33.

2. Ernst Haeckel was born in Gemuenden in 1890 and entered the Bavarian Army as a *Fahnenjunker* in 1909. He served in World War I and the Reichswehr,

196

and in 1937 he was commander of the 107th Infantry Regiment (1937–40). He led the 263rd Infantry Division (1940–42), the 158th Reserve Division (later the 16th Infantry Division and 16th Volksgrenadier Division) (1942–44), and ended the war commanding Division 471 (1945).

3. SS General Georg Keppler was an acting commander only. On October 24, he was replaced by SS Lieutenant General Hermann Priess, who led the corps for the rest of the war. Keppler was born in Mainz in 1894 into a military family (his father was a colonel) and had joined the Imperial Army in 1913 as a *Fahnenjunker* in the Fusilier Regiment Generalfeldmarschall Prince Albrecht of Prussia, the Hanoverian 73rd Fusilier Regiment. A lieutenant at the end of World War I, he had not been selected for the Reichswehr, so he joined the police and in 1935 returned to active duty—in the SS. By 1937, he was an SS lieutenant colonel, and he was promoted to full colonel the following year. He commanded the "Der Fuehrer" Infantry Motorized Regiment in the West (1940), was acting commander of the Totenkopf ("Death's Head") Motorized Infantry Division in Russia (1941), and commanded the 2nd SS Panzer Division "Das Reich" (1942–43). After commanding the I SS, he was commander of Waffen-SS in Hungary and Higher SS and Police Commander, Hungary. Keppler led the III SS (Germanic) Corps in Courland (1944–45) and ended the war commanding the XVIII SS Corps in the West (1945). He died in Hamburg on June 16, 1966. Nikolaus von Preradovich, *Die Generale der Waffen-SS* (Berg am See: 1985), pp. 39–40 (hereafter cited as "Preradovich"); Bender and Taylor, Volume II, p. 31; Kraetschmer, pp. 52–59.

4. Blumenson, *Breakout and Pursuit*, pp. 576–77.

5. Larry Collins and Dominique Lapierre, *Is Paris Burning?* (New York: 1965), p. 24 (hereafter cited as "Collins and Lapierre").

6. Keilig, p. 60. Choltitz was a Prussian, born in Silesia in 1894. He was educated in various cadet schools and entered the service as a senior officer cadet in March 1914. Commissioned second lieutenant in the 107th Infantry Regiment in September, he fought in World War I and served in the Reichswehr (1919–35). He was a major commanding the III Battalion, 16th Infantry Regiment, in 1937. Promoted to lieutenant colonel (1938) and colonel (1941), he took charge of the 16th Infantry in September 1940.

7. Collins and Lapierre, p. 24.

8. Robert Ley committed suicide in late 1945.

9. Collins and Lapierre, pp. 23–25.

10. Hubertus von Aulock was born in Kochelsdorf, Upper Silesia, in 1891. He joined the army as a *Fahnenjunker* in 1911 and was commissioned in the 22nd Infantry Regiment in 1912. He was discharged after World War I as a first lieutenant but rejoined the service in 1938 as a reserve captain. He was a corps supply officer when the war began. In late 1940, he became deputy commander of the Brandenburg Regiment and joined the staff of the Military Commander of Northwest France in 1941. For reasons that are not clear, Hitler promoted him directly from lieutenant colonel to major general, effective August 1, 1944. He was captured on September 2 and retired to Hamburg after the war. Keilig, p. 15.

11. Otto Dessloch was born on June 11, 1889. During World War I, he was a pilot and observer in the Flying Service. During World War II, he served as

commander of the 6th Air Division (1939), II Flak Corps (1940–41), I Flak Corps (1942), and 4th Air Fleet on the Russian Front (1943–44). Named commander in chief of the 3rd Air Fleet (later Luftwaffe Command West) in August 1944, he returned to the Eastern Front as commander of the 4th Air Fleet in late 1944. On April 27, 1945, when Field Marshal Ritter Robert von Greim succeeded Hermann Goering as Supreme Commander of the Luftwaffe, Dessloch replaced Greim as commander of the 6th Air Fleet, which he led until the end of the war. He was promoted to colonel general on March 1, 1944. He died on May 13, 1977. Absolon, p. 18; Dessloch Personnel Extract, Air University Archives.

12. Pierre Koenig was best known for his brilliant defense of Bir Hacheim during the Gazala Line campaign when, as commander of the 1st Free French Brigade, he frustrated Rommel and much of the Afrika Korps for 15 days. Finally surrounded, he nevertheless broke out with his entire command, except the wounded. After the war, he commanded the French zone of occupied Germany.

13. Miller, p. 162.

14. Keegan, p. 292.

15. Like Choltitz, Otto Abetz did not want Paris destroyed.

16. Blumenson, *Breakout and Pursuit*, p. 598, citing Dietrich von Choltitz, *Soldat unter Soldaten* (Konstanz: 1951), pp. 255–59.

17. Hamburg had been fire-bombed by the RAF in 1943. Roughly 50,000 people were killed and 40,000 were wounded. More than half of the city was destroyed.

18. Collins and Lapierre, p. 170.

19. Wilhelm Mohnke was born in Luebeck on March 15, 1911, the son of a master carpenter. He followed his father into this profession after dropping out of school. In 1931, Mohnke joined the NSDAP and, a few weeks later, the SS. He spent most of his career in the Leibstandarte Adolf Hitler, commanding the unit (now the 1st SS Panzer Division) during the Battle of the Bulge. Prior to that, he commanded the division's panzer battalion in Russia. In Normandy, however, he commanded the 26th Panzer Grenadier Regiment of the 12th SS Panzer Division. Mohnke was apparently responsible for a number of atrocities, including the murder of Canadian prisoners of war during the Battle of Normandy. He was promoted to SS-*Brigadefuehrer* (SS-major general) on January 13, 1945. He was commandant of the Reichchancellery in Berlin when Adolf Hitler committed suicide. Mohnke led the subsequent breakout, and although several of his people escaped, Martin Bormann was killed and Mohnke himself was captured. He remained in Soviet prisons until October 1955, when he returned to West Germany and set up a very successful export business. He was living in a suburb of Hamburg in the 1990s. Preradovich, pp. 181–82.

20. Blumenson, *Breakout and Pursuit*, p. 579.

21. Otto von Knobelsdorff was born in Berlin in 1886. Educated in cadet schools, he joined the 94th Infantry Regiment as a *Fahnenjunker* in 1905. He fought in World War I, served in the Reichsheer, and was a major general and commandant of the fortress of Oppeln when Germany mobilized. He was promptly named chief of staff of the XXXII Corps Command (1939–40) and became commander of the 19th Infantry Division in 1940. Late that year he was given command of the newly formed 19th Panzer Division, which he led on the Eastern Front. In January 1942, he became acting commander of the X Corps and

took charge of the II Corps (surrounded at Demyansk) in June. In October 1942, Knobelsdorff assumed command of the XXIV Panzer Corps and later led the XXXXVIII Panzer Corps (December 1942–October 1943) and XXXX Panzer Corps (February 1944–August 1944). He led 1st Army from September 6 to November 30, 1944, but was sacked because he protested too strongly when his army was stripped of its tank units, which were sent to the Ardennes. Knobelsdorff retired to Hanover and wrote a history of the 19th Infantry/Panzer Division. He held the Knight's Cross with Oak Leaves and Swords.

22. Tessin, Volume 5, pp. 160, 173.

23. The 199th Security Regiment was formed at Troyes on February 10, 1943. It absorbed the 339th, 763rd, 654th, and 722nd Landeschuetzen Battalions from the III, XII, X, and XI Military Districts, respectively. It had four battalions: the I at Troyes, the II at Chalons, the III at Chaumont and the IV at Bordeaux. It also had a 13th (Heavy Weapons) Company and a 14th (Engineer) Company. In May 1943, its staff was at Bar-sur-Aube, and presumably they took the 13th and 14th Companies with them. The original I/ and III/199th were sent to Marseilles in August 1943 and became part of Security Regiment Boehmer of Armeegruppe Felber. A new III Battalion was established at Joigny, and a new I/199th was formed at Troyes. After the Battle of Troyes, the 199th Security Regiment became the 199th Security Battalion and was assigned to 19th Army. It was dissolved in October. Ibid., Volume 7, p. 292.

24. Juin became the chief of staff of the French Defense Ministry in 1944.

25. Seaton, *Fortress*, p. 122.

26. Blumenson, *Breakout and Pursuit*, pp. 616–17. After the war, Choltitz quietly returned to Baden-Baden, where he wrote his memoirs. When he died on November 5, 1966, he was more greatly mourned in France than in Germany.

CHAPTER IX

BEYOND THE SEINE

The last rear guards of Army Group B fell back beyond the Seine on August 29, and the Normandy campaign was over. During the last 10 weeks, it had suffered 500,000 casualties, of which 210,000 had been captured. Virtually all of its panzer divisions had been smashed. It had also lost 2,300 tanks and assault guns, and according to Blumentritt, only 100 to 120 managed to escape behind the Seine. During that time, it received only 30,000 replacements. On August 29, Model reported to Hitler that the average strength of his 11 panzer and panzer grenadier divisions that had fought in Normandy was "five to ten tanks each." The 16 infantry divisions of the 5th Panzer and 7th Armies could muster only enough men to form four full-strength divisions, but with almost no artillery and few heavy weapons.[1] With such meager forces, Model was not in a position to halt the Allies' offensive, even on a formidable natural barrier such as the Seine.

For his drive beyond the river, General Eisenhower planned to advance on a broad front along two axes of advance: Montgomery's 21st Army Group (reinforced with the 1st Allied Airborne Army and the 1st U.S. Army under General Hodges) was to drive northeast from the Seine toward the Ruhr, with its main effort north of the Ardennes. To the south, Bradley's 12th Army Group was to drive to the east, in a secondary effort. Montgomery's initial objectives were the capture of the Channel ports, the destruction of the German 15th Army, and the seizure of the V-weapons launching sites.

Meanwhile, Model continued the retreat that had been in progress since he assumed command. All of the units under his command (including Army Groups B and G) were supposed to fall back to the Kitzinger Line, which was to be constructed along the Somme and Marne Rivers, under the supervision of the Military Governor of France. General Kitzinger, however, had been given little in the way of workers or construction materials and had to rely primarily on French laborers—and they were understandably reluctant to do anything that would delay their own liberation. Informed that little progress was being made, Hitler placed Kitzinger under Model's command on August 23, but this move had no effect upon the course of events. The Seine had already been breached, and Model told Jodl on August 28 that he did not believe it would be possible to stop the retreat short of the western approaches to the Rhine River. Only on German soil, he pointed out, could the Wehrmacht count upon civilian labor to perform their construction tasks effectively.

To defend the Kitzinger Line, Model demanded additional troops: 15 divisions in the Troyes-Dijon-Jura Mountains area and 30 to 35 divisions for the front, plus a new panzer army with 12 tank divisions as a mobile reserve. He would also need four additional army headquarters and 16 new corps headquarters (4 of them panzer) to successfully defend the line. This, he knew, was impossible. All Hitler could make available to him in August was 4 of the new Volksgrenadier divisions and roughly 80 partially trained replacement battalions from the Home Army. From Italy he had ordered the transfer of the veteran 3rd and 15th Panzer Grenadier Divisions, and 2 more divisions of replacement troops and two panzer brigades were slated to arrive at the end of August or during the first week in September: certainly not enough to hold the Kitzinger Line. Model, therefore, began to fall back to the next natural defensive line, which extended from the Schelde estuary in the Netherlands to the Albert Canal in Belgium, to the Meuse River in France. Even this line, he suspected, would soon be swamped by the fast-paced Allied advance.

Meanwhile, the Americans continued to advance rapidly. In the zone of Hodges's U.S. 1st Army, the U.S. 3rd Armored Division (now under the command of Major General Maurice Rose) crossed the Marne on August 27 and advanced 50 miles, capturing the cathedral city of Soissons on the Aisne before the end of the day. German resistance was nonexistent. The Americans even managed to bag three troop trains east of the city—OB West had no idea that the Americans were anywhere close to Soissons. Among other things, an entire SS panzer company was taken prisoner, and four of the latest model PzKw VI "Tiger" tanks were captured intact. In the meantime, the 7th Armored Division of Patton's army crossed the Marne on its way to Rheims, and the 4th Armored was closing in on Chalons. Hitler's policy of committing the panzer divisions to the hedgerow fighting of Normandy was now paying monstrous dividends: Model had almost nothing but nonmotorized infantry with which to defend this excellent tank country, and marching ("straight leg") infantry was of little use here, against the fully motorized American divisions.

It is one of the ironies of World War II that the German Army in the West in 1940 was little different from that of 1944 in terms of mobility, but the German Army of 1940 was the most mobile army in the world, whereas the army that defended France in 1944 was one of the worst, insofar as motorization was concerned. In 1940, only 10 of Germany's 136 divisions were panzer and perhaps the equivalent of 5 others were motorized. In May 1944, only 10 of OB West's 58 divisions were tank or motorized units. Army Group B was now something of a sitting duck for the rapidly moving British and American forces.

A typical example of what was happening to the Wehrmacht at this time is the story of Sergeant Helmut Hoerner. No recent draftee, he was a tough, competent veteran of a dozen campaigns. He had fought in the "Dash to the Channel," at Dunkirk, across Belgium and France, and was in the first rush of Operation "Barbarossa." He took part in the great encirclement at Smolensk, helped turn back the massive Soviet counterattacks at Vyazma, and pushed on to the gates of Moscow, before he was wounded at Volokolamsk. After recovering in Karlsruhe (and marrying his 18-year-old fiancée), he was sent back to the Russian Front, where he fought under Model in the desperate battles around Rzhev (1942–43). He was serving as a forward observer in the 77th Infantry Division during the Normandy campaign when he was wounded by an American hand grenade on July 4. Evacuated to the Reserve Hospital in Paris, he was inducted into an emergency battalion under Captain Nollte on August 19. It included remnants of the 77th Infantry. Hoerner was given command of an infantry platoon of 42 men, which had only one machine gun, one automatic pistol, and 12 rifles. Marching on foot (he did not have a single vehicle), Hoerner's battalion was overrun by Sherman tanks from Collins's U.S. VII Corps about 25 miles northeast of Château-Thierry on August 26. Although clearly trapped miles behind enemy lines, Hoerner and two of his comrades (both veterans of the Eastern Front) attempted to make their way back to German lines on foot. They were, however, cornered by a party of Frenchmen and Americans and raised their hands in the "double German salute" on August 29. Hoerner was soon relieved of all of his decorations and his wrist watch.[2]

"The thought comes: Why didn't I put a bullet into my head?" he wrote in his diary.

What purpose is there to living without freedom, especially now after the world in which I believed, for which I fought and bled, has collapsed? Who are these people, who, like highway bandits with no feeling of shame, plunder soldiers in their most bitter hour and enrich themselves in the most base manner.... What will happen to us, what must the homeland face if these Americans are successful in pushing into the Reich?

. . . It is true that today we have fallen into the hands of robbers, but the fair fight in Normandy brings the conclusion that not all Americans are such miserable highwaymen as these. The fact that they have a sense of humor was proven during an episode that occurred near Saint-Sauveur. At that time some Germans fell into their hands, including an eighteen-year-old who had the face of a child. After a quick decision they cut his pants off above the knee, filled his pack with chocolate, hung a sign around his neck that read "We do not fight children," and sent him back across no-man's land to his unit.[3]

While Sergeant Hoerner was trying in vain to escape Collins's tanks and motorized infantry, General Bradley assigned Patton objectives on the upper Rhine, 250 miles east of his bridgeheads on the Seine. To reach these objectives, Patton would have to cross several rivers, including the Marne, the Velse, the Aisne, the Meuse, and the Moselle. Although these rivers offered excellent possibilities for defense, von Knobelsdorff did not have the troops to take advantage of them. He tried to protect the left flank of his 1st Army by committing the 17th SS Panzer Grenadier Division (now reinforced almost to full strength but made up of men without unit training) and the battered 9th Panzer Division (down to a strength of one infantry battalion, four or five tanks and assault guns, and a single battery of artillery) along the Seine east of Montereau. He assigned the LXXX Corps the task of defending Reims (on the Velse River) and with establishing absorption points along the Marne from Melun via Château-Thierry to Chalons. At the same time, about 100 officers from the LVIII Panzer Corps set up roadblocks, in an attempt to stop the panic-stricken retreat toward Reims and the east.

The Luftwaffe was the worst offender. On D-Day, it had a strength of nearly 340,000 men (out of 1.4 million Wehrmacht troops in France), including a few hundred pilots, about 100,000 flak troops, and 30,000 paratroopers—leaving an inexcusably high number of supply and service troops for an air fleet of only 100 operational aircraft.[4] When the German Front in Normandy collapsed, the 3rd Air Fleet's ground and signals organizations simply took to their heels, heading east as rapidly as possible, without bothering to demolish anything. Even top-secret files were left behind and fuel dumps were abandoned, instead of being put to the torch. This was the last straw, as far as the air fleet commander was concerned. On August 19, Hitler relieved the lazy and indolent Field Marshal Hugo Sperrle of his command and replaced him with Dessloch (see Chapter VIII), but he could do nothing to stem the tide. On September 22, the Nazi dictator downgraded the 3rd Air Fleet and redesignated it Luftwaffe Command West.

For his drive on the Rhine, Patton initially had two corps south of Paris: the XII and the XX. (Later Haislip's XV would be returned to him.)

Supplies were a more serious problem to him than the German 1st Army. On August 25, for example, 207 air force transports had to land at Orleans and deliver him more than 500 tons of supplies to sustain the advance. Even then 3rd Army would have faltered, had it not captured a large German fuel train at Sens.

Between August 25 and 28, the U.S. 4th Armored Division advanced from Troyes to Vitry-le-Francois and crossed the Marne, as did the U.S. 80th Infantry Division. By then the U.S. XII Corps was virtually out of gasoline, but the capture of 100,000 gallons of German fuel at and near Chalons allowed it to continue the advance. The U.S. XX Corps ran into the remnants of the 48th and 338th Infantry Divisions, the horse-drawn artillery battalion of the 708th Infantry Division, and the panzer battalion of the 17th SS Panzer Grenadier east of Melun but was slowed down only briefly. The German resistance crumbled quickly, and the American 7th Armored Division pushed on to the Marne, captured Epernay, bypassed Reims to the east, and headed north toward the Aisne. The U.S. 5th Infantry Division, following the 7th, secured Reims on August 30 without much difficulty. By noon on August 31 the 7th Armored had captured the Meuse bridge at Verdun and by September 1 had crossed the river in strength. Patton was now in a position to attack toward the Moselle (between Metz and Nancy) and, from there, would have been barely 100 miles from the Rhine. In the meantime, the partially rebuilt 17th SS Panzer Grenadier Division had virtually been eliminated as a combat force, and the 48th and 338th Infantry Divisions had been reduced to two small Kampfgruppen. Unfortunately for the Americans, Patton was literally out of gas. Individual Shermans were already dropping out of formation, their fuel tanks completely dry. All across the front, in fact, Eisenhower's policy of blasting the French transportation network was now proving to be a two-edged sword. The destruction of the French transportation network had been a major contributing factor to the success of the D-Day landings and the subsequent Allied victory in Normandy. However, now that the Allies needed the French highways and railroads, they were in shambles—totally inadequate for the task of maintaining the advance of several Allied armies at the same time. In addition, no Allied general had expected the German defenses in France to collapse so suddenly and so completely; therefore, they did not have as many truck and transport units in France as they needed. Additionally, Eisenhower was now having to divert 3,000 tons of supplies a day just to feed Paris. At the same time, Patton's rapid drive had caused shock and consternation at OKW, because the U.S. 3rd Army now represented a threat to Dijon. Through this city ran the only escape route available to Wiese's 19th Army, which was falling back from southern France. Accordingly, Hitler rushed Knobelsdorff everything he could get his hands on, including the 3rd and 15th Panzer Grenadier Divisions from Italy, four recently formed Volksgrenadier divisions, and the 106th Panzer Brigade. Several divisions that were rebuilding from the Normandy debacle were also earmarked for 1st Army.[5] As a result, Patton's drive came to a sputtering halt west of the Moselle.

Montgomery was also suffering supply problems, but not to the extent Patton was. During the last week of August, he smashed General of Infantry Otto Sponheimer's LXVII Corps of the 15th Army, which was defending along the coast between the Seine and the Somme.[6] Meanwhile, the LVIII Panzer Corps rallied the remnants of the 18th Luftwaffe Field and 6th Parachute Divisions at Compiegne, where it was reinforced with the 348th Infantry Division, which was coming down from the north, too late to reinforce the Paris garrison, as Model had originally intended. Here the corps tried to form a breakwater position on the left flank of the 5th Panzer Army. At the same time, following its defeat at Vernon, the LXXXI Corps fell back cross the Seine and in the direction of the Somme with the remnants of several units that were no longer battleworthy. All of this left very little in the path of Hodges's U.S. 1st Army (forming Monty's right flank), which surged forward with the U.S. XIX and VII Corps (left to right). Collins's VII quickly broke through the LVIII Panzer Corps' line near Meaux on August 26. The American spearheads passed within a mile of Knobelsdorff's headquarters during their drive on Château-Thierry, which they captured on August 28. Two days later they reached Rethel and Montcornet, 100 miles beyond the Seine. That same day, elements of the 1st Canadian Army liberated Rouen, the river port of Paris.

Meanwhile, the U.S. V Corps (General Gerow) at last disentangled itself from the joyous mess that was Paris and joined the pursuit on August 29 (with the U.S. 5th Armored, 4th Infantry, and 28th Infantry Divisions), and Kuntzen's LXXXI Corps simply disintegrated. By the evening of September 1, the 1st U.S. Army was across the Aisne River and was closing in on Compiegne, 45 miles northeast of Paris. Three days later, Kuntzen was sacked and the remnants of his command were given to Lieutenant General Friedrich-August Schack.[7]

In the meantime, Montgomery began his main offensive. His primary objective was Antwerp. The British forces jumped off on August 29, spearheaded by the 600 tanks of Horrock's XXX Corps. By noon on August 30, the British 11th Armoured Division had broken through the front of the 5th Panzer Army, was 40 miles from Amiens, and was advancing on the city against light opposition. Horrocks ordered it to push forward through the night, because he wanted to take the bridges over the Somme by a surprise coup. Thanks to the help of the FFI, the British seized three of the four bridges at Amiens in the predawn darkness of August 31, before the Germans could blow them up. In the process the tankers of the 3rd Royal Tank Regiment overran the 7th Army's command post, where Sepp Dietrich was meeting with Heinrich Eberbach. Dietrich managed to escape in a sedan, but Eberbach was captured as he tried to get away in a Volkswagen. Most of the 7th Army's staff was also captured. Only Colonel von Gersdorff and one other officer managed to escape—on foot. (They later made their way back to German lines and joined General of Panzer Troops Erich Brandenberger, who was on September 3 charged with the task of rebuilding 7th Army.)[8] The Kitzinger Line was broken before it could be manned. Horrocks, meanwhile, continued his drive, and on September 2 the British Guards Armoured Division reached the Belgian border southeast of Lille. Farther east, American Shermans crossed into Belgium as far as the Lille- Mons road, by which thousands of Germans were trying to escape. There were now three Allied corps (the British XXX and the U.S. XIX and VII) within a day's march of Brussels. Only the chaotic state of the French road and railway systems had prevented Montgomery and Bradley from completing the destruction of the Wehrmacht in France. Even so, there was not much left of the 7th or 5th Panzer Armies, the 1st and 19th Armies were not in much better shape, and the 15th Army—still defending in the Pas de Calais area and along the Belgian coast—was now in danger of being cut off by a rapid British advance.

NOTES

1. Wilmot, p. 434.

2. Helmut Hoerner, *A German Odyssey: The Journal of a German Prisoner of War*, Allan K. Powell, trans. (Golden, Colo.), pp. 3–92.

3. Ibid., pp. 92–93.

4. Albert Seaton, *The German Army, 1933–45* (New York: 1982), p. 223. (hereafter cited as "Seaton, *German Army*").

5. As of September 16, 1944 (after 15th Panzer Grenadier Division had been transferred to the 19th Army), 1st Army consisted of:

> XIII SS Corps: SS Lieutenant General Hermann Priess
>> 3rd Panzer Grenadier, 17th SS Panzer Grenadier, and 462nd Infantry
>> Divisions
>
> LXXXII Corps: General of Artillery Johann Sinnhuber
>> 559th Volkgrenadier, 36th Infantry, and 19th Infantry Divisions
>
> LXXX Corps: General of Infantry Dr. Franz Bayer
>> 48th Infantry, Panzer Lehr, 5th Parachute Divisions (Tessin, Volume 2, p. 3).

6. Otto Sponheimer was born in Nuremberg in 1886. He joined the army as a volunteer in 1907 but nevertheless managed to earn a commission in the 14th Bavarian Infantry Regiment in 1909. In 1920, however, he was discharged from the army due to the Treaty of Versailles, after 13 years' service. Sponheimer

promptly joined the Bavarian police and served with them until 1935, when he rejoined the army as a colonel. By 1937, he was commander of the 24th Infantry Regiment, which he led in Poland. Later he commanded the 21st Infantry Division (late 1939–early 1943), was deputy commander of the XXVIII and X Corps (1943), commander of the LIV Corps in northern Russia (1943–44), and commander of the LXVII Corps (from June 1, 1944). He ran afoul of the Nazi leadership, however, was relieved of his command on December 17, 1944, and never reemployed. He was an excellent commander.

7. Adolf Kuntzen was never reemployed and on December 31, 1944, was dismissed from the service.

Friedrich-August Schack was born in 1892 and joined the army as a war volunteer in the 1st Hussars Regiment in 1914. He received a commission as a second lieutenant in the infantry in late 1915. Schack was selected for retention in the Reichsheer; during the World War II era, he commanded the 15th Machine Gun Battalion (1938–40); he commanded the 392nd Infantry Regiment (early 1940–42); he was commandant of the War School at Potsdam (1942–43); and he commanded the 216th Infantry Division (1943), the 272nd Infantry Division (1943–44), LXXXI Corps (September 4 to 21, 1944), LXXXV Corps (1944), and XXXII Corps (1945). Promoted to general of infantry on April 20, 1945, he retired to Goslar after the war.

8. Erich Brandenberger was born in Augsburg in 1892. He entered the army as an officer-cadet in the 6th Bavarian Field Artillery Regiment in 1911. He served in World War I and the Reichsheer and was chief of staff of the XXIII Corps when the war began. He later led the 8th Panzer Division (1941–43), the XVII Corps (1943), and the XXIX Corps (1943–44), all of the Eastern Front. Promoted to general of panzer troops on August 1, 1943, he led the 7th Army from August 28, 1944, to February 20, 1945. He was relieved of this command by Field Marshal Model due to a personality conflict—they never got along. Brandenberger, however, was named commander of the 19th Army on March 25, 1945, and led it until the end of the war. He died in Bonn in 1955.

CHAPTER X

THE ALLIES MOP UP IN FRANCE

THE 19th ARMY ESCAPES

While Eisenhower's armies were smashing Army Group B and the 1st Army, Sandy Patch's 7th Army was attempting to complete the destruction of Blaskowitz's Army Group G in the south of France. At this time, Army Group G consisted of Sacks's very weak LXIV Corps (retreating from the Bay of Biscay) and Wiese's 19th Army, which was falling back from the Mediterranean. As was typical of Hitler, Sacks had to leave behind detachments at La Rochelle and Royan (at the mouth of the Gironde River on the coast of the Bay of Biscay), and they were ordered to fight to the last man. As for the rest of the corps, everything depended on the 19th Army. If it could hold off the Americans long enough, Sacks's men could reach Dijon and make good their escape. If not, they would be captured, along with the bulk of Army Group G.

By August 18, Wiese's 19th Army was in fragments. General of Fliers Erich Petersen's IV Luftwaffe Field Corps (716th Infantry and 189th Reserve Divisions) was trying to escape to the northeast (from the area of the Spanish border),[1] while the 148th and 157th Reserve Divisions (in extreme southwestern France) had been driven into the zone of Kesselring's OB Southwest. The remnants of the 242nd Infantry Division were retreating into Toulon, while the 244th Infantry Division fell back into Marseilles. Hitler had ordered that both cities be defended to the last bullet. This left Wiese with only four divisions with which to face the Allied drive up the Rhone: the 198th Infantry, 158th Reserve, 11th Panzer, and 338th Infantry. All four divisions eventually were placed under the control of General of Infantry Baptist Kniess's LXXXV Corps, which formed the solid rear guard for Army Group G's evacuation of southern France.[2]

As we have seen, the Allied invasion of southern France was spearheaded by the three divisions of Truscott's U.S. VI Corps. After the destruction of the German LXII Corps (see Chapter VII), Truscott was opposed only by elements of Major General Otto Richter's 198th Infantry Division, which did a good job of delaying the Americans east of Aix-en-Provence. The city did not fall until August 21; then the 198th Infantry fell back to positions southeast of Avignon, where it joined the 11th Panzer and 338th Infantry for a defense of the city.

Meanwhile, between August 16 and 18, the 2nd Air Division made its last stand in southern France. It mustered its remaining 14 Do-217s, 65 Ju-88s, and several fighters in the Aix-en-Provence area and flew about 140 sorties against Allied ground and naval targets. By August 21, however, the Luftwaffe was evacuating its bases, and except for rare reconnaissance flights, air support for the 19th Army ceased altogether. In the meantime, General de Lattre's French II Corps landed and drove to the west, with the mission of capturing the ports of Toulon and Marseilles.

General Truscott began his drive up the Rhone on August 21, and he intended to accomplish nothing less than the destruction of what was left of the German 19th Army. On August 22 he took Grenoble without opposition as the 157th Reserve Division fell back into the mountains to the east, and by August 24, his forces had reached Antibes, 140 miles from the Mediterranean. His plan to destroy the 19th Army miscarried, however. He almost succeeded in surrounding the 198th Infantry, 338th Infantry, and 11th Panzer in an eight-day battle around Montelimar, but the Germans managed to keep a narrow corridor open and escaped to the north. The battle ended on August 28. The 198th, 338th, and 716th Infantry, 189th Reserve, and 11th Panzer Divisions had escaped. German losses were nevertheless very high: 2,000 motorized vehicles destroyed, 1,000 horses killed, and more than 40 guns lost along Highway 7 alone. General Wiese, however, was able to continue his retreat. On September 1, the Allied 6th Army Group was activated under the command of Lieutenant General Jacob L. Devers. Controlling the U.S. 7th Army and French 1st Army (General de Tassigny), it was to form the southern flank of Eisenhower's front until the end of the war.

After the Battle of Montelimar, events in southern France raced rapidly to their conclusion. Bordeaux was evacuated by the Germans and occupied by the French on August 24, and Nice fell on September 1. Lyon, the third largest city in France, was liberated the following day, and the entire French Mediterranean coast was in Allied hands by September 8. The spearheads of Patch's U.S. 7th Army joined up with the southern flank of Patton's 3rd Army near Dijon on September 12, completing the linkup between the Allied forces coming up from the Mediterranean and those that had broken out of Normandy.

Most of the 1st Army had already escaped by this time. The headquarters staff itself had already been sent to the north, to form the new left flank of Army Group B, leaving Sachs's LXIV Corps to direct the withdrawal from the Atlantic coast. It had very few combat units. The largest were the 716th Infantry Division (a Kampfgruppe smashed on D-Day) and the recently formed 30th SS Grenadier Division "Russische # 2." The 30th SS was made up of Osttruppen and was anything but an elite fighting organization and is a good example of how Himmler had polluted the Waffen-SS (Armed SS). On September 14, one of its battalions (mostly composed of Ukrainians) mutinied, murdered its officers, and joined the FFI.[3]

Like the 19th Army at Montelimar, the nonmotorized 1st Army moved with the speed of desperation. It headed for Dijon, which was held open by the 19th Army and its rear guard, the 11th Panzer Division. Most of the 1st Army made good its escape. Only the rear-most column under Major General Botho Elster, the former commandant of Biarritz, did not make good its getaway.[4] Elster's column, which consisted mostly of noncombat troops, lost contact with the screening force that was supposed to escort it to Dijon in early September. By September 5, the column stretched out over more than 30 miles of French roads and was being increasingly harassed by the FFI. Three days later, Elster made contact with 1st Lieutenant Samuel W. Magill, the commander of an American reconnaissance platoon, who had advanced south of the Loire on his own initiative. Elster preferred capture by the Americans to surrender (and probably eventual murder) by the FFI, so he agreed to capitulate to the U.S. 83rd Infantry Division. The surrender took place two days later. General Macon, the commander of the 83rd, captured 18,850 men (including 754 officers), 10 women, 400 automobiles, 500 trucks, and 1,000 horse-drawn wagons.[5]

Of the 100,000 men and 200 women who began the trek from the Bay of Biscay, most of them on foot, 65,000 escaped.[6] Most of the rest managed to surrender to the Americans. Between 10,000 and 15,000 were missing. Most of these were killed or murdered by partisans.

The U.S. 7th Army finally halted before the Belford Gap on September 15, ending the "Dragoon" campaign. It had destroyed several divisions and captured more than 75,000 prisoners—not as many as General Patch had hoped to capture, to be sure, but a tremendous Allied victory nonetheless. On the other hand, both the German 1st and 19th Armies—although badly battered—had escaped and "lived to fight another day."

THE BATTLES FOR THE PORTS OF TOULON, MARSEILLES, AND BREST

The rapid advance of the Allied armies had left several German garrisons cut off in French ports, miles behind enemy lines. Some of these ports, such as Lorient and St. Nazaire, the Allies were content to leave alone. They, in effect, became self-supporting prisoner-of-war camps and remained so until the end of the war. In other cases, however, the Allies felt that they needed the ports to help supply their armies. This particularly applied to Toulon, Marseilles, and Brest. Two other considerations also applied in the case of Brest. First, its commander, Lieutenant General Hermann Ramcke, was not only a fanatical Nazi; he was also a highly daring and innovative commander who was not likely to be content to sit out the rest of the war without taking offensive action.[7] Second, a large part of his garrison consisted of the troops of his own 2nd Parachute Division: an elite, pro-Nazi formation that would be able and more than willing to attack Allied forces in the rear, as ordered by Ramcke. Deciding that it was unsafe to allow the 2nd Parachute to remain at large, Eisenhower and Bradley ordered Middleton to destroy it.

The task of reducing the Mediterranean ports of Toulon and Marseilles fell to General de Lattre's II French Corps, which attacked Toulon with the 1st French, 9th Colonial, and 3rd Algerian Divisions, as well as several smaller units from Senegal and Morocco and elements of the 1st French Armored Division. At the same time, other French detachments, supported by American units, invested Marseilles, about 25 miles to the west. There were about 18,000 German soldiers and sailors in each city.

Toulon, the former base of the French Mediterranean Fleet, was well defended by Lieutenant General Johannes Baessler, a highly respected veteran of the Eastern Front, under the overall supervision of Rear Admiral Heinrich Ruhfus, the commandant of the fortress. Baessler had commanded the 4th Panzer Regiment prior to the outbreak of the war and served as chief of staff of the XI Corps in Poland, the Netherlands, Belgium, France, the Balkans campaign, and Russia. He was promoted to major general in February 1942 and assumed command of the 9th Panzer Division in the Kursk sector in April. On November 1, he was transferred to the command of the 14th Panzer Division at Stalingrad. Baessler took part in General Hans Valentin Hube's successful effort to prevent the Red Army's "inner" encirclement of the city but was seriously wounded in the process. On November 26, after only 26 days in command, he was flown out of the pocket and was judged medically not fit to return to active duty until July 20, 1943, when he assumed command of the 242nd Infantry. He was promoted to lieutenant general on February 1, 1944.

Baessler's men were of indifferent quality, but he seemed to be able to get the most out of them, and he took maximum advantage of the old French fortifications and the naturally excellent defensive terrain around the naval fortress-city. In addition, he had already strengthened the inner defenses of Toulon with minefields, trench systems, and barbed wire entanglements, and he had about 150 artillery pieces in support. On August 19, when the French launched a frontal assault on the city, Baessler repulsed them with heavy casualties. Still, the French had the city surrounded, they outnumbered Baessler more than 3 to 1, had dozens of tanks, and were supported by the devastating firepower of the Allied navies and air forces. Slowly they pushed their way into Toulon and ground the 242th Infantry to bits. General Baessler was critically wounded on August 26 and died later that year. All resistance ended on August 28. Admiral Ruhfus was among the 17,000 prisoners.

Like Toulon, Marseilles was well defended by a highly respected veteran of the Eastern Front. Lieutenant General Hans Schaefer had led the 251st Infantry Regiment in the French campaign and in Operation "Barbarossa" and had taken over the 252nd Infantry Division on the Moscow sector when Lieutenant General Diether von Boehm-Bezing's health cracked in early 1942. Promoted to major general in April 1942, Schaefer assumed command of the 332nd Infantry Division on January 1, 1943 (the day he was promoted to lieutenant general), and led it until June 5, when he was seriously wounded near Kharkov. He did not return to active duty until April 14, 1944, when he assumed command of the 244th Infantry.

The Siege of Marseilles also began on August 19, but General Schaefer did not have the natural advantages that existed at Toulon; still, he took full advantage of what nature offered him and put up a strong defense, which included especially fierce house-to-house fighting in the northern suburbs. By the night of August 27–28, however, the Germans held only the dock area, and Schaefer surrendered the city the next day. The French had taken more than 26,000 prisoners in the two cities and had reportedly killed perhaps 10,000, while suffering only 4,000 casualties themselves (excluding Resistance losses; an ill-advised FFI uprising in Marseilles on August 21 had been put down by General Schaefer with severe French casualties). U.S. Navy "Seebees," assisted by French volunteers and army engineer units, immediately began to repair the damaged ports.

Major General Troy Middleton, the commander of the U.S. VIII Corps, launched the major offensive against Brest on August 25, with the U.S. 8th, 2nd, and 29th Infantry Divisions. He was uneasy about the attack from the beginning. He had requested 20,000 tons of ammunition, but 3rd Army had only authorized him 5,000 tons. Middleton refused to start his offensive until Bradley and Patton agreed to supply him with 3,000 more tons. After three days of battle, during which the Germans yielded almost no ground, despite extremely heavy Allied air and naval support, the promised ammunition still had not been delivered. Middleton therefore suspended his offensive and, despite urging, cajoling, and vague threats from General Patton, refused to launch any more major attacks until he felt that he had adequate stockpiles to win the battle. Middleton was right: 5,000 tons of ammo would not be enough to take Brest. It would require 25,000 tons.

At last resupplied to his minimum requirements, Middleton resumed his offensive on September 7. As usual, and consistent with its entire history, the 2nd Parachute Division put up a fierce resistance. The other division in the fortress, the static 343rd Infantry, also fought very well. The 343rd's commander, Lieutenant General Erwin Rauch, had led the 123rd Infantry Division on the Eastern Front from August 1941 until January 1944 and had considerable experience in situations of this nature. He had fought in the Demyansk Pocket for more than a year.

The Battle of Brest was a struggle for 75 strong points. It was actually two battles, since the German defenses were cut in half by the Penfeld River. Progress was slow, but gradually the Americans crushed the fortress, strong point by strong point, by sheer weight of firepower. General Rauch was captured on September 17, and resistance in the western half of the pocket ended the next day. Colonel Erich Pietzonka, the commander of the 7th Parachute Regiment, surrendered the eastern part of the city on September 18, and nearly 10,000 men (mostly paratroopers) marched into Allied captivity—but not until after they had shaved, washed, put on clean uniforms, and fetched their suitcases. They presented a strange contrast to the dirty American infantrymen, who had just forced them to surrender. Major General Hans von der Mosel, the fortress chief of staff, surrendered the city garrison about the same time.[8] General Ramcke, meanwhile, escaped to the Crozon peninsula, where he finally surrendered on September 19. Ramcke was also ready for a long captivity: He reportedly had eight suitcases packed and brought along his fishing gear. The last pocket of resistance surrendered on September 20. Naturally, both the city and port of Brest were thoroughly demolished; it never did much toward alleviating the Allied supply problem, which was not solved until November, when Antwerp and the Channel ports were finally opened and operational.

The Americans suffered 10,000 casualties in the Battle of Brest—an extremely high total for a city that was more than 300 miles behind the front lines. On the other hand, they had captured more than 38,000 Germans, of which more than 20,000 were combat troops—and some of the Wehrmacht's best at that. The cost in terms of fuel and ammunition for the supply-strapped Allies, however, was very high: almost 500,000 rounds of artillery ammunition, 1.75 million rounds of small arms ammunition, and 360 tons of bombs. In addition, the port of Brest was so badly damaged and the front was moving east at such a rapid pace that the Americans abandoned the project of reopening the harbor before it was completed.

The fall of Brest also released three more American divisions and the veteran VIII Corps for use at the front. They did not arrive too late. In fact, by the time they went back into the line, the days of the great advances were over. The Germans had rallied, and stalemate had set in on the Western Front.

NOTES

1. The IV Luftwaffe Field Corps was transferred to the army and was redesignated LXXXX Corps on November 11, 1944. Erich Petersen (1889–1963) nevertheless continued to lead it until the end of the war. Tessin, Volume 2, p. 232; Absolon, p. 26.

2. Baptist Kniess was born in Gruenstadt in the Rhineland in 1885. He joined the Bavarian Army in 1906 and was commissioned in the infantry in 1908. After serving in World War I and the Reichsheer, he commanded the 63rd Infantry Regiment and was Landwehr Commander, Heilbronn. Upon mobilization, however, he assumed command of the 215th Infantry Division (1939–42). He was promoted to general of infantry in late 1942 and assumed command of the LXVI Corps. Later he led LXXXV Corps (July 10 to November 14, 1944). Relieved of his command (with little justification), he retired to Munich after the war.

3. Weigley, p. 236.

4. Botho Elster was born in Berlin in 1894 and entered the service as a *Fahnenjunker* in 1913. Commissioned in the infantry in 1914, he fought in World War I but was not chosen for the Reichswehr, so he joined the police. He returned to active duty in Hitler's military expansion of 1935, but this time as a major in the panzer branch. He was a colonel and commander of the 8th Panzer Regiment (1938–41) and briefly commanded the 101st Panzer Brigade (1941). Apparently not successful at this level, he was transferred to the staff of OB West. He commanded the 100th Panzer Brigade in France (1942–43) and was promoted to major general on March 1, 1943. He was acting commander of the 894th Field Administrative Command (1943) before assuming command of the 541st Field Administrative Command. He died in Boeblingen in 1952.

5. Blumenson, *Breakout and Pursuit*, p. 654.

6. Seaton, *Fortress*, p. 124.

7. Hermann Ramcke was promoted to general of parachute troops, effective September 1, 1944. He died on July 7, 1968, at the age of 79.

8. Hans von der Mosel was born in Bodenbach in 1898 and entered the army as an officer-cadet in 1916. He was commissioned in the 101st Grenadier Regiment in 1917. Retained in the Reichsheer, he was commandant of the Air Landing School and Maneuver Area Altwarp when the war began, although only a major. He later commanded I Battalion/234th Infantry Regiment (1940), II/156th Infantry Regiment (1940–42), and the 548th Infantry Regiment (1942–43). Named commandant of Brest on May 1, 1943, Mosel was not promoted to major general until September 1, 1944. He had, in the meantime, been superseded by Ramcke as commander of Brest (on August 12). Mosel served as Ramcke's chief of staff during the siege. He lived in Nienburg/Weser after the war. Keilig, p. 230.

CHAPTER XI

THE "MIRACLE OF THE WEST"

THE DRIVE TO THE WEST WALL

The forward elements of the British 2nd and U.S. 1st Armies reached the Belgian frontier on September 2 and pushed into the Low Countries without pause. Montgomery intended to capture the Belgian capital via airborne assault, but the armor of Horrocks's XXX Corps was moving so rapidly that this was not necessary. Early on the morning of September 3, it crossed the Scheldt at Tournai, and the last natural barrier to Brussels was breached. German resistance continued to be weak as Horrocks sent the British 11th Armoured Division (on the left) toward Antwerp and the Guards Armoured Division forward to Brussels, which was 70 miles away. By late afternoon, the Guards were entering the Belgian capital. The next day, the British 11th Armoured Division entered Antwerp. Responsibility for the city had been entrusted to Major General Count Christoph zu Stolberg-Stolberg's 136th Special Employment Division Staff in mid-June, but the speed of the Allied advance and an uprising by Belgian partisans had taken Stolberg by surprise.[1] As of the first of September, Stolberg had 15,000 to 17,000 men at his disposal, but they were poorly armed and of little or no combat value. By the time the British neared the city, Stolberg himself had been captured by the partisans. The British had been so fast that the Germans did not even have time to blow up the port installations. Intact the British captured one of the finest ports in the world. It is located 60 miles up the Scheldt River and is completely sheltered but deep enough to handle every kind of ocean vessel. The 11th Armoured captured intact the huge 1,000-acre harbor, along with 3.5 miles of wharves, quays, and drydocks. Four locks, which connected the river with another 25 miles of quays, were undamaged. All of the more than 600 hydraulic and electric cranes and all of the floating cranes were still operational. The railroad lines, which linked the harbor with the rest of Belgium and Europe, was also intact. Not even the bridges or giant cranes had been destroyed. Six thousand prisoners had been captured; initially they were locked up in the city zoo.

Meanwhile, panic and pandemonium broke out in Holland. It was triggered by Reichskommisar Dr. Arthur Seyss-Inquart and Anton Mussert, the brutal leader of the Dutch Nazi Party. Neither was noted for his physical courage. As early as September 1, Seyss-Inquart ordered all German civilians (including his own Nazi administrators) to leave the western part of the Netherlands for eastern Holland. Mussert followed his lead, and both officials were among the first to depart. Seyss-Inquart established his new headquarters in a lavish bunker at Apeldoorn, 15 miles north of Arnhem. Mussert moved to Twente, in Overijssel Province, even farther away from the Allied armies.

Although the situation deteriorated when the first rats left what appeared to be a sinking ship, it did not degenerate into absolute shambles until September 4, when Antwerp fell. Then the panic really set in. There were more Nazis in the Netherlands than any country outside Germany, and many of them were now fleeing for their lives, along with German civil administrators, labor battalions, Luftwaffe service personnel (always among the first to move smartly to the rear), Osttruppen, and even German soldiers—something unheard of just a short time ago. Railroad stations were overwhelmed with people trying to escape, many of them with their families. Many soldiers, mostly from security and rear area units, threw away their weapons; some even sold them to the Dutch! Some troops begged Dutch civilians for civilian clothing; others took it at gunpoint. Gangs of German soldiers stole horses, wagons, automobiles, trucks, and bicycles—anything that would help them get back to the Reich more quickly. At the same time, Nazi officials and some officers and sergeants tried to make off with their loot. One Dutch woman recalled seeing a German truck carrying off a large double bed—with a woman in it. "Scenes were witnessed which nobody would ever have deemed possible in the German army," Walter Goerlitz wrote.

Naval troops marched northward without weapons, selling their spare uniforms. . . . They told people that the war was over and they were going home. Lorries loaded with officers, their mistresses and large quantities of champagne and brandy contrived to get back as far as the Rhineland, and it was necessary to set up special courts-martials to deal with such cases.[2]

The Dutch civilians were also infected by excitement, but theirs was of an entirely different nature. They had liberation fever. Everywhere Dutch civilians were rejoicing, crowding the sideways, waving long-hidden Dutch flags and screaming, "Long Live the Queen!" Rumors that the British were just down the road swept every Dutch city and town, and crowds gathered, straining to catch their first glimpse of the liberators.

The Allies were not just down the road, however. They were back in Belgium.

Gradually discipline reasserted itself. Although their divisions were scattered, the German command system was still intact. Highly skilled and experienced divisional and regimental cadres were sent to the Netherlands, where they set up collection points, absorbed stragglers into new units, and gradually restored order. New units appeared on the scene, including paratroopers, Hitler Youth, and two SS panzer divisions. They were all obviously ready to fight and die for the Fuehrer. Lieutenant General Kurt Chill, the commander of the 85th Infantry Division, which had practically been destroyed in France, was ordered to return to Germany, to rebuild his shattered command. Instead, on his own initiative, he stayed in northern Belgium and set up reception stations on the northern end of every bridge north of the Albert Canal.[3] In this way he absorbed elements of two other divisions and hundreds of stragglers into the ad hoc Battle Group Chill. Order was restored to the German Front.

The news of the fall of Antwerp (Europe's second port after Rotterdam and third in the world after New York and Rotterdam)[4] was greeted with shock and consternation at Fuehrer Headquarters in East Prussia. Its loss not only held out to the Allies the immediate possibility of solving their supply problems; it also threatened to make the Albert Canal line (from Antwerp to Maastricht) useless and placed the 15th Army in imminent danger of being surrounded in the lowlands of Flanders. In two days, Montgomery had driven a 75-mile wedge between it and Dietrich's 5th Panzer Army, which was now retreating in the direction of Aachen. All Model had to cover the gap with was the low-quality 719th Infantry Division, a two-regiment unit that had been on guard duty along the Dutch coast since it was formed in the summer of 1941; a "Normandy" division at Kampfgruppe strength; a brigade of Dutch SS; and a few garrison and security units from the Netherlands. Himmler, in his capacity as commander in chief of the Home Army, could only offer one ad hoc convalescent division, the 176th Infantry, which was made up of soldiers who would not have been in the army four years before.[5] The men of this unit were grouped into battalions according to their ailments. The "stomach battalion," for example, consisted of men with ulcers who required special diets. There was also an "ear battalion," a "foot battalion," an "eye battalion," and so on. Not even the most optimistic Nazi believed they could stop (or even significantly delay) the British 2nd Army.

Hitler was in a temper that day, and, among others, he took his rage out on Hermann Goering and even threatened to end the Luftwaffe's existence as a separate branch of the service. At this point, Goering came to the rescue of the army. To the complete surprise of Guderian and the General Staff, he announced that he had six parachute regiments more or less ready for frontline duty and could raise two more from convalescent battalions, making a total combat force of 20,000 men. To this he could add as many as 10,000 from Luftwaffe air and ground crews whose training or operations had been stopped by a lack of fuel. In addition, he pointed out, these were Luftwaffe personnel, thoroughly indoctrinated with the spirit of National Socialism—they could be counted upon to fight to the end.

When he heard this news, an excited Hitler forgot all about letting the army absorb the Luftwaffe (as Goering had calculated). He immediately ordered Colonel General Kurt Student, the commander of the 1st Parachute Army, to move his headquarters (until then an administrative and training command) to the Netherlands and to defend the canal line. Model had planned to use this HQ to direct a Fuehrer-ordered counterattack against Patton's right flank and rear in the Nancy-Langres; now he transferred Dietrich's 5th Panzer Army Headquarters to eastern France for that purpose. Dietrich handed over his sector to Headquarters, 7th Army, which was now under the command of General Brandenberger, and left at once for Nancy. Finally, Model ordered General of Infantry Gustav-Adolf von Zangen, the newly appointed commander of the 15th Army,[6] to withdraw the bulk of its troops to the banks of the Scheldt estuary, leaving behind garrisons at Boulogne, Dunkirk, Le Harve, and Calais to deny the Channel ports to the Allies as long as possible. He also instructed the commander of the 15th Army to counterattack to the northeast, but these orders were countermanded on September 6, just as Zangen's troops were about ready to strike. The attack was called off because Model and OKW realized that the British were too strong to be dislodged. Also, Model probably did not want to call the attention of the Allied generals to this sector, for reasons explained below. Meanwhile, Hitler reinstated Field Marshal Gerd von Rundstedt as OB West, although Model remained commander in chief of Army Group B.

To Hitler, the aging Rundstedt had proven his political reliability as president of the "Court of Honor," which discharged the conspirators of July 20 from the Wehrmacht so that they could stand trial in Friesler's People's Court.[7] Rundstedt's appointment to supreme command in the West at this time, Hitler felt, would reassure the Officers' Corps and help restore its morale. The situation Rundstedt inherited now, however, was much worse than it had been in July, when he told Keitel to "end the war, you fools!" In Model's estimation, OB West now had only the equivalent of 25 full-strength divisions and needed 35 to 40 more to conduct an effective defense in the West. Since everyone knew that these were not available, he saw only one option: a retreat to the West Wall.[8] Model had made this recommendation to Fuehrer Headquarters the day before he was superseded by Rundstedt.

Hitler, for once, was correct in separating the posts of OB West and commander in chief, Army Group B. Commanding an army group and the entire Western Front was too big a job for anyone. Kluge probably realized this when he assumed both positions on July 17, the day Rommel was critically wounded. He apparently took personal command of Army Group B only because he was afraid that Hitler would give the post to the SS general, Hausser—and he was probably right. In the 18 days that he held both posts, Walter Model had proven that he could not handle both jobs at the same time, although in fairness to him, it must be pointed out that he inherited a battle already lost, and twice during this period Model had complained to Hitler about the difficulties of commanding both Army Group B and OB West at the same time.[9]

Hitler summoned Rundstedt to "Wolf's Lair" at the end of August and invited him to attend the daily situation conferences. According to General Warlimont, he treated Rundstedt with "unwonted diffidence and respect," even though the aging marshal sat through the sessions "motionless and monosyllabic." Rundstedt was kept in the dark about the reason for his presence in Rastenburg until the afternoon of September 4, when Hitler asked him to reassume command of the Western Front. Stiffly, with both hands on his marshal's baton, Rundstedt replied: "My Fuehrer, whatever you may command, I will do my duty to my last breath."[10] He left for the Western Front that same afternoon. The next day, even before the field marshal resumed his command, Hitler transferred his longtime chief of staff, General of Infantry Guenther Blumentritt, to the staff of the LXXXVI Corps (where he was to undergo training as a corps commander) and replaced him with Lieutenant General Siegfried Westphal, the former chief of staff of OB South, who had just recovered from the nervous breakdown he had suffered in Italy that summer during the battle for Rome.[11] Rundstedt protested the change but to no avail. He and Westphal, however, worked well together, and Westphal was certainly a better chief of staff than Blumentritt.[12] The appointment of Rundstedt, however, was not a fortunate one. The aging Prussian field marshal took one look at the decimated and dispirited forces and decided that the war was lost. When he arrived at OB West (now headquartered at Aremberg, a small town near Koblenz) on the afternoon of September 5, his operations officer, Colonel Bodo Zimmermann, gave him an inventory of his divisions. OB West now had 48 infantry and 15 panzer-type divisions, but only 15 of these were at anywhere near full strength. In all, OB West had a combat power equivalent to only 27 divisions. Eisenhower had an estimated 60 divisions on the

Table 11.1
OB West's Condition, September 5, 1944

	Infantry Divisions	Panzer Divisions	Panzer Brigades
Completely Fit	13	3	2
Partially Fit	12	2	2
Totally Unfit	14	7	—
Dissolved	7	—	—
Rebuilding	9	—	—

Source: Christopher Chant, ed., *The Marshall Cavendish Illustrated Encyclopedia of World War II* (New York: 1972), Volume 7, p. 1909.

Continent.[13] OB West's condition on September 5 is illustrated in Table 11.1.

On September 7, two days after he resumed command, Rundstedt informed Fuehrer Headquarters that the Allies were advancing with approximately 2,000 tanks (a very close estimate) but that he had only about 100 panzers fit for action.[14] He estimated that he was outnumbered more than 2 to 1 in men; 2.5 to 1 in artillery; 20 to 1 in tanks; and 25 to 1 in airplanes. Furthermore, his soldiers were worn out and exhausted, and there were serious shortages in transport, gasoline, and ammunition. He asked that all available tanks and assault guns be rushed to the Western Front, but Hitler had nothing left to give him in the way of armor. During the month of July, the army had lost 1,969 tanks and assault guns, but German industry could provide only 1,256 replacements, and nearly all of these had been sent to the Eastern Front, where Army Group Center was being crushed. In August, the army only received 1,122 replacements but lost twice that many. To make matters worse, the situation in the East was no less catastrophic than that in the West, so OB West could not claim priority for new tanks and panzer units. "As far as I was concerned," Rundstedt said later, "the war ended in September."[15] He retired to his headquarters with his cigarettes and cognac and seldom reemerged; he left the daily conduct of operations in the hands of his subordinates, his chief of staff, and OKW (i.e., Fuehrer Headquarters).

Like Rundstedt, Model received a new chief of staff on September 5, when Lieutenant General Dr. Hans Speidel was arrested in connection with the assassination attempt of July 20. He was replaced by the less capable General of Infantry Hans Krebs, who had been Model's chief of staff when he commanded the 9th Army on the Eastern Front.[16] Despite his Nazi sympathies, Model had tried to shield Speidel, but to no avail. He spent the rest of the war in prison and only escaped execution because he was lucky.[17]

Goering's "surprise" parachute regiments were not the only reinforcements Hitler sent to Rundstedt; the Replacement Army and the Wehrkreise continued to crank out Volksgrenadier divisions at an incredible pace, as it did throughout the war. Wave 30 consisted of the 12th, 16th, 19th, 36th, 560th, and 563rd Volksgrenadier Divisions, of which the 12th, 16th, and 36th were sent to the West. The 5 Wave 31 "shadow" divisions (i.e., partially formed units) were quickly absorbed by the 25 Wave 32 divisions: grenadier divisions numbered between 564 and 588. They, in turn, were absorbed by veteran infantry divisions (now designated Volksgrenadier divisions) that had been depleted in combat: the 9th, 18th, 26th, 47th, 62nd, 79th, 167th, 183rd, 212th, 246th, 256th, 257th, 271st, 272nd, 276th, 277th, 320th, 326th, 337th, 340th, 349th, 352nd, 361st, 363rd, and 708th—75 grenadier regiments in all.[18] Nine of these divisions were sent to the West; most of the rest were sent to Army Group South Ukraine, which had just suffered a catastrophic defeat in Rumania.

Hitler, meanwhile, ordered Rundstedt to restore the line and "to fight for time so that the West Wall can be prepared for defence." He also ordered him to launch an attack from the Epinal area against the right flank of Patton's 3rd Army, regardless of losses.[19]

General Student never had a chance to hold the 60-mile-long Albert Canal line. It would take at least a week for most of his new regiments to reach the front, and the British had already breached the canal line by September 6. He was, however, also given command of the Wehrmacht forces in the Netherlands, and owing to the British supply difficulties, Student felt that he might be able to establish a thin front near the Dutch-Belgian border.

Field Marshal Model, meanwhile, turned his attention to the rescue of the 15th Army—the strongest army left in Army Group B. It had been under the command of General von Zangen since the anti-Nazi General von Salmuth had been sacked on August 25, and it had 90,000 men, 600 guns, and more than 6,200 vehicles and horses. It was no longer possible for it to escape solely by land, however. To make good its getaway, 15th Army would have to cross the Scheldt estuary—a boat trip of 3.5 miles from Breskens to Flushing on Walcheren Island. The trip would be 13 miles for troops departing from Terneuzen. From Flushing, the troops would have to march over a narrow, open, unprotected causeway that connected Walcheren Island with South Beveland peninsula; then they would have to take a single road that led to the mainland, 15 miles north of Antwerp. (Had the British just driven 15 miles north after capturing Antwerp on September 3, they would have cut off the escape route of the 15th Army. The speed of their breakthrough had so surprised the Germans that there had been no troops in the critical sector at that time, but, like the Americans, the British were engaging in "pursuit thinking" and missed a major opportunity.) All of this would have to be gone in the flat, open terrain of the Netherlands in the face of an enemy who had absolute control of both the sea and the air. Even if everything went perfectly, it would take at least three weeks to complete the evacuation. Undaunted, Zangen posted a strong rear guard to check the Canadian and British forces advancing in his rear, and started the evacuation on September 6.[20]

Elsewhere, the battered units from Normandy were still trying to escape the Montgomery's juggernaut, which (unlike Patton's 3rd Army) had not yet completely run out of gas. On Montgomery's left flank, the 1st Canadian Army sealed off most of the escape routes of Zangen's 15th Army and besieged the ports of Le Harve, Dunkirk, Calais, and Boulogne and overran the V-1 sites around Pas de Calais. In his center, Dempsey's 2nd British Army advanced north of Antwerp, across the Albert Canal and the Meuse. On his right flank, Hodges's 1st U.S. Army took Mons on September 3 and surrounded the remnants of several German divisions and three German corps headquarters: the LXXIV (Straube), the LVIII Panzer (Krueger), and the I SS Panzer (Keppler). As the senior general, Straube assumed command of the encircled forces, which were much more interested in escaping than fighting.

Straube ordered his disorganized forces to break out, and a great many did, but 25,000 were captured. The U.S. IX Tactical Air Command later claimed the destruction of 851 motorized vehicles, 50 armored vehicles, and 652 horse-drawn vehicles in the Mons Pocket. All three corps commanders escaped, along with their staffs, but several divisions were smashed, including the elite 6th Parachute Division, which went into the battle with a combat strength of only two battalions. Its commander, Lieutenant General Ruediger von Heyking, was among the prisoners.[21] Its sister division, the 3rd Parachute, was at less than regimental strength but managed to escape, thanks to the leadership of its acting commander, Major General Walther Wadehn.[22] Lieutenant General Joachim von Treschow of the 18th Luftwaffe Field Division also escaped, but only 300 men came out of the pocket with him: Most of them preferred to surrender to the Americans.[23]

The 18th Field was dissolved after Mons. Major General Karl Wahle of the 47th Infantry Division and Lieutenant General Paul Seyffardt of the 348th Infantry succeeded in escaping the pocket but were captured before they could reach the safety of the West Wall.[24] The 47th Infantry had to be rebuilt as a Volksgrenadier Division, and the remnants of Lieutenant General Eugen-Felix Schwalbe's 344th Infantry Division (which was also at Mons) had to be taken out of the line.[25] Later it absorbed the remnants of the 91st Air Landing Division and elements of the 172nd Replacement Division and reemerged as the 344th Volksgrenadier Division. The 271st Infantry—also mauled at Mons—was sent to Slovakia, where it absorbed the 576th Volksgrenadier Division and was sent to the Eastern Front as the 271st Volksgrenadier Division.[26] Other German units were also pounded as they tried to reach the frontier. Kurt Meyer, who had spent years in the Leibstandarte Adolf Hitler (Hitler's SS bodyguard unit, now the 1st SS Panzer Division), visited his old outfit on August 20 and barely recognized it, so few of the "old hands" were left. When he heard who was missing or dead, tears poured down his cheeks. Indeed, Normandy was, in a very real sense, the graveyard of the Waffen-SS as an elite fighting force. A partial list of the key SS men killed in Normandy is shown below:

SS Captain Wilhelm Beck, commander of the 2nd Company, 1st SS Panzer Regiment and winner of the Knight's Cross on the Eastern Front, killed near Caen on June 10;

Reserve Captain Otto Toll, company commander in the 12th SS Panzer Engineer Battalion and winner of the Knight's Cross as a platoon leader in the Afrika Korps, an officer on loan from the army, killed on June 10;

SS Major General Fritz Witt, holder of the Knight's Cross with Oak Leaves and commander of the 12th SS Panzer Division, killed on June 12;

SS Master Sergeant Alfred Guenther, Knight's Cross holder from the Eastern Front and platoon leader in the 1st SS Assault Gun Battalion, killed in action in June;

SS Sergeant Emil Duerr, gun commander in the 4th (Heavy) Company, 26th SS Panzer Grenadier Regiment of the Hitler Youth Division, killed in action at St. Mauvieu (near Caen) on June 27 and awarded the Knight's Cross posthumously;

SS Major Georg Heinrich Karl Karck, commander of the II Battalion/2nd SS Panzer Grenadier Regiment of the 1st SS Panzer Division "Leibstandarte Adolf Hitler," killed in action in July;

SS Captain Karl Keck, commander of the 15th (Engineer) Company of the 21st SS Panzer Grenadier Regiment, 10th SS Panzer Division "Frundsberg," killed at Avenay, Normandy, and awarded the Knight's Cross posthumously;

SS Lieutenant Colonel Christian Tychsen, the scarfaced commander of the 2nd SS Panzer Division "Das Reich" and holder of the Oak Leaves, killed in action, July 28;

SS Master Sergeant Adolf Rued, a member of the staff of the 3rd SS Panzer Grenadier Regiment "Deutschland" of the 2nd SS Panzer Division, killed in action on August 2 and awarded the Knight's Cross posthumously;

SS Private First Class Hermann Alber of the 20th SS Panzer Grenadier Regiment, 9th SS Panzer Division "Hohenstaufen," killed in the Battle of Hill 176, August 2, and awarded the Knight's Cross posthumously;

SS Major Ludwig Kepplinger, commander of the 17th SS Panzer Battalion, 17th SS Panzer Grenadier Division, killed by Maquis seven miles southeast of Laval in August;

SS Lieutenant Helmut Wendorff, platoon leader in the 13th (Heavy) Company of the 1st SS Panzer Regiment LAH, who had knocked out 30 Soviet tanks on the Eastern Front, killed in action southeast of Caen, August 6;

SS Lieutenant Michael Wittmann of the 501st SS Heavy Panzer Battalion, the greatest tank ace of all time and a holder of the Knight's Cross with Oak Leaves and Swords, killed south of Caen, August 8, and posthumously promoted to SS captain;

SS Captain Karl Bastian, commander of the II Battalion, 21st SS Panzer Regiment, 10th SS Panzer Division "Frundsberg," killed in the Argentan-Falaise zone, August 10, and posthumously awarded the Knight's Cross;

SS Major Karl-Heinz Prinz, commander, II Battalion, 12th SS Panzer Regiment, killed in action, August 14;

SS Sergeant Hans Reiter, member of the staff company of the 21st SS Panzer Grenadier Regiment, 10th SS Panzer Division, killed in action at St. Clair and posthumously awarded the Knight's Cross;

SS Major Hans Becker, Knight of the Iron Cross and commander of I Battalion, 2nd SS Panzer Grenadier Regiment in the Leibstandarte Adolf Hitler, killed in action, August 20;

SS Major General Theodor Wisch, commander of the 1st SS Panzer Division, seriously wounded in both legs, August 20;

SS Reserve Technical Sergeant Josef Holte, platoon leader in the 9th SS Panzer Regiment, killed near Livarot, August 20, and posthumously awarded the Knight's Cross;

SS Major Heinrich Heimann of the 1st SS Assault Gun Battalion, 1st SS Panzer Division "Leibstandarte Adolf Hitler," killed in action west of Chambois, August 20;

SS Lieutenant Josef Amberger, commander of the 8th Company, 1st SS Panzer Regiment, killed in action, August 21, and posthumously awarded the Knight's Cross;

SS Colonel Max Wuensche, commander of the 12th SS Panzer Regiment and holder of the Knight's Cross with Oak Leaves, severely wounded in the Falaise Pocket and captured on August 24;

SS Lieutenant Colonel Otto Meyer, commander of the 9th SS Panzer Regiment, 9th SS Panzer Division "Hohenstaufen," killed in action northeast of Amiens, August 28, and posthumously awarded the Oak Leaves to the Knight's Cross; and

SS Lieutenant Colonel Hans Waldmueller, another Knight of the Iron Cross and commander of the I Battalion, 25th SS Panzer Grenadier Regiment, 12th SS Panzer Division "Hitler Youth," died of wounds on September 8.[27]

After Normandy, the Waffen-SS divisions had lost so many of their bravest men and best leaders and veterans, and Himmler and General of SS Gottlob Berger, the chief of the SS Central Office, were filling their places with so many substandard replacements, that they never performed at quite the same level again.[28] After Normandy, the SS divisions lost much of their former eliteness.

During the retreat through Belgium, casualties among the Waffen-SS units continued to mount, both in the upper and lower echelons. On

September 2, SS Major Erich Olboeter, the commander of the 26th SS Panzer Grenadier Regiment of the Hitler Youth Division, was retreating through a Belgian village when his vehicle ran over a mine laid by a partisan. Both of his legs were blown off. He died later that night in the hospital at Charleville.

On September 5, the remnants of the 12th SS Panzer Division tried to prevent the Americans from crossing the Meuse, but it simply no longer had the men to do so. The "Amis" managed to cross the river that night near Namur, only 55 miles from the German border. At first "Panzer" Meyer did not believe the news; his men had always held before. When it was confirmed, he ordered his division to retreat behind the Ourthe. Meyer himself went ahead of his unit with a small, motorized detachment, to make sure the Americans had not already captured the critical crossroads of Durnal. When he entered the village, however, he saw the people greeting the American vanguard. One of the Shermans spotted the SS general's column and blasted the first vehicle. "A few Volkswagen against a column of tanks is not very amusing," Meyer recalled later.

There was no time to turn around and escape. Meyer and his escorts took to their heels. It was every man for himself. The general jumped a fence, followed by one of his men, and hid in a chicken coop behind one of the houses. To them, minutes seemed like hours. By midnight a light rain was falling, and Meyer could bare it no longer—he left the shed to see what was happening in the street. Then his heart almost stopped beating: The village was in the hands of the partisans!

Meyer silently made his way back to the coop, but the wet chickens began to make a commotion—they wanted the shelter all to themselves. An old farmer finally came out to see what was the matter and found himself looking down the barrels of two pistols, held by desperate SS men. They decided to let the old man go, since his disappearance would cause others to come looking for him. First, however, they made him promise not to reveal their secret. Meyer and his comrade, Max Bornhoeft, did not take his promise at face value. As soon as the old man disappeared, they climbed a nearby wall and started running, passed the church where the partisans were headquartered, over another wall, into a compost heap, and into the cemetery. No further flight seemed possible. Meyer covered Bornhoeft with old wreaths and headed back in the direction of the church, intent upon ambushing the partisans, when he was spotted by two policemen, who had been summoned by the farmer. They pointed their gun at Meyer, but the SS general fired first, then ran to the southern wall of the cemetery, followed by Bornhoeft. Instantly they were almost surrounded by partisans. They jumped the center cemetery wall, fell 12 feet, and took off down an old road. There were several shots, and Bornhoeft cried out and fell to the ground. Meyer again turned on the partisans, who promptly took cover when his bullets came too close for comfort. The SS general took cover behind a small door in the wall, behind a tree and a large rock, but the partisans were all around him, searching everywhere. One of them, apparently the leader, loudly called upon Meyer to surrender. He promised that they would obey the law and turn him over to the Americans.

"There was a time when we swore never to be taken alive," Meyer recalled.

The cruel Russian experiences moved us to it. Now that is all so far away. One bullet. . . . Should I honor the oath? Or does it only apply to the Eastern Front? Minutes pass. My eyes are drawn repeatedly to the metal object in my hand. I think of my family and our coming child. It is difficult, so difficult to make a decision. The partisans are standing a few meters from my hiding place. I study their faces. A few are bitter and brutal while others seem to be no more than harmless burgers.

The leader walked to within a few yards of the trapped SS general without seeing him. Behind him, however, was his son, a lad of 14, who shouted that the rock had been moved; he had noticed the dry ground near the stone—the fugitive was behind the small wooden door.

Shots rang out and splintered the door, forcing Meyer into the corner. He screamed out to the father: "My weapon is pointing at your son. Will you keep your promise?!" The father immediately pulled his son behind him and repeated his promise. "Panzer" Meyer threw down his weapon and surrendered. Several of the partisans wanted to shoot him out of hand. "I look into the father's eyes. With a movement of his hand he forces his companions to lower their weapons. Grumbling, they obey. . . . The leader tells me that he was a worker during the war in Germany and experienced only good; he has no intention of leading a band of murderers."

Bornhoeft was severely wounded in the shoulder. He and Meyer spent an uncomfortable night in the partisan headquarters and in the village police station, where they deliberately handcuffed them so tightly that the metal cut into the flesh. The Wehrmacht's youngest general hoped that his troops would counterattack, recapture the village, and rescue him. Attack they did, but they were beaten back by the Americans. The next morning, Meyer was handed over to U.S. troops. The first American stole his Knight's Cross; the second, a lieutenant whose mother was German, told him: "For God's sake, don't say who you are. Your troops are receiving terrible treatment."

Meyer soon found out what he meant. One GI stole his wristwatch, another his SS ring, and a third slammed a rifle butt into his head and was about to shoot him when the lieutenant intervened. He and Bornhoeft were driven back to Namur and handed over to the military police, along with about 60 other prisoners. A Belgian mob attacked the helpless Bornhoeft as he was being lifted down in a stretcher, and a partisan shot him to death while the bloodthirsty mob roared its approval. The military police (MPs) shook their heads and shooed the crowd away. Then they took about 20 men in Waffen-SS and paratrooper uniforms out of the group and executed them. Some were only 18 years of age and had graduated from basic training just two weeks before. Meyer was saved only because his camouflage smock made the MP sergeant think he was a member of an army tank unit.

Kurt Meyer spent two weeks in the Catholic hospital at Namur, suffering from a fractured skull, still without revealing his identity. When asked about his papers, he told his captors that they had been stolen—a story they readily believed. He told them that he was Colonel Meyer of the 2nd Panzer Division. At last, Meyer was transported to the huge POW camp at Compiegne. On the trip, he recalled what he and his fellow prisoners observed:

[S]itting depressed in the corner of the truck we look at a gigantic Allied supply depot. Inconceivable piles of ammunition, fuel and other supplies lie on either side of the road. Depot follows depot at kilometer distances. In between are airstrips and large reserves of tanks and artillery. Traffic winds peacefully in and out of the depots. There is no trace of air cover, camouflage, or anti-aircraft guns. We are looking at the house of a rich man! Do the Americans really understand what kind of superiority in weapons and equipment they have at the German border?[29]

Meyer had hopes of escaping from Compiegne but was soon transferred to England. He was not identified as an SS officer until some time later. Meanwhile, his former division—or what was left of it—made its way behind the Meuse under the temporary command of SS Lieutenant Colonel Hubert Meyer, the division's operations officer.

If the Anglo-Americans (and the Canadians in particular) were shooting their SS and paratrooper prisoners (who were, with considerable justification, considered pro-Nazi) as early as June, they became much more apt to do so in the weeks ahead, after they got their first glimpses of a concentration camp. During the first week of November, the South Alberta Regiment of the 4th Canadian Armoured Division pushed into southern Holland and captured the recently evacuated camp at Vught, on the road between Breda and 's-Hertogenbosch. Major General Harry Foster, the divisional commander, recalled:

It was laid out like an army camp with barn buildings that housed up to 1,500 prisoners. A rail spur ran into workshops at the rear where slave workers rebuilt downed Allied aircraft for use as German spy planes. . . .

In the central yard stood eight strangling posts. Eight ropes dangled from a

6×6 overhead beam. Wood blocks, 18 inches square with foot staples, were set out under each gallows. Victims stepped up onto the blocks, received the noose, then had the blocks kicked from under their feet by the guards. As they hung slowly strangling ankle arteries were sliced open and their blood collected in a marble catch-basin through a series of connecting gutters. For what purpose the blood was taken we could only guess.

Close by were two banks of ovens for disposing of the bloodless corpses. Beside this crematory was a pile of human bones 8 feet long and 4 feet wide. Local village officials estimated that the Germans had disposed of over 10,000 victims at this camp; resistance fighters, students, government officials, many of them Jews. . . .

What sort of people do such things to their fellow humans? Why they are no better than animals. . . . [N]o, they are worse.[30]

In the meantime, the Allies' pursuit was slowing. On September 3, the U.S. 9th Infantry Division of Collins's VII Corps crossed the Meuse just south of Dinant, expecting no resistance. They were suddenly pounced upon by elements of the tough 2nd SS Panzer Division and the remnants of the 12th SS Panzer Division "Hitler Youth," both operating under Keppler's I SS Panzer Corps. One U.S. battalion was partially surrounded and lost more than 200 men. The 9th Infantry was forced to cling to a small foothold on the east bank for a day and a half before it could be rescued by a task force from the U.S. 3rd Armored Division, coming down from the north. Even so, Dinant was not captured until the morning of September 7. During this battle, the remnants of the 77th Infantry Division (about 4,000 men) were finally encircled and destroyed.

The Allied advance continued, and the U.S. VII Corps took Liege on September 7, but resistance seemed to be stiffening. To the south, Bastogne was captured by Leonard Gerow's U.S. V Corps on the September 8. Luxembourg, the capital of the Grand Duchy by the same name, was occupied on September 10, and by September 11, Malmedy was in American hands. The American soldiers were now in the Ardennes, only a few miles from the German border, and there was a noticeable chill in the air, not attributable solely to the changing season. A few days before, one American soldier wrote of a liberated town: "Once again cognac, champagne, and pretty girls." His tone was slightly bored because he had come to expect such things. Now, however, the attitude of the civilians had changed. "There were no more V-for-Victory signs, no more flowers, no more shouts of 'Vive l'Amerique,' " Blumenson recalled. "Instead, a sullen border populace showed hatred, and occasional snipers fired into the columns."[31] Meanwhile, the XIX Corps of Hodges's 1st Army ran out of gas and was immobilized for several days. The U.S. 5th Armored Division continued to push forward, however, and on the evening of September 11, one of its patrols crossed the German frontier near Stalzenburg. The Americans probed deeper the next day and discovered

Figure 11.1
The Western Front, September 15, 1944

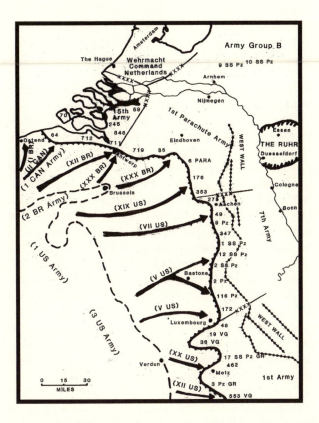

that the West Wall opposite the Ardennes was weakly manned and some of its fortifications were not occupied at all. Supply difficulties prevented an attack until September 14, however, and by that time, the situation had fundamentally changed. Model had been able to reinforce the threatened sector, and the American attack, which penetrated the first line of defenses, was beaten back to the outskirts of Pruem. The Americans were finally halted on the very fringes of the West Wall. Figure 11.1 shows the situation as of September 15.

Meanwhile, along the coast, the 1st Canadian Army (with six divisions) captured the city of Rouen (near the mouth of the Seine) on August 31, took the minor ports of Dieppe and Ostend a few days later, and prepared to attack the major Channel ports of Le Havre and Pas de Calais. In the zone of the British 2nd Army, the VIII British Corps, with two infantry divisions, two tank brigades, and most of the army's heavy and medium artillery, was still on the Seine, immobilized due to a lack of gasoline. The XII British Corps was still engaged in driving into the rear of Zangen's 15th Army but was meeting unexpectedly fierce resistance. This meant that out of the 14 divisions and seven armored brigades in 21st Army Group, Montgomery had only one corps left with which to continue the advance into Holland: Horrocks's XXX, with the 11th and Guards Armoured Divisions. It was not strong enough to sustain the momentum of the drive.

South of the Ardennes, Patton was also running into serious problems. His army had been largely immobilized due to a lack of fuel for several days. When he was at last able to resume his offensive on September 5, German resistance was no longer weak to nonexistent: It was very tough. One American effort to cross the Moselle (at Pont-a-Mousson) was beaten back with heavy losses, and although one U.S. force was able to seize Toul in the Moselle bend, the U.S. 3rd Army in general was tied down in heavy fighting between Metz and Nancy. Patton's great advance had also come to an end. It was the same story everywhere: Just as suddenly as it had started, it stopped. The Wehrmacht was no longer "on the run." Despite the Mons Pocket, Army Group B had managed to escape and was now digging in behind the West Wall. Army Group G (19th Army and LXIV Corps) had also escaped, bringing most of its combat units out with it, more or less intact. The two army groups linked up on September 12, establishing a continuous front from the North Sea to the Swiss border. Most of it was behind the West Wall (called the Siegfried Line by the Allies), which extended from the Dutch border near Kleve to the Swiss frontier, just north of Basle. The Germans once again had a continuous front, although it was not thickly held.

June, July, and August 1944 had been a disastrous period for the Third Reich. It had lost 55,000 men killed and 340,000 missing in the West and 215,000 killed and 627,000 missing on the Eastern Front. Counting wounded (which generally amounted to three times the number killed), the total casualties amounted to 2,047,000. OB West had also lost the use of 200,000 more men, cut off in Hitler's so-called fortresses on the Atlantic coast. The 2-million-plus casualties suffered from June to September were roughly equal to the losses the Wehrmacht suffered from the start of the war to February 1943, including Stalingrad. A quarter of a million horses had also been lost. Some 29 divisions had been lost or rendered impotent (including those trapped in the coastal fortresses), and 3 divisions had been disbanded in the Balkans, 2 in Italy, and 10 in the east, making the total losses for the three-month period 44 divisions. In all, the Reich would lose 106 divisions in 1944—more than it had in 1939.[32]

The loss of France also cost the Third Reich a major source of food, raw materials, industry, money, horses, and labor. France was, and is, the major agricultural nation in Europe and supplied as much food to

Germany as did the entire occupied East. It had also provided the Wehrmacht with 500,000 of its 2.7 million horses, upon which the German Army depended to move most of its artillery and supply columns. French industry and raw materials (especially iron ore) had also been ruthlessly exploited by the occupying power. Three-quarters of France iron ore produced in 1943, for example, was exported to Germany, as well as half of her bauxite. Half a million French laborers had been sent to Germany since 1940 (voluntarily and otherwise), to add to the 1 million prisoners of war whose labor continued to be exploited. France and Belgium together voluntarily contributed two SS divisions to the German cause, both of which were still fighting on the Eastern Front. Now, however, there would be no more replacement troops. (The Dutch contributed a third SS division, and there were many Dutchmen in the 5th SS Panzer Division "Viking.") There were enough men left in France, however, to add seven new divisions to the Allied cause by early 1945, and these exclude a number of colonial divisions, fighting primarily in Italy. The loss or isolation of the French ports further crippled an already devastated U-Boat branch, while the addition of new airfields placed the U.S. 8th Air Force and the British Bomber Command almost on the doorstep of the Ruhr, which they continued to reduce to rubble. Also gone was the string of radar posts in France that had tipped off the Germans that a major air raid was on the way.

Senior officer losses on the Western Front had not been light, either. They included Major General Wilhelm Falley, commander of the 91st Air Landing Division, killed in a firefight with U.S. paratroopers, June 6; Lieutenant Colonel Karl Meyer, commander of the 915th Grenadier Regiment, killed at Bayeux, June 7; Major General Ritter und Elder Sigismund-Helmut von Dawans, chief of staff of Panzer Group West, killed by Allied bombers, June 9; General of Artillery Erich Marcks, commander of the LXXXIV Corps, killed by a fighter-bomber, June 12; SS Lieutenant General Fritz Witt, commander of the 12th SS Panzer Division "Hitler Jugend," killed by Royal Navy gunfire, June 14; SS Major General Werner Ostendorff, commander of the 17th SS Panzer Grenadier Division, seriously wounded, June 16; Lieutenant General Heinz Hellmich, commander of the 243rd Infantry Division, killed by a fighter-bomber, June 16; Major General Rudolf Stegmann, commander of the 77th Infantry Division, killed by a fighter-bomber, June 17; Lieutenant Colonel Franz Mueller, acting commander of the 243rd Infantry Division, captured at Cherbourg; Lieutenant General Wilhelm von Schlieben, commander of the 709th Infantry Division and Fortress Cherbourg, surrendered, June 26; Rear Admiral Walther Hennecke, Naval Commander Normandy, captured in Cherbourg, June 26; Major General Robert Sattler, commandant of Cherbourg, captured June 27; Colonel General Friedrich Dollmann, commander of the 7th Army, died of a heart attack at his command post, June 29; SS Lieutenant General Heinz Lammerding, commander of the 2nd SS Panzer Division "Das Reich," seriously wounded in June; Lieutenant General Adolf Heusinger, chief operations officer of the High Command of the Army, seriously wounded on July 20 and never reemployed; General of Infantry Walter Buhle, chief of the Army staff at OKW, severely wounded, July 20; Colonel Heinz Brandt, principal assistant to the deputy chief of the General Staff of the army, mortally wounded on July 20 and died on July 22; General of Infantry Rudolf Schmundt, chief of the Army Personnel Office, blinded and mortally wounded, July 20, and died October 1; General of Artillery Theodor Geib, Army Rear Area Commander, Southern France, mortally wounded, July 30; Lieutenant General Dietrich Kraiss, the commander of the 352nd Infantry Division, mortally wounded near St.-Lô on August 2 and died August 6; Lieutenant General Karl Spang, commander of the 266th Infantry Division, captured, August 8; Colonel Andreas von Aulock, commandant of St. Malo, surrendered, August 17; Major General Leo Mayr, leader of the 659th Field Administrative Command, captured on August 20; SS Major General Theodor Wisch, commander of the 1st SS Panzer Division, critically wounded, August 20; Major General Johannes Schraepler, commander of the 120th Artillery Command, captured by the Americans on August 21; Major General Walter Gleininger, commander of the 586th Field Administrative Headquarters, committed suicide, August 21; Major General Claus Boie, commander of the 497th Field Administrative HQ, captured by the British on August 24; Major General Hans-Georg Schramm, director of FK 533 (the 533rd Field Administrative Headquarters), captured at Troyes, August 26; Lieutenant General Johannes Baessler, commander of the 242nd Infantry Division, mortally wounded at Toulon, August 26; Rear Admiral Heinrich Ruhfus, commandant of Toulon, surrendered, August 28; Lieutenant General Hans Schaefer, commander of the 244th Infantry Division and Fortress Marseilles, surrendered, August 28; Major General Edgar Arndt, commander of the 708th Infantry Division, killed in action on August 24; Major General Detlef Bock von Wuelfingen, acting commanding officer (CO) of the 681st Field Administrative Headquarters, captured near the West Wall, September 1944; General of Infantry Erwin Vierow, former commander of Northwest France and chief of the ad hoc "General Command Somme," captured, September l; Major General Fritz Reinhardt, commander of the 518th Field Administrative Headquarters, killed in action, September l; Major General of Reserves Hubertus von Aulock, Kampfgruppe commander in Paris and later northwestern France, captured, September 2; Major General Paul von Felbert, CO of the 560th Field Administrative Command in southwestern France, captured on September 5; Major General Axel Schmidt, commander of the 159th Reserve Division, killed near Belfort Gap, September 8; Lieutenant General

Conrad-Oskar Heinrichs, commander of the 89th Infantry Division, killed in action, September 8; Major General Botho Elster, commander of FK 541, captured on September 14; Major General Erwin Jolasse, commander of the 9th Panzer Division, seriously wounded on September 16; Lieutenant General Erwin Rauch, commander of the 343rd Infantry Division, captured in Brittany, September 18; Major General Hans von der Mosel, captured in Brest, September 18; Lieutenant General Hermann Ramcke, commander of the 2nd Parachute Division and commandant of Brest, surrendered, September 19; and FK 622 commander Major General Erich von Kirchbach, mortally wounded on September 24.

In addition, several commanders were sacked or forced into retirement. Some of these men were relieved for their part in the conspiracy of July 20, and some were dismissed for other reasons. The best of these was Baron Hans von Funck, veteran commander of the 7th Panzer Division and XXXXVII Panzer Corps and one of Germany's most competent tank commanders. Others (excluding those executed for their part in the anti-Hitler conspiracy) included General of Infantry Walter von Unruh, chief of the special manpower rationalization staff, involuntarily retired, July 14; General of Infantry Alexander von Falkenhausen, military governor of Belgium and northern France since 1940, relieved on July 14 and discharged from the service after July 20; Colonel General Friedrich Fromm, commander of the Replacement Army, relieved, July 20, and arrested the following day, later shot for cowardice; Colonel General Kurt Zeitzler, chief of the General Staff of the Army, relieved July 21; General of Panzer Troops Ferdinand Schaal, commander, Wehrkreis Bohemia and Moravia, relieved and arrested on July 21 for his part in the conspiracy of July 20; General of Artillery Fritz Lindemann, chief of the Artillery Directorate of the Replacement Army, a conspirator of July 20, deserted July 21, later wounded and captured by the Gestapo on September 3 but never executed; General of Panzer Troops Rudolf Veiel, anti-Nazi commander of Wehrkreis V and former member of the Afrika Korps, relieved in July for his part in the conspiracy of July 20; General of Infantry Walter Fischer von Weikersthal, commander of the LXVII Corps, relieved on July 24; Major General Wilhelm Kirchenpauer von Kirchdorf, chief of staff of Wehrkreis IV, relieved on July 28 and arrested for his part in the conspiracy of July 20; Major Joachim Kuhn, chief of operations of the 28th Jaeger Division on the Eastern Front and a conspirator of July 20, deserted to the Soviets, July 28; Lieutenant General Baron Hans-Karl von Esebeck, acting commander of Wehrkreis XVII, relieved and arrested for his part in the conspiracy of July 20; General of Infantry Erich Raschick, CO of Wehrkreis X (headquartered at Hamburg), retired on July 30; General of Artillery Curt Gallenkamp, commander of the LXXX Corps, sacked on August 10; General of Infantry Mauritz von Wiktorin, commander of Wehrkreis XIII, relieved on August

15 for his part in the conspiracy of July 20; Colonel Victor Kolbe, chief of staff, Wehrkreis XIII, relieved on August 15 for his part in the conspiracy of July 20; Colonel Hans Liphart, chief of the personnel office, Wehrkreis XIII, relieved on August 15 for his part in the conspiracy of July 20; Colonel General Hans von Salmuth, commander of the 15th Army, relieved of his command on August 25 for having knowledge of the conspiracy of July 20 but failing to report it;[33] General of Panzer Troops Adolf Kuntzen, commander of the LXXXI Corps, relieved September 4; Lieutenant General Dr. Hans Spiedel, chief of staff of Army Group B, relieved and arrested on September 5 for his part in the conspiracy of July 20; General of Infantry Kurt von der Chevallerie, commander of the 1st Army, relieved on September 5 and never reemployed; Major General Ernst von Poten, commandant of Metz, sacked on September 8; and General of Artillery Walter Warlimont, deputy chief of operations at OKW, sacked in September and never reemployed.

The list of senior officers who committed suicide or were executed for their part in the July 20 conspiracy is also most impressive and reads almost like a Who's Who in the German Army in 1944. A partial listing includes Colonel General Ludwig Beck, former chief of the General Staff of the Army, shot, July 20; Colonel Count Claus von Stauffenberg, chief of staff of the Home Army, shot, July 20; General of Infantry Friedrich Olbricht, chief of the General Army Office of the Replacement Army, shot, July 20; Lieutenant General Paul von Hase, arrested July 21 and later hanged; General of Signal Troops Erich Fellgiebel, chief signals officer for the army and the Wehrmacht, arrested July 20 and hanged in August; Major General Henning von Treschow, chief of staff of the 2nd Army, committed suicide, July 21; Lieutenant Colonel Hans-Alexander von Voss, staff officer with Army Group Center, committed suicide, July 21; Colonel Baron Wessel von Freytag-Loringhoven, chief of the Army Affairs Office at OKH, suicide, July 23; Lieutenant Colonel Werner Schrader, staff officer to the Quartermaster General of the Army, suicide, July 28; Major General Hellmuth Stieff, chief of the Army Organization Section at OKW, hanged, August 8; Luftwaffe Lieutenant Colonel Caesar von Hofacker, on the staff of the Military Governor of France, arrested in July and later hanged; Colonel Bodo von Harbou, chief of staff of the Artillery Directorate of the Home Army, arrested in late July and hanged himself in his cell shortly thereafter; Lieutenant General Baron Karl von Thuengen-Rossbach, inspector of the Berlin Recruiting Area, arrested on August 7 and hanged on October 24; Field Marshal Erwin von Witzleben, former OB West, hanged, August 8; Colonel General Erich Hoepner, former commander of the 4th Panzer Army, hanged, August 8; Lieutenant Colonel Robert Bernardis, staff officer to General Olbricht, hanged, August 8; Colonel Hahn, chief of staff to the chief signals officer of the army, arrested on August 12 and later executed; Lieutenant General Fritz

Thiele, chief signal officer at OKW after Fellgiebel's arrest, himself arrested on August 14 and hanged on September 4; Field Marshal Hans von Kluge, committed suicide, August 19; Colonel Meichssner, chief of the Organizations Section, OKW, hanged; Colonel Eberhard Finckh, deputy chief of staff of OB West, arrested and subsequently executed on August 30; Colonel von Linstow, chief of staff to the Military Governor of France, executed, August 30; General of Infantry Carl-Heinrich von Stuelpnagel, Military Governor of France, shot and blinded himself on July 21, hanged on August 30; and Field Marshal Erwin Rommel, committed suicide to save his wife and son from arrest by the Gestapo, October 14. In all, 21 generals and 33 colonels and lieutenant colonels were executed, and dozens of others committed suicide.[34]

In contrast to the German losses during the same period, Eisenhower had landed more than 2.1 million men and 460,000 vehicles on the European Continent as of September 11. This amounted to 49 full-strength combat divisions, with more Anglo-Saxons joining the fight every week, and the French Army reconstituting itself at a rapid pace for the Battle of Germany. Over roughly the same time period, Ike's forces had lost 40,000 killed, 164,000 wounded, and 20,000 missing—a total of 224,000 casualties, or less than half what Hitler's legions had suffered.[35] Small wonder the morale of the Allies soldiers was very high in early September 1944 even though their fuel tanks were very low. Bradley and Montgomery were already planning the crossing of the Rhine, and even Eisenhower was wagering that the war would be over by Christmas. Not even the worst pessimist among them would have guessed that it would be more than six months before they could even cross the Rhine.

As the Allies approached the West Wall, they simply ran out of gas. The damaged French ports, railway system, and highway system, coupled with the need to provide for Paris and other French cities and a shortage of trucks, had overtaxed the Allied logistical system to the point where the advance could no longer be sustained. There were a number of reasons for this phenomenon. First, the Allies had not landed enough trucks. No one had expected Army Group B to collapse so suddenly, so no one on the Allied side had prepared for it. The Normandy bridgehead was constricted enough without adding dozens of transportation companies into the mix.

The American and British trucks, for the most part, had to haul supplies from Cherbourg or points near to the invasion beaches, and the trip's distance grew longer the further their armies advanced. This, in turn, required more fuel. By early September, the U.S. transportation companies alone were consuming 300,000 gallons of fuel a day, just to deliver food, ammunition, fuel, and medical supplies, among other things, to the combat units. The Allied supply units responded by creating the "Red Ball Express" (a system of supply, transport, and delivery, including one-way roads) and pushing their men and vehicles harder and harder, until the trucks themselves began to fall apart mechanically. It was all mathematically predictable. Between August 26 and September 2, for example, Patton's 3rd Army consumed between 350,000 and 400,000 gallons of fuel per day but received an average of only 202,382 gallons a day. By September 2, it only had 25,390 gallons left—which was simply not enough to operate with.[36] Had it not been for captured German fuel, Patton would not have gotten as far as he did.

General Bradley and Montgomery (who became a field marshal on September 1) took some extraordinary measures to keep the advance going. When the U.S. 26th, 95th, and 104th Infantry Divisions arrived, for example, he immobilized them, took their trucks, and formed several new truck companies. Soon engineer units were temporarily converted to truck companies, and 18 artillery battalions were immobilized and their vehicles were used to haul supplies. A number of anti-aircraft battalions suffered the same fate. On the other flank of the Allied advance, Montgomery immobilized the British VIII Corps so that the XXX Corps could continue the advance on Brussels and Antwerp.

In addition, for once in history, Hitler's "fortress" policy was paying a positive dividend for the Third Reich. All the ports in northern France had been demolished or were under siege. They would have to be rehabilitated or captured and then rehabilitated. (The German combat and naval engineers had an undeniable talent for destruction and disorganization.) This process would take time, as well as resources that were already in short supply at the front. The exception was Antwerp, which the British had captured almost intact. The failure of every commander from Montgomery to the divisional commander who captured the place was now readily apparent. The Germans still held the approaches to the harbor; therefore, the harbor was of no value until the approaches were secured. This would take weeks, if not months. (It would be November before the Scheldt was cleared of German forces, and then it had to be cleared of mines.)

On the other side of the hill, the Germans were staging another one of their rapid recoveries. Whatever else can be said about it, the German Army in World War II was one of the most resilient in history. Under Himmler (who, one must admit, had a talent for organization), the Replacement Army continued to function as well or better than it did under Fromm. It produced 18 new Volksgrenadier "people's infantry" divisions in July and 25 more in August. In addition, 10 new panzer brigades, built around a Panther battalion, were created. Most of the units in both categories were sent to the West. Also, several old formations were rebuilt. The diversion of six French and American divisions from Italy to the south of France lessened the pressure on OB South, so it was able to transfer the veteran 3rd and 15th Panzer Grenadier Divisions to the Western Front. These, like two of the first Volksgrenadier divisions (the 553rd and 559th) and the 106th Panzer Brigade, were sent to the 1st Army, which was opposing Patton. Since he had one corps immobilized to the rear and two others that were running low on everything, Patton was unable to conquer Metz—much to his disgust. It was his first failure as a military commander.

To the north, Montgomery had been superseded by Eisenhower as Allied ground forces commander on September 1. He nevertheless wanted to continue to direct the focal point of the Allied war effort, and he came up with an idea of how to do it. Instead of turning west, to capture the Channel ports and the approaches to Antwerp, he wanted to advance northeast, penetrate across the Rhine via a combination of airborne landing and armored thrust, and capture the Ruhr, Germany's premier industrial region. If Germany lost the Ruhr, Germany lost the war. Of course, this would require concentrating Allied resources (i.e., supplies) on the left wing.

Much to the disgust of Bradley and Patton, Eisenhower approved the plan. Operations began on September 17.

The plan, Operation "Market-Garden," called for the U.S. 101st Airborne to seize critical bridges in and around Eindhoven, the U.S. 82nd to secure the area around Nijmegen, and the British 1st Airborne Division to capture the Lower Rhine (Neder Rijn) bridge at Arnhem. Meanwhile, the armor-heavy British XXX Corps was to break through German lines and drive 20,000 vehicles 60 miles down a single road in three days (!), linking up with each airborne division in turn, until the Rhine was finally breached at Arnhem. Then the British 2nd Army would be beyond the West Wall and in a position to turn east, against the Ruhr. Figure 11.2 shows the plan for Operation Market-Garden.

It was an ambitious plan and bold in the extreme. The ground forces would have to cross eight water obstacles, including three major rivers—the Maas (as the Dutch call the Meuse), the Waal (a major branch of the Rhine), and the Lower Rhine—as well as two smaller rivers (the Dommel and the Aa) and three large canals (the Wilhelmina, the Willems, and the Maas-Waal). Worse still, the advance would have to take place over swampy terrain, which would confine motorized units to the roads. Every advantage of terrain, in short, favored the defense. Even so, with an already beaten and routed enemy, it still would not affect the final outcome of the drive.

Ominously, however, German resistance was already stiffening. Just as had occurred many times before, beaten Germans did not stay beaten long, especially if Authority was nearby, to issue orders. And there was plenty of Authority nearby. The panzers, artillery, and heavy equipment

Figure 11.2
Operation "Market-Garden": The Plan

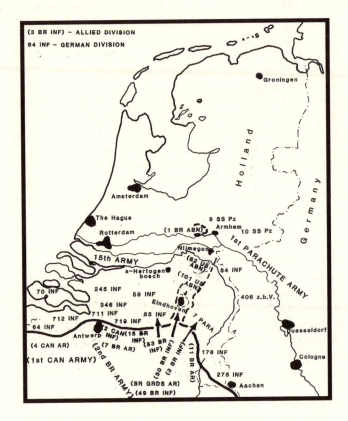

had been lost in Normandy, at Falaise, Mons, and in other battles, but the leadership had escaped. Model was still at large, as were his army headquarters: 1st Parachute, 15th, and 5th Panzer. Staff, 7th Army, was being rebuilt under General of Panzer Troops Erich Brandenberger, an officer who had proven himself countless times on the Eastern Front. Seventh Army would be directing three corps and 10 divisions in the line against the Americans within two weeks, and many of its troops would be heavily engaged in the Battle of Aachen. Only one corps had been destroyed at Falaise (the LXXXIV). Several divisions and their headquarters had been totally lost, but Rundstedt still had 12 panzer-type divisional headquarters and 55 infantry-type divisional HQs. True, many platoons were being led by staff sergeants and sergeant majors, companies were more often than not commanded by lieutenants, battalions were being led by captains, regiments by majors and lieutenant colonels, and (frequently) divisions by colonels, but that had been going on since

1941. In addition, there were plenty of sergeants and corporals around—veterans of the Eastern and Western Fronts—to make sure that the orders were passed on and obeyed. And the men in the ranks responded to their leadership. After all, these were the men who led them out of the hell that was Falaise.

Directly in the path of the British ground thrust lay Kurt Student's 1st Parachute Army, which included General of Infantry Hans Reinhard's LXXXVIII Corps. Reinhard had the 719th Infantry Division and Kampfgruppe Chill, now a division-sized force, led by a determined commander who was demonstrating a talent for rallying and organizing defeated units. In addition, Student's army included the 176th Infantry Division, the Parachute Training Division, and Kamfgruppe Walther. The 176th had only 7,000 men, and they were in poor physical shape. The Parachute Training Division consisted of three parachute regiments under the command of Student's own chief of staff, Lieutenant General Wolfgang Erdmann, and was of higher quality. Young Colonel Erich Walther, the tough and competent commander of the 1st Parachute Regiment, had formed Kampfgruppe Walther out of his own unit, one of Goering's "surprise" regiments and part of the 2nd Parachute Regiment.[37] The celebrated 6th Parachute Regiment, led by Lieutenant Colonel Baron Friedrich August von der Heydte, also joined Student's army, although it had lost much of its eliteness because it had left so many of its best men dead in Normandy.

Montgomery's plan called for the establishment of an armored corridor of 64 miles. He would not merely have to deal with the enemy to his front, but on both flanks as well. On the left lay most of General von Zangen's 15th Army, who was still extricating his legions from the trap the British had failed to close west of Antwerp. By September 22, he would have 86,000 men, 6,000 vehicles, 600 guns, and 6,000 horses on the mainland.[38]

On the British right flank, three to five miles from the Eindhoven-Arnhem Road, lay the Reichswald, a deep forest. No one knew exactly what was in it, but whatever was there would be able to launch forays against the road and cut it.

At this point in the war, the euphoria of "pursuit thinking" clearly dominated the minds of the Allied soldiers at all levels, from field marshal to private. Even the normally gloomy military intelligence staff officers were affected. For example, there was an unsettling report from the Dutch Resistance that the II SS Panzer Corps with the 9th SS Panzer Division was rebuilding in the Arnhem area. That suggested that the 9th's sister division, the 10th SS Panzer, was probably there as well. They had, after all, fought together as a team in Normandy, under the command of the II SS Corps. This unconfirmed report, however, was brushed aside.

It was known that the II SS Panzer had disappeared from the front. One British intelligence officer obtained aerial photographs of the Arnhem area, in which panzer forces were clearly present. He connected these two facts (and was the only one to do so) and was bold enough to suggest that the II SS might be in the Arnhem sector. His leaders suggested that he had overworked himself, and he was quickly sent back to the United Kingdom on an involuntary medical leave.

It had not yet occurred to the Allied commanders that they had underestimated their enemy—again. They had expected to capture Caen and be 30 miles inland by nightfall on D-Day. They gained only a maximum of six miles on D-Day and had to pay the price in the *bocage* country. That price was more than 100,000 men. Now they did it again, and the price would be a defeat at Arnhem. They would do it a third time in 1944, and the price would be another 100,000 men, lost in the Battle of the Bulge.

Perhaps the fatal flaw in Montgomery's plan was that it left no room for error. Among other things, it counted on a relatively slow German reaction. In this respect, it was plagued by just plain bad luck. On or about September 8, Field Marshal Model decided to relocate his headquarters. He delegated the task of finding one to his administrative and transportation officer, Gustav Sedelhauser, a 35-year-old lieutenant. Sedelhauser picked Oosterbeek, an upper-income residual village 2.5 miles west of Arnhem. Lieutenant General Hans Krebs, who had just replaced Speidel as the chief of staff of Army Group B, headquartered in the beautiful Hotel Hartenstein. Model chose to billet in the less ostentatious Tafelberg, just down the road to the west. The new HQ became operational on September 15. With the live-wire field marshal billeting 2 miles from the British drop zones, the Germans would be guaranteed a swift reaction when the British landed two days later. The worst piece of bad luck, however, was that the II SS Panzer Corps *was* located just north of Arnhem. Model had sent it there some days before. His selection of the Arnhem zone as a rest area for the SS Panzertruppen was quite arbitrary. Army Group B's front was 300 miles long, and it had only two divisions in reserve. Its only blind luck was that the only mobile reserve in the entire army group was within striking distance of Arnhem.

The British had also apparently failed to locate SS Major Sepp Krafft's 16th SS Panzer Grenadier Replacement Training Battalion, which was located seven miles west of Arnhem, on the very edge of the British drop zones. They were immediately engaged, and some paratroopers were shot before they could get out of their parachutes. Nevertheless, one British parachute battalion managed to capture the northern end of the Arnhem bridge, although they could not secure the south end. Here they were pinned down, and despite a truly heroic fight, every one of them was eventually killed, captured, or forced to surrender.

The II SS Panzer was not at full strength—far from it, in fact. The 9th SS Panzer Division "Hohenstaufen," which was commanded by 31-year-old SS Lieutenant Colonel Walter Harzer, had 3,500 men, perhaps five tanks and assault guns, and very few armored fighting vehicles or personnel carriers.[39] The 10th SS Panzer Division "Frundsberg," which was led by 38-year-old SS Brigadefuehrer (Major General) Heinz Harmel, had 6,000 men, 20 Panther tanks, 40 armored personal carriers, and several guns (both flak and howitzers).[40] To give an indication of what it had been through in France, when it had been committed to the Battle of Normandy on June 30, the 10th SS had a strength of 15,898 men.

As soon as the Allies landed, Model abandoned his headquarters and headed for the II SS Panzer. (He initially thought that his headquarters was the British objective but soon realized it was the bridge at Arnhem.) Oddly, the Armed Forces Netherlands reacted even more quickly. This Wehrmacht command was directed by General of Fliers Friedrich Christiansen, a naval aviation pioneer who had earned the Pour le Merité in World War I.[41] He was generally considered to be "over his head" in this assignment, which he owed solely to his friendship with Hermann Goering. One finds nothing to criticize in his actions during the Battle of Arnhem, however. As soon as he heard of the landings, Christiansen immediately rushed every unit he could lay his hands on to Arnhem. They were directed by the ad hoc Division von Tettau, which was well led by Lieutenant General Hans von Tettau, who had been General Student's Ia in 1940 and 1941.

SS Lieutenant General Wilhelm "Willi" Bittrich, the commander of the II SS Panzer Corps, sent the 10th SS Panzer Division to block the Nijmegen-Arnhem Road, while the 9th SS Panzer dealt with the British paratroopers at Arnhem.[42] Both assignments were difficult. Part of the 10th SS had already left for Germany, where it was to be rebuilt; now it had to be recalled. The entire division then had to ferry across the Rhine—not an easy operation, even without Allied aerial domination. By the end of the first day, however, the British 1st Airborne was largely contained, and new German units were appearing on the battlefield, including SS Major Hans Peter Knaust's 9th SS Panzer Grenadier Replacement Training Battalion (from Bittrich's reserve), the 102nd Heavy Rocket Launcher Battalion (from Bittrich), and the Tigers of Captain Bruhn's 506th Heavy Panzer Battalion (from Model's reserve). The 191st Artillery Command, a reinforced regiment, was on the way.

The Americans were not as unlucky as the British, but their lot was hard enough. Important bridges were blown up before they could seize them, and the U.S. 101st Airborne Division landed within 10 miles of Student's headquarters, after flying directly over it. They were also within 10 miles of Lieutenant General Walther Poppe's 59th Infantry Division (part of 15th Army), which soon brought them under heavy attack. The U.S. 82nd Airborne was also tied up in heavy fighting in Nijmegen against elements of the 9th SS Panzer Reconnaissance Battalion, which was reinforced by the I Battalion/22nd SS Panzer Grenadier Regiment (part of the 10th SS Division). Still the Allies might have won the battle, had the armored advance not been slow. They had a difficult time dealing with Colonel Walther, however, and by September 19, they were still 46 miles south of Arnhem, trying to push an entire corps down a single road.

The U.S. 82nd Airborne Division had hoped that the only troops in the Reichswald were Landesschuetzen: older-age security troops of marginal value. Sure enough, they were initially attacked by Lieutenant General Gerd Scherbening's 406th Infantry Division, which consisted of four Landesschuetzen battalions of about 500 men each. They were certainly no match for the young, superbly trained paratroopers, but even they were dangerous, because the nearly immobile paratroopers could not be everywhere at one, and the Germans could charge out of the Reichswald and cut the road without opposition anytime they chose. On September 20, however, things became more serious. The 406th was joined by Meindl's II Parachute Corps, which controlled four substandard Luftwaffe Field companies but also had two battalions from the famous 6th Parachute Division, whose men were on a par with those of the 82nd. As the campaign progressed, the ad hoc Corps Feldt (under General of Cavalry Kurt Feldt) from Wehrkreis VI began attacking the road, backed up by Major Baron von Maltzahn's 107th Panzer Brigade. Later, the armored corridor (called "Hell's Highway" by the Allied soldiers) was attacked by elements of General Obstfelder's LXXXVI Corps, the 245th Infantry Division (a Kampfgruppe), the 280th Assault Gun Brigade, the SS Lansturm Nederland (Netherland) Brigade, and the 642nd Marine Battalion (a naval unit), among others. The 180th and 190th Reserve Divisions joined the battle in its closing stages. As a result, the XXX Corps did not reach the Rhine until September 25. By then, the drive had become a rescue mission. The 1st British Airborne Division had been decimated and pushed back into a narrow perimeter on the edge of the river. It ferried across the Rhine that night, abandoning both its bridgehead and its wounded.

The 1st Airborne lost 7,842 of its 10,005 men. The Polish 1st Airborne Brigade, which supported it, also suffered heavy losses. Many of the British were worried about surrendering to the SS. They need not have. Hitler's elite shock troops were filled with admiration at the way the British paratroopers had fought and showered their prisoners with food, chocolates, and cigarettes. They had unwittingly made the moment even more bitter for their prisoners. The gifts were British or American supplies, captured when the supply drops meant for them had landed behind German lines. The division's communications failed early in the battle, and they had no way to inform the pilots of the transport airplanes that the Germans had overrun their drop zones.

With the end of the Battle of Arnhem, the rout of the Wehrmacht was over. The German Army had suffered a massive defeat—but not a decisive one. Once they reached the West Wall, neither the German soldier nor his Fuehrer was thinking about retreat any longer. The soldier was now back in the Reich and was concerned with defending his home, his family, and his Fatherland. The Fuehrer, on the other hand, was thinking about resuming the offensive. He was already planning his next military disaster, the Battle of the Bulge.

NOTES

1. Count Christoph zu Stolberg-Stolberg was born in Westheim, Westphalia, in 1898. He joined the army in late 1914 as a *Fahnenjunker* and was commanded in the Guards Rifle Battalion in 1915. He was accepted into the Reichsheer and, as a lieutenant colonel, took command of the 159th Infantry Regiment when the war broke out. He was not given command of a division until mid-1943, however, when he became acting commander of the 160th Mobilization Division. He was made commander of Eastern Troops in the 7th Army's zone in 1943 and became commander of Security Staff 136 in 1944. He assumed command of Antwerp on June 4, 1944.

2. Walter Goerlitz, *History of the German General Staff* (New York: 1953), p. 303.

3. Kurt Chill was born in Thorn in 1895 and volunteered for the army in 1913. Commissioned in the infantry in 1915, he was discharged in 1920 and joined the police. He reentered the army as a major in 1936. He was a battalion commander when the war broke out, successively commanding the 45th Infantry Regiment, the 122th Infantry Division, the 85th Infantry Division, and the LV Corps (February 1945). He was acting commander of the XXVI Corps on the Eastern Front at the end of the war. He was living in Groemitz, Holstein, in the mid-1950s. Keilig, p. 60; Mehner, Volume 12, p. 447.

4. In 1938, the port of Antwerp had been the destination of 12,000 ships that carried 60 million tons of cargo.

5. Known as "Division Number 176," it was not officially upgraded to the 176th Infantry Division until November 2, 1944; however, it had a strength of 10,637 men. Tessin, Volume 7, pp. 186–87.

6. Gustav-Adolf von Zangen was born in Darmstadt in 1892. He entered the Imperial Army as an officer-cadet in 1910 and was commissioned in the infantry. After World War I, he was discharged from the army, so he joined the police. Zangen reentered the army as a lieutenant colonel in 1935 and rose rapidly, commanding the 88th Infantry Regiment (1938–41), the 17th Infantry Division (1941–43), LXXXIV Corps (1943), LXXXVII Corps (1943), Army Detachment von

Zangen in northern Italy (1943–43), and 15th Army. Zangen was promoted to colonel (1938), major general (1942), lieutenant general (1943), and general of infantry (June 1, 1943). A talented commander, he was nevertheless forced to surrender 15th Army to the Americans at the end of the Battle of the Ruhr Pocket, April 1945.

7. Rundstedt later said that he acceded to Hitler's request that he serve as the president of the Court of Honor because, "If I had not, I too might have been considered a traitor." This explanation did not satisfy many of his fellow generals, who privately criticized him for knuckling under to the Fuehrer. Cornelius Ryan, *A Bridge too Far* (New York: 1959; reprinted ed., New York, 1974), p. 42.

8. Foster, p. 398.

9. Warlimont, p. 477.

10. Walter Goerlitz, ed. *In The Service of the Reich: The Memoirs of Field Marshal Keitel*. David Irving, trans. (Briarcliff Manor, NY: 1966; reprinted., 1979), p. 247.

11. Siegfried Westphal was born in Leipzig in 1902. He joined the 12th Grenadier Regiment as a *Fahnenjunker* in 1918, the day before the armistice. He was commissioned in the 11th Cavalry Regiment in 1922. He spent World War II in staff positions, serving as Ia of the 58th Infantry Division (1939–40); Ia, XXVII Corps (1940), of the staff of the Armistice Commission (1940–41); Ia, Panzer Group (later Army) Afrika (1941–42); chief of staff, 1st Italian-German Panzer Army (1942–43); and chief of staff, OB South (1943–44). He remained chief of staff of OB West until the end of the war. Westphal was promoted to lieutenant general on April 1, 1944, and to general of cavalry on February 1, 1945.

12. Later, Guenther Blumentritt was acting commander of the XII SS Corps (October 1944–January 1945), acting commander of the 25th Army (January–March 1945), and acting commander of the 1st Parachute Army (March–April, 1945). He ended the war as commander of the ad hoc Army Blumentritt (Keilig, p. 38). After the war, he wrote a laudatory biography of Field Marshal von Rundstedt, in which he compared their relationship to a father and son. He moved to Malburg after the war and died in 1967.

13. This estimate was wrong. Eisenhower actually had only 49 divisions on the European mainland at the time.

14. Wilmot, p. 480. Figures are for PzKw IVs, Panthers, Tigers, and 75mm assault guns.

15. Foster, p. 397.

16. Hans Krebs had previously served as the chief of the army's training branch (1939), chief of staff of VII Corps (1939–42), chief of staff of Model's 9th Army (early 1942–1943), chief of staff of Army Group Center (1943–44). He became acting chief of staff in late March 1945, replacing Heinz Guderian. Krebs committed suicide in Berlin on May 1 or 2, 1945. He was promoted to general of infantry, effective August 1, 1944.

17. Dr. Hans Speidel was freed by French troops in the spring of 1945. He was chief military negotiator in the European Defense Community discussions of 1952–53. He joined the Bundeswehr (the West German Armed Forces) when it was founded in 1955 and was promoted to full general in 1957. He was the first German to be commander of Allied Land Forces Central Europe, headquartered in Fontainebleau, France. Speidel retired in 1963 and died in 1984.

18. Tessin, Volume 1, pp. 89–93.

19. Wilmot, p. 480.

20. Zangen's rear guard included Lieutenant General Curt Eberding's 65th Infantry Division, which delayed the 1st Canadian Army for more than a week. Eberding's defense was critical for the 15th Army's escape, although he and his command could not escape. Eberding was captured on November 4, 1944, and the remnants of his division surrendered within the next two days.

21. Ruediger von Heyking (born 1894) was later handed over to the Russians. He was apparently not released from prison until October 1955. He died the following year. Absolon, p. 39.

22. Later acting commander of the 8th Parachute Division, Major General Wadehn was killed in action near Wesel (on the northern sector of the Western Front) on January 5, 1945. Absolon, p. 80.

23. Joachim von Treschow was born in Danzig in 1894. He was educated at various military schools and entered the army as a senior officer cadet in 1912. He was commissioned in the 73rd Fusiliers the following year. Treschow fought in World War I, served in the Reichsheer, and was a lieutenant colonel when World War II started. He commanded a battalion in the 58th Infantry Regiment (1939), the regiment itself (1939–42), and the 328th Infantry Division (1942–43). Later he was inspector of Italian units in Germany (1943–44), was commander of the 18th Luftwaffe Field (1944), and later commanded the LIX Corps. He was promoted to lieutenant general in 1943.

24. Karl Wahle was a native of Dresden. He was formerly military attaché to Bucharest (1938–40), commander of the 267th Infantry Regiment (1940–42), commandant of Hamburg (1942–43), and commander of the 214th and 719th Infantry Divisions, before assuming command of the 47th Infantry on August 1, 1944. He was promoted to major general in 1942 but seems to have been passed over for lieutenant general.

Paul Seyffardt was a signals officer in the 1930s. During World War II, he led the 111th Infantry Regiment (1940–42), the 205th Infantry Division (1942–43), and the 348th Infantry Division (1944).

25. Eugen-Felix Schwalbe was born in the Saar in 1892. He joined the army as an officer-cadet and earned a reserve commission in the infantry in 1914. He commanded the 461st Infantry Regiment (1939–40), the 109th Infantry Regiment (1941–42), the 344th Infantry Division (1942–44), the 719th Infantry Division (1944), and the LXXXVIII Corps (1945). He was promoted to general of infantry on March 1, 1945.

26. Tessin, Volume 8, pp. 302–3; Volume 9, pp. 343–44.

27. Kraetschmer.

28. Gottlob Berger was born in Gerletten, Wuerttemberg, in 1896. His father was a spy who was captured and executed by the Americans in 1918. His son, meanwhile, joined the army as a war volunteer in 1914 and was seriously wounded in the summer of 1916. He earned his commission later that year and was a company commander and battalion adjutant by the end of the war. Discharged in 1920, he was a reserve cavalry captain by 1938. An early Nazi and Storm Trooper, Berger joined the SS in 1936 as an *Oberfuehrer* (roughly a senior colonel). He rose rapidly after joining the staff of the Reichsfuehrer-SS in 1937 and was largely responsible for increasing the size of the Waffen-SS, but at the

cost of diluting its quality. He was promoted to SS-*Obergruppenfuehrer* and General of Waffen-SS in 1943 and directed military operations in Slovakia in 1944.

29. See Foster, pp. 411–12.

30. Ibid., p. 415.

31. Blumenson, *Breakout and Pursuit*, p. 695.

32. Seaton, *German Army*, p. 238.

33. Hans von Salmuth was born in Metz, then a German garrison town, in 1888. He entered the service as an officer-cadet in 1907 and was commissioned in the 3rd Grenadier Guards Regiment in 1909. During World War I, he served as a battalion executive officer and then as a General Staff officer. He served during the Reichsheer era and was chief of staff of Army Group North (later B) during the invasions of Poland and France. He was promoted to general of infantry in 1940 and commanded XXX Corps (1941), 17th Army (1942), 4th Army (1942), 2nd Army (1943–43), 4th Army again (1943), and 15th Army (1943–44). Promoted to colonel general on January 1, 1943, he was relieved of his command on August 25, 1944, when it was determined that he had been approached by the conspirators of July 20 and had not reported them. He was tried as a war criminal by the U.S. Military Tribunal at Nuremberg and was sentenced to 20 years' imprisonment in 1948; however, he secured an early release in 1953. Salmuth retired to Wiesbaden and died in Heidelburg on January 1, 1962.

34. Keilig.

35. Blumenson, *Breakout and Pursuit*, p. 695.

36. Weigley, p. 266.

37. Erich Walther, a tough, young paratrooper, was born on August 5, 1903. He participated in most of the major German airborne drops of World War II and distinguished himself in the Battle of Sicily, among others. A holder of the Knight's Cross with Oak Leaves and Swords, he was promoted to major general on January 1, 1945, and was given command of the 2nd Hermann Goering Parachute Panzer Grenadier Division. Walther surrendered to the Russians at the end of the war and was starved to death in captivity, dying on Christmas Day of 1947. He was 44 years old.

38. Weigley, p. 293.

39. Walter Harzer was born in Stuttgart in 1912. He joined the Reichsheer in 1934 but soon transferred to the SS-VT. He attended the Junkerschule (Officers' Training School) at Bad Toelz and was commissioned SS second lieutenant in 1936. He was a platoon leader and company commander in the SS "Deutschland" Motorized Regiment and was commander of the II Battalion, 4th SS Infantry Regiment, in 1941–42. After a brief General Staff course, Harzer became second General Staff officer in the 10th SS Panzer Division "Frundsberg" and became Ia of the 9th SS Panzer Division "Hohenstaufen" in May. He was acting divisional commander in September 1944 during the Battle of Arnhem. Harzer was promoted to SS colonel and was commander of the 4th SS Panzer Grenadier Division "Police" from December 4, 1944, until the end of the war. He died in Stuttgart on May 29, 1982. Kraetschmer, pp. 760–62; Preradovich, pp. 153–54.

40. Heinz Harmel was born in Metz in 1906, the son of a medical doctor. He joined the Nazi Party in 1926 and became an SS man in 1935. By early 1937 he was an SS second lieutenant and platoon leader, and in early 1941, he was on the staff of the II Battalion, "Der Fuehrer" SS Motorized Regiment. He rose rap-

idly during the campaigns in the East and in October 1942, he was commander of the SS "Deutschland" Motorized Regiment. On May 1, 1944, Harzer was given command of the 10th SS Panzer Division "Frundsberg" and was promoted to *SS-Oberfuehrer* 18 days later. On September 7, 1944, he was promoted to SS major general. He was awarded the Knight's Cross with Oak Leaves and Swords in late 1944. Kraetschmer, pp. 760–62.

41. Friedrich Christiansen was born on December 12, 1879, and joined the Imperial Army at the end of the century. During World War I, he commanded a coastal aviation detachment and was awarded the Pour le Merité. He commanded the Armed Forces Netherlands from May 29, 1940, until April 7, 1945. From November 10, 1944, to January 28, 1945, he was simultaneously commander of the 25th Army, until he was succeeded by Blumentritt. Christiansen died on December 3, 1972. Absolon, p. 20.

42. Wilhelm Bittrich was born in February 26, 1894, in Wernigerode am Harz, the son of a German trade representative. He joined the 19th Reserve Jaeger Battalion when World War I broke out and ended the conflict as a second lieutenant and a fighter pilot. He was a member of the Freikorps von Huelsen in the early 1920s and later was a civilian employee of the Luftwaffe, working as an instructor pilot. He joined the Nazi Party in 1932 and entered the SS in July 1933. A member of the SS-VT, the forerunner of the Waffen-SS, Bittrich was almost immediately given command of a battalion (I/SS "Germania" Regiment) because of his solid and varied military background. By October 1941 he was an SS major general commanding the SS "Deutschland" Motorized Regiment of the "Das Reich" Division. In May 1942, Bittrich assumed command of the 8th SS Cavalry Division "Florian Geyer," which he led against partisans in the Balkans. On February 15, 1943, he assumed command of the 9th SS Panzer Division "Hohenstaufen," which was just being formed. Bittrich assumed command of the II SS Panzer Corps when Hausser was promoted to the command of the 7th Army. Promoted to *SS-Obergruppenfuehrer und General der Waffen-SS* on August 1, 1944, he made a number of unguarded, derogatory remarks about Himmler and the Nazi leadership. The Reichsfuehrer-SS ordered him recalled to Berlin, but this move was blocked by Field Marshal Model, who protected him. Bittrich led the II SS until the end of the war and surrendered to the Americans, who handed him over to the French. Bittrich was kept in jail until 1954, when he was finally released. He held the Knight's Cross with Oak Leaves and Swords (which was awarded on May 6, 1945, a week after Hitler's suicide and several days after Himmler had been stripped of his posts). General Bittrich died on April 19, 1979, in Wolfratshausen, Upper Bavaria. Kraetschmer, pp. 220–23.

TABLE OF EQUIVALENT RANKS

U.S. Army	German Army
General of the Army	Field Marshal (*Generalfeldmarschall*)
General	Colonel General (*Generaloberst*)
Lieutenant General	General of (Infantry, Panzer Troops, etc.)
Major General	Lieutenant General (*Generalleutnant*)
Brigadier General*	Major General (*Generalmajor*)
Colonel	Colonel (*Oberst*)
Lieutenant Colonel	Lieutenant Colonel (*Oberstleutnant*)
Major	Major (*Major*)
Captain	Captain (*Hauptmann*)
First Lieutenant	First Lieutenant (*Oberleutnant*)
Second Lieutenant	Second Lieutenant (*Leutnant*)

*Brigadier in British Army.

APPENDIX II

GERMAN STAFF ABBREVIATIONS

Chief of Staff (Not present below the corps level)

Ia—Chief of Operations

Ib—Quartermaster (Chief Supply Officer)

Ic—Staff Officer, Intelligence (subordinate to Ia)

IIa—Chief Personnel Officer (Adjutant)

IIb—Second Personnel Officer (subordinate to IIa)

III—Chief Judge Advocate (subordinate to IIa)

IVa—Chief Administrative Officer (subordinate to Ib)

IVb—Chief Medical Officer (subordinate to Ib)

IVc—Chief Veterinary Officer (subordinate to Ib)

IVd—Chaplain (subordinate to IIa)

V—Motor Transport Officer (subordinate to Ib)

National Socialist Guidance Officer (added 1944)

Special Staff Officers (Chief of Artillery, Chief of Projectors [Rocket Launchers], etc.)

CHARACTERISTICS OF OPPOSING TANKS[1]

Model	Weight (in tons)	Speed (mph)	Range (miles)	Main Armament	Crew
British					
Mark IV "Churchill"	43.1	15	120	1 6-pounder	5
Mark VI "Crusader"	22.1	27	200	1 2-pounder	5
Mark VIII Cromwell	30.8	38	174	1 75mm	5
American[2]					
M3A1 "Stuart"[3]	14.3	36	60	1 37mm	4
M4A3 "Sherman"	37.1	30	120	1 76mm	5
German					
PzKw II	9.3	25	118	1 20mm	3
PzKw III	24.5	25	160	1 50mm	5
PzKw IV	19.7	26	125	1 75mm	5
PzKw V "Panther"	49.3	25	125	1 75mm	5
PzKw VI "Tiger"	62.0	23	73	1 88mm	5

[1]Characteristics of each tank varied somewhat from model to model.
[2]All American tanks were also in the British inventory. The British Shermans were sometimes outfitted with a heavier main battle gun. These Shermans were called "Fireflies."
[3]A reconnaissance tank.

BIBLIOGRAPHY

Absolon, Rudolf, comp. *Rangliste der Generale der deutschen Luftwaffe nach dem Stand vom 20. April 1945*. Friedberg: 1984.

Barnett, Correlli, ed. *Hitler's Generals*. London: 1989.

Bender, Roger James, and Hugh P. Taylor, *Uniforms, Organization and History of the Waffen-SS*. Mountain View, Calif.: 1971.

Berberich, Florian. "Gustav Wilke." In David G. Chandler and James Lawton Collins, Jr., eds., *The D-Day Encyclopedia*. New York: 1994.

Berberich, Florian. "Karl Wilhelm von Schlieben." In David G. Chandler and James Lawton Collins, Jr., eds., *The D-Day Encyclopedia*. New York: 1994.

Bidwell, S., and D. Graham. *Firepower: British Weapons and Theories of War, 1904–1945*. London: 1982.

Blumenson, Martin. *Breakout and Pursuit. United States Army in World War II. The European Theater of Operations*. Washington, D.C.: 1961.

———. "Recovery of France." In Vincent J. Esposito, ed., *A Concise History of World War II*. New York: 1964.

Blumenson, Martin, and the Editors of Time-Life Books. *Liberation*. Alexandria, Va.: 1978.

Blumentritt, Guenther. *Von Rundstedt: The Soldier and the Man*. London: 1952.

Bradley, Omar N. *A Soldier's Story*. New York: 1951.

Breuer, William B. *Death of a Nazi Army: The Falaise Pocket*. New York: 1985.

———. *Hitler's Fortress Cherbourg*. New York: 1984.

———. *Operation Dragoon*. Novato, Calif.: 1987. Reprint ed., New York: 1988.

Brown, Anthony C. *Bodyguard of Lies*. New York: 1975.

Buelowius Personnel File. Maxwell Air Force Base, Montgomery, Alabama, Air University Archives, n.d.

Carell, Paul. *Invasion: They're Coming!* Boston: 1965. Reprint ed., New York: 1966.

Chandler, David G., and James Lawton Collins, Jr., eds. *The D-Day Encyclopedia*. New York: 1994.

Chant, Christopher, ed. *The Marshal Cavendish Illustrated Encyclopedia of World War II*. New York: 1972. 20 Volumes.

Bibliography

Chant, Christopher, Richard Humble, William Fowler, and Jenny Shaw. *Hitler's Generals and Their Battles*. New York: 1976.

Choltitz, Dietrich von. *Soldat unter Soldaten* Konstanz: 1991.

Collins, Larry, and Dominique Lapierre. *Is Paris Burning?* New York: 1965.

Cooper, Matthew. *The German Army, 1933–1945*. Briarcliff Manor, N.Y.: 1978.

D'Este, Carlo. *Decision in Normandy*. London: 1983. Reprint ed., New York: 1983.

Dietrich, Wolfgang. *Die Verbaende der Luftwaffe, 1935–1945*. Stuttgart: 1976.

Eisenhower, Dwight D. *Crusade in Europe*. New York: 1948.

Ellis, L. F. *Victory in the West*. Volume I: *The Battle of Normandy*. London: 1962.

English, John A. "R.F.L. Keller." In David G. Chandler and James Lawton Collins, Jr., eds., *The D-Day Encyclopedia*. New York: 1994, pp. 328–29.

Essame, H. "Normandy Revisited." *Military Review*. Volume XLIII, No. 12 (December 1963), pp. 76–77.

Florentin, Eddy. *The Battle of the Falaise Gap*. Meryvn Savill, trans. New York: 1969.

Forman, James. *Code Name Valkyrie: Count von Stauffenberg and the Plot to Kill Hitler*. New York: 1975.

Foster, Tony. *Meeting of the Generals*. Toronto: 1986.

Fuerbringer, Herbert. *9.SS-Panzer-Division*. Heimdal: 1984.

Gavin, James M. *On to Berlin*. New York: 1978.

Geyr von Schweppenburg, Baron Leo. "Panzer Group West (Mid-1943–15 July 1944)." Foreign Military Studies *MS # 258*. Office of the Chief of Military History, Washington, D.C.

———. "Panzer Group West (Mid-1943–15 July 1944)." Foreign Military Studies *MS # 466*. Office of the Chief of Military History, Washington, D.C.

———. "Panzer Tactics in Normandy." U.S. Army ETHINT 3, an interrogation conducted at Irschenhausen, Germany, December 11, 1947. On file, U.S. National Archives.

Goerlitz, Walter. *History of the German General Staff*. New York: 1953.

Goerlitz, Walter, ed. *In the Service of the Reich: The Memoirs of Field Marshal Keitel*. David Irving, trans. Briarcliff Manor, N.Y.: 1966. Reprint ed., 1979.

Goralski, Robert. *World War II Almanac, 1931–1945*. New York: 1981.

Graber, Gerry S. *Stauffenberg*. New York: 1973.

Greenfield, Kent R., ed. *Command Decisions*. Washington, D.C.: 1960.

Guderian, Heinz. *Panzer Leader*. New York: 1957. Reprint ed., New York: 1967.

Harrison, Gordon A. *Cross-Channel Attack*. United States Army in World War II. European Theater of Operations, Office of the Chief of Military History. Washington, D.C.: 1951.

Hart, B. H. Liddell. *History of the Second World War*. New York: 1972. 2 Volumes.

———. *The Other Side of the Hill*. London: 1951.

Hastings, Max. *Das Reich*. New York: 1981.

Haupt, Werner. *Das Buch der Panzertruppe, 1916–1945*. Friedberg: 1989.

———. *Rueckzug im Westen, 1944*. Munich: 1978.

Hawser, Richard. *Putsch!* New York: 1971.

Hayn, Friedrich. *Die Invasion von Cotentin bis Falaise*. Heidelberg: 1954.

Hildebrand, Hans H., and Ernst Henriot. *Deutschland Admirale, 1849–1945*. Osnabrueck: 1990. 3 Volumes.

Hoehne, Heinz. *Canasis*. J. Maxwell Brownjohn, trans. Garden City, N.Y.: 1979.

Hoerner, Helmut. *A German Odyssey: The Journal of a German Prisoner of War.* Allan K. Powell, trans. Golden, Colo.: 1991.

Hoffmann, Peter. *The History of the German Resistance, 1933–1945.* Cambridge, Mass.: 1977.

Irving, David. *Hitler's War.* New York: 1977.

———. *The Trail of the Fox.* New York: 1977.

Jacobsen, H. A., ed. *July 20, 1944.* Bonn: 1969.

Jacobsen, H. A., and J Rohwer, eds. *Decisive Battles of World War II: The German View.* New York: 1965.

Jacobsen, Otto. *Erich Marcks, Soldat und Gelehrter.* Goettingen: 1971.

Keegan, John. *Six Armies in Normandy.* New York: 1982. Reprint ed., New York: 1983.

Keilig, Wolf. *Die Generale des Heeres.* Friedberg: 1983.

Keitel, Wilhelm. *In the Service of the Reich.* Briarcliff Manor, N.Y.: 1979.

Kluge, Guenther von. Personnel Record. Air University Archives, Maxwell Air Force Base, Ala.

Kraetschmer, E. G. *Die Ritterkreuztraeger der Waffen-SS.* 3rd ed. Preussisch Oldendorf: 1982.

Kramarz, Joachim. *Stauffenberg: The Architect of the Famous July 20th Conspiracy to Assassinate Hitler.* New York: 1967.

Kriegstagebuch des Oberkommando des Wehrmacht (Fuehrungsstab). Frankfurt-am-Main: 1961. 4 Volumes.

Kurowski, Franz. *Das Tor zur Festung Europa.* Neckargemuend: 1966.

Lucas, James, and Matthew Cooper. *Hitler's Elite Leibstandarte SS, 1933–1945.* London: 1975.

Luck, Hans von. *Panzer Commander.* New York: 1989.

Luettwitz, Heinrich von. "Avranches." Foreign Military Studies *MS # A-904.* Office of the Chief of Military History, Washington, D.C.

Luther, Craig W. H. *Blood and Honor: The History of the 12th SS Panzer Division "Hitler Youth," 1943–1945.* San Jose, Calif.: 1987.

MacDonald, Charles, and Martin Blumenson. "Recovery of France." In Vincent J. Esposito, ed., *A Concise History of World War II.* New York: 1964.

Mason, David. *Breakout: The Drive to the Seine.* New York: 1969.

Mason, Herbert Molloy. *To Kill the Devil: Attempts on the Life of Adolf Hitler.* New York: 1978.

McKee, Alexander. *Last Round against Rommel.* New York: 1966.

Mehner, Kurt, ed. *Die Geheimen Tagesberichte der deutschen Wehrmachtfuehrung im Zweiten Weltkrieg, 1939–1945.* Osnabrueck: 1984–90. 12 Volumes.

Mellenthin, Frederick Wilhelm von. *Panzer Battles: A Study in the Employment of Armor in the Second World War.* Norman, Okla.: 1956. Reprint ed., New York: 1976.

Messenger, Charles. *Hitler's Gladiator: The Life and Times of Oberstruppenfuehrer und Panzergeneral-Oberst der Waffen-SS Sepp Dietrich.* London: 1988.

———. *The Last Prussian: A Biography of Field Marshal Gerd von Rundstedt, 1875–1953.* London: 1991.

Mierzejewski, Alfred C. "Railroads." In David G. Chandler and James L. Collins, Jr., eds., *The D-Day Encyclopedia.* New York: 1994.

Miller, Robert A. *August 1944.* Novato, Calif.: 1988. Reprint ed., New York: 1989.

Bibliography

Mitcham, Samuel W., Jr. *Men of the Luftwaffe*. Novato, Calif.: 1988.

Montgomery, Bernard Law. *The Viscount of Alamein, Normandy to the Baltic*. London: 1958.

O'Neill, Robert J. *The German Army and the Nazi Party, 1933–1939*. New York: 1966.

Perger, Mark C. *SS-Oberst-Gruppenfuehrer und Generaloberst der Waffen-SS Paul Hausser*. Winnipeg, Canada: 1986.

Perrett, Bryan. *Knights of the Black Cross*. New York: 1986.

Poeppel, Martin. *Heaven and Hell: The War Diary of a German Paratrooper*. Louise Willmot, trans. London: 1988.

Preradovich, Nikolaus von. *Die Generale der Waffen-SS*. Berg am See: 1985.

Ritgen, Helmut. *Die Geschichte der Panzer-Lehr-Division im Westen, 1944–1945*. Stuttgart: 1979.

Rohmer, Richard. *Patton's Gap*. New York: 1981.

Rommel, Erwin. *The Rommel Papers*. B. H. Liddell Hart, ed. New York: 1953.

Ruge, Friedrich. "The Invasion of Normandy." In H. A. Jacobsen and J. Rohwer, eds., *Decisive Battles of World War II: The German View*. New York: 1965.

———. *Rommel in Normandy*. Ursula R. Moessner, trans. San Rafael, Calif.: 1979.

Ryan, Cornelius. *A Bridge Too Far*. New York: 1974.

———. *The Longest Day*. New York: 1959. Reprint ed., New York: 1959.

Scheibert, Horst. *Die Traeger des Deutschen Kreuzes in Gold: das Heer*. Friedberg: n.d.

Schlabendorff, Fabian von. *Revolt against Hitler*. Gero v. S. Gaevernitz, ed. London: 1948.

Seaton, Albert. *The Battle for Moscow*. Briarcliff Manor, New York: 1980. Reprint ed., Chicago: 1981.

———. *The Fall of Fortress Europe, 1943–1945*. New York: 1981.

———. *The German Army, 1933–45*. New York: 1982.

———. *The Russo-German War, 1941–45*. New York: 1971.

Shulman, Milton. *Defeat in the West*. London: 1947. Revised ed., New York: 1968.

Snyder, Louis L. *Encyclopedia of the Third Reich*. New York: 1976.

Speidel, Hans. *Invasion, 1944*. Chicago: 1950. Reprint ed., New York: 1950.

Stacey, C. P. *Official History of the Canadian Army in the Second World War*. Volume 3: *The Victory Campaign (The Operations in North-West Europe, 1944–1945)*. Ottawa: 1960.

Stauffenberg, Friedrich von. "Panzer Commanders of the Western Front." Unpublished manuscript in the possession of the author.

Stoves, Rolf. *Die Gepanzerten und Motorisierten deutschen Grossverbaende: Divisionen und selbstaendige Brigaden, 1935–1945*. Friedberg: 1986.

Stumpf, Reinhard. "Eugen Meindl." In David G. Chandler and James Lawton Collins, Jr., eds., *The D-Day Encyclopedia*. New York: 1994, pp. 360–61.

Stumpf, Richard. *Die Wehrmacht-Elite: Rang- und Herkunfstsstruktur der deutschen Generale und Admirale, 1933–1945*. Boppard am Rhein: 1982.

Taylor, Hugh Page. *Uniforms, Organization and History of the Waffen-SS*. San Jose, Calif.: 1982. 5 Volumes.

Taylor, Telford. *Sword and Swastika: Generals and Nazis in the Third Reich*. New York: 1952. Reprint ed., Chicago: 1969.

Tessin, Georg. *Verbaende und Truppen der deutschen Wehrmacht und Waffen-SS im Zweiten Weltkrieg, 1939–1945*. Osnabrueck: 1973–80. 16 Volumes.

Tippelskirch, Kurt von. *Geschichte des Zweiten Weltkrieges*. Bonn: 1951.

Toland, John. *Adolf Hitler*. New York: 1976. Reprint ed., New York: 1977.

Truscott, Lucian K., Jr. *Command Missions: A Personal Story*. New York: 1954.

Viebig, Wilhelm. "277th Infantry Division (13 Aug–8 Sep 1944)." Foreign Military Studies *MS # B-610*. Office of the Chief of Military History, Washington, D.C.

Warlimont, Walter. *Inside Hitler's Headquarters, 1939–1945*. R. H. Barry, trans. London: 1964. Reprint ed., Novato, Calif.: 1964.

Weigley, Russell F. *Eisenhower's Lieutenants*. Bloomington, Il.: 1981.

Wilmot, Chester. *The Struggle for Europe*. New York: 1952.

Wilt, Alan F. *The Riviera Campaign of August 1944*. Carbondale, IL: 1981.

Winterstein, Ernst Martin, and Hans Jacobs. *General Meindl und seine Fallschirmjaeger: Vom Sturmregiment zum II. Fallschirmjaegerkorps, 1940–1945*. Braunschweg: 1976.

Wistrich, Robert. *Who's Who in Nazi Germany*. New York: 1982.

Ziemke, Earl F. *Stalingrad to Berlin: The German Defeat in the East*. Washington, D.C.: 1966.

Zimmermann, Bodo. "OB West: Command Relationships." Foreign Military Studies *MS # B-308*. Office of the Chief of Military History, Washington, D.C.

INDEX

About the Author

SAMUEL W. MITCHAM, JR. is a Professor of Geography and a military historian at the University of Louisiana in Monroe. He has written 20 books, primarily about the German Wehrmacht and World War II. He is a former professor at Henderson State University in Arkadelphia, Arkansas.